I0331421

Lay Buddhism and Spirituality

Eastern Buddhist Voices

Series Editor: Michael Pye

Shin Buddhist Comprehensive Research Institute
Ōtani University, Kyōto, Japan

Volume 1
Beyond Meditation: Expressions of Japanese Shin Buddhist Spirituality

Volume 2
Listening to Shin Buddhism: Starting Points of Modern Dialogue

Volume 3
Interactions with Japanese Buddhism: Explorations and Viewpoints in Twentieth Century Kyōto

Volume 4
Buddhist Temples of Kyōto and Kamakura

Beatrice Lane Suzuki

Edited by Michael Pye

Volume 5
Lay Buddhism and Spirituality:
From Vimalakīrti to the Nenbutsu Masters.

Volume 6
Yinshun and his Exposition of Madhyamaka:
New Studies of the Da Zhidu Lun in twentieth-century China and Taiwan

By Stefania Travagnin

Lay Buddhism and Spirituality:
From Vimalakīrti to the Nenbutsu Masters

Edited by

Michael Pye

with the assistance of
The Eastern Buddhist Society

Eastern Buddhist Voices, Volume 5

equinox

SHEFFIELD UK BRISTOL CT

THE EASTERN BUDDHIST

Volume IV   October, 1927–March, 1928   Numbers 3 & 4

CONTENTS

PAGE

The Lankavatara Sutra, as a Mahayana Text in Especial Relation to the Teaching of Zen Buddhism.
DAISETZ TEITARO SUZUKI 199

The Chinese Tendai Teaching.
BRUNO PETZOLD 299

Vimalakirti's Discourse on Emancipation (concluded).
An English Translation by HOKEI IDUMI........ 348

NOTE.

Published for THE EASTERN BUDDHIST SOCIETY,
Kyoto, Japan.

Price, single copy, one yen fifty; yearly, six yen.
Annual subscription in foreign countries, including postage, is:
England, 15 shillings; France, 25 francs; special price for
India, 8 rupees; U. S. A., $3.50.

THE PRESENT DOUBLE NUMBER IS ¥3.00

Published by Equinox Publishing Ltd.

UK: Office 415, The Workstation, 15 Paternoster Row, Sheffield S1 2BX
USA: ISD, 70 Enterprise Drive, Bristol, CT 06010
www.equinoxpub.com

First published 2014

ISBN 978-1-908049-14-8 (hardback)
ISBN 978-1-908049-15-5 (paperback)

British Library Cataloguing-in-Publication Data

A catalogue record for this book is available from the British Library.

Library of Congress Cataloging-in-Publication Data

Lay Buddhism and Spirituality : from Vimalakirti to the Nenbutsu Masters /
Edited by Michael Pye with the assistance of The Eastern Buddhist Society.
pages cm — (Eastern Buddhist voices ; 5)
Includes bibliographical references and index.
ISBN 978-1-908049-14-8 (hb) — ISBN 978-1-908049-15-5 (pb)
1. Buddhism—Doctrines. 2. Spiritual life—Buddhism. 3. Buddhist laymen—Religious life. I. Pye, Michael.
BQ4150.L42 2014
294.3'8--dc23

2014010898

Typeset by Queenston Publishing, Hamilton, Ontario, Canada
Printed and bound by Lightning Source, Milton Keynes, UK and La Vergne, TN, USA.

Contents

List of Illustrations x
Preface with Acknowledgements xi
Conventions on Names, Titles and Scripts xiii
A Note on *The Eastern Buddhist* xvi

1 Introduction 1

Part I The Teaching of Vimalakīrti

2 Vimalakīrti's Discourse on Emancipation 21
Introduced and Translated by Izumi Hōkei
I On the Buddha-land 25
II The Way of the Necessary Means 35
III The Disciples 37
IV The Bodhisattvas 45
V Mañjuśrī 52
VI The Inconceivable Emancipation 58
VII On Beings 62
VIII The Way of the Buddha 68
IX On Entering the Doctrine of Non-duality 73
X Buddha Gandhakūṭa 77
XI The Life of a Bodhisattva 82

XII Buddha Akṣobhya 87
XIII On Paying Homage to the Law 91
XIV The Commission of the Law 94

Part II Related Strands in Early Mahāyāna Buddhism

3 The Heart Sūtra (*Prajñā-pāramitā-hṛdaya-sūtra*) 99
Shaku Hannya

4 Nāgārjuna's *Mahāyāna-viṃśaka* 107
Translated by Yamaguchi Susumu

5 Outline of the *Avataṃsaka Sūtra* (*Kegonkyō*) 115
Beatrice Lane Suzuki

6 The Hymn on the Life and Vows of Samantabhadra 121
Translated by Izumi Hōkei

Part III Hints of Laity in the Esoteric Tradition

7 Fudō the Immovable 133
Beatrice Lane Suzuki

8 Ceremonies for Disciples on Mount Kōya 149
Beatrice Lane Suzuki

Part IV Revisiting Masters of the Nenbutsu

9 The Pure Land Doctrine in Shōkū's "Plain Wood" Nenbutsu 167
Sugihira Shizutoshi

10 Myōe's Critique of Hōnen 181
Bandō Shōjun

11 Ippen Shōnin and the Nenbutsu 199
Yanagi Sōetsu

12 Shinran and his Song on Amida Buddha 221
Beatrice Lane Suzuki

13 On Steadfast Holding to the Name 231
Kakunyo Shōnin

14 Rennyo the Restorer 241
Kaneko Daiei

15 Asahara Saichi the Myōkōnin 259
Satō Taira

16 The Rite of Reception into Jōdo Shinshū 277
Dan Bornstein

Synoptic List of Text Titles 281
Character List for Historical Persons 299
Original Publication Details 307
Index 311

List of Illustrations

Frontispiece	Contents page of *The Eastern Buddhist* IV 3/4 1928	v
Figure 7.1	Fudō according to the Mystic Rites of Acala the Messenger	136
Figure 7.2	a) Another form of Fudō described in the Mystic Rites; b) Fudō in the Acala Kalpa; c) Fudō with sword in left hand and rope in right hand, sitting on a lotus-flower; d) Fudō with four faces and four arms.	137
Figure 7.3	Fudō trampling on Iśvara and his consort	141
Figure 7.4	Fudō with his two attendants	142
Figure 7.5	A form of Fudō preserved at the temple Miidera, at the foot of Mt. Hiei	144
Figure 7.6	Another form of Fudō preserved at Miidera, at the foot of Mt. Hiei	144
Figure 7.7	The form taken by the noted Yellow Fudō	146
Figure 10.1	Myōe Shōnin meditating in a tree (detail)	188
Figure 15.1	Asahara Saichi	261
Figure 15.2	Poem by Saichi pencilled on a wood-shaving	262
Figure 15.3	Poem by Saichi pencilled on wood	264
Figure 15.4	Asahara Saichi in group at the temple Anrakuji	270

Preface with Acknowledgements

This volume is the last in a set of five which present valuable materials from the early years of the journal *The Eastern Buddhist.* The overall project was designed in collaboration with The Eastern Buddhist Society to celebrate the 90th anniversary of its foundation in 1921. The book series Eastern Buddhist Voices is projected to continue, as circumstances permit, with works drawn from Japan and elsewhere in East Asia.

The Eastern Buddhist Society is located within Ōtani University in Kyōto, which also houses the invaluable Shin Buddhist Comprehensive Research Institute. Both the university and the institute have been extremely helpful. Further support was granted in various ways by the head temple of the Shinshū Ōtani-ha branch of Shin Buddhism, the Higashi Honganji 東本願寺, also in Kyōto. To each of these institutions, my gratitude is hereby most warmly expressed.

The advice of staff members of The Eastern Buddhist Society was most important in dealing with the resolution of various linguistic and other research questions, with data provision, and with the checking of drafts. In this regard I mention with warm gratitude Dr. Michael Conway, Sanskrit specialist Dr. Ōta Fukiko, Ms. Kisa Ito[1] and Mr. Dan Bornstein. Overall guidance and advice was given by Professor Inoue Takami and Professor Yasutomi Shin'ya of Ōtani University and The Eastern Buddhist Society. I also thank Dr. Elizabeth Tinsley for circumstantial information on ritual activities on Mount Kōya, and Norman Waddell and Thomas Kirchner for their translations of articles by Yanagi Sōetsu and Satō Taira respectively at the time of original publication in *The Eastern Buddhist.* Detailed responsibility for editorial decisions about the re-use of materials from the journal lies not with The Eastern Buddhist Society as such but with the editor of the volume. However, apart from the assistance already mentioned, the permission to present such valuable and

1. Japanese names are given in the Japanese order, family name first (as here Ōta), except in Americanized cases (as here Ito and without macron), but exceptions are sometimes made when the original authors provided the names with special titles.

interesting materials once again to a wider world is gratefully acknowledged.

Overall, the editor believes that this collection is a harvest of fine contributions by the Japanese scholars of those early times in the twentieth century, when the wish to tell the world about the traditions of eastern Buddhism was fired by youthful energy and by an evident commitment to lively cooperation with each other and the wider world.

Michael Pye
Kyōto 2014

Conventions on Names, Titles and Scripts

The following conventions have mainly been carried forward from previous volumes, but these explanations have been slightly revised. In principle, all words from Asian languages are shown in italics with diacritical marks as appropriate. In the first half of the twentieth century it was still quite common, in English, to capitalize all kinds of words deemed to be important, and this practice was imitated by non-native users with varying degrees of enthusiasm. Here, however, capital letters have usually been edited out in accordance with current style, unless kept in a particular context for the sake of the original flavour. Over the years some terms have been anglicized.

The following should be noted:

Buddha	for "the Buddha" or in names of particular buddhas
buddha/s	for any buddha or buddhas in the plural
Bodhisattva	in names of bodhisattvas
bodhisattva/s	for any bodhisattva or bodhisattvas in the plural
Dharma	meaning the Teaching (sometimes Law) of the Buddha
dharma/s	meaning elements or factors of existence
karma	anglicized, so not italicized
nenbutsu	sometimes as Nembutsu, if an author so used it.
nirvana	if so used in a very general context, otherwise *nirvāṇa*
Nirvana	if so used in a very general context, otherwise *nirvāṇa*
Samgha	only when capitalized in English as a proper noun for the Buddhist order, otherwise *saṃgha*

Similar considerations apply for Pāli forms: bodhisatta/s, Dhamma, dhamma/s, kamma, nibbana, Nibbana, Sangha. For both Sanskrit and Pāli words an English plural has been permitted, e.g. bodhisattvas, buddhas, sūtras, *devas*.

Policy on the presentation of personal names, the titles of Buddhist works and the scripts used to represent them have been guided by three considerations. First, we have tried to be fair to the authors, seeking to maintain the flavour of their writing while not encumbering them with correctable errors. Second, we have sought to be of service to readers, who may be coming to these writings for the first time. Third, we have aimed broadly at consistency throughout the volume.

Transliteration systems used here follow modern standards, i.e. by using the pīnyīn system for Chinese, and Sanskrit transliteration with diacritical marks as used by Indologists today. This is good practice for Buddhist Studies in general. For Japanese, the Hepburn system is used with slight modifications. The main modifications are the consistent use of "n" instead of the phonetically closer "m" in words such as nenbutsu (except when Nembutsu is maintained for period flavour) and the use of an apostrophe to separate potentially confused syllables when the letter "n" is followed by a vowel (e.g. *den'e*). While there is wide-ranging general agreement over the Hepburn system there is no completely authoritative guide to its modifications.[1]

In general, Chinese characters as used in Japan (*kanji*, or Sino-Japanese characters) follow the typographical reform undertaken in the post-war years. Alternatives may also be shown, especially in some historical China-related contexts. Some use is made of spaces and hyphens, even though these do not occur in the original languages. Thus endings in Japanese such as *-shū* (meaning denomination) are shown with a hyphen. Endings of Chinese text names such as *jīng* (sūtra) and *lùn* (treatise) are shown separated, but not in Japanese where they have become fully integrated. In general, the tendency to break everything up into its components has been resisted. Shinran's famous work *Kyōgyōshinshō* is therefore shown as a single unit and not as *Kyō Gyō Shin Shō*. Many of these things could be handled differently and are in the end a question more of "feel" than of ineluctable rules.

Since the translations included below reflect the high standards of *The Eastern Buddhist* in general, they have not been revised in their substance. However printing errors have of course been corrected, and the orthography has been regularised, as with the earlier volumes in this series. In the case of translations, the would-be "scriptural" archaic English verb-forms (dost, hast, beseecheth, etc.) and personal pronouns (thou, thee, thine, etc.) have been modernized, as these simply create an impenetrable fog for most contemporary readers, and in any case were not always consistently used. A number of syntactical corrections or adjustments were also necessary, mostly trivial, notably relating to the correct use of definite and indefinite articles. Any more extensive

1. This is explained in detail in Volume One of this series, *Beyond Meditation*.

re-phrasing has been signalled. In some cases the article titles have been revised to make them more compact and accessible, and precise details of the original publication are given in an appendix. The attempt has always been made to honour the intention of the author.

Japanese Buddhists typically use canonical texts in their Chinese form, even though many of them are presumed to have originated in India. When our authors were writing, the Sanskrit originals of such Chinese texts were still being identified for the first time, while in some cases it was becoming clear that no Sanskrit original could be found at all. There are two reasons why there may be no Sanskrit original for a Chinese Buddhist text. First, it may have been irretrievably lost. This can never be finally determined, as the very recent discovery of a Sanskrit manuscript of *The Teaching of Vimalakīrti* has shown. Second, however, a text may never have existed in Sanskrit to begin with, even though it was named as "a sūtra" of the Buddha or was a treatise ascribed to a famous Indian Buddhist personality. Reluctance to recognize such fictions led to the retrospective invention and use of Sanskrit titles to create an aura of authenticity, even though this misled students and other readers. In a number of cases the non-existence of a Sanskrit original has now become clear for very good reasons of language and content. Important examples of this are the *Sūtra on the Visualisation of Amitābha* (観無量寿経 *Guānwúliàngshòujīng*, Japanese: *Kanmuryōjukyō*), which is one of the three basic sūtras of Pure land Buddhism, and *The Awakening of Faith in the Mahāyāna* (大乘起信論 *Dàshèngqǐxìn lùn*,[2] Japanese: *Daijōkishinron*), a very popular text in East Asia which was piously ascribed to Aśvaghoṣa.

To some extent it is the notion of "authenticity" and the very respect in which Sanskrit is held which has led to unnecessary difficulties. As a matter of historical fact there are many sūtras in Sanskrit itself which are piously ascribed to the Buddha but do not in fact go back directly to him at all. The Sanskrit of the sūtras was in any case not the Buddha's own personal language. Given this, the mere fact that a sūtra developed or was composed in Chinese does not necessarily make it less "authentic" than one which first appeared in Sanskrit. Fortunately, in the pages of *The Eastern Buddhist*, while the assumptions of traditional piety continue to be evident to some extent, we also find a clear respect for the findings of modern scholarship. This is itself part of the voice of modern Buddhism.

2. Also pronounced *Dàchéngqǐxìn lùn.*

A Note on *The Eastern Buddhist*[1]

In 1921 a group of leading Buddhists in Kyōto founded The Eastern Buddhist Society in order to propagate the spirit of Buddhism in the modern world. The leaders of this group were Suzuki Daisetsu (D. T. Suzuki), Sasaki Gesshō, Akanuma Chizen and Yamabe Shūgaku. Suzuki's wife Beatrice Lane Suzuki and Yokogawa Kenshō also played a significant role. These writers were variously interested in Zen Buddhism and Shin Buddhism, and in the relations between these two and earlier forms of Buddhism. They were also concerned with the question of how best to express Buddhist teaching in a world which was becoming increasingly internationalized. The well-known journal *The Eastern Buddhist* was also founded in 1921, being edited in the first instance by Suzuki Daisetsu and Beatrice Lane Suzuki. In the Foreword to the first issue of the journal, Suzuki wrote as follows: "The Society has for its objects the study of Buddhism, the publication of the result of such study, and the propagation of the true spirit of Buddhism." These objectives have found ample expression in the pages of the journal over some ninety years so far. In their fulfilment, the journal carries articles on all aspects of Buddhism as well as English translations of classical texts and writings by modern Buddhist thinkers.

While the society became most widely known for *The Eastern Buddhist* it has also encouraged many other projects such as the translation of Buddhist texts and the arrangement of seminars and lectures. Its main office is housed in Ōtani University, Kyōto, and its researchers benefit from the fine library holdings which are easily accessible there. There is also a close connection with the Higashi Honganji and the leading branch of Shin Buddhism (Ōtani-ha) which is based there. At the same time the approaches of both the society and of the journal have always been open to, and widely appreciative of various aspects of the Buddhist

1. This note was first published in the first volume of this series. However some errors have been corrected relating to the launch of the New Series in the mid-sixties.

tradition. It is well known that Suzuki Daisetsu himself was devoted to the Zen tradition, while the traditions and texts of other branches of Mahāyāna Buddhism have frequently been presented as well.

The publication of the journal was interrupted by World War II. It was picked up again in 1949, under the editorship of Suzuki Daisetsu and Sugihira Shizutoshi, but the difficulties of the times led to irregularity of appearance and a new pause in 1958. *The Eastern Buddhist* was relaunched as a "New Series" in 1965, Vol. I No. 1 appearing in September of that year and Vol. I No. 2 one year later in September 1966. Shortly before the second issue appeared however, on July 12th 1966, Suzuki Daisetsu had passed away aged 96. Vol. II No. 1 was therefore designed as a memorial issue to him and appeared in 1967. The general editorship then passed through various hands, notably those of Nishitani Keiji (1900–1990), Abe Masao (1915–2006) and Nagao Gajin (1907–2005). Indeed, quite apart from the editorship, writings by some of the best known names in modern Japanese Buddhist thought may be found in its pages. Increasingly, non-Japanese advisors with excellent reputations in Indian, Japanese and Buddhist studies played supporting roles.

While there has often been a strong interest in Zen, matching the expectations of an international public at particular periods, the presentation of Shin Buddhism has also been actively pursued in the journal. Moreover, Japanese contributors have increasingly been joined by foreigners who have offered translations of texts as well as matters for discussion. If we consider the overall trajectory over many years, it may be said that the balance has shifted from the straightforward presentation of substance in the early years to an emphasis on interaction and dialogue later on. This movement is reflected and celebrated in volumes 1 to 3 of the present series of collected papers. At the same time, the original objectives of the Eastern Buddhist Society have by no means been forgotten, and the overall approach, integrating Buddhist scholarship and thought, is continued by the present editors under the leadership of Yasutomi Shin'ya. *The Eastern Buddhist* now looks back on a history of nearly a century and with some interruptions has flourished in an excellent manner. Long may it continue.

— 1 —

Introduction

There is a widely current image of Buddhism in the western world which sees it, above all, as a religion for monks who have "left the household life" in search of enlightenment and nirvana. They are supported and venerated by the laity, who for their part hope to accumulate merit or receive other blessings. There is considerable validity in this picture, even if the distinguishing robes of the monks vary from saffron to orange and brown, deep red or, as is usual in Japan, even black. What is less often perceived is a deep current of spirituality running through generations of laity.

It is fair to say that in general the classic image is characteristic for Theravāda Buddhism, while the opening up of new options for lay followers arises in the context of the bodhisattva path, which is relevant to ordained and lay alike. It is therefore a special feature of Mahāyāna Buddhism, the Buddhism of the "great vehicle" which encompasses a large variety of schools, denominations and sects spread through the whole of East Asia. It is true that in Mahāyāna Buddhism, too, there have been found innumerable monks, and nuns, who have separated themselves from "household" life following the example of the Buddha himself, famed for his "great renunciation." Such persons have frequently been a spiritual inspiration to others who, often for apparently good reasons, are still entangled in worldly affairs. And yet there have been countercurrents too, in the various countries.

This volume presents a variety of texts which express some of the spirituality of the Buddhist tradition in generally accessible forms. For this very reason, and sometimes intentionally, these texts point to a transcending of any distinction between monastic and lay persons. It is in this perspective that we are able to refer to "Lay Buddhism and Spirituality" in the title of the book.

How did it come about that the conceptual basis for the distinction between monk and lay was called into question, or even steadily undermined, and that with the very best of intentions? This is partly because a number of leading concepts in Buddhism are not particularly bound to the receiving of the precepts, or ordination. In Mahāyāna Buddhist literature of various kinds, key terms such as emptiness, enlightenment, insight and compassion have taken on a free-wheeling status. Such terms somehow transcend the listing of mere characteristics, for example in psychological analysis. It is also partly because the inner spiritual process of the Mahāyāna Buddhist follower involves not only the appropriation of a conceptual framework, but also its dismantling. This can be seen in the widely used *Heart Sūtra*, of which a translation will be found below. Here the deconstruction of traditional concepts is carried out ritually, and repetitively. Similarly we read in the *Exposition of Vimalakīrti*, near the beginning of its sixth chapter:

> He who seeks the Dharma never seeks the contemplation of suffering, never seeks the attainment of the cessation of suffering, and never seeks the walking on the path of cessation. And why? The Dharma is far above mere talk. If I should say that I see suffering, the cause of suffering, the cessation of suffering, and the path of cessation, it is mere talk and this is not seeking the Dharma.[1]

If the four noble truths can be relativized in this way, it is not surprising that the idea of the monastic community or order, i.e. the *saṃgha*, cannot be maintained as the unique or even dominant site of Buddhist spirituality. The same approach will be seen in all the interactions between the layman Vimalakīrti and his ordained interlocutors, as can be read in detail below.

Second, this conceptual shift is accompanied above all by the centrally important perspective of the path of the bodhisattva, which is not tied to the taking of restrictive monastic vows but over-arches the lives of lay and ordained in a single religious perspective. This may be seen below, for example in the vows of the mythical bodhisattva Samantabhadra, but also in ordination ceremonies for real laypersons in Shingon Buddhism and, in a reduced form, in Shin Buddhism. Such an approach to the making, or taking of vows makes it possible for a new kind of spirituality to emerge, which is not dependent on the ritual status of "leaving the household," in Japanese *shukke* 出家. On the contrary, the Buddhism of being in the household, *zaike bukkyō* 在家仏教, comes into its own.

Third, in the opposite direction and notably in the case of Japan, it has become widespread for ordained monks to be married. As a matter of personal decision this goes back to the time of Shinran Shōnin 親鸞聖人 (1173–1262), although in his case it is a matter of subtle definition as to whether he was in fact leaving the monkhood, even though he married. His own understanding was famously expressed in the words

1. For this quotation "Dharma" has been preferred to "Law."

"neither monk nor lay" (*hisō hizoku* 非僧非俗; or as these characters are read out discursively in Japanese, *sō ni arazu zoku ni arazu*).[2] In subsequent centuries there seems to have been a creeping toleration of clerical marriage in general, as well as a relaxation of other monastic rules such as the prohibition of meat eating. During the Tokugawa Period (1603–1867), clerical marriage became socially significant in connection with the increasingly widespread pattern of using small temples of various denominations to serve specific local communities in a kind of parish system (*danka seido* 檀家制度). This was universalized, through the required registration of the populace, in order to make the prohibition of Christianity efficacious. It was therefore widely assumed that such temples should be looked after by ordained Buddhist "monks" who became clerics in residence. At the same time, such clerics or ministers, being alone and with no shared monastic kitchen and so on, needed to be looked after themselves. Since the hereditary principle also came into play, as so often in Japan, progeny were also required to provide consistency in the care of the temples and their cemeteries. Finally, in 1872, an edict by the modernizing Meiji government specifically overrode traditional precepts by fully authorizing clerical marriage, which consequently became the widespread norm.[3] In fact it is also not unknown for monks in temples without any parochial functions, for example in the larger Zen clusters, to enter into long-term partnerships or to marry. Even after the compulsory registration of families through temples was abolished, not much has changed in this respect, because the tradition of funeral arrangements and ancestor loyalty focused on the local temples has continued by and large right down to the present day, giving rise, perhaps unfairly, to the expression "funeral Buddhism." In Shin Buddhism much of the care of traditionally parochial temples, including basic ritual services, is carried out by what may be called the temple wives, known as *bōmori* 坊守 in Japanese, that is, literally "protectors of the temple residence." The main qualification rites of Shin Buddhism are, after all, open to persons of either gender, and they can be celibate or married. Moreover some of the newer Buddhist movements of the twentieth century, especially those focused on the *Lotus Sūtra*, are self-consciously lay, emphasizing their character as household Buddhism or *zaike bukkyō*. All of these things together have led to a significant blurring of the ancient categories, although it remains the case that some denominations, especially the ones with the longest history, maintain the monastic/lay distinction more clearly than others.

2. The expression occurs in the *Kyōgyōshinshō*.

3. For a detailed study of the historical shifts in these matters see Richard Jaffe, *Neither Monk nor Layman. Clerical Marriage in Modern Japanese Buddhism* (Princeton, NJ: Princeton University Press) 2001.

In the early issues of *The Eastern Buddhist*, set unobtrusively between modern statements, dialogues and arguments, we find a number of translations from Buddhist texts which are relevant to this subject of lay spirituality in the Mahāyāna perspective. In spite of their interest, students and teachers alike have often failed to notice them or to make adequate use of them. By assembling them here, the intention is to present a spectrum of lay spirituality from the early Mahāyāna, with Vimalakīrti as our chief witness, right up to the *nenbutsu* masters of Pure Land and Shin Buddhism. This cannot in any sense amount to systematic research on lay Buddhist spirituality in East Asia. However the coexistence of these texts in the early years of *The Eastern Buddhist* is very suggestive. One might almost suspect that there was some kind of plan behind it. In fact it was surely accidental, because the various translators and presenters all had their own motivations such as the excitement of modern indological or buddhological research,[4] a fascination with Shingon iconography, or a keen interest in the variations of devotion to the vows of Amida Buddha. Yet drawing the texts together into one volume brings out the fact that these varied Buddhist subject-matters, though sometimes separated by academic or denominational custom, are in fact intricately related to each other.

Key themes which underlie all the texts in some way or another are: (a) non-dualism and emptiness, (b) vows of universal compassion towards all beings, and (c) the potential participation of all on the basis of a lay spirituality. The latter may be summed up in a pithy, paradoxical phrase found in the Chinese version of the *Exposition of Vimalakīrti*: *zài jiā chū jiā* 在家出家, read in Japanese as *zaike wa shukke nari*. This means, literally, "to be in the household life is to depart from the household life." Or we may leap forward to a statement by Shinran's great-grandson Kakunyo (from his text below, the *Shūjishō*):

> If Amida did not make His Vow to embrace all beings without a single exception, how could His devotees see their desire for Rebirth in the Pure Land fulfilled?[5]

4. This is evidenced in other articles which are not reproduced here, but which may be of interest to specialists for other reasons. See for example the "Gathas of Dasabhumika-sūtra" in a collaboration by Johannes Rahder and Susa Shinryū (Sanskrit only) in V/4 and VI/1 (1931/2). A pearl not to be overlooked is Ōchō Enichi's "Tao-an on Translation" in VIII/4 (1958) 1–7. Tao-an (Dào'ān 312–385) writes in salutary detail about what is going on when "we" translate from Sanskrit into Chinese, pointing out various pitfalls and reminding us both that while the Buddha made his teaching accord with the times, customs then change further; and that the sole purpose of translation is to make those who do not know the original language acquainted with the subject matter.

5. Capitals in the original, as in references to God in the English of the time of the translation.

This overrides any distinction between monk and lay. All are embraced by the great Vow of Amida Buddha, ascribed to him while yet having the status of a bodhisattva, i.e. prior to his attainment of buddhahood as such, and appropriated by others through the *nenbutsu*: Namu Amida Butsu 南無阿弥陀仏. It is this *nenbutsu* which forms the basis of all Pure Land and True Pure Land teaching, and is available to all. We may confidently speak therefore of a lay spirituality which runs from Vimalakīrti to the masters of the *nenbutsu*, a major connecting point being the very conception of the bodhisattva way and the bodhisattva vows.

Our first piece, and the longest one, is an early translation of the *Exposition of Vimalakīrti* by Izumi Hōkei 泉芳璟[6] (1884–1947). The main reason why this has been overlooked, even by scholars who are not usually slow to criticize earlier contributions, is probably because it appeared in separate parts, no less than eight in number, over a period of five years. Some parts of the work are more arresting than others, and so miscellaneous parts appearing randomly in a journal would not necessarily attract attention. But the complete work is not so long and therefore it is really worth reading it through as a unified piece. For many years, the dominant version in a European language was that of the Belgian scholar Étienne Lamotte, who turned it from Tibetan into French, but with such a spicing of speculative reconstructions of the presumed Sanskrit that it was difficult to read as a unified text. After some years an English translation was made from Lamotte's French, so that was at three removes from any Sanskrit original text. A little while after Izumi's work, the appearance of which spanned the years from 1923 to 1928, there was also an early translation from the Chinese into German by Yokota and Fischer,[7] but again this was often overlooked by users of English only, especially as it first appeared in the middle of a world war. In fact there are now other translations of varying quality, both from Chinese and Tibetan, but they cannot all be reviewed here. We believe that Izumi's translation, which seems to have been the first from the Chinese into English,[8] should at least take its place among the various attempts to do justice to what is an exciting text.

It should be remembered that until very recently there has been no extant Sanskrit text of the *Exposition of Vimalakīrti* except for a few fragments. Much is made of the literalness of Tibetan translations of Buddhist scriptures, but it must be remembered that these are usually much

6. An older transliteration gives the surname as Idumi (also in *The Eastern Buddhist*), but this form has been dropped since 1946.

7. Yokota Takezō and Jakob Fischer, *Das Vimalakirti-Sūtra*, Tokyo (Hokuseidō Press) 1943.

8. The translator's own footnote 3 refers to an even earlier, but obscure attempt, which I have also failed to locate.

later than the Chinese versions, which represent an older stage in the manuscript tradition. This commonly applies even to Sanskrit manuscripts of Buddhist scriptures, which can post-date Chinese versions by centuries. There has recently been much justified excitement over the discovery of a Sanskrit manuscript of the *Vimalakīrti* in 1999 in Tibet, at the Potala itself.[9] At the same time it should not be forgotten that though the sheer fact of a text's being Sanskrit is often taken to imply priority *per se*, this manuscript may also have gone through some textual developments in the course of the centuries.

There is certainly much work ahead for the detailed study of the *Vimalakīrti*, but in the meantime translations such as the one presented here can still be read for a reliable orientation, and with pleasure. Few can fail to warm to this lay figure, Vimalakīrti, who feigns illness so that the Buddha has an opportunity to send one of his disciples to enquire after his health. But these monastic contemporaries demur, one by one, citing encounters in which Vimalakīrti had mercilessly exposed the rigidity of their assumptions. By the time this is finished it seems that there is little left of a Buddhist religion based on abandoning the household life. Only the wise Mañjuśrī has the nerve to visit him on his sick-bed. When he does, Vimalakīrti "empties" his household through a feat of supernatural power, just to illustrate the emptiness of things. Then the two have a Dharma conversation, mainly about non-duality. Mañjuśrī asks kindly about Vimalakīrti's well-being, and also inquires how long the bodhisattva expects to be ill. The answer to this will be found in the text, but as a clue it may be recalled that he was only pretending to be ill. Vimalakīrti may or may not have existed in reality; about that we have no independent evidence. Just as he was only pretending to be ill, perhaps he was only pretending to exist! On the other hand, the way he is presented seems to be legendary, rather than mythical, and so the narrative may be the literary working up of real encounters between an advanced lay follower of the Mahāyāna and various monks who were still beholden to pre-Mahāyāna ways of thinking. It is notable that iconographic presentations of this lay bodhisattva have always shown him as a real person and not as a celestial being of any kind. The idea of having Buddhism without necessarily having monks seems to have gone down well in China, where the idea of leaving the household life was greeted with some suspicion.[10]

---

9. Published in a transliterated form as *Vimalakīrtinirdeśa: A Sanskrit Edition Based upon the Manuscript Newly Found at the Potala Palace* by Study Group on Buddhist Sanskrit Literature, Institute for Comprehensive Studies of Buddhism, Taishō University, Tokyo (Taishō University Press) 2006.

10. Cf. Sinologist Paul Demiéville's essay "Vimalakīrti en Chine" which was published together with Lamotte's translation as Appendix II, 438–455.

A few words may be added about the translator Izumi Hōkei, who was a professor of Sanskrit literature, of course including much Buddhist literature, at Ōtani University in Kyōto for about thirty years. Having been a pupil of Nanjō Bun'yū 南条文雄 (1849–1927), who learned much from Max Müller in Oxford, Izumi also went abroad to India and Europe for two years. He produced revised editions of the Sanskrit texts of the *Rishukyō* 理趣経 and the *Nyūhokkaibon* 入法界品 (*bon*: chapter) of the *Kegonkyō* 華厳経. The latter sūtra will be taken up again below under "Hymn on the life and vows of Samantabhadra." Izumi also translated a number of well-known Mahāyāna texts directly from Sanskrit into Japanese and compared these in parallel in the printed form. This process was a modern development which enabled Japanese readers to get "behind" the language of the Chinese versions, even though the latter in many cases represent an older stage in textual transmission. Such translations into modern Japanese included *The Sūtra of Brilliant Golden Light*[11] and *The Lotus Sūtra.* A well-known book in Pure Land Buddhist circles is his *Bonbun Muryōjukyō no kenkyū* 梵文無量壽經の研究 (1939), i.e. "Studies in the Sanskrit *Sūtra on Unlimited Life*" and he also published an influential introduction to Sanskrit in 1944. Izumi was therefore very well qualified and experienced in the linguistic tools needed for translating Buddhist texts, the Chinese versions also being easily accessible to him; yet it remains a mystery as to how the final English text of the *Vimalakīrti* could become quite as good as it did. Even if there was some further polishing process which is now lost to view, as may be surmised, it reached an impressive standard which many Japanese scholars would work hard to emulate today.

The *Vimalakīrti* is associated with the Perfection of Insight (Prajñāpāramitā) literature, a class of Buddhist sūtras which range extremely in length from very long, namely three substantial volumes in the modern Japanese printed edition of the Chinese Buddhist Canon (*Taishō Shinshū Daizōkyō*), to very short as in the *Heart Sūtra* which will be found below. The *Heart Sūtra* has been translated and commented upon many times, but it is very convenient to be able to draw, for this collection, on a presentation by Shaku Hannya, an otherwise unidentified author contemporary with Izumi. This contains an introduction, an edition of the Sanskrit text, an English translation from a widely used Chinese version and notes on the content. Readers will see that while the non-dualism which features prominently in the *Vimalakīrti* does not occur exactly in the *Heart Sūtra*, there is nonetheless a profound similarity in the attitude taken towards the standard teachings of older Buddhism. It is regarded as of central importance, spiritually, to achieve a state of detachment

11. In 1929 he published a short section of the Sanskrit text of this sūtra in *The Eastern Buddhist* (Vol V 1, 102–120) together with Nanjō Bun'yū, but unfortunately the project was not continued.

from specific concepts which, though once helpful, may themselves become obstacles in the bodhisattva path. The bodhisattva who depends on the perfection of insight has no obstacles in his mind.

While sūtras are in principle anonymous, such thoughts are also the trademark of the famous second century Indian Buddhist thinker Nāgārjuna. Here we are able to adduce a short text known as the *Mahāyānaviṃśaka* (Twenty Verses on the Mahāyāna) which was translated and introduced by Yamaguchi Susumu 山口益 (1895–1976). Being a Tibetologist, Yamaguchi based his translation on two Tibetan versions which he also carefully compared. It may be interesting for advanced students to compare this translation with one which was published four years later by Vidhusekhara Bhattacharya, who was working directly from a Sanskrit text.[12] Yamaguchi points out that an "idealistic tendency" can be noticed in this text, bringing it close to the Yogācāra school, while at the same time Nāgārjuna uses the similes for *śūnyatā* (emptiness) which are regularly found in the *Prajñā-pāramitā Sūtra*, namely that all things are like dreams, visions, the moon reflected in water or images in a mirror.

We come next to a brief consideration of three texts which are incidentally linked through one particular figure: the bodhisattva Samantabhadra, known in Japanese as Fugen Bosatsu 普賢菩薩. While the name Samantabhadra means "universally worthy," its Chinese rendering *Pǔxián*, giving Japanese Fugen, bears the slight nuance of "universally wise" in the sense of maturely wise and thereby worthy. Though also extant in Chinese versions, the "Hymn on the life and vows of Samantabhadra" was edited and translated from Sanskrit by Izumi Hōkei. We give Izumi's introduction and English translation below. It is notable that the text ends with the repeated notion that Samantabhadra would eventually be born in the world of Amitābha Buddha. The bodhisattva vows for which he is noted (see the text) bear the implication of a universal availability of salvation regardless of monastic or lay status.

The hymn on Samantabhadra has been associated with the huge *Avataṃsaka Sūtra*, which is in effect a collection of texts; it has sometimes been included within it and sometimes circulated separately. However, Samantabhadra, or Fugen, is also the chief figure in two further texts. First, he is the key character in the closing chapter of the *Lotus Sūtra*, being Chapter 28 in the widely current translation by Kumārajīva. This chapter was evidently appended at an intermediate stage in the development of that composite sūtra (before Kumārajīva's time) and was then, after further expansions, repositioned at the end.

Fugen also appears in a short text, which in some traditions is placed together with the *Lotus Sūtra*, known as the *Kanfugenbosatsukyō* (Ch. *Guān*

---

12. Calcutta 1931; also available at www.huntingtonarchive.osu.edu (viewed 2013).

pŭxián púsà jīng 觀普賢菩薩經) the "Sūtra on the Visualization of Fugen" which is not extant in Sanskrit. Although neither of these texts was taken up in the early contributions to *The Eastern Buddhist*, it is interesting to note that Samantabhadra provided a focus for such a "visualization sūtra." It is thought that the visualization sūtras, as a class, originated at least partly in China. Such visualization is a particular form of meditational practice, which in turn has a close affinity to the relevant iconography. Equally well known in Japanese Pure Land Buddhism and Shin Buddhism is the similar "visualization" sūtra focused on Amitābha, the *Kanmuryōjukyō* (Ch. *Guānwúliàngshòu jīng* 観無量寿経), in which the key person who receives instruction on the meditation is the imprisoned Queen Vaidehī, a lay woman. Such works were no doubt originally recited and used as meditational guides by monastics, but they have also fed into lay spirituality in the course of the centuries.

Looking on now to the *Avataṃsaka Sūtra* we are able to include here a brief introduction to it by Beatrice Lane Suzuki, which was described as an "outline." In fact she dwells particularly on a long element within it known as the *Gaṇḍavyūha*, which at the time of her writing was being translated by her husband Suzuki Daisetsu into English. It is of interest to the theme of this book when she emphasizes the large number of lay persons among the "good friends" of the central figure of Sudhana. In her introduction she writes:

> In regard to the good friends whom Sudhana visited, besides Mañjuśrī who appeared three times and Samantabhadra who appeared as the first and the last, there were fifty in all. What kind of persons were they? If we classify them we will find that there were five Bodhisattvas, five monks, one nun, eight householders, a physician, a perfume seller, a sailor, two kings, two laymen, four laywomen, three of whom were ladies and one a heavenly maiden, several children, a number of deities, a mendicant, a hermit, and two Brahmins.
>
> In the *Gaṇḍavyūha*, we find the Mahāyāna tendency to lay stress upon lay people rather than upon monks, and among all the friends we find only five monks. Not all of the friends were aristocratic and wealthy. One was a perfume seller, one a sailor, and one woman a courtesan.

We can see from this how the concept of Buddhist discipleship cut right across any apparent division between monks and lay persons. Note too that Samantabhadra is one of the two named bodhisattvas, together with Mañjuśrī, the same as the one who had been able to visit Vimalakīrti and converse with him on non-duality.

Suzuki Daisetsu evidently had various translation and publication projects which took a somewhat meandering course depending on the circumstances. He first wrote on the *Avataṃsaka Sūtra* in 1921 in Volume 1 of *The*

Eastern Buddhist (in four parts), while his presentation of the *Gaṇḍavyūha* was later lodged in the third series of *Essays in Zen Buddhism* (1934). Similarly, he is well known for his translation of the *Laṅkāvatāra-sūtra*, while it is remarkable that his volume *Studies in the Laṅkāvatāra Sūtra* in fact contains a great deal about later Zen Buddhism. It seems that here it was the idea of the non-discrimination of oppositional factors which fascinated him as a key element of Zen or more generally "eastern" thought.

Rather less well known is Suzuki's apparent promotion of the *Sūtra on Unlimited Life*, one of the three key sūtras of Pure Land Buddhism and hence of Shin Buddhism. Lengthy but incomplete sections of this were published in *The Eastern Buddhist* in 1957 under the title "Fo-shuo Wu-liang-shou-ching."[13] There is no question of reproducing these sections here, since there are various other leading translations in use today. However we may briefly recall main ideas of the sūtra, as they also fit to some extent with the themes of the present volume. The story line is the account of how the bodhisattva Dharmākara emerged from within a mighty number of bodhisattvas and buddhas to become Amitāyus ("Immeasurable Life") and Amitābha ("Immeasurable Light"), simplified in Japanese to Amida Buddha. The bodhisattvas and buddhas all follow a pattern similar to that of Śākyamuni himself, the historical Buddha, beginning as lay persons hearing the teaching, and going right through to their own enlightenment or buddhahood and subsequent proclamation of Dharma. An important feature of this bodhisattva path, which straddles the concepts of lay and ordained, is the formulation of vows or resolves. Like Samantabhadra therefore, the bodhisattva Dharmākara is known for his vows, and these provide the basis for the faith of Pure Land Buddhism including Shin Buddhism. This faith is founded above all on the famous Eighteenth Vow which runs:

> If, upon my attaining Buddhahood, all beings in the ten quarters aspiring in sincerity and faith to be born in my country, and calling me to mind up to ten times, were not to be born there, then may I not attain supreme enlightenment.[14]

---

13. Volume VIII/3, 10–27, continued in VIII/4, 10–17. These translations are not ascribed to a specific person, but an introduction was provided by Nogami Shunjō. The prefixed expression "Fo-shuo" (J. *bussetsu* 仏説) simply indicates that a sūtra is regarded as an "utterance of the Buddha" but since all Buddhist sūtras are theoretically regarded as utterances of the Buddha, it is usually omitted in mere bibliographies. The text in question is regularly referred to as the *Dàwúliàngshòu jīng* 大無量壽經, J. *Daimuryōjukyō* 大無量寿経.

14. This minimal translation owes something to that of D. T. Suzuki in his translation of Shinran's *Kyōgyōshinshō*, (Suzuki, new edition 2012, 114); but here the capital letters are cut out, not having any basis in the original, one or two other adjustments are made, and above all *nen* is translated as "calling to mind" rather than with "meditating [i.e. pronouncing my Name: *nenbutsu*]" which seems unnecessarily unwieldy.

It is of course this adducing, meditatively calling to mind, or as some have it "calling" on the name of Amida, which finds expression in the formula known as the *nenbutsu*: Namu Amida Butsu or in real voice: Na-M(u)-A-Mi-Da-Bu. This came to be the subject of much repetition. However, while "calling" became important throughout the variations of Pure Land Buddhism, it should be noted that in Shin Buddhism there is a particularly strong emphasis on the inner attitude of *shinjin* which accompanies it. Indeed it is questionable whether it is necessary to physically utter the *nenbutsu* at all, if the attitude is right. Indeed, on some accounts the idea of "hearing" the *nenbutsu* was given prominence over the action of uttering it, with Amida Buddha effectively saying it for us, within us, if we are able to hear. This is explained in the article entitled "Shin Buddhism as the Religion of Hearing" by Yokogawa Kenshō 横河顕正 (1916–1940) which was republished from *The Eastern Buddhist* in *Beyond Meditation*.[15]

Beatrice Lane Suzuki was already mentioned above in connection with the "Outline of the *Avataṃsaka Sūtra* (*Kegonkyō*)" but altogether we have four pieces in this volume which stem from her pen. She was evidently an enthusiastic and integrative member of the original editorship of *The Eastern Buddhist* and contributed in various ways to its early success. Though not herself a trained philologist of the classical languages of Buddhism, she was able to work with others to make things accessible in English, and it is a happy coincidence that the themes of our present volume are reflected in the pieces which she authored, two of which alone make up our Part Three, "Hints of Laity in the Esoteric Tradition."

In Part Three we continue to be treated to the interplay between the supernatural beings of Buddhism and the devotion and discipline of lay persons. For this we turn now briefly to Shingon Buddhism or, as one might say, the Esoteric Buddhism (*mikkyō* 密教) defined by Kōbō Daishi 弘法大師 (Kūkai 空海). This tradition stands in some tension both with the Zen Buddhism of Suzuki Daisetsu, and with the Shin Buddhism of the employers and sponsors of the Suzukis at Ōtani University, which of course has the Higashi Honganji of the Shinshū Ōtani-ha in the background. It is not quite clear just why Beatrice Suzuki developed an inter-

---

It is notable that Suzuki did not shrink from using the word "meditating" though it does not normally take a direct object in English, and in fact no object is specified in the original. In the translation for the Numata series, veteran translator and Shin Buddhism scholar Inagaki Hisao simply goes for "...and call my Name even ten times..." which fits with the developed practice of actually saying or reciting the *nenbutsu*. (Inagaki 1995, 34). However the basic meaning of *nen*, in the text (*naishi jūnen* 乃至十念, Japanese pronunciation), does not necessarily imply that. Moreover there is nothing corresponding to "name" in the original, and here we simply add "me" to complete the sense without going too far.

15. Pye (ed.), *Beyond Meditation. Expressions of Japanese Shin Buddhist Spirituality (Eastern Buddhist Voices 1)*, (Sheffield, Equinox), 2011, 217–249.

est in Shingon. Quite likely the use of the word "esoteric" had something to do with it, for we must remember that she was a Theosophist as well as a Buddhist sympathizer. Other Theosophists world-wide were showing an interest in Tibetan Buddhism, which in many ways is a parallel to Shingon Buddhism and to "Esoteric Tendai" (Tendai Mikkyō). We also know that she was simply impressed and inspired by Mount Kōya itself, the main religious centre of Shingon–and who can fail to be? Beatrice Suzuki's own description of Mount Kōya was included in the book *Buddhist Temples in Kyōto and Kamakura* (2013)[16] which presents anew her enthusiastic descriptions of a number of temples, mainly in those two cities and including the Shingon temple Tōji in Kyōto. Nowadays there is a very strong element of tourism on Mount Kōya, it must be admitted, and yet there remain beautiful sites which many tourists pass by without noticing: the Kongō Sanmai-in 金剛三昧院, for example, which is only a couple of hundred metres from the main road, and of which the pagoda is a national treasure. Even the beautiful path for walkers through the great cemetery up to the mausoleum of Kōbō Daishi is often abbreviated by visitors in coaches, who are deposited at an entry point near the goal and so miss many of the extremely impressive memorials surrounded by the huge cryptomerias which cover the mountain. Mount Kōya is of course at a considerable distance from Kyōto, and even now the cable car journey helps one to imagine the remoteness of earlier centuries.[17]

Although Shingon Buddhism is very different from the Pure Land tradition, especially in the Shin Buddhist form, Beatrice Suzuki's two articles relating to Shingon are of particular interest with reference to the theme of laity in Buddhism. The divinity Fudō Myōō 不動明王, Bright King Immovable, a figure well-known to all lay devotees of Shingon Buddhism, is particularly close to their interests, and indeed appears as something like a common person. Though fierce in the destruction of the passions, he has a rather rough and simple face, with a squint, and seems when all is said and done to be quite kindly and close to the people. This is explained in detail in "Fudō the Immovable" with reference to or quotations from various texts such as the *Commentary on the Vairocana Sūtra* by Yīxíng 一行 (J. Ichigyō). Given the interplay with images of Fudō we could think of this contribution in terms of *iconography as text.*

Correspondingly, *ritual as text* may be discerned in Beatrice Suzuki's second article in this section, which records the liturgical sequence of ordination and retreat ceremonies on Mount Kōya for those who seek to enter more fully into the esoteric stream. The ordination procedure

16. Beatrice Lane Suzuki, *Buddhist Temples in Kyōto and Kamakura (Eastern Buddhist Voices 4)*, Sheffield (Equinox) 2013.

17. For circumstantial descriptions see Chapters 17 and 18 of *Buddhist Temples in Kyōto and Kamakura.*

is quite complex, far more complex for example than any similar ceremonies in Shin Buddhism and there is in fact a problem about whether these ceremonies are even open to lay persons at all. Beatrice Suzuki's very clear understanding was that they were, at least under some circumstances, and she even entitled her article "Ceremonies for Lay Disciples at Kōya-san," although they were presumably not *only* for lay disciples. By contrast, current information is that these ceremonies are not now open to lay participation, and the title has therefore been simplified for this republication. It is possible that there was a little international misunderstanding back in the 1930s (which would not be for the first time!), but it is also possible that the management of the rituals has changed somewhat since then. The issue cannot be finally resolved here, but some further details will be found in the footnotes below. In general, however, it may be acknowledged that the underlying concept of bodhisattva-hood is not precisely related to a distinction between monk and lay, and it is of interest to see how the bodhisattva precepts are formulated in a ritual context.

The Buddhism of Mount Kōya had come to be of particular interest to Beatrice Suzuki, and it seems that she had been doing extended research about it, visiting the mountain regularly. According to her husband's brief obituary for her in *The Eastern Buddhist*[18] her main thoughts during the closing months of her life in St. Luke's Hospital in Tokyo had been with a study of "the Shingon practice and philosophy of Buddhism"—which however remained uncompleted. In fact her last contribution to *The Eastern Buddhist* was a brief introduction to Shinran Shōnin, the founder of Shin Buddhism, and his Song on Amida, which appeared in Volume VII 3/4 (1939). Beatrice had already been taken ill in 1938 and died on July 16, 1939, just before that issue appeared in print, dated the same month. The article will be referred to again below.

We now turn finally, in Part Four, to Pure Land Buddhism and Shin Buddhism under the general heading "Revisiting Masters of the Nenbutsu." In the first book of this series, *Beyond Meditation* (Eastern Buddhist Voices 1), five "masters of the *nenbutsu*" were introduced: Hōnen, Shōkū, Ippen, Shinran and Rennyo. Here we revisit this foundational history in other ways.

So we now find ourselves in the conceptual domain of Pure Land Buddhism in general and Shin Buddhism in particular. The reader will find a spectrum of articles, mainly from the early days of *The Eastern Buddhist*, which, though not encyclopedic, provide an introduction to the variety found within the Pure Land Buddhist tradition of Japan. The pieces selected include important short texts, or substantial quotations from texts, so that the reader is led into original materials. It is fascinating to see in what varied ways the simplicity of non-duality can be linked

18. Volume VII 3/4, 376.

with the consciousness of a lay orientation and the comprehensiveness of bodhisattva vows. For this and other reasons it is quite evident that, contrary to many facile misrepresentations, the Pure Land tradition in general (including Shin Buddhism) has been a significant vehicle for the conveyance of the central import of the "great vehicle" or Mahāyāna.

By now we are finding modern explorations of older themes, in an expanding thought-world. These are not the expressions of any kind of naïve faith but, rather, searching examinations of the thought and practice of various well-known figures. Such writings provide a fine introduction to the spiritual world of Shin Buddhism, which has stood the test of time and now stands adjacent to the world of Zen, often interlocking with it. While the issues addressed by the modern authors are to a large extent intellectual, they bear on the nature of mythology and the ways in which a spiritually conceived message can be stated in a secular world.

First we learn from Sugihira Shizutoshi 杉平顗智 (1899–1984) about the "Plain Wood" Nenbutsu of one of Hōnen's leading disciples, Shōkū (1177–1247). A general account of Shōkū's life and thought, also by Sugihira, was published in *Beyond Meditation.*[19] In this new piece we get extensive quotations from his own writing, centred on the idea of the *nenbutsu* being available to all when set forth like plain wood without any paint. Additions and decorations are not required. While Shōkū came to be regarded as the patriarch of the Seizan branch of Pure Land Buddhism, his teaching was not really in conflict with that of Hōnen, but may be seen rather as an exposition of it.

It was very different with Myōe Shōnin 明恵上人 (1173–1232) who mounted a sustained, even fierce critique of Hōnen's teaching. This is presented by Bandō Shōjun 坂東性純 (1932–2004) in an article originally entitled "Myōe's Criticism of Hōnen." Myōe sought to emphasize the continuing value of meditation in a more traditional Buddhist sense, regarding Hōnen's emphasis on the *nenbutsu* as an unwelcome diversion. There is a painting of Myōe seated at meditation in the intertwined branches of a tree which is justly famous and of which we are able to show a reduced detail in the context of the article.[20] What the story of Myōe's critical, acute intervention shows is that the development of Pure Land Buddhism in Japan was by no means a simple sentimental story, but a strongly contested one. It is well known that an oppositional approach was also mounted by Nichiren 日蓮 (1222–1282) in his own inimitable style. However, with Myōe the opposition is not sūtra-based, as it mostly was (in a certain sense) for Nichiren, but practice-based. These were all options within the great cathedral of Tendai doctrine and practice, already cele-

19. Volume 1 of this series (2011).

20. The original publication in *The Eastern Buddhist* (1974) included this frequently reproduced colour painting as a frontispiece, but separate from the article itself.

brated by Bruno Petzold in his "Dengyō Daishi and German theology."[21]

We also take another look here at the approach of Ippen Shōnin 一遍上人 (1239–1289), this time through the eyes of Yanagi Sōetsu 柳宗悦 (1889–1961). This can be read profitably as a complement to that of Sugihira Shizutoshi, which was republished in *Beyond Meditation*. It is quite significant that Yanagi was not merely a founder of the folk craft (*mingei*) movement in Japan, and a specialist in aesthetics who interpreted simple artefacts in terms of the Pure Land, as in his "The Pure Land of Beauty."[22] He also took careful note of the details of the emergence of the *nenbutsu* tradition. When Yanagi's article on Ippen first appeared in *The Eastern Buddhist* in 1973, a coloured illustration from a painting of Ippen himself was also provided, but here the reader is referred to a very similar painting which was already reproduced in *Beyond Meditation* (Portraits of the Saintly Figures 3).

For Shinran Shōnin, who in terms of age was Ippen's senior by some years, we first make use of the conveniently brief introduction by Beatrice Lane Suzuki who is introducing here one of Shinran's *wasan*—a hymn of praise composed in Japanese. It seems that she particularly appreciated the *shōnin*[23] as a composer of *wasan*, Japanese songs of a religious nature. The whole point of composing a *wasan* was of course to make the teaching more accessible to lay persons than it could ever be in the sūtras chanted in a Japanese version of Chinese. Here we include just the *Amida Wasan* in a translation which apparently stems from her, though no doubt on the basis of information and advice from the Japanese side. It gives a reliable and readable first impression of the contents. A detailed comparison of older and newer translations is not the intention here, and for further study those of the Ryūkoku Translation Series are recommended.[24] The collections of *wasan* are quite important in any study of Shinran's religious thought or of Shin Buddhism in general and it is extremely instructive to see precisely what themes Shinran chose when writing them. They were intended to provide orientation for lay followers who were not in a position to pursue scholarly monastic stud-

21. *Interactions with Japanese Buddhism* (Eastern Buddhist Voices 3), 24–31.

22. *Interactions with Japanese Buddhism* (Eastern Buddhist Voices 3), 183–206.

23. The word *shōnin* when used of Shinran, as of Nichiren, is usually written as meaning "saintly person" while in other cases such as Hōnen, it is written as which means an "elevated person" and hence a respected religious leader.

24. Fujimoto, R., Inagaki, H. and Kawamura, Leslie H., *Jōdo Wasan* (Ryūkoku Translation Series IV), Kyōto 1965. This presentation has the advantage of showing the original text on the same page, and also the stanzas by Donran (Tánluán 曇鸞, 476–542) on which this *wasan* is based. A small selection of the *wasan* translated by Yamabe Shūgaku was published in the very first issue of *The Eastern Buddhist* in 1921. Although they could not have been reproduced here without more re-editing than desirable, it is of interest to see that the editors considered it valuable enough to include them immediately.

ies, praising the key texts and patriarchs of the tradition. In the *Amida Wasan*, note the reference to Fugen in Stanza 15, i.e. to the bodhisattva Samantabhadra who was already featured in this book. Innumerable bodhisattvas are said to "take refuge" to his virtues before returning from Amida's Pure Land for the salvation of living beings. Also evident is the now familiar transcendence of the distinction between monk and lay. This may be seen in references to the equalizing power of Amida Buddha, for whom such distinctions play no further role (cf. Stanza 16). The idea is based on the "original vow" of Amida, relevant to all living beings of whatever status, which is conveniently summarized in Stanza 24.

This is followed with a kind of homily by Kakunyo 覚如 (1270–1351), Shinran's great-grandson,[25] entitled "On Steadfast Holding to the Name" in which he seeks to clarify the correct understanding of the founder's teaching. The Japanese title is *Shūjishō* 執持抄 which more literally means "notes on holding fast," i.e. to the name of Amida. Kakunyo Shōnin, being the third head priest of the then still undivided head temple, the Honganji, evidently felt a strong responsibility for the stability of the emerging new Buddhist denomination. He is also known for his work the *Kudenshō* 口伝鈔 ("Record of Oral Tranmission") which sought to present an authoritative collection of the key teachings of Shinran together with some incidents from his life. In spirit this is close to the justly famous *Tannishō* 歎異抄, the collection of sayings collected by Yuien 唯円 (died 1290). The concern for reliable doctrinal precision is shared. The *Kudenshō* represents oral traditions in so far as Kakunyo was able to garner information from Yuien and from Shinran's grandson Nyoshin Shōnin 如信上人 (1239–1300). Here, however, we restrict ourselves to the *Shūjishō*, which first appeared in this form in 1939. Unfortunately the introductory note and the translation were published anonymously, and as with some other cases the oral tradition of the Eastern Buddhist Society does not extend back far enough for further information to be recovered.

A later, particularly strong combination of doctrinal clarity and institutional leadership was provided by Rennyo Shōnin 蓮如上人 (1415–1499), now seen as a key figure in the establishment of the leading Shin Buddhist denominations. The article presented as "Rennyo the Restorer" was published in two instalments in English translation in 1998, but the Japanese original stems from 1915. The author, Kaneko Daiei 金子大榮 (1881–1976), was a leading Shin Buddhist thinker of modern times whom we already introduced in *Listening to Shin Buddhism* (Eastern Buddhist Voices 2). It is of great interest to see his steady picture of Rennyo Shōnin, and as with Yanagi on Ippen, students will find this to be an interesting complement to the presentation of Rennyo by Sugihira Shizutoshi in *Beyond Meditation*.

25. He was the grandson of Kakushin-ni, Shinran's daughter.

The broadening consciousness of Shin Buddhist circles is markedly illustrated by Satō Taira's article on "The Awakening of Faith in the Myōkōnin Asahara Saichi" which introduces an exponent of a particular form of Shin Buddhist spirituality. Readers of Suzuki Daisetsu will recall that he had devoted considerable attention to Saichi in his comparative work on Buddhist and Christian mysticism, as can be seen in his work *Mysticism, Christian and Buddhist*,[26] and Suzuki's stimulus is picked up eagerly by Satō Taira 佐藤平 (born 1939). Although the present article is much later than our other materials, having been published in Japanese as late as 1981 and then in English translation in *The Eastern Buddhist* in 1985, it provides a summary introduction to a theme which had been previously appreciated in Suzuki's circle, to which Satō Taira belonged. In general, the *myōkōnin* 妙好人 might be referred to in English as *nenbutsu* mystics,[27] and the tenor of their spirituality was presented by Suzuki Daisetsu in an article entitled simply "The Myōkōnin" which appeared in *The Eastern Buddhist* in 1950.[28] Here he writes of Saichi, but pays most attention to a lay woman living in the countryside who dictated instructions in mystical verse to her son who was to go and work in the city. This woman, Mrs. Mori, moved from self-reliance and religious carelessness into a consciousness of new joy when sensing dependence on the vow of Amida. The *myōkōnin* illustrate above all that the *nenbutsu* tradition is not one which inevitably suffers ritualized ossification. Rather, its meaning emerges from within the familiar ritual into a new experience of joyful freedom. There might appear to be a certain danger of rigidity in that there are indeed various tightly structured routines in Shin Buddhist religious ceremonies, even if they are not supposed to be regarded as "practice" or *gyō* 行. What we see in the figures of *myōkōnin* such as Mrs. Mori or Asahara Saichi however is that, without any interest in doctrinal change or ritual deviation, a repeated deepening of Shin Buddhist spirituality is possible and leads to ever new vitality. This is independent of any identification of a person as "monk" or "lay" or of whether a person has any particular liturgical status.

As a coda to this collection it is a pleasure to include the outline of the *kikyōshiki* 帰敬式, the first incorporation rite of a novice follower in the Ōtani branch of Shin Buddhism. This rite is sometimes referred to in English as a kind of "confirmation" by analogy with the Christian rite

26. New York (Harper and Brothers) 1957. See especially Section 10, which includes a number of Saichi's sayings.

27. Care should be taken not to mentally translate the English term "mysticism" into Japanese as *shinpi*, for this implies a specific proximity to "esoteric" Shingon Buddhism and the like, which is by no means implied in the English usage.

28. VII 2, 1–21. Unfortunately we cannot reproduce this article here for copyright reasons, and so it is particularly valuable to be able to include the presentation by Satō Taira.

which "confirms" a person in the faith, subsequent to baptism. Technically however (from the point of view of the study of religions) these are all incorporation rites, as opposed to reinforcement rites, which are repeatable. The reader will be able to compare this *kikyōshiki* with the rite for ordinations on Mount Kōya which was presented earlier in the volume. The Shin Buddhist rite is considerably shorter. Nevertheless, in spite of the rather large doctrinal, and indeed spiritual distance between the Shingon tradition of Mount Kōya and the Buddhism of Shinran Shōnin, some overlaps can be seen. In particular, through the lines on *ekō* 回向, meaning "redirection,"[29] or more literally "turning over towards," the path to participation in the bodhisattva vows is opened to all. While there is no reliance in Shin Buddhism on the personal achievement of merit, the merit which is *received* may nevertheless be "turned over" for the benefit of all living beings everywhere—a sentiment with which we may well conclude this introduction.

29. A common translation for the term *ekō*, which is used in all Buddhist denominations in Japan, is "transfer of merit." However in Shin Buddhism care is always taken to avoid any presumption that the Buddhist follower has managed to *produce* any merit which could be transferred. Hence "redirection" or "turning over" is preferred. The sense is that each lay follower is able to share in the on-going transfer of what he or she has received from Amida Buddha.

Part I

The Teaching of Vimalakīrti

— 2 —

Vimalakīrti's Discourse on Emancipation

Izumi Hōkei

Introduction[1]

This is an English translation of the *Vimalakīrti-nirdeśa* (Nanjio 146),[2] being the first attempt to introduce the text to Western readers.[3] Strangely, no one has so far tried to translate it into any of the European languages—a book so full of interest in various ways and so largely contributing to the foundations of Oriental philosophy and religion.

The sūtra was probably first composed in Sanskrit or in some Indian dialect much earlier than the time of Nāgārjuna, which was in the second century CE; for it is frequently quoted by him in his commentary on the *Prajñāpāramitā-sūtra* (Nanjio 1169). How much earlier it was composed we have no means to ascertain; but there is no doubt that the compi-

1. Ed. This introduction has been slightly edited linguistically while retaining the flavour of the original. A technical portion at the end has been simplified, see note 7 below.

2. Ed. This refers to the catalogue of the Chinese Buddhist Canon prepared by Nanjō Bun'yū 南条文雄, which was frequently used at the time. The transcription "Nanjio" is that used on the publication. This catalogue is now widely regarded as superseded because of the publication of the *Taishō Shinshū Daizōkyō.*

3. I did not know when I wrote these lines that an English translation by Mr. Kakichi Ōhara appeared in the *Hansei-Zasshi* for 1898–1899, which is now extremely difficult to obtain. I have had so far no opportunity to read it, but the translator, I am told, was a young and sincere Buddhist who unfortunately died prematurely some fifteen years ago. Some passages from this sūtra are also translated in the *Outlines of Mahayana Buddhism*, London, 1907, by Prof. D. T. Suzuki, to which I have referred in the text. In any case, my translation, which was done quite independently, may be judged on its own merits. Ed. For a brief indication of other English translations see the Introduction to this volume.

lation took place some centuries before Nāgārjuna, because it requires some considerable time for a sūtra to grow worthy of being quoted as a sacred authority.

King Aśoka, a patron of Buddhism, who flourished in the third century BCE and who was a great propagator of the faith throughout India even beyond the northern frontiers, over the Himalayan ranges, never mentions this sūtra; nor does King Kaniṣka of the first century CE. But there is no reason why we should deny the existence of the *Vimalakīrti* in those days simply from this fact, because there are in this sūtra remarkable characteristics which are quite different from those recognized as orthodox by these kings; it is quite likely that they would ignore the canons of the other sects though such might have already been in actual existence.

We may however say, with some hesitation, that this sūtra existed already in the thought of lay Buddhists, though not in the circle of the monastic orthodoxy at the times of the kings mentioned, to whom it seems to have remained quite unknown.

I now propose to point out some of the outstanding characteristics of the sūtra which distinguish themselves from those of the Buddhist doctrine known to Aśoka or Kaniṣka.

(1) We see in this sūtra very frequently the phrase "skilful means"[4] the full original meaning of which is difficult to reproduce in English except by this literal rendering, so dry and altogether inadequate. But this is made to include every legitimate practice issuing from a perfectly religious life. From the first chapter to the last we often meet also with a "supernatural power" which a Bodhisattva or a Buddha exercises. What does this supernatural power mean? It has no meaning by itself. If it had any at all it would be merely to please ignorant and childish people, which is absurd and ridiculous in serious literature. The supernatural power exercised by the principal figures in this sūtra is an indispensable expedient for leading beings to the realization of the highest truth. The Mahāyānistic ideal of a Bodhisattva is to sacrifice his own selfish happiness for a greater cause, and his efforts are concentrated in this self-sacrifice. He does not even extirpate his passions, quite contrary to the ideal of the Hīnayānists; for otherwise he could not feel any sympathy with the lower beings suffering from passions and deliver them from pain. He incarnates himself in any being, even in a medical herb (Chapter VIII) in order to save all beings and lead them to the higher stage of religious life. These sacrificial deeds are never or hardly known in the doctrine of the Hīnayāna.

4. Upāya-kauśalya in Sanskrit. Upāya means "coming near," "approach," "a means," or "expedient," and Kauśalya, "cleverness," "skilfulness," or "expediency"; they are rendered in Chinese as *shànqiǎo fāngbiàn* 善巧方便 (Japanese pronunciation *zengyō hōben*). Ed. The Chinese term does mean skill/ful + means, but strictly speaking, the Sanskrit term meant skillfulness as pertaining to means, i.e. skill in means.

(2) The Six Pāramitās, being the preliminary means for attaining Buddhahood, are never sought by the Hīnayānists, whose final goal is to become an Arhat; but in the present sūtra these Pāramitās are most strongly emphasized. In fact they are one of the signs distinguishing Mahāyāna from Hīnayāna. Charity, discipline, patience, diligence, meditation, and wisdom which are repeatedly taught in the text, form the highest standard of the religious life of a Bodhisattva. And we may take them as standard ethical teachings even when they are interpreted in a modern sense.

(3) Great mercy and compassion towards all beings is most highly recommended in this sūtra. These are cherished only by a Bodhisattva, who belongs to the Mahāyāna; but no Śrāvaka or Pratyeka-Buddha can cherish it inasmuch as he belongs to the Hīnayāna. A Śrāvaka or a Pratyeka-Buddha acts only for himself, not for others; his Nirvāṇa is a complete extinction which is the final goal to his life. But a Bodhisattva does not enter into Nirvāṇa—for the sake of beings who suffer in this life and whose salvation is his sole duty.

(4) Lastly, this sūtra frequently makes reference to a certain mental outlook in which attachment finds no place. This state is beyond either words or thought (Chapter IX, etc.). In fact even the Hīnayāna speaks of freeing oneself from attachment, but to cling to a state of non-attachment is still an attachment, which is always condemned in this sūtra. True non-attachment is absolute, it is not only free from all forms of attachment but free from non-attachment itself. Here is an absolute freedom of the Bodhisattva in all his life-activities, and this is what has never been known to the Hīnayānists.

All these characteristics above mentioned, which are never found in Hīnayāna Buddhism, are products of "the Supreme Enlightenment" which Mahāyānists designate as "Anuttara-samyak-saṃbodhi." To cherish the thought which will lead to this enlightenment is the first step to be taken by all Mahāyānists.

On the whole, what is most emphatically insisted upon in the sūtra before us is the practising of the life of a Bodhisattva as against that of a Śrāvaka or a Pratyeka-Buddha, that is to say, the Mahāyāna is strongly upheld against the Hīnayāna; the religion of laymen against the ascetic life of the monastery. The Fourfold Noble Truth, the Twelve Chains of Causation, and the Eightfold Right Path, which are found everywhere in the Buddhist teaching as preached in Ceylon or Burma, disappear in this sūtra, or at least they are presented in different forms, and in their place are taught the Fourfold Acceptance[5] (*Saṃgraha*), the Ten Pāramitās, and

5. "Acceptance" [as is sometimes translated] is not a good word for *Saṃgraha*, which primarily means "seizing," or "holding." In this case, it is to accept or receive kindly, or to have good understanding, and four modes of it are enumerated by Buddhists: 1. giving, 2. speaking kindly, 3. beneficent deeds, and 4. impartiality.

the Thirty-Seven Requisites (*bodhipākṣika*) for Attaining Supreme Enlightenment. We can also point out how the human Gautama gradually gives way to a superhuman Buddha, who in turn assumes many forms—not as historical Buddhas who are said to have preceded Gautama Buddha, but as manifestations of the eternal truth (Chapter III). It is always the way with a Mahāyāna sūtra that an exceedingly long list of Buddhas is given, and that finally their number grows so enormously large—millions, trillions, or even equal to the sands of the Gaṅgā—that the individual naming is now quite impossible. It shows how Buddhism developed in its ontology from the historical conception of one teacher to that of the Highest Being.

One thing however we should not overlook here, is that this sūtra has contributed much to the popularization of Buddhism. We can imagine how, at the time of its appearance, the monks became corrupted, since they hid themselves behind the walls of their monastery, lost the influence and power which, owing to the virtue planted by the Buddha, they had exercised over the outside world. The lay-brothers of Buddhism were quite dissatisfied with this inactivity of the priests, and united themselves to take the scepter away from the monks now powerless in the propagation of a living faith. Religion ought not to be made the monopoly of the priests, but the possession of all who seek in earnest, either monks or laymen.

As the Vimalakīrti is the production of such a movement started by the laity, those who have always been considered the great disciples of Śākyamuni and the leaders of the priesthood, Śāriputra, Mahāmaudgalyāyana, and Mahākāśyapa, are now treated in this sūtra as miserable ignoramuses destitute of supernatural powers, which fact they themselves confess either by compulsion or on their own account.

It is due to the influence of this movement of the laity that, in Japan, Shōtoku Umayado (574–622), the crown prince of the Emperor Yōmei, who was a great patron of Buddhism, thought himself to be a Vimalakīrti, and wrote a commentary on this sūtra . He was never ordained as a priest but did far more than a professional priest in propagating Buddhism in Japan, and even now many a layman following the example of this devout prince-Buddhist takes pleasure in reading this sūtra above all others.

In this connection it may also be recalled that, in the ancient history of Japan, there was a ceremony called the Yuima-e, which was performed by order of the Imperial Court during certain periods of the Nara and the Heian reign. This was the ceremony of reciting the *Vimalakīrti-nirdeśa-sūtra*, Yuima being the Japanese pronunciation of Vimalakīrti. With reference to the origin of the ceremony, we are told that in the third Year of the Empress Saimyō (655–661)[6] the chief minister Kamatari became ill, and Hōmyō (Beomyeong), a nun who had come from Korea, persuaded the

6. Ed. 斉明天皇, otherwise read as Saimei Tennō.

Empress to recite this sūtra for the recovery of the sick minister, saying that the *Discourse* originated in the sickness of Vimalakīrti and its recitation would be efficacious in the present case. The Empress, therefore, commanded this to be done, and Kamatari was restored to health even before the recitation was over. Then he as an act of gratitude began the ceremony of reciting the *Vimalakīrti-nirdeśa* in the temple which he had erected as a thanksgiving offer to the Buddha. Since that time this became one of the chief ceremonies to be performed annually by order of the Court.

The Sanskrit text was lost a long time ago, and there is very little hope of discovering it;[7] therefore the Chinese translations made directly from the original should be taken as the texts for a translation, as here. Fortunately the style of these translations is so simple that we can see without much difficulty what the original might have been. The sixth translation came from the pen of Kumārajīva in three volumes, in 406 CE. This is the one most widely read and studied, and is the basis for the present English translation, while I did not neglect consulting the other translations wherever necessary.[8]

Vimalakīrti's Discourse

I

On the Buddha-land

Thus it was heard by me. At one time the Blessed One dwelt at Vaiśālī,[9] in the grove of Āmrapālī,[10] together with eight thousand great Bhikṣus and thirty-two thousand Bodhisattvas. These Bodhisattvas were well known to the world; they were endowed with profound wisdom and fundamental duties,[11] and supported by the power of all the Buddhas; they were the maintainers of the true Law which they preached, like the roaring of a lion, for the protection of the Law-fortress; their names were heard in all

7. Ed. So it seemed; but recently a manuscript has been found! See the Introduction to this volume.

8. Ed. This paragraph is a much abbreviated redaction. Izumi originally set out details of the Chinese versions, although four out of seven were "lost" ones, and also of a number of commentaries (not comprehensive), and of a few references in Indian Buddhist literature. The reader is referred to the original publication for his overview. Izumi also noted that the *Śikṣāsamuccaya* by Śāntideva (11th century, as edited by C. Bendall in "Bibliotheca Buddhica," Vol. I. Petrograd, 1897) contains a few passages from the Sanskrit *Vimalakīrti sūtra*, but scattered. A promise to collect these up in an appendix was unfortunately never realized.

9. This is a town on the eastern bank of the Gandak in the district now known as Vihar.

10. A courtesan who offered her garden to the Buddha.

11. Ed. Or "virtues."

the ten quarters; though not requested they made themselves advisers of all people, giving them peace; transmitting and elevating the Three Treasures[12] they rendered them immortal; conquering the Evil Ones and repressing all the heresies; they were all pure and undefiled, ever free from all the hindrances,[13] and their minds were abiding in unimpeded emancipation; they were never interrupted in their recollection, meditation, self-control, and eloquence; they were endowed with [the virtues of] Charity, Discipline, Patience, Energy, Meditation, Wisdom, and Capacity for devising Skilful Means[14]; they attained to recognition in the Law[15] which is uncreated and unobtainable; they were obedient to [the doctrine of all the Buddhas] in rolling the Wheel[16] which never turns back; comprehending the nature of things, they were acquainted with the capacity of all beings; they could never be excelled by any, as they attained to the state of fearlessness; they cultivated their minds with virtues and wisdom; endowed with grandeur and beauty, they were supreme in mien and form; they abandoned all worldly ornaments; their reputation reached far and wide, surpassing even Mount Sumeru; their faith was profound and as strong as a diamond; the Treasure of the Law [in their possession], showering rain of ambrosia, illumined all the world over; their voice was so exquisite that no other could excel; comprehending deeply the causation of things they were free from all false ideas; the two heresies [of positivism and negativism] left no traces in them; they

12. The Buddha, the Law (*dharma*), and the Brotherhood (*saṃgha*).

13. The five impediments (*nivāraṇa*) are: covetousness, anger, sleep, restlessness, and doubt; and the ten entanglements (*paryavanaddha*) are: anger, concealment, not to be ashamed of oneself, not to feel shame towards others, envy, stinginess, regretfulness, sleepiness, restlessness, and dejection.

14. This (*upāya*) is a spiritual faculty to be exercised by the Bodhisattva for the weal of his fellow-beings, when he finishes fulfilling all the six self-benefitting virtues of perfection (*pāramitā*).

15. *Anutpattika-dharma-kṣānti* in Sanskrit. *Kṣānti* is generally translated "patience" or "long-suffering," but when it stands in this combination, it presents some difficulties. According to Xiánshǒu (Genju 賢首), the noted commentator of the *Avataṃsaka-sūtra, kṣānti* here means "to accept the truth patiently and to feel easy and undisturbed at heart" (忍受眞理情安不動). If so, *Anutpattika-dharma-kṣānti* will mean a state of perfect reconciliation to the absolute and uncreated Dharma (Law or truth). The Mahāyānists recognize two stages leading up to the final reconciliation (*kṣānti*): one is through the sense of hearing and the other is affective. In the beginning one attentively listens to the discourses on the Dharma, which gradually takes hold of his entire heart, and finally his whole being grows reconciled to the truth uncreated (*anutpattika*) and therefore eternally abiding.

16. The Buddha's discourses on the Dharma have been likened, ever since his first sermon to his five disciples, to the revolving of the wheel. When one makes this Wheel of the Dharma move on for ever without any set-back, that is, when one's heart is firmly established in the truth, one is said to have attained the stage of *Avinivartanīya*.

fearlessly expounded the Law as a lion roared; their discourse sounded like a peal of thunder; as they were beyond all measure no standard could be applied to them; they gathered the treasures of the Law like the sea-leaders; they thoroughly understood the deep significance of all things; they were acquainted with all the places occupied by all beings and their mental dispositions; they approached the omnipotent knowledge of peerless Buddha who is in possession of the Ten Powers, [four kinds of] Fearlessness, and the Eighteen Special Faculties;[17] capable of closing the gates of all the evil regions, yet they manifested themselves in the five paths of existence;[18] they healed, as great physicians did, all who suffered, bestowing medicine on them as their circumstances demanded and making them obedient to their orders; completing immeasurable qualities, adorning the innumerable Buddha-lands, they made all those who saw or heard them share in their benefits; all their works never were in vain; those Bodhisattvas who were thus endowed with these qualities were:—(1) Samatāvalokita-Bodhisattva [one who sees equality], (2) Asamatāvalokita-Bodhisattva [one who sees non-equality], (3) Samatāsamatāvalokita-Bodhisattva [one who sees both equality and non-equality], (4) Samādhīśvararāja-Bodhisattva [one who is powerful as a king in meditation], (5) Dharmeśvara-Bodhisattva [one who is powerful in righteousness], (6) Dharmalakṣaṇa-Bodhisattva [one who comprehends the nature of things], (7) Prabhālakṣaṇa-Bodhisattva [one who

---

17. These virtues and faculties are exclusively possessed by the Buddha. The ten powers (*bala*) are: (1) the knowledge of what is fit and unfit, (2) of the consequences of karma, (3) of all degrees of meditation and concentration, (4) of the relative powers of the sense-organs, (5) of the various dispositions of beings, (6) of the different elements or realms of existence, (7) of the process leading to any end, (8) of remembering former abodes, (9) of birth and death, and (10) of extinguishing evil overflows (*āsrava*).

    Vaiśāradya means "confidence," "assurance" or "consciousness," but according to the Chinese translators it is "fearlessness" (*wu wei* 無畏), that is, freedom from all the inhibitory feelings born of the sense of limitation. Four kinds of it are mentioned as characteristic of the Buddha: (1) the consciousness that he has the most perfect knowledge, (2) that his evil overflows are eternally stopped, (3) that he has shown the hindrances to the attainment of Nirvāṇa, and (4) that he has shown the right way to escape sufferings.

    The eighteen *avenika* dharmas are (1) faultless behaviour of the body, (2) faultlessness of speech, (3) of thought, (4) firmness of intention, (5) of memory, (6) of samādhi, (7) of energy, (8) of emancipation, (9) of wisdom, (10) freedom from fickleness (11) from noisiness, (12) from confusedness, (13) from heaviness, (14) from heedlessness, (15) from inconsiderateness, (16) the seeing of all things past, (17) of all things future, and (18) of all things present.

18. The five forms of existence (*gati*) are generally reckoned: Hells (*naraka*), Hungry Ghosts (*preta*), Animal Life (*tiryak*), Human Life (*manuṣya*), and Gods (*deva*). When Demons (*asura*) are counted in, we have six *gatis*.

comprehends the nature of light], (8) Prabhāvyūha-Bodhisattva [light-adorned one], (9) Mahāvyūha-Bodhisattva [majestically adorned one], (10) Ratnakūṭa-Bodhisattva [treasure-heaped one], (11) Supralāpakūṭa-Bodhisattva [lord of eloquence], (12) Ratnahasta-Bodhisattva [treasure-laden one], (13) Ratnamudrāhasta-Bodhisattva [treasure-seal-handed one], (14) Sadotthitahasta-Bodhisattva [one with ever-lifted hands], (15) Sadāvalambitahasta-Bodhisattva [one with ever-let-down hands], (16) Sadāprarudita-Bodhisattva [one ever weeping for those who suffer], (17) Harṣendriya-Bodhisattva [one with joyful sense-organs], (18) Harṣarāja-Bodhisattva [king of joy], (19) Supralāpaghoṣa-Bodhisattva [one with eloquent voice], (20) Ākāśagarbha-Bodhisattva [one who conceives the sky], (21) Ratnadīpadhara-Bodhisattva [one who holds the treasure-torch], (22) Ratnaśūra-Bodhisattva [one who is a hero as precious as a jewel], (23) Ratnadarśana-Bodhisattva [one whose understanding is like a jewel], (24) Indrajāla-Bodhisattva [one who is like Indra's jeweled net], (25) Prabhājāla-Bodhisattva [one who is like a jeweled net of surpassing brilliancy], (26) Nālambanasamāhita-Bodhisattva [one who meditates on the causelessness of things], (27) Jñānakūṭa-Bodhisattva [one with a mass of wisdom], (28) Ratnavijaya-Bodhisattva [one who possesses treasure surpassing that of the world], (29) Devarāja-Bodhisattva [king of deities], (30) Mārapramardana-Bodhisattva [one who smashes the Evil One], (31) Vidyutprāpta-Bodhisattva [one who holds lightning], (32) Īśvararāja-Bodhisattva [mighty king], (33) Guṇālaṃkāra-Bodhisattva [one who is adorned with all qualities], (34) Siṃhanada-Bodhisattva [one who roars as a lion], (35) Stanitaghośa-Bodhisattva [one whose voice is like thunder], (36) Parvatasaṃghātaghoṣa-Bodhisattva [one whose voice is like that of crashing mountains], (37) Gandhahastin-Bodhisattva [one whose fragrance is like that of an elephant], (38) Śvetagandhahastin-Bodhisattva [one whose fragrance is like that of a white elephant], (39) Nityodyukta-Bodhisattva [ever-diligent one], (40) Anikṣiptadhura-Bodhisattva [one who is never at rest], (41) Sujāti-Bodhisattva [one who is of excellent birth], (42) Puṣpavyūha-Bodhisattva [one adorning himself with flowers] (43) Avalokiteśvara-Bodhisattva [the lord of mercy for all sufferers], (44) Mahāsthāmaprapta-Bodhisattva [one possessing mighty power], (45) Brahmajāla-Bodhisattva [one resembling Brahma's jeweled net], (46) Ratnadaṇḍa-Bodhisattva [one possessing a jeweled scepter]; (47) Ajita-Bodhisattva [the unconquered one], (48) Alaṃkārakṣetra-Bodhisattva [the possessor of the land of splendour], (49) Suvarṇacūḍa-Bodhisattva [one with golden locks], (50) Maṇicūḍa-Bodhisattva [one whose hair is adorned with a precious gem], (51) Maitreya-Bodhisattva [a descendant of Mitra], (52) Mañjuśrīkumārabhūta [Mañjuśrī, one endowed with excellent virtue, the prince of the Law].

He dwelt together with those thirty-two thousand Bodhisattvas and ten thousand Brahman gods including Śikhins and others, all of whom came from the four quarters of the other worlds, in order to hear him preach; and there were also twelve thousand Indra gods who came from the four quarters of the other worlds as well as other powerful gods, serpent gods, Yakṣas, Gandharvas, Asuras, Garuḍas, Kiṃnaras, Mahoragas, and with them there were many Bhikṣus, Bhikṣuṇīs, Upāsakas, and Upāsikās.[19]

Then the Blessed One, surrounded by this assembly of innumerable hundred-thousands of beings, was preaching the Law; seated on the lion-throne adorned with many jewels, towering over all those who were assembled there, like the mount Sumeru, the king of mountains, making its appearance in the great ocean.

At that time there was in Vaiśālī a son of a wealthy merchant named Ratnakūṭa [heap of treasure]. He came to worship the Blessed One together with five hundred sons of other wealthy merchants, each bringing a canopy adorned with seven precious jewels. They all worshipped the Blessed One touching his feet with their faces, each offering his own canopy to the lord. Then the supernatural power of the Blessed One, acting upon these jeweled canopies, transformed them into one mighty canopy, covering the whole three thousand great Chiliocosms, and on the canopy was seen manifested in all its details, every feature of the worlds. And also there was seen manifested on the canopy all the Sumeru mountains, Himālaya mountains, Mucilinda mountains, Mahāmucilinda mountains, Gandha mountains, Ratna mountains, Kanaka mountains, Kāla mountains, Cakravāḍa mountains, Mahācakravāḍa mountains, oceans, rivers, streams, springs, suns, moons, stars, constellations, palaces of the serpent gods, and many other gods, as well as all the Buddhas and their discourses.

At that time the whole assembly, seeing the supernatural power of the lord, admired it saying that they had never seen such a wonder before, and worshipped him with their folded hands, and looked up into the face of the lord with eager eyes which never turned away from him.

Then Ratnakūṭa, the son of a wealthy merchant, praised the lord in his presence with these verses:

1. Adoration to him whose eyes are pure, wide, and long as the leaves of the blue lotus, whose mind is pure and ever wrapped in fullness of meditation, whose meritorious deeds infinite in number were accumulated by him for ages, and who leads all beings with the ways of perfect peace.

2. We behold the wonderful miracle wrought by the Great Sage, showing the countless lands of all the ten quarters and many a Buddha preaching the Law therein, even here in the presence of all of us.

3. The righteous power of the King of Righteousness far surpasses those of all beings; he, unmoved in the comprehension of the fundamental truth, ever bestows on all beings the wealth of righteousness; he

19. Laymen disciples of the Buddha are called *upāsaka*, and women disciples *upāsikā*.

attains to the state of sovereignty in all things. Therefore adoration is due to the King of Righteousness.

4. He discourses on the truth which is both affirmation and negation; for all things come from causes and conditions and there is neither actor nor action nor sufferer, and yet karma good or bad, is never lost.

5. Since he, first conquering the Evil One under the Bodhi tree, obtained the ambrosia of tranquility and reached the path of supreme enlightenment, he has entirely ceased to have [selfish] will and its activities. And yet he is capable of repressing all the heresies which oppose him.

6. Thrice he rolled the wheel of the Law in the world, the wheel ever pure and testified by gods and men, who through it attain their goal. Thence the Three Treasures made their appearance in the world.

7. He saves all beings from sorrow through this excellent doctrine, which when once given brings them to peace, from which they never fall. He is the Great Physician King who delivers us from old age, disease, and death. Adoration is due to him whose virtues are infinite as the ocean.

8. He, like Mount Sumeru, unmoved by worldly fame or slander, shows mercy equally to the good and the wicked; his mind, like the sky, shows no partiality. Who reveres not this jewel among men?

9. Now I dedicate this humble canopy to the World-honoured One, whose tenfold supernatural power, shown by his compassion towards us, manifests in it our three chiliocosms, palaces of deities, serpent gods, and beings such as Gandharvas and Yakṣas.

10. All things which the world can produce, are seen manifested therein; all assembled praise the lord beholding the wonder which has never been seen before. Adoration is due to the Honoured One in the three worlds.

11. The Great Sage, the king of righteousness, is the only refuge of all beings; there is none who remains unhappy when once he with serene mind beholds the lord; everywhere he beholds the lord before him; this is a special feature of his supernatural powers.

12. The lord preaches with one language, one only; yet beings who hear him preach, deeming it their own, understand him according to their kind; this is a special feature of his supernatural powers.

13. The lord preaches with one language, one only; yet each one who practises according to his own understanding, obtains the advantage to the full; this is a special feature of his supernatural powers.

14. The lord preaches with one language, one only; yet in it some fear, some rejoice, some renounce the world, and some resolve their doubts; this is a special feature of his supernatural powers.

15. Adoration to you who possess the ten powers and are ever diligent. Adoration to you who have obtained the four kinds of fearlessness. Adoration to you who have obtained supernatural power. Adoration to you who are the great leader.

16. Adoration to you who are capable of breaking all the fetters of passion. Adoration to you who have reached the other shore. Adoration to you who are the saviour of the world. Adoration to you who are forever free from the way of birth and death.

17. He thoroughly knows the coming and going of all beings; he is ever emancipated in all things; stainless in the world as a lotus; walks the path of tranquility, comprehending the nature of things; free from hindrance, he is independent as the sky—to him adoration is due.

Then Ratnakūṭa, son of a wealthy merchant, having uttered these verses, spoke to the lord and said: "O Blessed One, these five hundred sons of wealthy merchants have cherished the thought of obtaining supreme enlightenment and wish to hear about the pureness of the land of the Buddha; I only pray this, that the Blessed One preach the way to the pure land, which the Bodhisattvas ought to walk."

The Buddha spoke: "Rightly said, O Ratnakūṭa, you have inquired the way to the pure land for the sake of all the Bodhisattvas; listen carefully! listen carefully! Ponder well on what you hear, and now I will preach for your sake." Then Ratnakūṭa, together with the five hundred sons of wealthy merchants, listened to his preaching.

The Buddha continued: "O Ratnakūṭa, beings of all kinds are the Buddha-world of the Bodhisattvas. And why? A Bodhisattva establishes his world according to the beings who are to be taught; he establishes his world according to the beings who are to be disciplined; he establishes his world according to whether or not beings are to enter into the wisdom of Buddha; he establishes his world according to whether or not beings through any world awaken the faculties of the Bodhisattva. And why? That the Bodhisattva establishes these lands of purity is to benefit all beings. Just as a man can freely build a palace upon a vacant land as he wills, but not in the sky where such things are not possible; so the Bodhisattva wishes to establish his world in order to perfect all beings, for he cannot establish his Buddha-land in the emptiness of sky.

You should know, O Ratnakūṭa, the sincere mind is the pure land of the Bodhisattva; when he shall arrive at full enlightenment, beings who never flatter will be born in that land. The firm mind is the pure land of the Bodhisattva; when he shall arrive at full enlightenment, beings who are endowed with virtues will be born in that land. The Mahāyāna-mind is the pure land of the Bodhisattva; when he shall arrive at full enlightenment, beings who belong to the Mahāyāna will be born in that land. Charity (*dāna*) is the pure land of the Bodhisattva; when he shall arrive at full enlightenment, beings who are capable of renouncing all will be born in that land. Discipline (*śīla*) is the pure land of the Bodhisattvas; when he shall arrive at full enlightenment, beings who fulfill the practice of the ten good deeds will be born in that land. Patience (*kṣānti*) is the pure land of the Bodhisattva; when he shall arrive at full enlightenment, beings who are endowed with the thirty-two excellent features will be born in that land. Diligence (*vīrya*) is the pure land of the Bodhisattva; when he shall arrive at full enlightenment, beings who practise all virtues will be born in that land. Meditation (*dhyāna*) is the pure land of the Bodhisattva; when he shall arrive at full enlightenment, beings who can concentrate their minds without distraction will be born in that land. Wisdom (*prajñā*) is the pure land of the Bodhisattva; when he shall arrive at full enlightenment, beings who attain to the true knowledge of things will be born in that land. The Fourfold Immeasurable Mind[20] is the pure land of the Bodhisattva; when he shall arrive at full enlightenment, beings who complete Mercy, Compassion, Joy and Impartiality will be born in that land. The Four Ways of Acceptance[21] are the pure land of the Bodhisattva; when he shall arrive at full enlightenment, beings who are encompassed by the power of Emancipation will be born in that land. The way of Necessary Means (*upāya*) is the pure land of the Bodhisattva; when he shall arrive at full enlightenment, beings who are well acquainted with the expedient means in all things will be born in that land. The thirty-seven requisites for attaining Supreme Enlightenment are the pure land of the Bodhisattva;[22] when he shall arrive at full enlightenment, beings who exercise the Meditation, the Righteous Work, the Energy, the Sense, the Faculties, the Seven Branches of Knowledge, and the Right Paths will be born in that land. The intention of bringing one's own merits [to the Mahāyāna] is the pure land of the Bodhisattva; when he shall arrive at full enlightenment, he will obtain the land endowed with all the virtues. To preach how to be delivered from the eight disadvantages is the pure land of the Bodhisattva; when he shall

20. *Catvāriy apramāṇāni*: Charity (*maitrī*), Compassion (*karuṇā*), Joy (*muditā*), and Impartiality (*upekṣā*).

21. *Saṃparigrahavastu*. This is the embracing of others with kindly feelings: liberality in giving (*dāna*), affability (*priyavacana*), useful deeds (*arthacaryā*), and taking part in another's joy and sorrow (*samānārthatā*).

22. The thirty-seven *Bodhipakṣadharmas* which are spiritual qualities conducive to the attainment of enlightenment, comprise seven categories: I: The four kinds of *smṛty-upasthāna*, presentness of memory, thoughtfulness: (1) in regard to the body, (2) to sensations, (3) to rising thoughts, and (4) to Dharma. II: The four kinds of application (*samyakprahāṇa*) are: (1) to keep down evil thoughts that have not yet been put into effect, (2) to do away with evil deeds already executed, (3) to cherish good thoughts that have not yet been put into effect, and (4) to cultivate good deeds already executed. III: The four *Riddhis* whereby one can accomplish whatever one wishes: (1) will, (2) thought, (3) exertion, and (4) reflection. IV: The five *Indriyas*, mental faculties, are: (1) faith, (2) energy, (3) memory, (4) concentration of mind, and (5) wisdom. V: The five Balas, or energies, not differing from the above but considered from the point of view of doing actul work. VI: The seven constituents of Bodhi (*bodhyaṅga*) are: (1) memory, (2) investigation, (3) energy, (4) contentment, (5) calmness, (6) concentration of the mind, and (7) equanimity. VII: The eightfold path.

arrive at full enlightenment, there in that land he will find neither the three unhappy regions nor the eight misfortunes.[23] To discipline oneself in morality and never to blame others for their faults is the pure land of the Bodhisattva; when he shall arrive at full enlightenment, there in that land he will not even find the expression 'breach of precepts.'[24] The ten acts of Goodness[25] are the pure land of the Bodhisattva; when he shall arrive at full enlightenment, beings who are born in that land will never suffer untimely death, will be abundantly rich, doing good, truthful and sincere, tender in talk; their families and relatives will never be scattered; they will be skilful in reconciling quarrels, ever benefiting others when speaking; they will never be envious, or angry, but ever maintaining right principles.

Thus, O Ratnakūṭa, the Bodhisattva with sincere mind begins his work; from this beginning he obtains a firm mind; through the firm mind he becomes the master of his will; with his will mastered he follows the true doctrine; following the true doctrine he brings himself towards the Mahāyāna; and as a consequence he learns the Necessary Means (*upāya*); with the Necessary Means he brings all beings to perfection, by this perfection his Buddha-land is purified; as his Buddha-land is purified, his preaching is purified; as his preaching is purified, his wisdom is purified; as his wisdom is purified, his mind is purified; as his mind is purified, all virtues are purified. Therefore, O Ratnakūṭa, when the Bodhisattva wishes to obtain a pure land, he should purify his mind, and as his mind is purified, purified is his Buddha-land."

At that time Śāriputra, through the power of Buddha, thought within himself thus: "If it be true that when the Bodhisattva is pure in mind, then his world is pure, why is this Buddha-land of ours so impure as we see it, which was established by the Buddha out of his pure mind when he was a Bodhisattva?" The Buddha knowing his thought spoke to him and said: "What do you think, O Śāriputra, is it the fault of the sun or moon that the blind cannot see the brightness thereof?" Śāriputra replied: "No, O lord, it is not the fault of the sun or moon, but it is the fault of the blind." The Buddha continued, "Then, O Śāriputra, it is not the fault of the Tathāgata that beings, because of their sins, cannot see

23. The eight misfortunes consist in not being able to see the Buddha and listen to his discourse on the Dharma. This is the fate of those beings who are in the hells, among the hungry ghosts, and in the brute creation, (because in these places there is nothing but pain), in the heaven of longevity, and in the country of the northern Kurus, (because people here are too contented); the deaf, dumb, and blind, too worldly intelligent ones, and those born before and after the Buddha.

24. Ed. Originally: "even the name of breach of precepts."

25. They are: not to destroy life, not to steal, not to commit adultery, not to speak falsehood, not to slander, not to report evil of others, not to talk incoherently, to be free from covetousness, from anger, and from folly.

the pureness of this Buddha-land of ours. Really, O Śāriputra, this land of ours is ever pure; but it is you that cannot see its purity."

Then Śaṅkhacūḍa, a Brahman king, spoke to Śāriputra and said: "You should not cherish such a thought as this, that this Buddha-land of ours is impure. And why? As I behold this world of ours established by the lord Śākyamuni, it is pure without blemish, as pure as the palaces of the Vaśavartin deities." Śāriputra said: "As I behold this world of ours, it is full of hills, mountains, dens, pits, thorns, pebbles, clay, rocks, and many other uncomely things." Śaṅkhacūḍa said: "Inequalities are in your own mind. You see this land not through the wisdom of the Buddha; therefore you think it impure. I tell you, O Śāriputra, the Bodhisattva pure in his firm mind looks upon all things impartially with the wisdom of a Buddha, and therefore this Buddha-land is to him pure without blemish."

At that time the Buddha touched the earth with his toes, and, lo, all the three thousand great Chiliocosms were seen adorned with many a hundred-thousand precious jewels, as the Treasure-adorned land of the Treasure-adorned Buddha possessing countless qualities; the entire assembly finding each seated upon a jewelled lotus-flower praised the Buddha saying that such had never before been seen. The Buddha then spoke to Śāriputra and said: "Now have you seen this world of ours pure and adorned?" Śāriputra said: "Well, O Blessed One, it is what I have never seen the like before, never even heard of such a wonder as this splendour now unfolded before us." The Buddha spoke to Śāriputra: "This world of ours is ever as pure as this; Yet to save beings of inferior capacities, this wicked and impure world is shown. As when the gods take their food from one and the same treasure-bowl, Yet the lustre of food is different according to their virtues, so, O Śāriputra, if one is pure in mind, then he can see the qualities of this world adorned."

At that time, when the Buddha showed the pureness of this land, five hundred sons of wealthy merchants led by Ratnakūṭa, attained to acquiescence in the uncreated Dharma, and eighty-four thousand men cherished the thought of supreme enlightenment.

As soon as the Buddha ceased to exercise his supernatural powers, the world became as it had been before. And thereupon thirty-two thousand gods and men who were striving after the Śrāvakayāna, perceiving that all component things are transient in their nature, and becoming free from desire and passion, attained to the purity of the Law-eye. Eight thousand Bhikṣus were freed from all [relative] things, had their passions extinguished; and their minds liberated.

II

The Way of the Necessary Means[26]

At that time, there dwelt, in the great city of Vaiśālī, a wealthy householder named Vimalakīrti. Having done homage to the countless Buddhas of the past, doing many good works, attaining to acquiescence in the eternal Law, he was a man of wonderful eloquence, exercising supernatural powers, obtaining all the Dhāraṇīs, arriving at the state of fearlessness, repressing all evil enmities, reaching the gate of profound truth, walking in the way of wisdom, acquainted with the necessary means, fulfilling the great vows, comprehending the past and future of the intentions of all beings, understanding also both their strength and weakness of mind, ever pure and excellent in the way of the Buddha, remaining loyal to the Mahāyāna, deliberating before action, following the conduct of Buddha, great in mind as the ocean, praised by all the Buddhas, revered by all the disciples and all the gods such as the Śakra and Brahma kings, the lord of this world, residing in Vaiśālī only for the sake of the necessary means for saving creatures, abundantly rich, ever careful of the poor, pure in self-discipline, obedient to all precepts, removing all anger by the practice of patience, removing all sloth by the practice of diligence, removing all distraction of mind by intent meditation, removing all ignorance by fullness of wisdom; though he is but a simple layman, yet observing the pure monastic discipline; though living at home, yet never desirous of anything; though possessing a wife and children, always exercising pure virtues; though surrounded by his family, holding aloof from worldly pleasures; though using the jeweled ornaments of the world, yet adorned with spiritual splendour; though eating and drinking, yet enjoying the flavour of the rapture of meditation; though frequenting the gambling house, yet leading the gamblers into the right path; though coming in contact with heresy, yet never letting his true faith be impaired; though having a profound knowledge of worldly learning, yet finding pleasure in things of the spirit as taught by Buddha; revered by all as the first among those who were worthy of reverence; governing both the old and young as a righteous judge; though profiting by all the professions, yet far above being absorbed by them; benefitting all beings, going wheresoever he pleases, protecting all beings as a judge with righteousness; leading all with the doctrine of the Mahāyāna when in the seat of discussion; ever teaching the young and ignorant when entering the hall of learning; manifesting to all the error of passion when in the house of debauchery; persuading all to seek the higher things, when at the shop of the wine dealer; preaching the Law, when among wealthy people as the most honourable of their kind;

26. Ed. I.e. skilful means.

dissuading the rich householders from covetousness, when among them as the most honourable of their kind; teaching Kṣatriyas patience when among them as the most honourable of their kind; removing arrogance when among Brahmans as the most honourable of their kind; teaching justice to the great ministers when among them as the most honourable of their kind; teaching loyalty and filial piety to the princes when among them as the most honourable of their kind; teaching honesty to the ladies of the court when among them as the most honourable of their kind; persuading the masses to cherish the virtue of merits when among them as the most honourable of their kind; instructing the highest wisdom to the Brahman gods when among them as the most honourable of their kind; showing the transient nature of the world to the Śakra gods when among them as the most honourable of their kind; protecting all beings when among the guardians as the most honourable of their kind: thus by such countless means Vimalakīrti, the wealthy householder, rendered benefit to all beings.

Now through those means he brought on himself sickness. And there came to inquire after him countless visitors headed by kings, great ministers, wealthy householders, lay-disciples, Brahman princes and other high officials. Then Vimalakīrti taking the opportunity of his sickness, preached to any one who came to him, and said: "Come, you gentlemen, the human body is transient, weak, impotent, frail, and mortal; never trustworthy, because it suffers when attacked by disease; you gentlemen, an intelligent man never places his trust in such a thing; it is like a bubble that soon bursts. It is like a mirage which appears because of a thirsty desire. It is like a plantain tree which is hollow inside. It is like a phantom caused by a conjurer. It is like a dream giving false ideas. It is like a shadow which is produced by Karma. It is like an echo which is produced by various relations. It is like a floating cloud which changes and vanishes. It is like the lightning which instantly comes and goes. It has no power as the earth has none. It has no individuality, as fire has none. It has no durability as the wind has none. It has no personality, as water has none. It is not real and the four elements are its house. It is empty when freed from the false idea of me and mine. It has no consciousness, as there is none in grasses, trees, bricks or stones. It is impotent, as it is revolved by the power of the wind. It is impure and full of filthiness. It is false and will be reduced to nothingness, in spite of bathing, clothing or nourishment. It is a calamity and subject to a hundred and one diseases. It is like a dry well threatened by decay. It is transient and surely to die. It is like a poisonous snake or hateful enemies or a deserted village, as it is composed of the (five) Skandhas, the (twelve) Āyatanas and the (eighteen) Dhātus.

O you gentlemen, this body of ours is to be abhorred, and the body of a Buddha is to be desired. And why? The body of a Buddha is the body of the Law. It is born of immeasurable virtues and wisdom. It is born of discipline, meditation, wisdom, emancipation, wisdom of emancipation. It is born of mercy, compassion, joy, and impartiality. It is born of charity, discipline, patience, diligence, meditation, emancipation, Samādhi, learning, meekness, strength, wisdom, and all the Pāramitās. It is born of the necessary means. It is born of the six supernatural powers. It is born of the threefold intelligence. It is born of the thirty-seven requisites of enlightenment. It is born of the concentration and contemplation of mind. It is born of the ten powers, threefold fearlessness and the eighteen special faculties. It is born by uprooting all wicked deeds and by accumulating all good deeds. It is born of truth. It is born of temperance. Of these immeasurable pure virtues is born the body of Tathāgata. You gentlemen, if one wishes to obtain the body of a Buddha and exterminate the diseases of all beings he should cherish the thought of supreme enlightenment."

Thus Vimalakīrti, the wealthy householder, rightly preached for the profit of those who came to visit him on his bed of sickness and made all these countless thousand people cherish the thought of supreme enlightenment.

III

The Disciples

At that time, Vimalakīrti, the wealthy householder, thought to himself thus: "I am on a bed of sickness; surely the Blessed One who possesses great mercy would never leave me unregarded."

Buddha knowing his thought said to Śāriputra: "Go you to Vimalakīrti and inquire after his health." Śāriputra replied to Buddha and said: "No, O Lord, I am not worthy to go and inquire after his health. And why? I remember one day I was quietly seated meditating under a tree in a forest; then Vimalakīrti came to me and said: 'Well O Śāriputra, to sit thus is not necessarily a quiet sitting. To sit quietly means to withdraw both mind and body from the triple world. Not to rise from the meditation of cessation [i.e., absolute tranquility] and yet to exercise all manners of daily life—this is to sit quietly. Following the manner of ordinary people without renouncing the righteous Law—this is to sit quietly. Not to make the mind abide either within or without—this is to sit quietly. Not to be influenced by the heretical views and yet to practise the thirty-seven requisites for attaining the supreme enlightenment—this is to sit quietly. If one should thus sit he would be approved by Buddha.' At that time, O Blessed One, hearing these remarks, I remained in silence and was unable to reply. Therefore, I am not worthy to go and inquire after his health."

Buddha then said to Mahāmaudgalyāyana: "Go you to Vimalakīrti to inquire after his health." Mahāmaudgalyāyana replied to the Buddha and said: "No, O Lord, I am not worthy to go and inquire after his health. And why? I remember one day when I went into the great city of Vaiśālī and was preaching the Law to the people in the streets, Vimalakīrti came to me and said: 'Well, O Mahāmaudgalyāyana, to preach the Law to the people should not be done in the manner you do. If the Law should be preached at all, it should be done in accordance with the Dharma. There are no created beings in the Law, because it is free from their taints. There is no self in it, because it is free from its taints. There is no durability in it, because there is neither birth nor death. There is no personality in it, because there is neither the past nor the future. The Law is ever serene, as it is far above all forms. The Law has no name, as it is above words. There is no preaching in it because it is beyond sense and meditation. It has no form, as it is like the sky. There is no idle talk in it, as it is absolute emptiness. There is no thought of selfhood in it, as it is free from the thought of selfhood. It has no discrimination, as it is free from all consciousness. There is no object of comparison in it, as there is no relativity. It is subject to neither primary nor secondary causation. It is identical with the essence of things, as it is immanent in them all. It is in accordance with the truth, as it has nothing to be in accordance with. It abides in the ultimate reality, as it remains unmoved on all sides. It is immovable, as it does not depend on the six sense-objects. It neither comes nor goes, as it is ever changing. It is in accordance with emptiness, formlessness, and aimlessness. It is above handsomeness or ugliness. It knows neither increase nor decrease. It knows neither birth nor death. It has no place of attachment. It is beyond eye, ear, nose, tongue, body, and mind. It knows neither altitude [nor profundity]. The Law ever is, ever abiding and immovable. The Law is far above all thought and all work. Well, O Mahāmaudgalyāyana, the nature of the Law being thus, how can we preach it? On the part of the preacher there is nothing to preach or declare, and on the part of the hearer nothing to hear or to obtain. Like a magician who preaches to an audience created by magic, so are we to preach the Law to a phantom audience. One should preach the Law in this spirit. Indeed, to preach the Law, one should understand various degrees of capacity in beings, be well provided with an intelligence which knows no impediment, with a great heart of compassion, and praise the Mahāyāna, thinking how to requite the grace of Buddha and how to make the three treasures abide.' When Vimalakīrti spoke thus, eight hundred householders cherished the thought of supreme enlightenment. As I have no such eloquence, I am not worthy to go and inquire after his health."

Buddha then said to Mahākāśyapa: "Go you to Vimalakīrti to inquire after his health." Mahākāśyapa replied to Buddha and said: "O Blessed One, I am not worthy to go and inquire after his health. And why? I remember once I was begging alms in a poor village, when Vimalakīrti came to me and said: 'Well, O Mahākāśyapa, though you possess a compassionate heart, yet your compassion cannot be universal, because abandoning the rich you seek only the poor in your begging of alms. O Mahākāśyapa, you should abide in the way of sameness and beg alms of all, each in its turn. The begging of alms should be done not for the sake of merely bodily nourishment. You should receive the rice-ball in order to break up the form of combination. You should accept food not cherishing the thought of acceptance. You should enter into a village as if it were deserted. Colours should be perceived as if by a blind man. Voice should be heard as if it were an echo. Odour should be perceived as if it were a wind. Taste should be tasted without being affected by taste. You should regard all things as illusory, as destitute of selfness as well as otherness, as neither burning by themselves nor going to extinction. O Kāśyapa, if you, not abandoning the eightfold path of wrong-doing, enter into the eightfold emancipation, and not abandoning false forms enter into the true Law, and give one dish of food to all beings and make offerings to all the Buddhas and Holies then you may take food. One who eats in such a manner, neither with passions nor without them, is neither engaged in meditation nor awakened from it, abides neither in this world nor in Nirvāṇa. In giving there are no merits, great or small, nor should the giver have any thought of gain or loss. This is the way of directly entering the path of Buddha and not that of the Śrāvakas. O Kāśyapa, if you eat in such a manner you partake not in vain of others' alms.'

When, O Blessed One, I heard these remarks, I felt that I had never heard the like before, then began deeply to revere all the Bodhisattvas and thought thus: 'Though still remaining as a simple layman, yet such is his eloquence. Who [hearing him] cherishes not the thought of supreme enlightenment?' Since that time, I have never persuaded people to the practice of Śrāvakas or the Pratyeka-Buddhas. Therefore, I am not worthy to inquire after his health."

Buddha then said to Subhūti: "Go you to Vimalakīrti to inquire after his health." Subhūti replied to Buddha and said: "O Blessed One, I am not worthy to go and inquire after his health. And why? I remember one day I went into his house begging for alms. Then Vimalakīrti, taking the bowl from me and having filled it with boiled rice, said to me: 'Well, O Subhūti, if a man is able to see sameness in food he will see sameness in everything too. If a man sees sameness in everything, he sees sameness in food too. By begging for alms in this manner he is able to take food.

If, O Subhūti, you be above lust, anger, or ignorance, without extirpating them; if you assume an absolute form without destroying the body; if you attain to intelligence and emancipation without exterminating ignorance and desire; if you obtain emancipation of the five unpardonable sins in spite of being in a state neither released nor bound; if you never see the four noble truths and yet remain not blind to them; if you attain to the result of full enlightenment without going above your mortal nature; if you be neither a common being nor a no-common being; if you be neither a saint nor a no-saint; if you be endowed with things yet transcend their nature—then you can take this food.

O Subhūti, if you see not Buddha, hear not his doctrine, but follow the six teachers of heresy such as Pūraṇa-Kāśyapa, Maskari-Gośālīputra, Sañjya-Vairāṣṭrikaputra, Ajita-Keśakambala, Kakuda-Kātyāyana, and Nirgrantha-Jñati-putra, making them your teachers, entering into their orders, following what they erroneously teach, then you would be able to take this food.

O Subhūti, if you follow heresy and arrive not at the other shore; if you abide with the eight difficulties and never strive to be free from them; if you caress passions and keep yourself away from impure objects—then you obtain the Samādhi of non-resistance, and all beings will also obtain the Samādhi. One who gives alms to you never makes for himself a heap of merit; one who offers food to you enters the three unhappy regions. If you should make yourself a friend of all passions helping all the evil ones; if you render yourself entirely identical with all the evils and all the passions; if you cherish a hostile heart against all beings; and abuse all the Buddhas and their doctrines; if you should never enter into the order and never enter into Nirvāṇa—if you should be thus, then you would be able to take this food.'

Then, O World-honoured One, hearing these words I remained stupefied, not understanding what was meant and not knowing what answer to make; but silently leaving my bowl I was about to depart from his house, when Vimalakīrti said: 'Well, O Subhūti, take your bowl and fear not. What think you if a phantom being produced by Tathāgata spoke those words? Is there any fear in your mind?' I replied: 'No.' Vimalakīrti said: 'All things are of illusory character. You need have no fear. And why? All things are never above such illusory nature. An intelligent man never adheres to words; therefore he has no fears. And why? The nature of words is not characterized by such words such as being or non-being. [When this is understood] there is emancipation, and emancipation manifests itself in all things.'

When Vimalakīrti spoke thus, two hundred deities attained to the pure-eye of the Law. Therefore, I am not worthy to go and inquire after his health."

Buddha then said to Pūrṇa-Maitrāyaṇīputra, "Go you to Vimalakīrti and inquire after his health." Pūrṇa replied to Buddha and said, "O World-honoured One, I am not worthy to go and inquire after his health. And why? I remember one day I was preaching the Law to the novices under a tree in a forest. Then Vimalakīrti came to me and said:

'Well, O Pūrṇa, you should enter into meditation and examine the minds of those people before you would preach. Filthy food should never be put into a jewelled bowl. You should know the thoughts of those Bhikṣus. A beryl should not be taken for a crystal. You can not know the sources of those beings. Never try to awaken them to enlightenment by the doctrine of the Hīnayāna. Never hurt him whose body is unwounded. A narrow path should not be shown to him who wishes to walk a broad path. A great ocean can never be put into the foot-print of a cow. The light of a fire-fly should never be deemed equal to the light of the sun.

O Pūrṇa, those Bhikṣus cherished the thought of the Mahāyāna in days gone by, yet forgot it only for a period. How can they be taught and led by the doctrine of the Hīnayāna? I know that the Hīnayāna knowledge is, like the blind, limited, superficial, and cannot discern different capacities of all things.'

Then Vimalakīrti, having entered into meditation, restored to those Bhikṣus the consciousness of their former existences, during which they had done many meritorious works under five hundred Buddhas, whereby they wished to turn their minds towards the attainment of supreme enlightenment. When they suddenly thus realized the true nature of their minds they prostrated themselves and worshipped Vimalakīrti with their faces touching his feet. Then Vimalakīrti preached the Law unto them and their minds never retreated in supreme enlightenment. Since that time, I am convinced that no Śrāvakas, being incapable of understanding others' faculties, ought to preach the Law. Therefore, I am not worthy to go and inquire after his health."

Buddha then said to Mahākātyāyana, "Go you to Vimalakīrti to inquire after his health." Mahākātyāyana replied to Buddha and said: "O Blessed One, I am not worthy to go and inquire after his health. And why? I remember one day I was discoursing on the ideas of transitoriness, suffering, emptiness, selflessness, and tranquillity. Then Vimalakīrti came to me and said: 'Well, O Kātyāyana, measuring with your mortal ideas you should not preach the Law which is absolute. O Kātyāyana, the Law is in its nature neither mortal nor immortal; this is the meaning of suffering. All things have ultimately no reality; this is the meaning of emptiness. Self and selflessness are identical; this is the meaning of selflessness. Nothing has either beginning or end; this is the meaning of annihilation.' When he had preached thus, the minds of the Bhikṣus attained to emancipation. Therefore, I am not worthy to go and inquire after his health."

Buddha then said to Aniruddha, "Go you to Vimalakīrti and inquire after his health." Aniruddha replied to Buddha and said: "O Blessed One, I am not worthy to go and inquire after his health. And why? I remember once I was walking in a certain place.[27] At that time, a Brahman deity, all

27. Walking was the daily custom among Buddhist mendicants. They circulate after

shining in pure brilliance, came to me, and worshipping me with his face which touched my feet, said to me, 'Tell me how many regions you can see, O Aniruddha?'[28] I replied to him, 'Well, O Angel, I can see these three great Chiliocosms belonging to the land of Śākyamuni even as at an Amra fruit in the hand.'[29] Then Vimalakīrti came to me and said: 'Well, O Aniruddha, tell me, is your supernatural sight a created thing, or is it one of the five miraculous powers of the heretical teachers? If it is not a created thing, it would be functionless, and should be incapable of being seen.' Then, O Blessed One, I remained silent. But those Brahman deities, having heard his words, thought that they had never heard the like before and asked him with bowed heads, 'Tell me who of all men in the world has the true supernatural sight.' Vimalakīrti replied, 'Buddha, the World Honoured One, alone, has attained to the true supernatural sight. Ever in contemplation, he sees all the Buddha countries far beyond the duality of things.' Then Vyūha-Śuddha, the Brahman deity and his relatives, the five hundred Brahman deities, all cherished the thought of supreme enlightenment, worshipping Vimalakīrti with their faces touching his feet, and they suddenly disappeared. Therefore, I am not worthy to go and inquire after his health."

Buddha then said to Upāli, "Go you to Vimalakīrti and inquire after his health." Upāli replied to Buddha and said: "O Blessed One, I am not worthy to go and inquire after his health. And why? I remember at one time there were two Bhikṣus who had committed a breach of discipline.[30] Full of shame they dared not confess it in the presence of Buddha but came to me and said: 'O Upāli, we have committed a breach of discipline and are too ashamed to confess it in the presence of our Lord. We beseech you for this only that you will show us how to be made free from the sin which causes us doubt and contrition.' I preached to them the Law according to the doctrine of discipline. Then Vimalakīrti came to me and said: 'Well, O Upāli, you should not increase the burden of those poor Bhikṣus, rather should you directly exterminate their pain of contrition instead of disturbing their minds. And why? The nature of sin is neither

meals about the temple or in the forest near the monastery. During their walk they recite certain holy names or some portions of the scriptures.

28. It is said that Aniruddha was the one who was most richly endowed with supernatural sight among the disciples of Śākyamuni.

29. Amra, *Mangifera indica*, Linn. mango fruit.

30. Nothing is mentioned in the original text as to what trespass against this discipline they have committed. But one of the commentators tells us that one of them was in doubt whether he had committed misconduct with a woman who was gathering fagots while he was sleeping in a shade; and the other was full of contrition as if he had murdered that woman because he, seeing her coming to him for the purpose of seducing him, had struck her in his anger so violently that she ran away from him, fell into a pit, and died.

within nor in the midst; as it is taught by Buddha, all beings are unclean when their minds are unclean; all beings are pure when their minds are pure; the mind is neither within nor without nor in the midst, and so all things are as the mind is. O Upāli, when one's mind attains to emancipation by means of meditation, is there any uncleanliness in the mind?' I replied, 'No, none.' Vimalakīrti said: 'Even so it is with the minds of all beings. O Upāli, a false idea is uncleanliness, being free from false ideas is pureness; O Upāli, all things are transient; nothing remains unchanged; they are like a phantom or a flash of lightning; nothing waits for another; nothing continues in a state of staying; all things are illusions; they are as dreams, a mirage, the moon reflected in the water, reflections in a mirror, caused only by false ideas. One who knows this is said to be obedient to discipline, and one who knows this is said to be learned.'

Then those two Bhikṣus said: 'What profound wisdom he possesses, even Upāli cannot be his equal; Upāli who is the first among all the disciples in the observance of discipline, cannot discourse with him.' I remarked, 'Except for Tathāgata there are no Śrāvakas or Bodhisattvas who can stand his irrepressible eloquence which can fulfill every desire, such is his wisdom.' At that time the two Bhikṣus had their fear and contrition terminated and thereby the thought of supreme enlightenment was awakened in them; they made this vow: 'May all beings attain such eloquence as that!' Therefore, I am not worthy to go and inquire after his health."

Buddha then said to Rāhula; "Go you to Vimalakīrti to inquire after his health." Rāhula replied to Buddha and said: "O Blessed One, I am not worthy to go and inquire after his health. And why? I remember one day the sons of the wealthy householders of Vaiśālī came to me with bowed heads and questioned me: 'Well, O Rāhula, you are the only son of Buddha who has relinquished the throne of a Cakravartin king and has renounced the world for the purpose of attaining enlightenment. Now tell us what are the advantages of renunciation according to the doctrine.'

At that time Vimalakīrti came to me and said: 'Well, O Rāhula, you should not preach to them the advantages of renunciation. And why? Not to have any advantages or merits—this is renunciation. It is a created thing of which we can speak as having any advantages or merits; but renunciation is an uncreated thing, and in an uncreated thing, there are neither advantages nor merits to talk about. O Rāhula, renunciation is neither this nor that nor between. It is beyond the sixty-two heresies. It abides in Nirvāṇa, attained by the intelligent only. It is walked by the saints alone. If you could subdue evil ones, transcend the five paths of existence, purify the five sights,[31] acquire the five powers, establish the

31. The five sights: fleshly, divine, true, intelligent, and enlightened sights.

five faculties, were not annoyed by outside things; if you could deliver one from all kinds of wickedness, crush all the heresies, go beyond the unsubstantiality of names, be emerged from muddy pollution; if you were without attachment, free from the idea of possession, free from clinging, not disturbed, and could feel inward joy, watch over others, abide in contemplation, and keep yourself away from all faults—if you could do these, then you would be said to have true renunciation.'

Vimalakīrti then spoke to the sons of the wealthy householders and said: 'You shall practise renunciation according to the true Law. And why? A Buddha is seldom seen in this world.' The sons of the wealthy householders said: 'O Sir, we have heard that the Buddha said that if it were not permitted by parents no one could renounce the world.' Vimalakīrti said: 'Well, yet if you cherished the thought of supreme enlightenment this is renunciation, this is perfect fulfillment.' At that time thirty-two sons of the wealthy householders all cherished the thought of supreme enlightenment. Therefore, I am not worthy to go and inquire after his health."

The Buddha then said to Ānanda: "Go you to Vimalakīrti and inquire after his health." Ānanda replied to the Buddha and said: "O Blessed One, I am not worthy to go and inquire after his health. And why? I remember one day my Lord had been somewhat indisposed. Some milk was required to restore him to health. Therefore, holding a bowl in my hand, I stood at door of a wealthy Brahman. Then Vimalakīrti came to me and said: 'Well, O Ānanda, why do you stand here so early in the morning with a bowl in your hand?' I replied: 'O Sir, our Lord is somewhat indisposed. Some milk is inquired to restore him to health. Therefore, I am here with a bowl in my hand!' Vimalakīrti said: 'Stay! stay! Ānanda, never utter such words; the body of the Tathāgata possesses the nature of adamant, as in him all wickedness is exterminated, and all goodness is combined together: What illness, what suffering could he suffer? Go you away in silence. O Ānanda, you should not insult the Tathāgata; you should not let strangers hear these coarse words, you should not let the deities who have great dignity, or Bodhisattvas who have come from the pure lands of the other quarters, hear these words. O Ānanda, even Cakravartin, the sacred king, even on account of his little merit, is free from illness; how much more would it not be so with the Tathāgata who, having accumulated infinite merits, surpasses all? Go you away, O Ānanda: let us not endure such an insult. If the heretical teachers hear this, they might think thus: "Could he be a teacher, who is incapable even of curing his own illness, while pretending to cure the diseases of others?" Go you away in haste and in silence; never again be heard by anybody. O Ānanda, you should know that the body of the Tathāgata is the body of the Law. It is not the body of desire; the Buddha is the world-honoured one above the three states of existence. The body of the

Tathāgata is above numbers.[32] The body of the Tathāgata is uncreated. What illness can such a body suffer?'

Then, O Blessed One, I was full of shame, thinking thus: 'Might it not indeed be that I have misunderstood our Lord even in spite of my nearness to him?'[33] And there was heard a voice from above, declaring: 'O Ānanda, true is that which is said by this man; yet the Buddha who made his appearance in the wicked world of the fivefold corruption[34] has brought illness on himself only in order to awaken all beings to emancipation. Go you, O Ānanda; never be ashamed of begging for milk.' O Blessed One, such is his wisdom and eloquence. Therefore, I am not worthy to go and inquire after his health."

Thus five hundred great disciples each relating his story, praising the words of Vimalakīrti, declared themselves unworthy to go and inquire after his health.

IV

The Bodhisattvas

The Buddha then said to Maitreya Bodhisattva: "Go you to Vimalakīrti and inquire after his health." Maitreya replied to the Buddha and said: "O Blessed one, I am not worthy to go and inquire after his health. And why? I remember one day I was preaching on the life at the Never-Returning Stage to the god-king and his kinsmen of the Tuṣita heaven. Then Vimalakīrti came to me and said: 'O Maitreya, the Blessed One assured you that you should obtain supreme enlightenment after only one birth; now tell me what birth does that assurance refer to. Does it belong to the past, or to the future, or the present? If it be of the past, it is already past. If it be of future, it is not yet come. If it be of the present, it never abides. It is taught by Buddha: O Bhikṣus, at this very moment you are being born and growing old and dying. If the assurance be of no-birth, no-birth is of the true order, and in the true order[35] there is neither the assurance of enlightenment nor even the supreme enlightenment itself. O Maitreya, how can you obtain your assurance in one birth? Did you obtain the assurance at the birth of Suchness or at its extinction? If you did obtain the assurance at the birth of Suchness, Suchness has no birth. If you did obtain the assurance at its extinction, Suchness has

32. Numbers mean the five Skandhas, the twelve Āyatanas, and the eighteen Dhātus, which are the component parts of the human body.

33. Ed. This sentence has been slightly recast.

34. Fivefold corruption: corruption of the present Kalpa, mankind, belief, life, and passions. *Sacred Books of the East* XLIX. Part 2, 102.

35. Ed. I.e. "no-birth is the true status of existence, and in the true status of existence there is neither..."

no extinction. All beings are of Suchness. All things too are of Suchness. All the sages and worthy men[36] are of Suchness. Even you, Maitreya, are of Suchness. If you are capable of obtaining the assurance, all beings too should be capable of obtaining the assurance.

And why? Suchness is one and not divisible nor is it differentiated. If you O Maitreya, can attain to the supreme enlightenment, all beings too can attain to it. And why? All beings have the nature of enlightenment. If you, O Maitreya, can attain to Nirvāṇa, all beings too can attain to it. And why? All the Buddhas know that all beings have ultimately the nature of tranquility, that is Nirvāṇa, and are never to be annihilated again. Therefore, O Maitreya, you should not tempt those gods with your doctrine. In reality, there is none cherishing the thought of supreme enlightenment, nor is there any who retreats. O Maitreya, you should strive to make those gods abandon the false idea that there is Bodhi distinct by itself. And why? Bodhi cannot be obtained by the body or the mind. Tranquility is Bodhi, as in it all things are tranquilized. Not-seeing is Bodhi, as it is beyond all relations. Not-working is Bodhi, as it is beyond thought. To cut [off] is Bodhi, as it exterminates all heresies. To separate is Bodhi, as it is free from all false ideas. To prevent is Bodhi, as it prevents all desires from rising. Not-entering is Bodhi, as it is free from covetousness. Accordance is Bodhi, as it is in accord with the truth. To abide is Bodhi, as it abides in the nature of things. To reach is Bodhi, as it reaches the ultimate. Non-duality is Bodhi, as it is separated from consciousness and its object. Equality is Bodhi, as it is equal to the sky. Uncreated[37] is Bodhi, as there is neither birth nor death. Knowledge is Bodhi, as it understands the mental dispositions of all beings. Not-coming-in-contact is Bodhi, as it is not to be known by any senses. Non-union is Bodhi, as it is detached from the influence of passion. Non-abiding is Bodhi, as it is without figure or form. Unreality of name is Bodhi, as names are empty. Being like a phantom is Bodhi, as it is far above grasping and abandonment. Not being disturbed is Bodhi, as it is eternal calm. Serenity is Bodhi, as it is pure in nature. Non-grasping is Bodhi, as it is far above all attachments. The absence of difference is Bodhi, as all things are same. The incomparability is Bodhi, as it is beyond analogy. Subtility is Bodhi, as all things are unknowable.'

O Blessed One, when Vimalakīrti preached this doctrine, two hundred gods attained to acquiescence in the eternal Law. Therefore I am not worthy to go and inquire after his health."

Buddha then said to a young man called Prabhāvyūha: "Go you to Vimalakīrti to inquire after his health." Prabhāvyūha replied to Buddha and said: "I am not worthy to go to inquire after his health. And why? I remember one day I was about to go out of the great city of Vaiśālī

36. Ed. Arhats, those who have achieved a state of being worthy to achieve nirvāṇa.

37. Ed. The original has "An uncreate is Bodhi, as there is neither birth nor death."

when Vimalakīrti was about to enter into it. I asked him with bowed head, 'Sir, tell me whence have you come?' He replied: 'I have come from the Bodhimaṇḍala, place of enlightenment.' I inquired: 'Where is the Bodhimaṇḍala?' He replied: 'Sincere mind is the Bodhimaṇḍala, as it is without falsehood. Activity is the Bodhimaṇḍala, as it accomplishes all works. The deep mind is the Bodhimaṇḍala, as it increases merits. The enlightened mind is the Bodhimaṇḍala, as it is without errors. Charity is the Bodhimaṇḍala, as it expects no rewards. Morality is the Bodhimaṇḍala, as it fulfills all vows. Patience is the Bodhimaṇḍala, as it knows no impediment in all beings. Diligence is the Bodhimaṇḍala, as it is never slothful. Meditation is the Bodhimaṇḍala, as it controls the mind. Wisdom is the Bodhimaṇḍala, as it directly sees all things. Mercy is the Bodhimaṇḍala, as it treats all beings with equality. Compassion is the Bodhimaṇḍala, as it endures exhaustion and pain. Joy is the Bodhimaṇḍala, as it finds pleasure in the Law. Impartiality is the Bodhimaṇḍala, as it destroys both love and hatred. Supernatural power is the Bodhimaṇḍala, as it is endowed with the six supernatural faculties. Emancipation is the Bodhimaṇḍala, as it is able to turn away and leave out. The Necessary Means is the Bodhimaṇḍala, as it teaches all beings. The Fourfold Acceptance is the Bodhimaṇḍala, as it embraces all beings. Much-hearing is the Bodhimaṇḍala, as it practises what is heard. Self-control is the Bodhimaṇḍala, as it rightly observes all things. The Thirty-seven Requisites for attaining supreme enlightenment are the Bodhimaṇḍala, as they adorn the created things. The fourfold noble truth is the Bodhimaṇḍala, as it never defrauds the world. The twelvefold chain of causation is the Bodhimaṇḍala, as it repeats endlessly beginning with ignorance till we come to old age and death. Passions are the Bodhimaṇḍala, as it knows them to be realities. All beings are the Bodhimaṇḍala, as it knows them to be selfless. All things are the Bodhimaṇḍala, as it knows them to be empty. Vanquishing the Evil Ones is the Bodhimaṇḍala, as it is immovable. The three states of existence are the Bodhimaṇḍala, as they have no fixed abodes for beings. Roaring like a lion is the Bodhimaṇḍala, as it knows no fears. The [ten] powers, the [fourfold] fearlessness, and the [eighteen] special faculties—they are the Bodhimaṇḍala, as they are without faults. The threefold knowledge is the Bodhimaṇḍala, as it is without obstacles. Knowing all things with one thought is the Bodhimaṇḍala, as it attains to omniscience. Thus O noble youth, you should know that all actions of a Bodhisattva who teaches all beings in accordance with all the Pāramitās, even to the raising and putting down of his feet, should be known as coming from Bodhimaṇḍala and abiding in the Law of Buddha.'

When he had preached this doctrine, five hundred gods all cherished the thought of supreme enlightenment. Therefore I am not worthy to go and inquire after his health."

The Buddha then said to Vasuṃdhara Bodhisattva: "Go you to Vimalakīrti to inquire after his health." Vasuṃdhara replied to the Buddha and said: "O Blessed One, I am not worthy to go and inquire after his health. And why? I remember one day, when I was staying in a quiet chamber, Māra Pāpīyas, the evil one, assuming the form of Indra, and accompanied by his kinsfolk and twelve thousand heavenly maidens who sang and played musical instruments, came to me, worshipped me, touching my feet with their faces, and stood to one side with folded hands in reverent attitude. I thought to myself that he was indeed Indra, and spoke to him thus: 'O Kauśika, welcome to you! Though you are richly endowed with happiness, yet you should not give yourself up to pleasures, and seeing how transient the five sensual enjoyments are, you should seek the root of merit and observe the eternal Laws even at the cost of your body, your life and your property.' Then he replied to me: 'Well, O true one, accept these twelve thousand heavenly maidens to attend on you.' I then said: 'O Kauśika, you should not bestow such an unLawful gift upon a Śramaṇa who has entered the order of Śākyamuni. They are of no use to me.' I had scarcely finished these words when Vimalakīrti came to me and said: 'This is not Indra but Māra the evil one who has come to tempt you.' And he turned to the evil one and said: 'Well, you should give me these heavenly maidens. I am worthy to accept this your gift.' Then the evil one, being astonished and fearing, thought to himself: 'Vimalakīrti intends to afflict me!' And he eagerly strove to disappear and depart but all his strivings were in vain. In spite of his utmost supernatural power he could not depart. Then he heard a voice in the air declaring: 'If you would give him these maidens, you could depart.' At last Māra, the evil one, seized with fear, gave his consent reluctantly.

At that time Vimalakīrti spoke to the maidens: 'Māra the evil one gave you all to me. Now all of you should cherish the thought of supreme enlightenment.' Then he preached to them according to their capacities, and persuaded them to cherish the thought of supreme enlightenment. Again he spoke: 'You have now begun to cherish the thought of supreme enlightenment. Now you should enjoy the pleasures of the Law, and give up the pleasures arising from the five senses.' The heavenly maidens inquired: 'What are the pleasures of the Law?' He replied: 'There is the pleasure of ever believing in Buddha. There is the pleasure of desiring to hear the Law. There is the pleasure of revering the order. There is the pleasure of being far above the five senses. There is the pleasure of regarding the five Skandhas as enemies. There is the pleasure of regarding the four elements as if they were venomous snakes. There is the pleasure of regarding the twelve Āyatanas as if they were a deserted village. There is the pleasure of regarding and guarding the thought of supreme enlightenment. There is the pleasure of bestowing happiness on all beings. There is the pleasure of revering the teacher. There is the pleasure of practising universal charity. There is the pleasure of being faithful to discipline. There is the pleasure of being patient and meek. There is the pleasure of being diligent in accumulating merits. There is the pleasure of being not distracted in meditation. There is the pleasure of wisdom clear and without blemish. There is the pleasure of spreading the thought of enlightenment. There is the pleasure of repressing all Evil Ones. There is the pleasure of destroying passions. There is the pleasure of purifying the Buddha-land. There is the pleasure of practising good works for the sake of perfection of forms. There is the pleasure of adorning the Bodhimaṇḍala. There is the pleasure of fearlessness even in hearing the profound Law. There is the pleasure of the threefold emancipation. There is the pleasure of not wishing to reach the goal before maturity. There is the pleasure of being friendly to one's fellow-believers. There is the pleasure of cherishing an unimpeded mind among the teachers of heresy. There is the pleasure of guiding misled friends back to the path. There is the pleasure of approaching good friends. There is the pleasure of being joyous in purity. There is the pleasure of practising the Laws of the numberless requisites which lead to enlightenment. These are called the pleasures of the Law for a Bodhisattva.'[38]

At that time Pāpīyas the evil one said to the maidens: 'Now let us go back to the heavenly palaces.' The maidens said to him: 'You did give us to this man who possesses the pleasures of the Law. We find great joy in his company and would no more take interest in the pleasures of the five senses.' Then Māra the evil one said to Vimalakīrti: 'Sir you ought to give these maidens back to me, because it is the principle of Bodhisattvahood that all things should be given to those who ask for them.' Vimalakīrti said: 'Well I have already given them up; you may take them away. May all beings fulfill their desires according to the Law.' Then the maidens asked Vimalakīrti, 'Tell us how we should conduct ourselves in the palace of the evil one.' Vimalakīrti said: 'Well sisters, you should know that there is the doctrine named the inextinguishable light. By the inextinguishable light is meant this—just as from one light we can produce a hundred or even a thousand other lights, brightening up darkness, yet the original light is not thereby exhausted; thus O sisters, a Bodhisattva can teach a hundred or even a thousand beings to cherish the thought of supreme enlightenment; though his own thought of enlightenment is not at all extinguished, they grow in their merits according to the doctrine. This is [what is meant by] the inextinguishable light. Though you be in the palace of the evil one, yet possessing this inextinguishable light

38. Ed. Though the original does not distinguish between the singular and plural of pleasure/s, the following passage refers to a number of specific pleasures, and so the plural has been corrected to the singular where appropriate.

you can make the innumerable gods and maidens cherish the thought of supreme enlightenment. Thus can you recompense the grace of Buddha and also greatly benefit all beings.'

At that time those heavenly maidens worshipped Vimalakīrti by touching his feet with their faces and suddenly disappeared, accompanying the evil one to his palace. O Blessed One, such is his supernatural power and wondrous eloquence. Therefore I am not worthy to go and inquire after his health."

The Buddha then said to Sudatta a son of a wealthy merchant: "Go you to Vimalakīrti to inquire after his health." Sudatta replied to the Buddha and said: "I am not worthy to go and inquire after his health. And why? I remember once at my father's house, I performed a great charity festival for full seven days, offering food to all Śramaṇas, Brahmans and heretics as well as to the poor, the humble, the suffering, and beggars. When the period of seven days expired, Vimalakīrti came into the assembly and said to me: 'O son of the wealthy merchant, the great charity festival should not be conducted in such a manner as you had. You should conduct a charity festival of spiritual gifts. What have we to do with the bestowal of material wealth?' I inquired: 'Sir, What is the spiritual charity festival?' [He replied:] 'The spiritual charity festival is not carried out in succession but simultaneously. It is looking after the welfare of all beings at one and the same time. This is called the spiritual charity festival.'

'What does it mean? For the sake of enlightenment you should cherish the thought of mercy. For the sake of salvation you should cherish the thought of great compassion. For the maintenance of the true Law you should cherish the thought of joy. For the attainment of knowledge you should dwell in the thought of impartiality. Removing all covetousness, virtue of charity should be practised. To teach the trespassers of morality, rules of discipline should be observed. Possessing the doctrine of selflessness, cherish the Kṣānti Pāramitā. Being far above the forms of body and mind, cherish the Vīrya Pāramitā. Obtaining the form of Bodhi, cherish the Dhyāna Pāramitā. Obtaining omniscience, cherish the Prajñā Pāramitā. Teaching beings, [the thought of] emptiness should be cherished. Not abandoning the created things, cherish [the thought of] formlessness. Manifesting human birth, cherish [the thought of] non-action. For the maintenance of the true Law, necessary means should be cherished. To save all beings, cherish the four deeds of acceptance. To revere all beings, cherish the means of removing arrogance. On the foundation of the body, life and wealth, the threefold Law of permanency should be established. In the sixfold remembrance memory should be exercised. Cherish the sincere mind in the possession of the sixfold peace. Abide in right living while practising the true Law. Be near to the intelligent and the holy with a pure and joyous mind. Cherish the thought of self-control without hating the wicked. Cherish the profound mind, while practising the way of mendicants. Cherish the thought of readiness to hear, while practising according to the doctrine.

Establish a quiet hermitage, while abiding in peace. Be seated in meditation, following the wisdom of the Buddha. Set up your place of holy work, liberating all beings from bondage. Accumulate merits, being endowed with splendour and purifying the Buddha-land. Follow judgment knowing the thoughts of all beings and preaching the Law according to each one's need. Follow the discriminating intelligence, knowing how all things, being far beyond either giving or taking, enter the domain of the one form. Bring forth all goodness exterminating all passion, every obstacle and all wickedness. Bring forth all causes which help the Law of enlightenment, while possessing all intelligence and all goodness. O noble youth, thus is the ceremony of gifts of spiritual things. If a Bodhisattva performs the ceremony of gifts of spiritual things he is called a great giver and he is also the cause of the merits of all the worlds.'

O Blessed One, when Vimalakīrti had spoken thus, two hundred Brahmans all cherished the thought of supreme enlightenment. My mind then obtained purity, and I praised him saying that I had never heard the like before, and bowed to him touching his feet, and took from my neck a necklace worth a hundred thousand [gold pieces] and presented it to him; but he would not accept it. Then I said: 'Sir, I pray only that you would accept my gift and do with it as you please.' Vimalakīrti then accepting the necklace, divided it into two parts, and offered one part to the meanest beggar in the assembly and the other to the Tathāgata Durdharṣa. All the assembly saw the Tathāgata Durdharṣa of the land of light, and also saw the necklace on that Buddha transformed into a jeweled terrace supported by four columns, and adorned on all sides and even transparent and visible. Then Vimalakīrti manifesting this miraculous power said: 'When a giver with equanimity gives even to the meanest beggar, he is like the Tathāgata himself, in his stock of merits there is no trace of discrimination, his great compassion is like [that of the Tathāgata] and he expects no reward; this is called perfecting the spiritual gift.' Then all in the city even to the meanest beggar seeing his miraculous power and hearing his speech awakened the thought of supreme enlightenment. Therefore I am not worthy to go and inquire after his health."

Thus all the Bodhisattvas each relating his story, praised the words of Vimalakīrti, and declared themselves unworthy to go and inquire after his health.

V

Mañjuśrī

The Buddha then said to Mañjuśrī: "Go you to Vimalakīrti to inquire after his health." Mañjuśrī replied to the Buddha and said: "O Blessed One, it is very difficult to discuss with that excellent man; he has attained to such a profound knowledge of the true nature of things; he is able to preach the essence of the Law; he is in possession of unchecked eloquence and unimpeded wisdom; he is well acquainted with the Lawful manners of a Bodhisattva; he has unraveled all the secrets of the Buddhas; he has subdued all evil ones; he is free in supernatural powers; he is perfect in wisdom and the necessary means; yet in compliance with the order of the Buddha, I will go to inquire after his health."

At that time all the Bodhisattvas, all the great disciples, the Śrāvakas, the Brahmans, and the four guardian gods in the assembly, thought within themselves thus: "Now if those two great sages, Mañjuśrī and Vimalakīrti converse together, surely there must be an excellent discourse." So at that moment eight thousand Bodhisattvas, five hundred Śrāvakas, and a hundred thousand deities all wished to follow him. Thus Mañjuśrī, being reverently greeted and surrounded by those Bodhisattvas, great disciples and deities, entered the great city of Vaiśālī.

At that time Vimalakīrti the wealthy merchant thought to himself: "Now Mañjuśrī, together with the large assembly, will come here." And by his supernatural power he made his chamber bare, removing all things together with his attendants and retaining only a sick bed, on which he laid himself. Mañjuśrī then entered the chamber, which had been made bare, leaving nothing but a sick bed. Then Vimalakīrti spoke thus: "Welcome, O Mañjuśrī, you come hither as if you come not, and you are seen as if you are not seen." Mañjuśrī said: "Sir, you speak rightly; if a man has already come, then he comes not; and if he has already gone, then he goes not. And why? One who comes comes from nowhere, and one who goes reaches nowhere; what is seen is not seen. But let us leave this matter aside for a while. Sir, how do you bear your sickness, or may it not be growing more severe by improper treatment? The Lord being exceedingly anxious about you, sends me most cordially to inquire after your health. Sir, what is the cause of your sickness? How long has it lasted? How can it be cured?" Vimalakīrti replied: "From ignorance comes our attachment, and my sickness is thus caused. Since all beings are sick, I am sick. If they were no more sick then my sickness would cease. And why? A Bodhisattva enters [a life of] birth and death for the sake of all beings; where there are birth and death, there is always sickness. If all beings were free from sickness, then there would be no more sickness for a Bodhisattva. Just as when the only son of a wealthy merchant becomes sick, then his parents [out of anxiety] become sick also, and when he is restored to health, then they also recover their health; even so a Bodhisattva loves all beings as parents love their only son; as long as all beings are sick he is sick, when they recover their health, he also recovers his health. Again, you have inquired about the cause of my sickness. The sickness of a Bodhisattva is caused only by his great compassion."

Mañjuśrī asked: "Sir, why is this chamber empty and without attendants?" Vimalakīrti replied: "Even the lands of all the Buddhas are also empty." He asked: "What is [the meaning] of emptiness?" He replied: "It is empty because it is empty." He asked: "How is it that emptiness is empty?" He replied: "It is empty, because non-discrimination is empty." He asked: "Can emptiness be discriminated?" He replied: "To discriminate is also empty." He asked: "Where is this emptiness to be sought?" He replied: "In the sixty-two heresies." He asked: "Where are the sixty-two heresies to be sought?" He replied: "In the emancipation of all the Buddhas." He asked: "Where is the emancipation of all the Buddhas to be sought?" He replied: "In the mind of all beings. Again, you asked why here I have no attendants; but all evil ones and all heretics are my attendants; and why? All evil ones find pleasure in birth and death; and a Bodhisattva never abandons birth and death. All heretics find pleasure in heresies and a Bodhisattva is never moved by heresies."

Mañjuśrī asked: "What is the form of your sickness?" Vimalakīrti replied: "My sickness has no form and cannot be seen." He asked: "Is your sickness connected with body or mind?" He replied: "It is not connected with the body because it is beyond the body; nor is it connected with the mind, because the mind is like a phantom." He asked: "To which of the four elements does your sickness belong, earth, water, fire, or air?" He replied: "This sickness [of mine] does not belong to the earth element, nor is it separated from it; so with water, fire and air elements. But the sickness of all beings is caused by the four elements, and as they are sick therefore am I sick."

Then Mañjuśrī asked Vimalakīrti: "How should a Bodhisattva console another Bodhisattva who is not well?" Vimalakīrti replied: "Preach to him about the impermanency of the body but not about abandoning the body. Preach to him about the liability of the body to suffer but not about the enjoyability of Nirvāṇa. Preach to him about selflessness of the body and preach how to teach and lead beings. Preach to him emptiness of the body but not about the ultimate annihilation. Preach to him about his past sins but not about fixing his thought. Sympathize with others who are sick, because of your own sickness. You should remind him of the suffering undergone in past existences through countless ages. You should let him remember that all beings are to be benefited, remember the merits accumulated in the past, and remember his pure life. Let him not cherish sorrow, but always [seek] to be diligent. You should enable him to make himself even a king among physicians and cure all diseases. Thus a Bodhisattva should console another Bodhisattva who is sick and encourage him to be joyous."

Mañjuśrī asked: "Sir, how should a Bodhisattva who is sick conquer his mind?" Vimalakīrti replied: "A Bodhisattva who is sick should dwell upon such thoughts as these: this sickness of mine has been caused by illusions, errors and passions in my past existences, and it has no real substance. Who is the sufferer in sickness? [No one]. And why? Because the four elements are combined together, there is the combination provisionally called the body. There is no ruler of the four elements besides themselves; nor is there any self in the body. Again, that which we call sickness comes from attaching oneself to Self. Therefore let him not be attached to Self. When the cause of sickness is known, then he should abandon all the thoughts both of Self and beings, and cherish the thought of objectivity. He should dwell upon such thoughts as these: 'body consists of several constituent parts combined together. When it is produced, it is objects only that are produced; and when it perishes it is objects only that perish. Again, those constituent parts are strangers to one another; when they are produced, they do not say so, and when they perish they do not say so.'

Then again, he should abandon even the thought of objectivity and dwell upon such thoughts as these: 'the thought of objectivity is also an error, and this error is a great calamity; it should be removed; how should it be removed? Free yourself from the ideas of me and mine. How can the ideas of me and mine be removed? It means to be removed from two things. What is meant by being removed from two things? Think of neither things within nor without and live the life of equity. How is [the thought of] equity to be dwelt upon? There is equity in self. There is equity in Nirvāṇa. And why? Both self and Nirvāṇa are empty. Why are they empty? They are empty because they are mere names. These two things have no definite nature. If a Bodhisattva would attain to this equity there would be no more sickness but that of emptiness; and this emptiness is also empty.' This sick Bodhisattva receives sense-impressions as if he did not. Not being endowed yet with the Buddha's Law he does not exterminate sensations to attain to the state of enlightenment. If he suffers he should cherish great compassion, comparing himself with those who are in unhappy existence, thinking 'Having conquered myself I will cause all beings to conquer themselves.' He ought only to remove his disease but not things themselves. In order to exterminate the origin of disease it should be taught [thus]: What is the origin of disease? It is bondage. Where there is bondage there is disease. By what is it bound? It is bound by the three states of existence. How is it exterminated? It is exterminated by [the thought of] nothing to obtain. Where there is nothing to obtain there is no bondage. What is [the meaning of] nothing to obtain? It is to be free from the two [opposing] heresies. They are [false ideas] of both things within and things without; they are nothing. Mañjuśrī, this is the means by which a Bodhisattva who is sick can conquer his mind and exterminate the sorrows of old age, disease and death. This is the Bodhi of a Bodhisattva. If he does not do thus, that which is exercised is destitute of efficient result. Just as one who conquers his enemy is said to be courageous, even so he is a true Bodhisattva who conquers both [his mind and] old age, disease and death.

Again, a Bodhisattva who is sick should cherish such thoughts as these. This sickness of mine is neither real nor existent and the sickness of all beings is also neither real nor existent. When he thinks thus, if he cherished a compassion born of passion, it should be abandoned. And why? Exterminating all passions which are like external dusts a Bodhisattva should awake great compassion. So far as the compassion born of passion is concerned, there is in his mind abhorrence of birth and death. If he is free from [passion] there is no more abhorrence. And whatever birth he may undergo is never affected by his passion. As his birth is free from bondage he is able to preach the Law to all beings and make them free, as Buddha taught. It is untrue to say that one who is bound can make another free from his bondage. It is true to say that one who is not bound can free another from his bondage. Therefore a Bodhisattva should not be bound. What is bondage? What is deliverance? To covet the taste of meditation is the bondage of a Bodhisattva. The birth of necessary means is the life of deliverance for a Bodhisattva. The wisdom destitute of the necessary means is bondage. The wisdom endowed with the necessary means is deliverance. The necessary means destitute of wisdom is bondage. The necessary means endowed with wisdom is deliverance.

Why is it that the wisdom destitute of the necessary means is bondage? When a Bodhisattva adorns the land of a Buddha and perfects beings therein, with his mind born of passion, and conquers his mind according to the Law of emptiness, no-form and no-work, he then is said to have the wisdom destitute of the necessary means which is bondage.

Why is it that the wisdom endowed with the necessary means is deliverance? When a Bodhisattva adorns the land of a Buddha, perfects beings therein, with his mind not born of passion, and conquers his mind without ever feeling tired according to the Law of emptiness, no-form, and non-action, he then is said to have the wisdom endowed with the necessary means, which is deliverance.

Why is it that the necessary means destitute of wisdom is bondage? When a Bodhisattva, still governed by passions such as covetousness, anger, and evil thoughts, accumulates a stock of merits he then is said to have the necessary means destitute of wisdom, which is bondage.

Why is it that the necessary means endowed with wisdom are deliverance? When a Bodhisattva is far above all passions such as covetousness, anger, and evil thoughts, accumulating a stock of merits, and turning it to the attainment, of supreme enlightenment, he then is said to have the necessary means endowed with wisdom, which is deliverance. O Mañjuśrī, a Bodhisattva who is sick should look upon things in such a manner.

Again, to look upon the body as transient, sorrowful, empty, and selfless, this is said to be wisdom. To benefit untiringly all beings though a Bodhisattva may be sick himself in this world of birth and death, this is the necessary means. Again as we look upon the body, the body is not separated from sickness, nor is sickness separated from the body; here is sickness, here is the body, the one neither precedes nor follows the other, this is said to be wisdom. Though he may be sick in his body, not to enter into Nirvāṇa, this is the necessary means.

O Mañjuśrī, a Bodhisattva who is sick should conquer his mind in such a manner: he should live neither in the conquered mind nor in the unconquered mind. And why? If he lives in the unconquered mind, he follows in the way of the ignorant, and if he lives in the conquered mind he follows in the way of the Śrāvakas.

Therefore a Bodhisattva should live neither in the conquered mind nor in the unconquered mind. To be far above these two states of mind is said to be the life of a Bodhisattva. Not to commit impure deeds even in [the world of] birth and death, and never to enter into Nirvāṇa, while he is living in Nirvāṇa, this is the life of a Bodhisattva. Doing neither the deeds of an ordinary man, nor the deeds of a saint, is the life of a Bodhisattva. Committing neither impure deeds nor pure deeds is the life of a Bodhisattva.

Though far above all evil deeds, but manifesting himself as repressing evil ones is the life of a Bodhisattva. Seeking omniscience, but never making untimely demands is the life of a Bodhisattva. Though knowing that all things are not created, yet not entering the rank of certainty is the life of a Bodhisattva. Though contemplating the twelve chains of causation, yet allowing himself to enter all evil thoughts is the life of a Bodhisattva. Though accepting all beings, yet never himself attaining to them is the life of a Bodhisattva. Though wishing renunciation, yet never extinguishing the body and mind is the life of a Bodhisattva. Though living in the three worlds, yet never going against the nature of things is the life of a Bodhisattva. Though realizing the emptiness of things, yet accumulating a stock of merits is the life of a Bodhisattva. Though realizing the formlessness of things, yet saving all beings is the life of a

Bodhisattva. Though realizing the non-acting of things, yet manifesting in the body which suffers is the life of a Bodhisattva. Though realizing the causelessness of things, yet achieving all good deeds is the life of a Bodhisattva.

Though realizing the six Pāramitās, yet comprehending all mental conditions of beings is the life of a Bodhisattva. Though realizing the six supernatural powers, yet never making passion extinct is the life of a Bodhisattva. Though realizing the fourfold infinite mind, yet never coveting to be born in the world of the Brahman is the life of a Bodhisattva. Though realizing the Dhyāna and Samādhi of deliverance, yet never being reborn in their respective worlds is the life of a Bodhisattva. Though realizing the fourfold meditation, yet never being separated either from the body or the sensation or the mind or the external objects is the life of a Bodhisattva. Though realizing the fourfold diligence, yet never abandoning the diligence of the body and mind is the life of a Bodhisattva. Though realizing the fourfold practice which fulfils any desire, yet attaining to fullness of supernatural power is the life of a Bodhisattva. Though realizing the five senses, yet discerning the intelligence or the ignorance of all beings is the life of a Bodhisattva. Though realizing the five powers, yet wishing to obtain the tenfold power of Buddha is the life of a Bodhisattva. Though realizing the seven requisites for attaining supreme enlightenment, yet understanding the wisdom of Buddha is the life of a Bodhisattva. Though realizing the eightfold right path, yet desiring to walk the innumerable ways of Buddha is the life of a Bodhisattva. Though realizing the [twofold] equipment, that is, the control of mind and the meditations, yet never attaining to absolute annihilation is the life of a Bodhisattva.

Though realizing that things have neither beginning nor end, yet adorning himself with splendour is the life of a Bodhisattva. Though appearing as a Śrāvaka or a Pratyeka-Buddha, yet never abandoning the Law of Buddha is the life of a Bodhisattva. Though following the absolute purity of all things, yet, when necessary, appearing as himself for the sake of others is the life of a Bodhisattva. Though comprehending all the Buddha-lands as absolutely empty, yet showing all the pure Buddha-lands is the life of a Bodhisattva. Though attaining to the ways of Buddha, rolling the wheel of the Law, and entering into Nirvāṇa, yet never abandoning the ways of a Bodhisattva is the life of a Bodhisattva."[39] When he had spoken these words eight thousand deities in the large assemblies which had accompanied Mañjuśrī all cherished the thought of supreme enlightenment.

39. Ed. Slight syntactic adjustments were necessary in the above three paragraphs.

VI

The Inconceivable Emancipation[40]

At that time Śāriputra, not seeing any seat in the chamber upon which they might sit, thought to himself thus: "Where can these assemblies of Bodhisattvas and disciples be seated?" Vimalakīrti, the wealthy householder, knowing his thought spoke to Śāriputra and said: "Why have you come here, is it to hear the Law [i.e. the Dharma][41] or to search for seats?" Śāriputra replied: "I have come here to hear the Law and not to search for seats." Vimalakīrti spoke: "O Śāriputra, he who seeks the Law never spares either life or body; how much less should he think about seats. He who seeks the Law has no desire either for form or sensation or perception or conformation or consciousness; also he has no desire either for the twelve organs and objects of sense (*āyatanas*) or eighteen elements (*dhātus*); no desire even either for the world of desire (*kāma*) or the world of form (*rūpa*) or the world of non-form (*arūpa*). O Śāriputra, he who seeks the Law has neither attachment to the Buddha nor to the Law nor to the Order. He who seeks the Law never seeks the contemplation of suffering, never seeks the attainment of the cessation of suffering, and never seeks the walking on the path of cessation. And why? The Law is far above mere talk. If I should say that I see suffering, the cause of suffering, the cessation of suffering, and the path of cessation, it is mere talk and this is not seeking the Law.

O Śāriputra, the Law is called complete annihilation; if either birth or death be realized it is either birth or death that is sought for and that is not the Law. The Law is that which knows no attachments; if there be attachments in the Law, Nirvāṇa itself is an attachment; this is not seeking the Law. There is no tracing in the Law; if the Law be traced, that is tracing and not seeking the Law. There is neither taking nor giving in the Law; if there be either taking or giving in the Law, this is either taking or giving and not seeking the Law. There is no refuge in the Law; if there be any refuge in the Law, this is attachment to the refuge and not seeking the Law. The Law is formless; if there be recognition of form, this is seeking the form and not seeking the Law. The Law knows no abodes; if it knows an abode, this is abiding and not seeking the Law. The Law is impossible to be seen, heard, or known; if there be something to be seen,

40. Ed. Izumi's original chapter heading was "Miracles" but the literal meaning of the term is "inconceivable" and it leads into the concept of "inconceivable emancipation." There are miracles worked by supernatural powers both in this and in later chapters.

41. Ed. The word "Dharma" has been added in this instance, but "Law" in the sense of a normative teaching was commonly used in Izumi's times. "Dharma" had not yet become established, and "Law" has therefore been left in place below as a characteristic term for the present translation.

heard, or known, this is seeing or hearing or knowing, and not seeking the Law. The Law is uncreated; if it be created this is seeking the created and not seeking the Law. Therefore, O Śāriputra, he who seeks the Law should not seek any thing in the Law. When he had spoken these words, five hundred deities attained the pure eye of the Law in all things."

Then Vimalakīrti, the wealthy householder, asked Mañjuśrī: "You have been to countless, non-calculable (*asaṃkhyeya*)[42] countries, even tens of thousands of millions; in what country is the lion-throne endowed with the most excellent qualities?" Mañjuśrī replied: "O Sir, after passing through countries equal in number to the sands of the river Gaṅgā, there is in the eastern quarter a world named Sumerudhvaja, and there a Buddha called Sumerupradīparāja now dwells. His body is eighty thousand Yojanas in height, and his lion-throne is also eighty thousand Yojanas in height, the most excellent in adornment." Then Vimalakīrti, the wealthy householder, manifested his supernatural power. And at that moment thirty-two thousand lion-thrones, high, broad, excellent, and pure were sent to him by the Buddha Sumerupradīparāja and were brought there into the chamber of Vimalakīrti. Neither all the Bodhisattvas nor the disciples nor Śakra nor Brahman nor the four guardian gods had seen the like before. That chamber now became so spacious that it contained all the thirty-two thousand lion-thrones without difficulty. In the city of Vaiśālī or even in the Jambudvīpa and in the four worlds there was nothing diminished, all being seen as it had been.

Then Vimalakīrti spoke to Mañjuśrī and said: "Take one of those lion-thrones together with all Bodhisattvas and excellent men, and sit on it, posing yourself as if you were the image of that [Tathāgata]." Then the bodies of those Bodhisattvas who possessed supernatural power suddenly increased in size to the height of forty-two thousand Yojanas and seated themselves on those lion-thrones, but novices among the Bodhisattvas and the disciples could not ascend those thrones. Then Vimalakīrti spoke to Śāriputra and said: "Take one of those lion-thrones." Śāriputra replied: "O sir, this seat is so high and broad that I can not ascend." Then Vimalakīrti said: "O Śāriputra, salute the Tathāgata Sumerupradīparāja that you may ascend the throne." Then all the novices among the Bodhisattvas and the disciples saluted the Tathāgata Sumerupradīparāja and seated themselves on the lion-thrones.

Śāriputra spoke: "O sir, I have never seen before so small a chamber able to contain [so many] thrones, so high and so broad. And in the city of Vaiśālī or even in the villages and towns of the Jambudvīpa and the four worlds and in the palaces of deities, kings of serpents and goblins, there is nothing diminished."

42. Ed. These (and other terms) all mean beyond countability, but the Chinese version simply transliterated *asaṃkhyeya*, which is why it remains in Izumi's translation.

Vimalakīrti spoke: "O Śāriputra, there is an emancipation of all the Buddhas and Bodhisattvas called the Inconceivable. If a Bodhisattva realizes this emancipation, he can enclose within a mustard seed even Mount Sumeru, so high and so broad, and thereby nothing is either increased or diminished. Mount Sumeru the king of the mountains remaining as it was, even the four guardian gods and the gods of the Trayastriṃśa [who live therein] recognize not and know not that they are enclosed therein. But only the being who is to be taught sees the fact that the Sumeru is contained in a mustard seed. This is called the doctrine of the Inconceivable Emancipation.

Again, he can enclose the waters of the four great oceans within a single pore of the skin and there is no disturbance among the beings of the water, whether fishes or turtles or great turtles or crocodiles, the nature of the great oceans remaining as it was; even those beings such as goblins and Asuras [who live therein] do not recognize or know they are enclosed and never disturb the being in whom they are enclosed.

Again, Śāriputra, a Bodhisattva who has realized the Inconceivable Emancipation cuts out the three great chiliocosms [from the universe] even as does the turner of porcelain, and holding them in the palm of his right hand, he casts them forth outside the worlds exceeding in number the sands of the river Gaṅgā; but the beings contained therein recognize not and know not the place where they are cast; when he again restores them to their former place there is no consciousness either of going or of coming in those beings, the nature of the worlds remaining as it was.

Again, Śāriputra, if there be any who ought to be taught and who wish to live long in this world, a Bodhisattva, prolonging seven days even to a kalpa, can make them believe those seven days to be a kalpa; or if there be any who is to be taught and who wish not to live long in this world, a Bodhisattva, reducing a kalpa to be but seven days, can make them believe a kalpa to be seven days.

Again, Śāriputra, a Bodhisattva who has realized the Inconceivable Emancipation, can show to all beings all the adornments of the lands of Buddha concentrated in one country; or he can take all beings of the land of Buddha in the palm of his right hand, and not moving from his original abode, can fly through all the ten quarters showing all things to all beings.

Again, Śāriputra, a Bodhisattva can manifest in a single pore of his skin all the instruments with which all beings in all the ten quarters honour all the Buddhas; or he can manifest in a single pore of his skin all the lands in all the ten quarters, even the sun, moon, and stars.

Again, Śāriputra, a Bodhisattva inhales from his mouth all the winds in all the ten quarters without injury to his body, whereby none of the trees outside him are destroyed.

Again, when the worlds in all the ten quarters come to their end and begin to burn, he takes into his body all the fires; but the conflagration remains unchanged, nor does it do any harm to him.

Again, in the nadir, passing through the countries equal in number to the sands of the river Gaṅgā, he may take a Buddha-land [among them], and deposit it anywhere, at any height, passing through the countries equal in number to the sands of the river Gaṅgā, as if he were lifting a leaf of the date with a needle, no disturbance being caused thereby in the land.

Again, Śāriputra, a Bodhisattva who has realized the Inconceivable Emancipation makes himself visible by his supernatural power, as a Buddha body, or a Pratyeka-Buddha body, or a Śrāvaka body, or Śakra body, or a Brahman body, or a Sahāṃpati body, or a sacred Cakravartin body; again he can produce all the sounds, from the highest to the lowest through all the middle grades, which can be produced in all the worlds of the ten quarters, and turning them even into the voice of a Buddha, he can produce the sounds of impermanence, pain, emptiness, and selflessness in which all the teachings proclaimed by all the Buddhas in the ten quarters can universally be heard. O Śāriputra, I have preached in outline the power of the Inconceivable Emancipation of a Bodhisattva; if it is preached in detail, we can never come to an end even when the present kalpa expires."

At that time Mahākāśyapa having learned what the Inconceivable Emancipation is, praised it saying that he had never heard the like before, and spoke to Śāriputra and said: "Just as a blind man cannot see all the coloured figures which may be presented before him, so all the Śrāvakas may listen to discourses on Inconceivable Emancipation, yet they are incapable of comprehending them. But what wise men hearing this would not cherish the thought of supreme enlightenment? How is it that we have cut down the root [of Bodhi] so that we are rotten seeds in the Mahāyāna? All the Śrāvakas listening to the discourses on the Inconceivable Emancipation should wail so loudly that the three great chiliocosms would be shaken, while all the Bodhisattvas would rejoicingly and reverentially accept this doctrine. If a Bodhisattva understands and believes in the doctrine of the Inconceivable Emancipation, no Evil Ones are able to do anything with him." When Mahākāśyapa had spoken these words thirty-two thousand deities all cherished the thought of supreme enlightenment.

Then Vimalakīrti spoke to Mahākāśyapa and said: "O sir, many of the Evil Ones living in the countless *asaṃkhyeya* worlds in the ten quarters, are such Bodhisattvas as have realized the Inconceivable Emancipation; they manifest themselves as the Evil Ones in order to preach and convert all beings through the necessary means.

Again, Mahākāśyapa, someone may demand of those countless Bodhisattvas in the ten quarters that they offer up one of their hands, legs, ears, nose, eyes, brains, heads, blood, flesh, skin, bones, villages, towns, wives, children, male and female slaves, elephants, horses, vehicles, gold, silver, beryl, precious shells, agate, coral, amber, pearl, mother of pearl, clothes, beverages or food. But the ones who make such demands upon the Bodhisattvas are in many cases Bodhisattvas themselves, who have realized the Inconceivable Emancipation; they manifest themselves in this way in order to strengthen the minds of other Bodhisattvas with their skillful means. And why? Bodhisattvas who have realized the Inconceivable Emancipation are possessors of mighty powers, and being of set purpose, can oppress other beings by making such calamitous demands. If they were really powerless and inferior beings they could never threaten Bodhisattvas in such a manner; just as an ass can never resist the kick of an elephant.[43] This is called the way of wisdom and 'the necessary means of a Bodhisattva who has realized the Inconceivable Emancipation.'"

VII

On Beings

Then Mañjuśrī asked Vimalakīrti: "How should a Bodhisattva regard all beings?" Vimalakīrti replied and said: "A Bodhisattva should regard all beings as a magician regards his magical creations created by himself; he should regard them as a wise man regards the moon in water, as his own reflections in a mirror, and again as a mirage in the summer season, as the echo of a calling voice, as clouds in the sky, as foams in the stream, as bubbles on the surface of water, as the solidity of the plantain tree, as the durability of lightning, as a fifth Element, as a sixth Skandha, as a seventh Consciousness, as a thirteenth Āyatana, as a nineteenth Dhātu.[44] And again a Bodhisattva should regard all beings as forms in the Formless World (*arūpa-dhātu*), as a sprout of burnt seed, as egoism held by the Srotāpanna[45] sages, as a rebirth of the Anāgāmin[46] sages, as the three passions entertained by Arhat sages, as a feeling of greed and anger and an idea of violating rules in the mind of a Bodhisattva after attaining to the state of Acquiescence, as residual impressions in a Buddha, as col-

43. Ed. This paragraph has been recast in some respects to ease the flow. The point is that one set of bodhisattvas tests another set of bodhisattvas with such oppressive demands, which however never disturb the latter who are themselves strong in the inconceivable emancipation.

44. Ed. The point of these numbers is that they exceed the traditional lists of analysis by one, thereby referring to a non-existent extra.

45. Ed. *Srotāpanna*: stream-winners, those who have entered the stream which will carry them along to nirvāṇa.

46. Ed. *Anāgāmin*: non-returners, those who will not need to be reborn in the present world of existence.

ours seen by the blind, as the breathings of one who has entered the meditation of complete annihilation, as the traces of birds in the sky, as the conception of a barren woman, as passions felt by a magically created person, as dream visions after awaking, as the rebirth of one who has entered Nirvāṇa, as smokeless fire."

Mañjuśrī then asked: "When a Bodhisattva regards [all beings thus], how can he practise mercy?" Vimalakīrti replied: "Having thus regarded all beings a Bodhisattva should think this: 'I should now preach this Law for the sake of all beings;' this is true mercy. Practise the mercy of complete annihilation, as there is no birth. Practise the mercy of no-heat, as there is no passion. Practise the mercy of equity, as the past, present, and future are the same. Practise the mercy of non-resistance, as there is nothing produced. Practise the mercy of non-duality, as things within and without do not coalesce. Practise the mercy of indestructibility, as all things are ultimately extinguished. Practise the mercy of solidity, as the mind is never destroyed. Practise the mercy of purity, as the nature of things is pure. Practise the mercy of infinity, as [individual works] are like the sky. Practise the mercy of the Arhat, as he slays passions which are enemies. Practise the mercy of the Bodhisattva, as he bestows peace on all beings. Practise the mercy of the Tathāgata, as he attains to the nature of suchness. Practise the mercy of the Buddha, as he enlightens all beings. Practise the mercy of spontaneity, as it is to be attained without effort. Practise the mercy of Bodhi, as [all things] are equal and of one taste. Practise the mercy of peerlessness, as all desires are exterminated. Practise the mercy of great compassion, as it leads all beings to the Mahāyāna. Practise the mercy of indefatigability, as it makes one contemplate the emptiness and the selflessness of things. Practise the mercy of Giving,[47] as nothing should be grudged. Practise the mercy of Morality, as it effects the conversion. Practise the mercy of Patience, as it protects himself and others. Practise the mercy of Diligence, as it protects all beings. Practise the mercy of Meditation, as he enjoys no sensuous pleasure. Practise the mercy of Wisdom, as he knows what the proper time is. Practise the mercy of the Necessary Means, as he manifests himself in all things. Practise the mercy of non-concealment, as his straight mind is pure. Practise the mercy of profound mind, as he is free from mixed deeds. Practise the mercy of non-deception, as he is free from falsity. Practise the mercy of peacefulness, as he helps us to obtain the happiness of Buddha. Thus is shown the mercy of a Bodhisattva."

47. Ed. Izumi translated this "mercy" as "Law Charity," but the reference here is to the first of the six, or ten perfections, usually referred to simply as "giving." The capital letters used for these by Izumi are retained; the use of capitals for Necessary Means (i.e. skillful means) indicates that this was regarded as a seventh perfection, to balance Wisdom.

Mañjuśrī again asked: "What is compassion?" Vimalakīrti replied: "When a Bodhisattva shares with all beings whatever merits he has acquired by his doings—this is called compassion. [Mañjuśrī again asked:] "What is joy?" [Vimalakīrti] replied: "When others are benefited, a Bodhisattva rejoices in it showing no reluctance whatever." "What is indifference?" He replied: "Whatever happiness and bliss may accrue from his deeds he has no desire to appropriate [it to himself]."

Again Mañjuśrī asked: "In what should a Bodhisattva who fears mortal existence find his refuge?" Vimalakīrti replied: "A Bodhisattva who is in fear of mortal existence should rely upon the power of the merits of Tathāgata." Mañjuśrī again asked: "If he wishes to rely upon the power of the merits of Tathāgata, what should he abide in?" He replied: "A Bodhisattva who relies upon the power of the merits of Tathāgata should abide in saving all beings." Again he asked: "If he wishes to save all beings, what should he remove?" He replied: "A Bodhisattva who wishes to save all beings should remove his passions." Again he asked: "If he wishes to remove his passions, what should he practise?" He replied: "He should practise right thought." Again he asked: "How should he practise right thought?" He replied: "He should realize that there is neither birth nor death." Again he asked: "What is that which has no birth and what is that which has no death?" He replied: "The evil is never born and the good never dies." Again he asked: "What is the root of the good and the evil?" He replied: "The body is the root of both." Again he asked: "What is the root of the body?" He replied: "Desire is the root." Again he asked: "What is the root of desire?" "False judgment is the root." "What is the root of false judgment?" "Erroneous perception is the root." "What is the root of erroneous perception?" "No-abiding is the root." "What is the root of no-abiding?" "As to no-abiding, it has no root. O Mañjuśrī, all things come from the root of no-abiding."

At that time there was in the chamber of Vimalakīrti a heavenly maiden who, having beheld those great persons and heard the Law preached, manifested herself there. She now scattered heavenly flowers upon all the Bodhisattvas and great disciples. When the flowers touched those Bodhisattvas they fell from them, but when they touched any one of those disciples they clung to him and did not fall. All the disciples strove to remove the flowers with their supernatural power but in vain.

Then the heavenly maiden asked Śāriputra: "Why are you striving to remove the flowers?" He replied: "These flowers are unLawful; therefore I must remove them." The heavenly maiden said: "You should not deem these flowers unLawful. And why? These flowers discriminate not between one thing and another; it is you yourself that cherishes the thought of discrimination. So far as the Law of Buddha is concerned, if any mendicant has discrimination in his mind he is said to be unLawful; if there be no discrimination nothing is unLawful; behold those Bodhisattvas to whom the flowers never cling, it is because they have exterminated all thoughts of discrimination. Just as when a man has fear in his mind evil spirits take the opportunity to enter into him, even so since these disciples cherish fear of mortal existence, things such as form, sound, odour, flavour, and touch take the opportunity to tempt them. With those who are far above fear, the passions of the five senses can do nothing with them. If passion remains the flowers cling; when passion is extinguished the flowers can no longer cling."

Śāriputra asked: "How long have you remained here in this chamber?" She replied: "I have remained here in this chamber since your liberation." Śāriputra asked again: "How long have you remained here?" She asked: "How long is it since your liberation?" Śāriputra, remaining silent, gave no reply. The heavenly maiden asked again: "Why are you silent in spite of being the most venerable and intelligent?" Śāriputra said: "Liberation is beyond words. Therefore I know not what to say." The heavenly maiden said: "All words and letters are aspects of liberation. And why? Liberation is neither within nor in the midst; letters are also neither within nor without nor in the midst. Therefore O Śāriputra, it is impossible to speak of liberation separated from letters. And why? All things are aspects of liberation." Śāriputra asked: "Is it not liberation to be free from passion, anger and ignorance?" The heavenly maiden said: "Buddha calls it liberation to be free from passion, anger, and ignorance, only for the sake of beings who are self-assertive. To those who are not self-assertive, Buddha declares that the nature of passion, anger, and ignorance is liberation itself."

Śāriputra said: "O maiden, rightly said! rightly said! What has made you so eloquent?" She replied: "I have obtained nothing; and I have attained to nothing. Therefore am I so eloquent. And why? If one thinks that he has either obtained or attained to something, then he is said to be self-assertive in the Law of Buddha." Śāriputra said: "Which of the three vehicles do you desire?" She replied: "I become a Śrāvaka when I lead beings by the teaching of Śrāvakas; I become a Pratyeka-Buddha when I lead beings by the doctrine of causation; I become the great vehicle when I lead beings by the doctrine of great compassion. O Śāriputra, just as a man having entered a forest of Campaka blossoms smells only the odour of these blossoms and nothing else, even so one having entered this chamber inhales only the odour of the virtues of Buddha, and is no longer desirous of the odour of other virtues, either of Śrāvakas or Pratyeka-Buddhas. O Śāriputra, any [beings], either Śakra, or Brahman, or the four guardian gods, or deities, or serpents, or goblins, all entering this chamber, hear only this excellent man preaching the Law; and when they go out, they all cherish the thought of supreme enlightenment, finding pleasure in the odour of the virtues of Buddha. O Śāriputra, I have stayed here in this chamber for twelve years and have never heard the doctrine either of the Śrāvaka or the Pratyeka-Buddha, hearing only the Law of the Bodhisattva which has been taught by all Buddhas and is unfathomable, full of great mercy and compassion.

O Śāriputra, in this chamber are for ever manifested the eight unobtainable things which have never existed before. What are they? This chamber is ever illumined with golden light both by day and night, the light neither of the sun nor the moon being regarded as bright; this is the first of those things which are unobtainable and have never existed before. He who enters this chamber never suffers from passion; this is the second of those things which are unobtainable and have never existed before. This chamber is ever frequented by such beings as Śakra, Brahman and Bodhisattvas of different regions; this is the third of those things, which are unobtainable and have never existed before. In this chamber is always proclaimed the Law of the six Pāramitās which enables one to the state of infallibility; this is the fourth of those things which are unobtainable and have never existed before. In this chamber excellent music is ever performed by heavenly beings, countless sounds of converting doctrines being sent forth from the strings; this is the fifth of those things which are unobtainable and have never existed before. There are in this chamber four great stores full of treasures which are never exhausted, however liberally they are given away to the poor and needy; this is the sixth of those things which are unobtainable and never existed before. There are in this chamber all the Buddhas of all the ten quarters led by Śākyamuni, Amitābha, Akṣobhya, Ratnaśrī, Ratnatejas, Ratnacandra, Ratnavyūha, Durdharṣa, Siṃhaghoṣa and Sarvārthasiddha, who come, at any moment this excellent man wills, to expound the mine of the Law which is the secret essence of all the Buddhas; and they return when their task is done; this is the seventh of those things which are unobtainable and have never existed before. In this chamber are manifested all the magnificent heavenly palaces and all the pure lands of all the Buddhas; this is the eighth of those things which are unobtainable and have never existed before.

O Śāriputra, there are ever manifested in this chamber these eight unobtainable things which have never existed before. Who, witnessing these miraculous phenomena, finds pleasure in the Law of Śrāvakas?"

Śāriputra asked "Why do you not change your form of womanhood?" The heavenly maiden replied: "During these past twelve years I have seen no womanly form; into what form shall I change? When a magician produces an apparition of a woman, if some one should ask him: 'Why do you not change this womanly form?' would such a question be right?" Śāriputra replied: "No, the creation of a magician has no fixed form; what is there that is to be changed here?" She then said: "Even so, all things have no fixed form; why do you dare to ask me to change my woman-form?"

At that moment the heavenly maiden through her supernatural power, transformed Śāriputra into a form like herself, and she manifested herself as Śāriputra and asked him: "Why do you not change your form of womanhood?" Then Śāriputra in the form of the heavenly maiden replied: "I know not what to change, being transformed into the form of a woman." She said: "O Śāriputra, if you could change this your form of woman then all women could be changed; just as you appear in the form of a woman without being a woman, even so all women only appear to be women; though they appear to be so, yet they are not. Therefore Buddha has spoken, 'all things are neither male nor female.'" As soon as the heavenly maiden withdrew her supernatural power the form of Śāriputra became as before. She asked Śāriputra: "Now where is your form of woman?" Śāriputra replied: "The form of woman is neither existing nor not existing." She said: "Even so, all things are neither existing nor not existing. This is what is taught by Buddha, that [things] are neither existing nor not existing."

Śāriputra asked the heavenly maiden: "In what place will you be reborn after you go hence?" The heavenly maiden replied: "I follow the way of birth as taught by Buddha." Śāriputra said: "The way of birth as taught by the Buddha is never to quit the world." The heavenly maiden said: "Even so, all beings are never annihilated." Śāriputra asked: "When will you attain to supreme enlightenment?" She replied: "When you become again an ignorant man, then shall I attain to supreme enlightenment." Śāriputra said, "It is against reason that I shall again become an ignorant man." She said: "It is also against reason that I shall attain to supreme enlightenment. And why? Bodhi has no abode; therefore there is no one who attains." Śāriputra said: "All Buddhas equal in number to the sands of the river Gaṅgā are attaining to or have attained to or will attain to supreme enlightenment—what does that then mean?" She said: "It is because of the letters and numbers of those worlds that we speak of the past, the present, and the future; but in enlightenment there is neither past nor present nor future." She asked: "O Śāriputra, have you attained to the way of Arhat?" He replied: "I have attained to it because there is nothing to attain." She said: "Even so it is with all the Buddhas and Bodhisattvas; they have attained to supreme enlightenment because there is nothing to attain."

Then Vimalakīrti spoke to Śāriputra and said: "This heavenly maiden, having honoured ninety-two millions of Buddhas, is now able to exercise the supernatural powers of a Bodhisattva; having realized all her desires she has obtained acquiescence in the eternal Law, and having realized the state of steadfastness she manifests herself as she wills and in consequence of her original vows she teaches all beings."

VIII

The Way of the Buddha

Then Mañjuśrī asked Vimalakīrti: "In what manner does the Bodhisattva practise the way of the Buddha?"

Vimalakīrti replied: "When the Bodhisattva practises no-way he is said to practise the way of the Buddha."

Again Mañjuśrī asked: "In what manner does he practise 'no-way'?"

Vimalakīrti replied: "The Bodhisattva is said to practise the way of the Buddha, when he feels no anguish, no anger in the commission of the five grave sins; when he enters hell even without the defilement of sin; when he enters the animal world without errors of ignorance and arrogance, etc.; when he enters the world of hungry ghosts though himself endowed with merits; when he practices such acts as may lead him to heaven either with form or without form, though he does not himself consider heaven an excellent abode; when he is free from defilements, while appearing as if practising covetousness; when he is free from impediments of anger, while appearing as if practising anger; when he controls his mind in wisdom, while appearing as if practising ignorance; when he abandons his possessions, both inner and outer, and does not spare even his body nor his life, while appearing as if practising avarice; when he abides in pure morality and trembles with great fear even for a minor misdemeanour, while appearing as if practising trespasses; when he is ever merciful and patient, while appearing as if practising anger; when he is diligent in virtue, while appearing to be slothful; when he is ever abiding in meditation, while appearing to be distracted in mind; when he is in possession of the wisdom both of this world and that of the world beyond, while appearing to be ignorant; when he follows the teaching of the scripture in accordance with the necessary means, while appearing as if practising flattery and hypocrisy; when he is even like a bridge for all beings, while appearing to be arrogant; when he is pure in mind, while appearing to practise passions; when he is obedient to the wisdom of Buddha, never following the doctrines of the heretical teachers, while appearing to be with the evil one; when he is preaching for the sake of all beings, the Law which has never been heard before, while appearing to be with Śrāvakas; when he is endowed with great compassion and teaches all beings, while appearing to be with Pratyeka-Buddhas; when his hands are bejeweled and his virtues are inexhaustible, while appearing to be with poor people; when he is endowed with excellent forms with which he is adorned, while he looks as if defective in the body; when he is endowed with virtues and born in the race of Buddhas, while appearing to be of mean birth; when he is regarded by all beings with pleasure having obtained the body of the Nārāyaṇa, while appearing to be weak and uncomely; when he eradicated the root of disease and is gone far beyond the fear of death, while appearing to be subject to old age and disease; when he is ever meditating on the transiency of things and is never covetous, though in possession of property; when he is far above the mire of the five senses, though he possesses wives and children; when he is endowed with eloquence and memory which never fails, while appearing to be slow in speech; when he saves beings and leads them in the right path, while appearing to be in the wrong path; when he has exterminated causes for the evil paths, while manifesting himself everywhere in all those paths; when he has exterminated birth and death, while manifesting Nirvāṇa. Mañjuśrī, when the Bodhisattva realizes the no-way in these manners, he is said to comprehend the way of Buddha."

Then Vimalakīrti asked Mañjuśrī: "What are the seeds of Tathāgata-hood?"

Mañjuśrī replied: "To possess the body is the seed. Ignorance and thirst are the seeds. Covetousness, anger, and ignorance are the seeds. The fourfold false idea is the seed. The fivefold passion is the seed. The six Āyatanas are the seed. The sevenfold abode is the seed. The eight wicked paths are the seeds. The ninefold passion is the seed. The tenfold wickedness is the seed. To speak briefly, the sixty-two heresies and all passions are the seeds of Buddhahood."

Mañjuśrī asked: "What is the meaning of this?"

Vimalakīrti replied: "He who enters into the 'state of fixedness' by seeing the uncreated, can never awaken the thought of supreme enlightenment. Just as a lotus flower can never grow on a high dry land but only in the filthy mire, even so he who enters the 'state of fixedness' by seeing the uncreated can never bring forth the Law of Buddha; it is only the mire of passion that beings bring forth the Law of Buddha. Again, seeds sown in the sky can never grow, but only in manured soil can they grow and bring forth fruit; even so he who enters the 'state of fixedness' by [seeing] the uncreated, does not bring forth the Law of Buddha; but it is in those beings who caress selfishness as high as Mount Sumeru that the Law of Buddha grows, cherishing the thought of supreme enlightenment. Therefore, it should be known that all passions are the seeds of Tathāgatahood. Just as one cannot obtain the inestimable treasure buried in the deep ocean unless one dives into it, even so no one can obtain the treasure of omniscience unless one enters the great ocean of passions."

Then Mahākāśyapa praised him by saying: "Rightly said! Rightly said! O Mañjuśrī, you have spoken excellently. What you have spoken is true. All passion is the seed of Tathāgatahood. While we Śrāvakas can never cherish the thought of supreme enlightenment, those beings who commit even the five unpardonable sins are able to cherish the thought [of supreme enlightenment] and bring forth things relating to Buddhahood. But we are forever incapable of cherishing it. Just as a man who is defective in his sense-organs can never again enjoy the advantages of the five senses, even so Śrāvakas and those who have exterminated passions can never partake in the advantages accruing from things relating to Buddhahood and cherish forever no desire [for higher things]. Therefore, O Mañjuśrī, ordinary men know how to return what they have received, while the Śrāvakas do not. And why? Ordinary men hearing the Law of Buddha and cherishing the thought of supreme enlightenment will never let the three treasures be discontinued, but the Śrāvakas, even when they have heard throughout their lives of the Buddha's [tenfold] power and [fourfold] fearlessness, can never cherish the thought of supreme enlightenment."

At that time there was in that assembly a Bodhisattva named Samantadarśanarūpakāya who asked Vimalakīrti: "O sir, who are your father, mother, wife, children, relatives, kinsfolk, officers, and friends, and where are your servants, maids, elephants, horses, and vehicles?"

Vimalakīrti replied in the following gāthās:

"1. Prajñāpāramitā is the mother of the Bodhisattva; Upāya is his father; all the leaders of men are born of such [parents].

2. The joy of hearing the Law is his wife: the mind of mercy and compassion is his daughter; and to possess good will and sincerity is his son; absolute emptiness is his house.

3. Passions are his disciples; they are obedient to the intentions of his will; the [thirty-seven] branches of knowledge are his friends by whom he attains to supreme enlightenment.

4. All the Pāramitās are his friends of righteousness; the four acceptances are his singing maidens who sing in concert the song of the Law.

5. There are the gardens of the Dhāraṇīs; the trees of the Law far above passion, the pure and excellent flowers of the mind of Bodhi, and the fruits of wisdom of emancipation.

6. There in the bathing lake of the eightfold deliverance the water of meditation runs over, strewn with the flowers of the sevenfold purity.[48] Those who bathe [in that water] are men free from the filth of passion.

7. Elephants and horses of the five supernatural powers yoked to the Mahāyāna vehicles, driven by intent mind, serve for the journey to the quarters of the eightfold righteousness.

8. He is endowed with a form adorned with excellent things; the best garment of penitence and the garlands of profound mind [are for him to wear].

48. The sevenfold purity is: (1) the purity of the body, speech, and mind; (2) the purity of being separated from passions; (3) the purity of seeing truth; (4) the purity of being without doubt; (5) the purity of discriminating the way of enlightenment; (6) the purity of comprehending conduct leading to enlightenment; and (7) the purity of Nirvāṇa.

9. There is the wealth of the sevenfold treasure;[49] to teach beings is the interest brought forth therefrom; to make them practise according to the Law and bring these merits to maturity are the great profit.

10. The fourfold meditation is the seat born of pure living; much learning and increase in wisdom serve as the awakening music.[50]

11. The food of the immortal Law he takes; the savour of emancipation is the sauce; the purity of mind is the bath, the anointing is the chapters of the Law of discipline.

12. Destroying all the enemies of passion, there are none who surpass him in courage and strength; repressing the four evils he sets up the banner of victory in the Bodhimaṇḍala.

13. Though he understands that there is neither birth nor death, yet he manifests himself in all lands as the sun is seen from every quarter.

14. Honouring countless millions of Tathāgatas in all the ten quarters, in him there is no idea of partiality because he distinguishes not between those Buddhas and himself.

15. Though he comprehends the emptiness of the nature of those Buddha-lands and beings therein, yet he ever realizes the land of purity for the sake of beings who ought to be taught.

16. He is the Bodhisattva who possesses the power of fearlessness and manifests even in one moment all beings with their forms, voices, and behaviour.

17. Though being conscious of [the evil one] yet he follows the evil deeds of [the evil one];[51] and he manifests those evils according to his will, through his wisdom of the necessary means.

18. He shows himself as subject to old age, disease, and death in order to teach all beings; though he knows that [things are] even as a phantom, yet he understands their real nature in a most thorough manner.

19. He causes a world conflagration and reduces the universe to nothing; this is to make all beings realize the transiency of things, as they are possessed by the idea of permanence.

20. When countless millions of beings come to invite the Bodhisattva, he goes to all their houses, even simultaneously, and makes them walk in the way of Buddha.

---

49. The sevenfold treasure: (1) faith, (2) discipline, (3) hearing, (4) indifference, (5) wisdom, (6) penitence, and (7) penance.

50. Kumārajīva commentating on this passage says that the nobles of India in his time had in their house a professional musician, whose duty it was to awaken them in the morning by soft music.

51. Ed. This passage was originally obscure, running "Though being conscious of evil, yet he follows the evil deeds of evil." The words in brackets have been added on the assumption that this passage is hinting, once again, at the ability of the bodhisattva to outwit Māra.

21. He produces all books of spells and all kinds of arts, making use of all these things in order to benefit all beings.

22. He mixes himself among all the heretics of the world, becoming himself one of the mendicants, and helps others to be freed from errors, while he himself never falls into any of these heresies.

23. He manifests himself as the sun or moon, or Śakra, or Brahman who is the lord of this world, or sometimes even as earth or water, or again as fire or wind.

24. When there is a plague in this kalpa, he shows himself as a medicinal herb; those who use it will be cured of disease and all poisonous [effects] will be nullified.

25. When there is a famine in this kalpa, he shows himself as food; and delivering people from hunger and thirst, he preaches the Law to them.

26. If there be a war in this kalpa, he shows mercy and compassion to all beings, and teaches them to enter a state of non-resistance.

27. If a great battle takes place, the Bodhisattva opposes the enemy with an equal force; manifesting a mighty power he subdues them and restores peace.

28. To all the lands where there are infernal regions the Bodhisattva will go and be busily engaged in saving all the suffering beings.

29. In all the lands where the beasts devour one another, he will manifest himself among them and benefit them.

30. Though he appears as if enjoying the five senses, yet he practises meditation; thus causing confusion in the mind of the evil ones, he gives them no chance to assert their power.

31. To see a lotus flower blooming right in a fire, this is indeed a rare thing; even so to practise meditation while leading a sensuous life, this is rare indeed.

32. Manifesting himself as a harlot he attracts those sensuously minded; this is to catch them by the hook of sensuality, and induce them later into the wisdom of Buddha.

33. He will sometimes be manifested as a burgomaster, or as a leader of traders, or as a national teacher, or as a minister of state, and benefit all beings.

34. He manifests himself as an inexhaustible store of treasure for all who are in need, and by this means persuades them to cherish the thought of enlightenment.

35. He manifests himself as a hero in possession of mighty power and suppresses all the arrogant spirits cherished by those that are egotistic and conceited; and makes them abide in the supreme enlightenment.

36. To those who are timorous he manifests himself before them and gives them comfort: he first bestows fearlessness on them and then lets them awaken the thought of supreme enlightenment.

37. Showing himself as a hermit, free from sensuality and in possession of the five supernatural powers, he leads all beings to realize discipline, patience, and mercy.

38. If there is any who requires attendants, he will be manifested to him as a servant; first he satisfies him in his needs, and then persuades him to cherish the thought of supreme enlightenment.

39. Whatever beings desire he bestows upon them; he induces them to the way of Buddha, and by the power of the good necessary means he provides them with everything they are in need of.

40. Thus infinite are the ways of the Bodhisattva and measureless his deeds; and innumerable are the beings he thus delivers; limitless is his wisdom.

41. Though all the Buddhas through countless millions of kalpas praise the virtues of the Bodhisattva, yet the limits will never be reached.

42. Who but the foolish, ignorant, and unintelligent, hearing such excellent teachings as these, cherish not the thought of supreme enlightenment?"

IX

On Entering the Doctrine of Non-duality

Then Vimalakīrti spoke to all the Bodhisattvas and said: "O sirs, how can a Bodhisattva enter the doctrine of non-duality? I beg of you to explain it according to your way of understanding."

There was in the assembly a Bodhisattva named Dharmeśvara who spoke thus: "O sirs, birth and death make a duality; but things are essentially uncreated, and therefore now they are not to be annihilated. To attain to the acquiescence in the Law of no-birth—this is to enter the doctrine of non-duality."

Śrīgupta Bodhisattva said: "I and Mine make a duality; because there is no I there is no Mine. This is said to enter the doctrine of non-duality."

Animeṣa Bodhisattva said: "Perceiving and not perceiving make a duality; if there is no perceiving of things they are unobtainable; as they are unobtainable there is neither seizing nor abandoning; there is no working, nor is there any function. This is to enter the doctrine of non-duality."

Śrīsiras Bodhisattva said: "Purity and impurity make a duality; if one penetrates into the true nature of impurity, one sees that there is no purity and thus attains to the state of annihilation. This is to enter the doctrine of non-duality."

Sunakṣatra Bodhisattva said: "Moving and remembering make a duality; if there is no moving, there is no remembering, and if there be no remembering, then there is no discrimination. This is to enter the doctrine of non-duality."

Sunetra Bodhisattva said: "Oneness and nothingness make a duality; if we know oneness that is nothingness, and if we do not get attached to nothingness, we enter into the state of sameness. This is to enter the doctrine of non-duality."

Subāhu Bodhisattva said: "The Bodhisattva-mind and the Śrāvaka-mind make a duality; if we understand that the nature of mind is empty like a phantom, there is neither the Bodhisattva-mind nor the Śrāvaka-mind. This is to enter the doctrine of non-duality."

Puṣya Bodhisattva said: "Good and not-good make a duality; if we entertain no thought of good and not-good, then we attain the realm of unconditionality and have a thorough understanding of truth. This is to enter the doctrine of non-duality."

Siṃha Bodhisattva said: "Sin and morality make a duality; when one fully understands that the nature of sin is not different from that of morality and penetrates this characteristic (of the truth) by the diamond-wisdom, he realizes that there is neither bondage nor deliverance. This is to enter the doctrine of non-duality."

Siṃhamati Bodhisattva said: "Passion and passionlessness make a duality; when one understands that all things are equal, then he cherishes not the ideas of passion and passionlessness, and neither does he attach himself to form nor does he abide in formlessness. This is to enter the doctrine of non-duality."

Śuddhamati Bodhisattva said: "The created and the uncreated make a duality; when one is separated from all ideas, then his mind becomes like the sky, and, being in possession of pure wisdom, it is not hindered by anything. This is to enter the doctrine of non-duality."

Nārāyaṇa Bodhisattva said: "Worldliness and unworldliness make a duality; when one comprehends that the nature of this-worldliness is empty, then he attains unworldliness; there is neither coming nor going from one to the other, and there is also neither overflowing nor scattering. This is to enter the doctrine of non-duality."

Sādhumati Bodhisattva said: "Saṃsāra (transmigration) and Nirvāṇa make a duality; but when one understands the nature of Saṃsāra, then he understands that there is neither Saṃsāra nor bondage nor liberation nor burning nor extinction. To understand thus is to enter the doctrine of non-duality."

Pratyakṣa Bodhisattva said: "The exhaustible and the inexhaustible make a duality. But whether things are ultimately exhausted or not exhausted, there is really nothing exhausted. As there is really nothing exhausted there is emptiness; and there is thus neither exhaustion nor non-exhaustion in emptiness. To understand thus is to enter the doctrine of non-duality."

Samantagupta said: "Self and selflessness make a duality. But as self is unobtainable how can selflessness be obtainable? When one understands the true nature of self he no longer cherishes [the idea of] duality. This is to enter the doctrine of non-duality."

Vidyuddeva Bodhisattva said: "Knowledge and ignorance make a duality. But the true nature of ignorance is knowledge; knowledge is not obtainable as it is beyond all ideas. In this to remain the same and be free from the thought of duality is to enter the doctrine of non-duality."

Priyadarśana Bodhisattva said: "Form and emptiness of form make a duality. But form itself is emptiness; and that emptiness is not form extinguished, but the nature of form is in itself emptiness. And the same may be said of the other Skandhas: mind, conception, conformation, and consciousness. For instance, consciousness and the emptiness of consciousness make a duality. But consciousness itself is emptiness; and emptiness is not consciousness extinguished but the nature of consciousness is in itself emptiness. To understand this is to enter the doctrine of non-duality."

Aruṇa Bodhisattva said: "[Of the five elements] the transiency of the first four and that of the fifth element, ether, make a duality. The nature of the first four elements is in itself that of the ether element; because the present is as empty as the past and the future. When the nature of the elements is comprehended, then he is said to enter the doctrine of non-duality."

Sumati Bodhisattva said: "Eye and form make a duality. When one comprehends the nature of the eye, then he no longer desires form, nor is he offended, or infatuated with it. This is called annihilation. The same may be said of the twelve Āyatanas: ear and sound, nose and odour, tongue and taste, body and touch, or mind and ideas; that is: mind and ideas make a duality. When one comprehends the nature of the mind, then he no longer desires ideas, nor is he offended or infatuated with them. This is called annihilation. To abide in this comprehension is to enter the doctrine of non-duality."

Akṣayamati Bodhisattva said: "Charity and transference of its merits towards [the acquirement of] omniscience make a duality. Charity is in itself the transferring of merits towards omniscience. The same may be said of the other Pāramitās: discipline, patience, diligence, meditation, and wisdom. They and the transferring of their merits towards omniscience make a duality. They are in themselves the transferring of merit towards omniscience. To enter thus into the oneness of things is to enter the doctrine of non-duality."

Gambhīramati Bodhisattva said: "Emptiness, formlessness, and aimlessness make a set of dualities. Emptiness is formlessness, and formlessness is aimlessness. When emptiness, formlessness, and aimlessness are attained, thoughtlessness and mindlessness are realized. To have the three ways of emancipation in each one of them—this is to enter the doctrine of non-duality."

Śāntendriya Bodhisattva said: "Buddha, the Law, and the Brotherhood make a a set of dualities. Buddha is the Law, and the Law is the Brotherhood; this triple treasure is in nature uncreated like the emptiness of space; even so are all things. To behave in accordance with this view is to enter the doctrine of non-duality."

Cittānāvaraṇa Bodhisattva said: "The body and its annihilation make a duality. The body is in itself its annihilation. And why? When one understands the true nature of the body, then he cherishes no longer the idea that there is the body and there is its annihilation. There is no duality or distinction between the body and its annihilation. Not to be astonished at this, nor to be afraid of it, is to enter the doctrine of non-duality."

Pradhānakuśala Bodhisattva said: "Body, speech, and mind make a set of dualities. This triple activity has no character of action in it. The non-activity of the body is the non-activity of speech, and the non-activity of speech is the non-activity of mind. This triple non-activity is the non-activity of all things. When one is in accordance with the wisdom of non-activity, this is to enter the doctrine of non-duality."

Puṇyakṣetra Bodhisattva said: "Meritorious deeds, demeritorious deeds, and indifferent deeds—they make a set of dualities. This triplicity of deeds is in itself empty, as they are neither meritorious, nor demeritorious, nor indifferent. He whose mind is not disturbed by these deeds is said to enter the doctrine of non-duality."

Puṣpavyūha Bodhisattva said: "From the idea of self there arises the idea of self and not self, which makes a duality. He who understands the true nature of self does not cherish the idea of this duality. When he does not abide in either of these, he has no consciousness. When there is no such consciousness one is said to enter the doctrine of non-duality."

Śrīgarbha Bodhisattva said: "When a man thinks that he has taken hold of something, there is a duality in his mind; when he has no such consciousness he has no consciousness of attainment, nor of abandonment. This is to enter the doctrine of non-duality."

Candrottama Bodhisattva said: "Darkness and light make a duality. When there is neither darkness nor light, then this duality disappears. And why? When one enters the contemplation of the extinction of sense and thought he sees neither darkness nor light; even so are all things. He who comprehends equality therein is said to enter the doctrine of non-duality."

Ratnamudrāhasta Bodhisattva said: "To be attached to Nirvāṇa and not to be detached from the world—these make a duality. When he is not attached to Nirvāṇa and renounces not the world, there is no longer duality. And why? If there is bondage then there is deliverance. If there is nothing bound from the beginning, who will seek for deliverance?

When there is neither bondage nor deliverance then there is neither attachment nor detachment. This is said to enter the doctrine of non-duality."

Cūḍamaṇirāja Bodhisattva said: "Righteousness and falsehood make a duality. He who abides in righteousness makes no distinction between righteousness and falsehood. When he is free from this duality he is said to enter the doctrine of non-duality."

Tattvarata Bodhisattva said: "Reality and non-reality make a duality. He who sees a reality as it is, does not even see it as distinct from another reality. How much more so with non-reality? And why? Reality cannot be seen by the fleshly eye; it is only seen by the eye of wisdom. And in this eye of wisdom there is nothing seen nor unseen. This is to enter the doctrine of non-duality."

Thus all the Bodhisattvas having each expressed his own view, Mañjuśrī was now asked: "What is meant by a Bodhisattva's entering into the doctrine of non-duality?" Mañjuśrī replied: "According to my view, with regard to all things there is nothing to be said nor to be expressed, nor to be thought about them; they transcend all questioning and answering. This is to enter into the doctrine of non-duality."

Then Mañjuśrī asked Vimalakīrti: "Now each of us has expressed his view; O sir, I wish you will express your view as to what is meant by a Bodhisattva's entering into the doctrine of non-duality." Vimalakīrti remained silent and said not a word.

Then Mañjuśrī praised him saying: "Well done, well done, ultimately not to have any letters or words, this is indeed to enter the doctrine of non-duality."

When this lesson concerning the entering into the doctrine of non-duality was preached to the five thousand Bodhisattvas in the assembly, all entered into the doctrine of non-duality and obtained acquiescence in the uncreated Law.

X

Buddha Gandhakūṭa

At that time Śāriputra thought to himself: "The meal time draws nigh; where should those Bodhisattvas take their meal?" Then Vimalakīrti knowing his thought thus spoke to him: "The Eightfold Liberation is preached by the Buddha and you should receive and practise it; why should you think of material food when you desire to hear the Law? But if you would eat, wait for a space, when I shall be able to obtain such food as you have never tasted before."

Then Vimalakīrti, having entered into a Samādhi, manifested to the great assembly a country called Sarvagandhasugandha, which is situated in the upper regions beyond the Buddha-countries exceeding in number even the sands of forty-two Gaṅgā rivers; and there is in that land a Buddha living at present, known as Gandhakūṭa, and the perfume of that land excels even the perfume of men and deities of the worlds of all the Buddhas in all the ten quarters.

There in that land neither the name of Śrāvaka nor of Pratyekabuddha is heard; there is only a great assembly of Bodhisattvas. The Buddha preaches the Law to [those Bodhisattvas]. Everything in that land is made of perfume. All over the land towers and terraces are built of perfume. People walk on a perfume-ground: All the gardens are of perfume. The savoury perfume of food fills the countless worlds in all the ten quarters. At that time the Buddha [Gandhakūṭa] was seated himself to partake of food with the Bodhisattvas. There were also present many deities each called Gandhavyūha; all of them, having cherished the thought of supreme enlightenment, did homage to each one in this great assembly.

Then Vimalakīrti asked the Bodhisattvas: "O sirs, who is able to bring here the food of that Buddha?" All the assembly remained silent through the supernatural power of Mañjuśrī. Vimalakīrti said: "How pitiful, O you Bodhisattvas! Are you not ashamed of yourselves?" Mañjuśrī said: "'Do not despise these novices,' this being the Buddha's command."

Then Vimalakīrti, without raising himself from his seat, manifested in the presence of the assembly an incarnate Bodhisattva, whose form, splendour, and dignity were magnificent, far surpassing any in the assembly. He then spoke to the Bodhisattva and said: "Go you there in the quarters on high, beyond the Buddha-countries exceeding even in number the sands of forty-two Gaṅgā rivers, to the country named Sarvagandhasugandha, where a Buddha named Gandhakūṭa now dwells, seated at table to take refreshments together with the Bodhisattvas, and on your arrival tell him these words of mine saying: 'Vimalakīrti, touching your feet with his bowed head, greets you with all reverence and wishes to inquire whether you are assailed with few ailings, few illnesses, and whether your spirits are in good condition as ever. He prays that you bestow upon him a portion of your food if you can spare it, that he might perform a religious work in the Sahā world, enabling all those who find pleasure in the inferior Law only, to open their eyes to the great religion, thus helping to spread the fame of Tathāgata throughout [the world].'"

Then at that time the incarnate Bodhisattva ascended on high in the presence of the assembly, and every one in the assembly could see him reach the country of Sarvagandhasugandha and greet that Buddha, touch his feet with his bowed head, and speak thus: "Vimalakīrti, touching your feet with his bowed head, greets you with all reverence and wishes to inquire whether you are assailed with few ailings, few illnesses, and whether your spirits are in good condition as ever. He prays you to bestow upon him some portion of your food if you can spare it, that he might perform a religious work in the Sahā world, enabling all those who find pleasure in the inferior Law only, to open their eyes to the great religion, thus helping to spread the fame of Tathāgata throughout [the world]."

The great men in that country, having beheld this incarnate Bodhisattva, praised him saying that they had never seen the like before, and asked the Buddha: "Whence comes this superior man? Where is the Sahā world? What does it mean to find pleasure only in the inferior Law?"

The Buddha replied and said: "In the lower region beyond the Buddha-countries even equal to the number of the sands of forty-two Gaṅgā rivers there is a world called Sahā; and there dwells, now, a Buddha called Śākyamuni; in the wicked age of five corruptions, he teaches the doctrine for the sake of those who find pleasure in the inferior Law only. There is a Bodhisattva called Vimalakīrti, who, abiding in the Inconceivable Emancipation, preaches the Law for the sake of the Bodhisattvas; now he specially sends this incarnate Bodhisattva to us, to praise my name and this land in order to help the Bodhisattvas there to increase virtue and merit." The Bodhisattva asked: "What wonderful virtue is possessed by him who is able to make an incarnate Bodhisattva fearless in virtue and endowed with such supernatural power?" The Buddha said: "Great indeed [is his virtue]! He sends the incarnate Bodhisattva to all the ten quarters in order to perform religious work and benefit all beings."

Then Gandhakūṭa Tathāgata having filled up a perfume-bowl with perfume-food gave it to the incarnate Bodhisattva. Then those nine millions of Bodhisattvas shouted together saying: "We would go to the Sahā world in order to do homage to Buddha Śākyamuni, and see those Bodhisattvas led by Vimalakīrti." The Buddha said: "Go you [Bodhisattvas]. Keep back the fragrance of your bodies lest those beings feel attachment [towards you] in their minds. Again you should abandon your real forms lest those who seek to be Bodhisattvas in that land should cherish [the feeling of] self-abasement. Again, you should not be contemptuous of them and thus create a hindrance-thought. And why? All the lands in all the ten quarters are [equal] even as the sky, but only for those beings who find pleasure in the inferior Law Buddhas do not manifest their lands of purity."

Then the incarnate Bodhisattva, having received that bowl of food accompanied by those nine millions of Bodhisattvas through the grace of the Buddha and Vimalakīrti, disappeared from that world and in an instant returned to the house of Vimalakīrti. Then forthwith nine millions of lion-thrones, magnificent as before, were manifested by

Vimalakīrti, and all those Bodhisattvas seated themselves thereon. Then the incarnate Bodhisattva handed Vimalakīrti that bowl filled with perfume-food; the fragrance of the food filled the entire city of Vaiśālī and all the three great Chiliocosms. Then Brahmans and wealthy householders of Vaiśālī inhaling the fragrance were gratified both in body and in mind, and gave praise, saying that they had never inhaled the like before.

At that time Candracchatra, a leader of wealthy house-holders, followed by eighty-four thousand men, came into the house of Vimalakīrti. Beholding in that chamber the multitude of the Bodhisattvas and lion-thrones, so high and so broad and so magnificent, and being pleased in mind, he seated himself on one side and greeted that great multitude of the Bodhisattvas and great disciples. [Besides], all the gods of earth, the gods of the sky, and the gods of the worlds of Form [and Formlessness], all inhaling the fragrance, came into the house of Vimalakīrti.

Then Vimalakīrti spoke to those great Śrāvakas led by Śāriputra and said: "Sirs, eat of the food of the Tathāgata which has the flavour of immortality (*amṛta*); it is born of the great compassion [of the Tathāgata]. Eat not with a divided mind, or it will not be digested." There were some Śrāvakas who thought to themselves: "The food is but little, and would it be possible for each one in this great assembly to share it?" The incarnate Bodhisattva said: "Measure not the infinite virtue and wisdom of the Tathāgata by the finite virtue and wisdom of the Śrāvaka; though the four great oceans might become dry, yet this bowl of food would never be exhausted. All men [in all the worlds] may eat of it even as much as a quantity equal to Mount Sumeru, and for a period lasting a Kalpa, yet it could never be exhausted. And why? The food spared by one who is infinitely endowed with the virtues of discipline, meditation, wisdom, liberation, and knowledge of liberation, could never be exhausted."

Then that bowl of food satiated all the assembly, yet remained as before not in the least impaired in quantity. All those Bodhisattvas, Śrāvakas and deities who ate of this food were gratified in body and felt happy just as did those Bodhisattvas of the world called Sarvasukhamaṇḍita; and from all the pores of their skin an excellent fragrance issued forth, like that from the trees in the world known as Sarvagandhasugandha.

Then Vimalakīrti asked the Bodhisattvas from Sarvagandhasugandha: "How does the Tathāgata Gandhakūṭa preach the Law?" They replied: "The Tathāgata in our country preaches without words; he enables all beings to attain the virtue of discipline only by means of perfume. The Bodhisattvas, each sitting under a lofty tree, inhale the excellent perfume and enter a Samādhi called the mine of virtues. Those who enter this Samādhi are endowed with all the virtues of a Bodhisattva."

Then the Bodhisattva asked Vimalakīrti: "In what manner does the world-honoured Śākyamuni preach the Law here?" Vimalakīrti replied:

"Beings of this world are very self-willed and difficult to teach. Therefore, the Buddha preaches to them in severe words in order to subdue them: unhappy regions such as hell, the animal world, and the world of hungry spirits are the regions for the ignorant; evil deed is the result of evil deed; evil speech is the result of evil speech, evil thought is the result of evil thought; murder is the result of murder; robbery is the result of robbery; adultery is the result of adultery; lying is the result of lying; duplicity is the result of duplicity; abusing is the result of abusing; idle word is the result of idle word; covetousness is the result of covetousness; anger is the result of anger; misconception is the result of misconception; avarice is the result of avarice; the breach of precepts is the result of breach of precepts; quick temper is the result of quick temper; slothfulness is the result of slothfulness; distraction of mind is the result of distraction of mind; ignorance is the result of ignorance; and so with initiation into disciplinary life, living disciplinary life, violation of disciplinary life, what ought to be done, what ought not to be done, the obstacles, absence of the obstacles, guiltiness, purity or impurity, passion or passionlessness, right or wrong, the created or the uncreated, the world or Nirvāṇa—with these divers doctrines he subdues the minds of all beings and conquers them; because they are as difficult to subdue as those of monkeys. Just as severe pain which penetrates even to the bone is to be inflicted upon an elephant or a horse in order to bring it to complete subjection as it is so obstinate and difficult to subdue, even so severe words must be spoken to discipline those beings who are obstinate and difficult to subdue."

Those Bodhisattvas having heard these words praised him saying: "We have never heard the like before; Śākyamuni, the world-honoured one, concealing his infinite power of independence which is never restricted, and manifesting only those things desired by the poor delivers them [from suffering], and also these Bodhisattvas of this world who are never wearied and always ready to condescend to become poor, are born in this land of Buddha cherishing infinite great compassion."

Vimalakīrti said: "It is even as you say that the Bodhisattvas of this world are firm in their great compassion towards all beings; and the happiness which is bestowed on all beings by them throughout their lives is of greater worth than all the deeds wrought in your land during hundreds of thousands of Kalpas. And why? In the Sahā world there are ten kinds of goodness which are never found in other lands of purity. What are they? (1) To treat the poor with charity, (2) to treat trespassers with pure discipline, (3) to treat the angry with patience, (4) to treat the indolent with diligence, (5) to treat the distracted with meditation, (6) to treat the ignorant with wisdom, (7) to save those who are in the eight difficulties by the Law which removes them, (8) to save those who find pleasure in the Hīnayāna by the Law of the Mahāyāna, (9) to save those who are destitute of virtue by a stock of merit, and (10) ever to perfect all beings with the Fourfold Acceptance—these are ten kinds of [goodness]."

Then those Bodhisattvas said: "How many Laws ought to be practised by a Bodhisattva in this world in order to be perfect in deeds and to be reborn in the pure land?" Vimalakīrti said: "A Bodhisattva who would be perfect in deeds and be born in the pure land must practise the eightfold Law in this world. What is the eightfold Law? (1) To bestow happiness on all beings without expecting reward, to endure all suffering for the sake of all beings, and to bestow on them all the stock of merit one has achieved; (2) to bring his mind down to the minds of those beings, ever in perfect humiliation; (3) to regard Bodhisattvas as if they were Buddhas themselves; (4) not to cherish doubt in his mind when listening to a scripture which he never heard before; (5) not to contradict Śrāvakas; (6) not to be jealous of the honour given to them, not to be arrogant over the benefit enjoyed by oneself and thereby subdue one's own mind; (7) ever to reflect upon his faults and never talk about others' shortcomings; and (8) ever to seek a stock of merit with intent mind—this is called the eightfold Law."

When Vimalakīrti and Mañjuśrī spoke these words, one hundred thousand deities in the great assembly all cherished the thought of supreme enlightenment, and ten thousand Bodhisattvas attained to acquiescence in the eternal Law.

XI

The Life of a Bodhisattva

At that time the Buddha was preaching the Law in the grove of Āmrapālī. Then suddenly the earth was seen broad and magnificent and the whole assembly became tinted with golden colour. Ānanda asked the Buddha, "O Blessed One, for what reason is there such an auspicious omen, that this earth is seen broad and magnificent, and why has the whole assembly become tinted with golden colour?" The Buddha spoke to Ānanda and said: "It is for this reason that Vimalakīrti and Mañjuśrī, revered and surrounded by the whole assembly, intend to come here, by first producing this auspicious omen."

Then Vimalakīrti spoke to Mañjuśrī: "Let us go and see the Blessed One and revere and honour him together with those Bodhisattvas." Mañjuśrī said: "Well said! Let us go; now it is the due time." Then Vimalakīrti through his supernatural power, holding in the palm of his right hand the whole assembly together with the lion-thrones, went to the place where the Buddha was; having arrived there, he got down on the earth; he saluted him touching his feet with bowed head; and walking round him seven times keeping him to his right side, stretching his folded hands towards him with intent mind, he stood on one side; then all those Bodhisattvas leaving their seats greeted the Buddhas, each touching his feet with bowed head and walking round him seven times and standing on one side; and all the great disciples, Śakra, Brahman, and the four guardian gods also, leaving their seats, saluted the Buddha touching his feet with bowed heads and standing on one side.

Then the Blessed One duly returned his salutation to those Bodhisattvas and commanded them to resume their seats. The whole assembly obeying his command resumed the seats. Then the Buddha spoke to Śāriputra: "Have you seen that which was wrought by the mighty supernatural power of those Bodhisattvas and those excellent men?" [He replied]: "Yes, I have seen it." "What do you think of it?" "O Blessed One, I see it; but it is inconceivable to me and beyond my mind and beyond my power of measurement."

Then Ānanda asked the Buddha: "O Blessed One, the perfume which we now inhale has never been inhaled before; what perfume may it be?" The Buddha spoke to Ānanda and said: "This [perfume] issues from the pores of the skin of those Bodhisattvas." Then Śāriputra spoke to Ānanda and said: "Even from the pores of our skin this perfume is issuing." Ānanda asked: "Whence comes this perfume?" He said: "Vimalakīrti, the wealthy householder, had received the portion of food from the Buddha of Sarvagandhasugandha and those who partook of the food in his house produce such a perfume from every pore [of the skins of their bodies]." Ānanda asked Vimalakīrti: "How long does this perfume last?" Vimalakīrti replied: "It will last until the food is exhausted." "When will this food be exhausted?" "Seven days will pass before the energy of this food will be exhausted; again Ānanda, if a Śrāvaka who has not yet entered into the ranks of steadfastness partakes of this food, he can attain to the ranks of steadfastness before it is exhausted; if [a Śrāvaka who] has entered into the ranks of steadfastness partakes of this food, he can obtain liberation of mind before it is exhausted; if one who has not yet cherished the thought towards the Mahāyāna partakes of this food, he can cherish the thought before it is exhausted; if one who has cherished the thought [towards the Mahāyāna] partakes of this food, he can attain to the acquiescence in the eternal Law before it is exhausted; if one who has attained to the acquiescence partakes of this food, he can attain to the state in which he is bound by one birth only before it is exhausted; just as a medicine called 'the excellent flavour' which has such a peculiarity that one who has taken it can exterminate all poison of passions before it is exhausted, even so this food exterminates all poison of passions before it is exhausted."

Ānanda spoke to the Buddha and said: "O Blessed One, I have never heard that the food of perfume performs such religious work." The Buddha said: "Indeed it is so, indeed it is so! O Ānanda there is a Buddha country which performs religious work by means of the light of a Buddha; there is another which performs religious work by means of the Bodhisattvas who are therein; there is another which performs religious work by means of the beings whom the Buddha teaches; there is another which performs religious work by means of a Bodhi tree; there is another which performs religious work by means of clothes and beds; there is another which performs religious work by means of food; there is another which performs religious work by means of gardens, forests and terraces; there is another which performs religious work by means of the thirty-two signs of perfection and the eighty minor marks of excellence; there is another which performs religious work by the body of a Buddha; there is another which performs religious work by means of the sky; by these means all beings are persuaded to the practice of discipline; there is another which performs religious work by means of parables, such as dreams, phantoms, shadows, echoes, reflections in a mirror, moon in water; there is another which performs religious work by means of sounds, words or letters; there is another pure land of a Buddha which performs religious work by means of silence, wordlessness and uncreatedness. Thus O Ānanda, conduct, movement and all that which has been done by all the Buddhas are nothing but religious works; O Ānanda there are the four evils, the eighty-four thousand ways of passion which all beings suffer from; yet Buddhas perform religious works even with these. These are performed in order to make beings enter the teaching of all the Buddhas.[52]

A Bodhisattva who has entered this doctrine seeing all the pure and excellent lands of the Buddhas neither attaches himself to it nor covets it nor is arrogant, and seeing all the impure lands of the Buddhas he neither grieves nor cares for nor avoids them. He raises the pure mind towards all the Buddhas rejoicing in and revering them as those whom he has never seen before. All Buddha-Tathāgatas are equal in virtues, but it is only in order to teach all beings that they manifest the Buddha-lands in different ways.

O Ānanda, behold all those Buddha-lands; there is variety on the earth, but there is none in the sky, even so there is variety in the physical bodies of the Buddhas, but there is none in their unobstructed wisdom. O Ānanda, all the Buddhas are equal in their physical bodies, in their dignity and births, in their discipline, meditation, wisdom, liberation, and wisdom of liberation, in their ten powers, the [fourfold] fearlessness, and the attributes of their extraordinary qualities, in their greatness of mercy and compassion, in their attitudes, conduct, and longevity of life, in their discourses, teachings, in the perfection of beings, in the purification of the Buddha-lands, and in the equipment of Buddha quality.

52. Ed. This sentence has been retranslated.

Therefore the Buddhas are called Samyak-saṃbuddhas, Tathāgatas, and Buddhas. O Ānanda, if I should explain fully the meaning of these three words, it would be impossible for you to comprehend even though you should live for a kalpa; it would be impossible to comprehend it even for all beings in the three great chiliocosms, who might obtain an excellent memory like Ānanda himself, and who might be endowed with a life lasting a kalpa. Thus, O Ānanda, the Anuttara-samyaksaṃbodhi[53] of a Buddha is infinite and his wisdom and eloquence are inconceivable."

Ānanda spoke to the Buddha and said: "From this time forth I will never call myself one who has learned much." The Buddha spoke to Ānanda: "No, you should not be discouraged. And why? Among Śrāvakas I speak of you as one who has learned much, but not among Bodhisattvas. Stay a while, O Ānanda, as intelligent ones are not to measure Bodhisattvas. Even though all the oceans could be measured, yet meditation, wisdom, memory, eloquence, and all the virtues of Bodhisattvas could never be measured. O Ānanda, you [Śrāvakas] ought to leave alone the deeds of Bodhisattvas. The supernatural power which this Vimalakīrti manifested for a moment could not be manifested by all the Śrāvakas and Pratyeka-Buddhas even with their utmost effort counting through hundreds of thousands of Kalpas."

Then those Bodhisattvas who came from Sarvagandhasugandha spoke to Buddha with folded hands and said: "O Blessed One, when we saw this land we cherished the thought that it was inferior to ours; but now we repent and renounce this thought. And why? The necessary means of all the Buddhas are so inconceivable that they manifest, in order to save all beings, different lands of their own according to the needs of all beings. O Blessed One, we pray that you would give some few words on the Law that we may think of [you], oh Tathāgata, when we return to our land."

Buddha then spoke to those Bodhisattvas: "There is a doctrine which is hindered neither by things limited and things unlimited; and this you ought to know. What is meant by things limited? They are things created. What is meant by things unlimited? They are things uncreated. A Bodhisattva ought neither to abandon the created nor to attach himself to the uncreated. What is it not to abandon the created? It is this: not to abandon great mercy and compassion; to cherish the thought of omniscience and never to be negligent; ever to teach all beings without weariness; ever to remember and practise the Law of the fourfold acceptance; not to spare body and life for the protection of the true Law; to accumulate a stock of merit without weariness; ever to have the mind abiding in peace with the necessary means and the transference of one's merit to others; to seek the Law diligently; to preach the Law without sparing; not to fear entering a life of birth and death as he strives to honour all the

53. Ed. Supreme perfect enlightenment.

Buddhas; to be far above either sorrow in poverty or joy in prosperity; not to despise novices; to revere sages like the Buddhas; to make those who fall into passion return to the right thought; not to deem the pleasure of renunciation the best; not to get attached to one's own pleasures but to rejoice at others' pleasures; to regard meditation as the hell; to regard a life of birth and death as a pleasure garden; to regard those who come to seek [the Law] as good teachers; to abandon all possessions with the thought of the acquirement of omniscience; to cherish the thought of rescue and protection when seeing those who break the precepts; to regard the Pāramitās as parents; to regard the Laws of requisites for attaining the supreme knowledge as kinsfolk; to do good without limit; to perfect one's own land of Buddha with all adornments of the pure land; to be endowed with perfect signs by practising infinite charity; to purify body, speech and mind by removing all wickedness; to undergo bravely the countless kalpas of birth and death; never to be weary in hearing of the infinite virtue of Buddha; to slay the enemy of passion with the sword of wisdom; to be far above the Skandhas, the Āyatanas and the Dhātus; to care for all beings for their eternal liberation; to vanquish the army of evil with great diligence; ever to seek the wisdom of unconscious reality; not to abandon things of the world, abiding in self-contentment with the fewest possible desires; to follow the world without injuring one's dignity; to lead beings by means of supernatural wisdom; not to forget what has been learned, being in possession of a retentive memory; to exterminate doubts as entertained by all according to their capacities; to preach [the Law] without impediments with the perfect eloquence that fulfills every desire; to enjoy the happiness belonging to gods and men by practising the tenfold goodness with a pure heart; to open the way of the Brahman god by practising the fourfold infinite [mind]; to pray [to a Buddha] to preach the Law that he may rejoice at it and praise goodness; to obtain the voice of a Buddha whereby body, speech and mind are improved; to obtain the dignity of a Buddha whereby good virtues are intensely practised, ever in enhancement of his behaviour; to found an order of Bodhisattvas by teaching the Mahāyāna; not to lose the stock of merit, with a mind free from dissipation—when these things are practised by a Bodhisattva, he is said not to have abandoned the created.

What is it not to abide in the uncreated? It is not to regard emptiness as something attained, even though one practises emptiness; not to regard formlessness and aimlessness as something attained, even though one practises them; not to regard causelessness as something attained, even though one practises it; not to shun the accumulating merits, though realizing the transiency [of things]; not to abhor birth and death, though meditating on the pains of this world; never to become weary of teaching others though realizing selflessness [of things]; not to pass into annihilation forever, though meditating on annihilation; to practise goodness both in the body and mind, though meditating on abandonment; to take refuge in the Law, though there is no refuge; to care for all beings with the Laws of the world, though seeing that life has no existence; not to exterminate passions, though seeing passionlessness [of things]; to teach beings with the Laws of practice, though seeing that there is no practice; not to abandon great compassion though seeing emptiness; not to follow the Hīnayāna, though seeing the ranks of certainty; not to neglect merit, meditation and wisdom so long as the original vow is not fulfilled, though seeing that all things are false, having neither substance nor personality nor master nor form; to practise such things is said of a Bodhisattva [who is] not abiding in the uncreated.

Again he abides not in the uncreated, as he is endowed with a stock of merit; he abandons not the created, as he is endowed with wisdom; he abides not in the uncreated, as he possesses great mercy and compassion; he abandons not the created, as he fulfills the original vow; he abides not in the uncreated, as he accumulates the medicine [of the Law]; he abandons not the created, as he distributes the medicine [of the Law]; he abides not in the uncreated, as he knows the maladies of beings; he abandons not the created, as he extirpates the maladies of beings. All the Bodhisattvas, excellent men practising such things, neither abandon the created, nor abide in the uncreated; this is the way of the Law called the liberation from the extinguishable as well as from the inextinguishable [which] you ought to know."

Then those Bodhisattvas, having heard this Law preached [by the Buddha], were filled with great joy, strewed beautiful flowers of many colours and many perfumes all over the three great chiliocosms, and having honoured the Buddha, his doctrine, and the Bodhisattvas, worshipped the Buddha by touching his feet with their bowed heads, praised him saying they had never heard the like before, and spoke thus; "Śākyamuni Buddha has here well exhibited his necessary means." Having spoken thus, they suddenly disappeared and returned to their country.

XII

Buddha Akṣobhya

Then the Blessed One asked Vimalakīrti: "You wish to see the Tathāgata; in what manner do you regard the Tathāgata?" Vimalakīrti said: "Just as I regard the reality of my body even so do I regard the Tathāgata. I regard the Tathāgata in this manner: he came not in the past, will not go in the future, and stays not in the present; I regard him neither as form nor as that-ness of form, nor as the nature of form; neither as sensation nor as conception nor as confirmation; neither as consciousness nor as that-ness of consciousness nor as the nature of consciousness; he is not caused by the four elements; he is even as the void; he is not an aggregate of the six Āyatanas as he is far above eye, ear, nose, tongue, body and mind; he is beyond the three worlds of existence; he is separated from the three dirts; he is in accordance with the three ways of liberation; he is endowed with intelligence yet he is as if not intelligent; he is neither of oneness nor of duality; he is neither of selfhood nor of otherness; he is neither formless nor attached to form; he is neither on this shore nor on that nor in midstream; yet he teaches all beings; he is never annihilated even though realizing complete annihilation, he is neither this nor that; he is depending neither on this nor on that; he is known neither by intelligence nor by consciousness; he is neither darkness nor light; he is neither name nor form; he is neither strong nor weak; he is neither pure nor impure; he is not in a definite place yet he is not separated from place; he is neither created nor uncreated; he neither manifests himself, nor is he explainable; he neither gives nor grudges; he neither observes nor violates the precepts; he is neither patient nor impatient; he is neither diligent nor slothful; he is neither collected nor confused; he is neither intelligent nor ignorant; he is neither true nor false; he neither comes nor goes; he neither goes out nor returns; he is beyond all modes of speech; he is neither a stock of merit nor not a stock of merit; he is neither deserving of homage nor undeserving of homage; he neither possesses nor abandons; he is neither endowed with form nor formlessness; he is identical with truth and equal to the nature of the Law; he can neither be measured nor be weighed, being far above all degrees and measures; he is neither great nor small; he is neither to be seen nor to be heard; neither to be felt nor to be known; he is liberated from all bondage; he is equal both to the intelligent and to the ignorant; he does not discriminate in anything; in all things he has no attainment, no loss, no corruption, no suffering; in him there is no acting, no doing, no birth, no death; no fear, no sorrow; no joy, no dislike; he knows no past, no future, no present; he is not to be discriminated nor manifested by any words; O Blessed One, such is the personality of the Tathāgata; thus should one regard him; those who regard him thus are said to have right understanding, those who regard him otherwise are said to have false understanding."

Then Śāriputra asked Vimalakīrti: "Whence have you come to be born here?" Vimalakīrti said: "Is there either going or coming in the Law which you have obtained?" Śāriputra said, "There is neither going nor coming." [Vimalakīrti said]: "When there is neither going nor coming, why do you ask me saying 'Whence have you come to be born here?' What do you think when a conjurer produces either a man or a woman, is there any going or coming?" Śāriputra said: "There is neither going nor coming; have you not heard that the Buddha taught that the form of all things was like a phantom?" He replied: "Even so it is; when the form of all things is like a phantom, why do you ask me saying 'whence have you come to be born here?' O Śāriputra, to leave is a form of destruction shown in unreal objects; to be born is also a form of continuation shown in unreal objects. A Bodhisattva never exterminates his stock of merit even when he goes out, he never lets evils grow even when he is born."

Then the Buddha spoke to Śāriputra and said; "There is a land called Abhirati; the Buddha there is called Akṣobhya. This Vimalakīrti comes from that land and is born here." Śāriputra said: "I have never heard the like before, O Blessed One, why should this man wish to leave his pure land and come here into a world full of anger and danger?" Vimalakīrti spoke to Śāriputra: "What do you think when the sun rises? Does it unite with darkness?" He replied: "No, when the sun rises there is no longer darkness." Vimalakīrti again asked: "Why does the sun go round the Jambudvīpa?" He replied: "In order to remove darkness by its brightness." Vimalakīrti said: "Even so is it with a Bodhisattva; though he is born in the land of impurity in order to teach all beings, he is never united with the darkness of ignorance, and he only exterminates the darkness of the passions of all beings."

At that time all the assembly earnestly longed to see the Tathāgata Akṣobhya and his assembly of Bodhisattvas and Śrāvakas in the land of Abhirati. The Buddha, knowing the thought of all the assembly, spoke to Vimalakīrti and said: "O noble youth, for the sake of all this assembly, let the Tathāgata Akṣobhya and his assembly of Bodhisattvas and Śrāvakas in the land of Abhirati be manifested here, all are earnestly longing to see them."

Then Vimalakīrti thought to himself: "I will without rising from my seat, manifest all the land of Abhirati including the Cakravāḍa mountains, the sun, moon, and stars, palaces of deities, serpent-gods, goblins, Brahman deities, the assembly of Bodhisattvas, Śrāvakas, towns, villages, men and women, young and old, even the Tathāgata Akṣobhya himself in the Bodhi tree and excellent lotus flowers which perform religious works in all the ten quarters; and the three jeweled stairs which connect this Jambudvīpa with the Trayastriṃśa heaven, and by which all the deities descend to honour the Tathāgata Akṣobhya and hear him preach, and by which all beings of this Jambudvīpa ascend to Trayastriṃśa heaven and see the deities of that heaven and the world Abhirati endowed with these infinite virtues; I will snatch that world with my right hand as the turner of porcelain snatches his clay and bring it here including its highest heaven Akaniṣṭha as well as its lowest sea level, and show them to all the assembly as one shows a garland in his hand." Having thought thus he entered a contemplation and, exercising his supernatural power, he transferred the land Abhirati into this world. The Bodhisattvas, Śrāvakas, deities and men in that world who possessed the supernatural power, cried out together and said: "O Lord, we are being carried away!" Buddha Akṣobhya said: "It is not I that is doing this; it is due to the supernatural power of Vimalakīrti." The other beings who did not possess the supernatural power did not recognize it and knew nothing about their being carried away; there was neither increase nor decrease in the land of Abhirati though it was transferred into this world; there was also no squeezing or compression in this world; it remained as before.

Then Buddha Śākyamuni spoke to the assembly and said: "Have you seen the Tathāgata Akṣobhya and his magnificent land Abhirati and his Bodhisattvas pure in life, and disciples who are pure and stainless?" They replied: "O verily we see." The Buddha then said: "If a Bodhisattva wishes to obtain such a pure land of Buddha, he should know the path on which the Tathāgata Akṣobhya walks."

When the world Abhirati was manifested, fourteen *nayutas* of men in this Sahā world cherished the thought of supreme enlightenment. They all wished to be born in the land of Abhirati, and Buddha Śākyamuni gave them his assurance and said: "You shall all be born in that land." Then [Akṣobhya of] the world Abhirati, having finished what he had to do in this world, returned to his abode. [This] was witnessed by all the assembly.

The Buddha spoke to Śāriputra and said: "Have you seen the Abhirati world and the Buddha Akṣobhya?" He replied: "O Blessed One, verily I have seen them; may all beings obtain the pure land even as the land of the Buddha Akṣobhya, and obtain supernatural power even as that of Vimalakīrti. O Blessed One, we have received so great a privilege that we could see this man and make ourselves acquainted with him and honour him; but all beings who even hear this scripture, in the present age or after the passing of the Buddha, will also obtain excellent profit. How much more meritorious would it be for them who having heard it, would comprehend, hold, recite, preach, and practise it according to the Law. If there be one who has held this scripture in his hand he is said to obtain the mine of the Law-treasure. When he recites or explains the meaning of it and practises it according to the doctrine, he will be protected by all the Buddhas. If there be one who honours such a man, he is said to honour the Buddha. If there be one who copies and holds this scripture, his room will be inhabited by the Tathāgata. If there be one who rejoices in hearing this scripture, he will attain omniscience. If he comprehends even one Gātha of four lines of this scripture and preach it to others, he will receive from the Buddha the assurance of attaining supreme enlightenment."

XIII

On Paying Homage to the Law

Then Śakra, the king of deities, who was among the assembly, spoke to the Buddha and said: "Though I have heard several hundred thousands of scriptures while I was waiting on Buddha and Mañjuśrī, yet have I never heard such a scripture as this—the Sūtra of ultimate reality ascertained by the supernatural faculty of Inconceivable Self-Existence. If I understand the meaning proclaimed by the Buddha rightly, he who hears, comprehends, holds, and recites this scripture will obtain the Law without fail; how much more [valuable] would it be to practise according to the doctrine! [Such a practitioner] can close [the gate of] the unhappy existences; he is protected by all the Buddhas; he can repress all the heresies, conquer the enmity of evil, realize Bodhi, abide in the Bodhimaṇḍala, and walk in the path along which the Tathāgata has walked. O Blessed One, if there be one who holds, recites, and practises this Sūtra, according to the doctrine, I will honour and serve him together with my kinsfolk; whenever this scripture may be found, either in the village, town, forest, or wilderness, I will go thither in order to hear the Law together with my kinsfolk and will cause him to believe who has not believed before, and will protect him who already believes."

The Buddha spoke to him and said: "Rightly said! Rightly said! O king of deities, I share your joy; here in this scripture the inconceivable and supreme enlightenment of all the Buddhas of the past, the present, and the future is fully set forth. Therefore, O king of deities, he who holds, recites, and reveres the scripture is said to honour all the Buddhas of the past, the present, and the future.

O king of deities, if there be as many Tathāgatas in number as there are bushes, whether of sugar-cane, bamboo, reed, paddy, or hemp, and the three great chiliocosms were to be full of them, and a son or daughter of a noble family were to honour, revere, praise, and pay homage to them and dedicate their dwellings to them for the space of one kalpa or thereabout, and after the passing of those Buddhas, he or she would erect a Stūpa of seven jewels containing the perfect body of each of the Tathāgatas as wide as the four worlds and as high as the heaven of Brahman, erecting a pole adorned with all magnificence and do homage to them with all the rarest flowers, all kinds of incense, garlands, banners and music, for the space of one kalpa or thereabout; what do you think, O king of deities, would the merit planted by this man be much or little?" Śakra, the king of deities, said: "Much indeed, O Blessed One, it would be impossible to enumerate his merits even in one hundred thousand millions of kalpas." The Buddha spoke to the king of deities: "It should be known that the merits of a son or daughter of a noble family who, hearing this scripture of Inconceivable Emancipation, comprehends, holds, recites and practises it would obtain greater merits than those. And why? The Bodhi of all the Buddhas springs forth from it; and the essence of the Bodhi is infinite. For this reason the merits are immeasurable."

The Buddha again spoke to the king of deities: "Once in the past immeasurable *asaṃkhyeya* kalpas ago, there was a Buddha called Bhaiṣajyarāja, a Tathāgata, an arhat, one who is perfect in knowledge, and a Sugata, knower of the world, an incomparable one, a tamer of men, teacher of gods and men, Buddha and Bhagavat. His world was called Mahāvyūha. The length of life of that Buddha was twenty shorter kalpas. There were thirty-six million *nayutas* of disciples and twelve million Bodhisattvas. O Indra, king of deities, at that time there was a Cakravartin king named Ratnacchatra, endowed with the seven treasures, who was the lord of four worlds. There were born of him a thousand princes who were all comely, courageous, and able to repress their enemies. Then Ratnacchatra [the king] with his kinsfolk, honoured the Tathāgata Bhaiṣajyarāja dedicating a dwelling to him during five kalpas; when those five kalpas had elapsed, he spoke to his thousand princes and said: 'You should also honour the Buddha with profound mind even as I do.' Then those thousand princes according to their father's command honoured the Tathāgata Bhaiṣajyarāja during five kalpas, dedicating a dwelling to him and other things. There was one among those princes named Candracchatra who [one day] sat alone and thought to himself: 'Can any homage be superior to this [homage]?' Then through the supernatural power of that Buddha there appeared in the sky a deity who declared: 'No homage is superior to homage to the Law.' He asked: 'What is homage to the Law?' The deity replied: 'You had better go to the Tathāgata Bhaiṣajyarāja to inquire concerning this matter; he would fully tell you what is meant by homage to the Law.' Then Candracchatra the prince having gone to the Tathāgata Bhaiṣajyarāja, greeted him touching his feet with bowed head, sat down on one side and asked the Buddha: 'O Blessed One, of all homages, homage to the Law is most excellent; what is meant by homage to the Law?'

The Buddha replied: "O noble youth, homage to the Law is this: the profound scriptures preached by the Buddha are so subtle and so difficult to understand that all the world is unwilling to accept and believe them; so they are pure without blemish; they are unobtainable by mere discrimination or thought; they are enclosed in the treasury of virtues of a Bodhisattva; they are sealed with the seal of Dhāraṇī; they lead to the state from which one never retreats; they perfect the six Pāramitās; they correctly discriminate the meaning [of all things]; they are in accordance with the Law of Bodhi; they are superior to all other scriptures; they lead to great mercy and compassion; they are far above all the temptation of evils and heresies; they are in harmony with the Law of causation; they transcend self, individuality, personality and durability; they are empty, formless, aimless and causeless; they are capable of elevating beings to a seat in the Bodhimaṇḍala and turn the wheel of the Law; they are praised by all deities, serpent gods, and Gandharvas; they are capable of leading beings to the mine of virtues of the Buddha; they comprehend all wisdom of the wise and the holy; they preach the paths walked by Bodhisattvas; they are based on the doctrine that all things are real; they unmistakably proclaim the doctrine of transiency, sorrow, emptiness, selflessness, and annihilation; they are capable of saving all who are guilty of trespassing the precepts; they are capable of causing fear to evil ones, heretics and those who are greedy; they are praised by all the Buddhas and saints; they turn against the sorrows of birth and death, and show the happiness of Nirvāṇa; they are preached by all the Buddhas of the three worlds in the ten quarters—if a man hear such scriptures as these, comprehends, holds, recites, and through the power of necessary means, discriminates, explains, and makes them manifest clearly to all beings, and thereby preserves the Law, he for these reasons is said to pay homage to the Law.

Again, to practise according to the teaching of all the Law, to be in accordance with the twelve links in the chain of causation, to be far above all heresies, to attain to acquiescence in the eternal Law, to be absolutely selfless, to be without personality, yet to be free from dissension, free from discord concerning the Law of cause and effect, to be free from ideas of possession, not to depend on words but to depend on meaning, not to depend on knowledge but to depend on wisdom, not to depend on incomplete scriptures but to depend on complete scripture, not to depend on man but to depend on the Law, to be in accordance with the nature of things, not to cherish any heretical views, to have no abode, and no refuge, to regard the twelve links of causation as working in an endless circle thus, as follows: as ignorance is completely annihilated, all component things are completely annihilated, until we come to, as birth is completely annihilated, old age and death are also completely annihilated. This is paying homage to the Law, which is superior to all other homages."

The Buddha again spoke to Indra, the king of deities, and said: "Candracchatra the prince, having heard such doctrines as these from the Buddha Bhaiṣajyarāja, attained to acquiescence in meekness; then, having removed the jewelled raiment and ornaments from his body, he offered them to the Buddha and spoke to him saying: 'O Blessed One, after the complete passing of Tathāgata I will pay homage to the Law and protect the true Law; I pray that you, through your power, would show me your compassion and raise me up so that I may be able to repress the enmity of evil and realize the life of a Bodhisattva.' Knowing his profound thought the Buddha prophesied for him and said: 'You will guard the fortress of the Law in the latter days.' O Indra, king of deities, then Candracchatra the prince, seeing the purity of the Law and hearing the prophecy from the Buddha, became a mendicant because of his faith; diligently practised the true Law, and in due course obtained the five supernatural powers, and walking in the path of a Bodhisattva, attained the unimpeded eloquence of Dhāraṇī; after the passing of the Buddha, through his supernatural power and the power of eloquence of Dhāraṇī, during ten shorter kalpas, he propagated the wheel of the Law which the Tathāgata Bhaiṣajyarāja had caused to roll.

Having protected the Law and having been diligent in practice, Candracchatra the Bhikṣu taught millions of millions of men enabling them to raise their minds to a state of never retreating[54] from supreme enlightenment, and enabled fourteen *nayutas* of men to cherish deeply the thought of Śrāvaka and Pratyeka-Buddha, and caused countless beings to be born in the heavens.

O Indra king of deities, you should not think that Ratnacchatra the [Cakravartin] king,[55] is any other than the Tathāgata Ratnatejas who has attained to Buddhahood; the thousand princes are but the thousand Buddhas in the Bhadrakalpa, beginning with Krakucchanda down to the last Tathāgata Ruci. The Bhikṣu Candracchatra is no other than myself.

Thus, O Indra king of deities, you should know the essence of this [doctrine] that paying homage to the Law is superior to all other homages, and unique and incomparable. Therefore, O Indra king of deities, [it is] by paying homage to the Law [that] you should honour the Buddha."

XIV

The Commission of the Law

At that time the Buddha spoke to Maitreya and said: "Maitreya, I now give over to you the Sūtra leading to supreme enlightenment, which I have gathered during countless millions of *asaṃkhyeya* kalpas of the past. In the generations that follow after the passing of Buddha, you should all widely proclaim and propagate this scripture through your supernatural powers in this Jambudvīpa, and never permit it to become extinct. And why? If there be in the later generations, either sons or daughters of a noble family, or deities or serpent-gods, or goblins, or Gandharvas, or Rakṣasas, who cherishing the thought of supreme enlightenment, find pleasure in the great Law, but fail to hear such scripture as this, great benefits would be lost to them. Such men as these, hearing such scriptures, will surely entertain great faith in them, cherish the rare thought [of enlightenment], and reverently preach them in detail

54. Ed. Rephrased for syntactical reasons.

55. I.e. a wheel-turning monarch, the secular equivalent to a Buddha who sets the wheel of Dharma rolling.

to all beings so that they will derive benefits therefrom.

O Maitreya, it should be known that there are two kinds of Bodhisattvas. Who are they? The ones are those who are fond of phrase and rhetoric, the others are those who can really and unflinchingly attain to the truth with all its deep meaning. Those who delight in phrase and rhetoric should be known as but novices among Bodhisattvas. Those who can understand [the knowledge of] such a profound scripture as this, stainless and free from attachment, and who are ever fearless, are able to enter it, who by hearing become pure in mind, who hold it, recite it, and practise it according to its teaching, should be regarded as having been long in the discipline of the ways of Bodhisattvahood.

O Maitreya, there are two ways by which novices among Bodhisattvas may fail to attain to the conviction in this profound doctrine. What are they? First, when they hear this scripture which has never been heard before, they may fear and doubt that they may not be able to follow it, and not believing it they may slander it saying: I have never heard the like before; whence comes it? Secondly, although they may hold and explain this profound scripture, yet they are not intimate with it, nor do they honour it, nor do they revere it, but often do they find fault with it. Those who behave either in one way or in the other should be known as novices among Bodhisattvas; they harm themselves and can never conquer their minds in the profound doctrine.

Again, O Maitreya, there are two ways by which Bodhisattvas, though comprehending the profound doctrine, yet harm themselves and can never attain to acquiescence in the eternal Law. What are they? To despise novices among Bodhisattvas and not to teach them is the one, and although they comprehend the profound doctrine, yet to explain it according to their own ideas is the other; these are the two ways."

Maitreya Bodhisattva, having heard these words, spoke to the Buddha and said: "O Blessed One, I have never heard the like before. It is indeed as the Buddha has spoken. I will remove with my utmost effort such false conceptions as these and hold fast to the works of supreme enlightenment which were accumulated by the Tathāgata during these countless *asaṃkhyeya* kalpas of the past. If there be in the future a son or daughter of a noble family who should seek the Mahāyāna I will enable them to put this scripture even in their own hands, so that they can hold it, recite it, and fully explain it for the sake of others. O Blessed One, if there be in the future any one who can hold it, recite it, and fully explain it for the sake of others, it should be known that he is established by the supernatural power of Maitreya."

The Buddha said: "Rightly said! Rightly said! O Maitreya, it is indeed as you say. I rejoice in it, sharing your joy." Then all the Bodhisattvas stretching forth their folded hands said to the Buddha: "We, after the passing of the Tathāgata, will widely proclaim and propagate the Law of supreme enlightenment in the lands of all the ten quarters, and enable those who preach the Law to obtain this scripture."

Then the four guardian gods spoke to the Buddha: "O Blessed One, if there be any who recite and explain this scripture anywhere, either in the town or village or forest or wilderness, I will go thither together with all my retinue and kinsfolk, in order to hear the Law and to protect him, so that as far as a hundred *yojanas* from his presence no [evil one] may have the opportunity to tempt him."

Then the Buddha spoke to Ānanda: "You should widely proclaim and propagate this scripture." Ānanda said: "Well [O Lord], I have already grasped the essence of this scripture; but, O Blessed One, what should this scripture be called?" The Buddha spoke to Ānanda: "This scripture should be called 'That Which is preached by Vimalakīrti (Vimalakīrti-nirdeśa)' and also 'The Doctrine of Inconceivable Emancipation.' You should remember it thus."

When the Buddha preached this scripture, Vimalakīrti, the wealthy householder, Mañjuśrī, Śāriputra, Ānanda, and all the deities, Asuras, and all of the great assembly, having heard that which was preached by the Buddha, greatly rejoiced in it, believed in it, and practised it.

the end of *The Exposition of Vimalakīrti*

Part II

Related Strands in Early Mahāyāna Buddhism

— 3 —

The Heart Sūtra (*Prajñā-pāramitā-hṛdaya-sūtra*)

Shaku Hannya

Introduction

One of the most popular and at the same time the most important canonical books adopted by the Far Eastern Buddhists is the *Prajñā-pāramitā-hṛdaya-sūtra* (the *Heart Sūtra*), in which the doctrine of *śūnyatā* (emptiness) is most concisely stated. The whole text does not exceed two printed pages in Sanskrit, and in the shorter Chinese version it consists of only two hundred and sixty-two characters.[1] This brevity must have helped its wide circulation among the Mahāyānists all over the East. It is recited by them on almost all occasions.[2]

We do not know when the compendious literature belonging to the Prajñā-pāramitā class was reduced to this abridged form, for as such the present sūtra is to be regarded. When Nāgārjuna laid the foundation of his Madhyamika philosophy on the doctrine of *śūnyatā* as expounded in the *Prajñā-pāramitā* and executed his work in such a masterly and consummate manner as to silence his more conservative brethren in faith, the sūtra must have become the central object of attention and veneration among his followers. But the original sūtra is a great bulky literature supposed to be consisting of 200,000 *ślokas* [verses] in Sanskrit and

1. Ed. In the original publication the article and the English translation were followed by the Sanskrit text and a Tibetan version. Here we include a transcription of the author's edited Sanskrit text. For the Tibetan, which is not romanized, please refer to the original publication. The opening paragraph above and other relevant references have been edited accordingly. The English has also been smoothed out in a few places.

2. Ed. It is recited by Japanese Buddhists of various denominations, but rarely in the Pure Land schools and especially not in the context of Shin Buddhism.

600 fasciculi in Chinese. It is no easy task to peruse the whole work, and it was quite natural that some pious soul would rise up and try to reduce it to a far less formidable size. In fact the conception of *śūnyatā* is not a very complicated one to explain, for a series of denials in regard to the main theses of Mahāyāna philosophy will suffice. The *Hṛdaya* was the rational outcome of this movement; the term means "gist," "kernel," or "essence."[3]

There is however another interpretation concerning the purport of this epitomized Sūtra which is made by the followers of the Shingon Sect. Seeing what a weighty position is occupied by the *dhāraṇī* or mantra [at the end of the text], they would regard the whole Sūtra as a Shingon text in which the power of the mystic formula is exalted.

At present we have two Sanskrit texts of the *Prajñā-pāramitā-hṛdaya-sūtra*, a shorter one and a fuller one, both of which were recovered in Japan. The original palm-leaves are said to have been brought to Japan in 609 CE (the shorter one) and in 850 CE (the fuller one). The earlier ones are the oldest palm-leaf manuscripts still in existence anywhere, in which, according to Max Müller and G. Bühler, we find the earliest specimens of a Sanskrit alphabet for literary purposes (cf. *Buddhist Texts from Japan*, edited by Max Müller, Oxford, 1881[4]). The difference between the fuller and the shorter *Hṛdaya* is that the first has a usual opening passage as in other Sūtras as well as concluding remarks after the Mantra while the shorter Sūtra opens abruptly and ends with the Mantra, the main text alone being preserved intact. The following Sanskrit text is the fuller one chiefly based upon Max Müller's recovery of the ancient palm-leaf manuscript found at [the temple] Hōryūji, Nara, Japan; but in two or three places his reconstruction has been revised since his reading is not in accordance with the spirit of the Prajñā-pāramitā philosophy. [On Tibetan versions see note.][5]

The English translation below is made from the shorter Chinese version, i.e. the translation by Kumārajīva in 400 CE, known in Japanese as the *Shingyō* (心經, i.e. *Hṛdaya-sūtra*).[6] To understand the Sūtra fully requires some knowledge of Mahāyāna Buddhism, especially as presented by Nāgārjuna in his *Madhyamika-Śāstra*, but in the present article

3. Ed. This is the term frequently translated as "heart" as in the adjusted title of this article.

4. In the well-known series The Sacred Books of the East, being Part 2 of Vol. 49.

5. Ed. The original article also contained a Tibetan text, concerning which the author wrote as follows: "The Tibetan text that follows the Sanskrit is also that of the fuller Sūtra. Prof. Teramoto, through whose kindness the present writer is able to reproduce the Tibetan version, has not yet recovered the shorter one."

6. Ed. Frequently also a little more fully as the *Hannya Shingyō* 般若心経 (i.e. "Prajñā Heart Sūtra").

only such technical terms as are referred to in the text will be briefly explained, leaving a systematic exposition of the *śūnyatā* philosophy to the future.[7]

English translation of the *Prajñā-pāramitā-hṛdaya-sūtra*

(Figures in brackets refer to notes which follow)

When the Bodhisattva Avalokiteśvara was engaged in the practice of the deep Prajñā-pāramitā, he perceived that the five skandhas (1) were all empty, and he was saved from all misery and suffering (2). "O Śāriputra," said he, "form is no other than emptiness (3), and emptiness is no other than form; what is form that is emptiness, and what is emptiness that is form. The same can be said of sensation, thought, confection, and consciousness. O Śāriputra, all things are characterized by emptiness: they are not born, they are not annihilated; they are not tainted, they are not immaculate; they do not increase, they do not decrease; therefore, in emptiness there is no form, no sensation, no thought, confection, consciousness; no eye, ear, nose, body, and mind (4); no form, sound, odour, taste, touch, and objects (5); no element of vision, etc., till we come to no element of consciousness (6); there is no ignorance, nor is there the extinction of ignorance, etc., till we come to there is no old age and death; nor is there the extinction of old age and death (7); there is no suffering, accumulation, annihilation, path (8); there is no knowledge, nor is there any obtaining, because there is nothing to be obtained. The Bodhisattva, depending on (9) the Prajñā-pāramitā, has no obstacles in his mind (10); and because he has no obstacles, he has no fear, and, going beyond all perverted and unreal views, reaches final Nirvana. All Buddhas of past, present, and future, depending on the Prajñā-pāramitā, attain to the highest perfect wisdom. Therefore, we know that the Prajñā-pāramitā is a great divine mantra, a mantra of great intelligence, the highest mantra, the peerless mantra, which is capable of putting aside all suffering, it is truth and not falsehood. Therefore, I proclaim the mantra of Prajñā-pāramitā (11). The mantra to be proclaimed then is: "Gate, gate, pāragate, pārasaṃgate, bodhi, svāhā!" (O wisdom, gone, gone, gone to the other shore, landed at the other shore, Svāhā!)

The longer text

The opening passage in the fuller text in Sanskrit and Tibetan which is missing[8] in the shorter one is:

---

7. Ed. The author referred here to a project for *The Eastern Buddhist*, which however was not realized.

8. Ed. It would be more accurate to refer to these sections as "lacking" in the shorter

"Adoration to the All-wise! Thus I heard. At one time the World-honoured One dwelt at Rājagṛha, on the Mount of Vulture, together with a large number of Bhikṣus and a large number of Bodhisattvas. At that time the World-honoured One was absorbed in a samādhi (Meditation) known as Deep Enlightenment. And at the same moment the Great Bodhisattva Āryāvalokiteśvara was practising himself in the deep Prajñāpāramitā."

In place of "Adoration to the All-wise!" the Tibetan version has:

Adoration to the Prajñāpāramitā, which is beyond words, thought, and praise, whose self-nature is, like unto space, neither created nor destroyed, which is a state of wisdom and morality evident to our inner consciousness, and which is the mother of all Excellent Ones of the past, present and future. Thus I heard...

The [additional] concluding passage runs as follows:

O Śāriputra, thus should the Bodhisattva practise himself in the deep Prajñāpāramitā. At that moment the World-honoured One rose from the samādhi and gave approval to the Great Bodhisattva Āryāvalokiteśvara, saying: Well done, well done, a noble son! So it is! So should the practice of the deep Prajñāpāramitā be carried on. As it has been preached by you, it is applauded by Tathāgatas and Arhats. Thus spoke the World-honoured One with joyful heart. The venerable Śāriputra and the Great Bodhisattva Āryāvalokiteśvara together with the whole assemblage, and the world of gods, men, asuras, and gandharvas all praised the speech of the World-honoured One.

Notes on the text

(Figures refer to those shown in the text above)

1. The five skandhas (aggregates or elements) are form (*rūpa*), sensation or sense-perception (*vedanā*), thought (*saṃjñā*), confection or conformation (*saṃskāra*), and consciousness (*vijñāna*). The first skandha is the material world or the materiality of things while the remaining four skandhas belong to the mind. *Vedanā* is what we get through our senses; *saṃjñā* corresponds to thought in its broadest sense or that which mind elaborates; *saṃskāra* is a very difficult term and there is no exact English equivalent, it means something that gives form; and *vijñāna* is consciousness, of which six kinds are ordinarily distinguished by scholars: eye-consciousness, ear-consciousness, nose-consciousness, tongue-consciousness, body-consciousness, and mind-consciousness.

---

text, because the likelihood is that they were later additions. These will have been made precisely because, as the author says, it was more usual for a sūtra to have such an opening. The reality is that the sūtra is an excerpt from the large *Prajñāpāramitā* and as such did not originally have the usual sūtra form.

2. This last clause ["and he was saved from all misery and suffering"] is missing in all the Sanskrit and Tibetan texts.[9]
3. "Empty" (*śūnya*) or "Emptiness" (*śūnyatā*) is one of the most important notions in Mahāyāna philosophy and at the same time most puzzling for non-Buddhist readers to comprehend. Emptiness does not always mean relativity or phenomenality, but often means absoluteness or transcendentality. When Buddhists declare all things to be empty, they are not advocating a nihilistic view; on the contrary they are assuming an ultimate reality which cannot be subsumed in the categories of logic. With them, to proclaim the conditionality of things is to assert the existence of something altogether unconditioned and transcendent of all determination. Śūnyatā may thus often be most appropriately rendered by the Absolute. When the Sūtra says that the five skandhas have the character of emptiness, or that in emptiness there is neither creation nor destruction, neither defilement nor immaculacy, etc., the sense is: no limiting qualities are to be attributed to the Absolute; while it is immanent in all concrete and particular objects it is itself not at all definable. Universal negation, therefore, in the philosophy of Prajñā is an inevitable outcome.
4. No eye, no ear, etc., refer to the six senses. In Buddhist philosophy, mind (*manovijñāna*) is the special organ or sense for the apprehension of dharma, or objects of thought.
5. No form, no sound, etc., are the six qualities of the external world, which become objects of the six senses.
6. "Element of vision, etc., till, we come to, no element of consciousness" is a reference to the eighteen *dhātu* or elements of existence, which include six senses, six qualities, and six consciousnesses. "Till we come to" (*yāvat* in Sanskrit, and 乃至 in Chinese[10]) is quite frequently met with in Buddhist literature to avoid repetition of well-known subjects. These classifications may seem somewhat confusing and overlapping.
7. "There is no ignorance," etc., is the wholesale denial of the Twelve Chains of Causation (*Nidāna*), which are ignorance (*avidyā*), confection (*saṃskāra*), consciousness (*vijñāna*), name and form (*nāmarūpa*), six sense-organs (*ṣaḍāyatana*), contact (*sparśa*), sense-perception (*vedanā*), desire (*tṛṣnā*), attachment (*upādāna*), being (*bhava*), birth (*jāti*), and old age and death (*jarāmaraṇa*). These Chains have been a subject of much discussion even among Buddhist scholars. *Pratītyasamutpāda* is the technical term in Sanskrit for the Chain of Causation.
8. The allusion is of course to the Fourfold Noble Truth (*satya*): 1. Life is suffering; 2. Because of the accumulation (*samudaya*) of evil karma; 3. The cause

9. Ed. It is unlikely that this clause was purposely omitted. The likelihood is rather that it was added in the course of a textual transmission independent of that which led to what we now have as the Sanskrit texts or the Tibetan version. Cf. Note 4 above.
10. Ed. *Nǎizhì*, Japanese pronunciation *naishi*.

of suffering can be annihilated (*nirodha*); 4. And for this there is the path (*mārga*).

9. Āśritya is rendered by Max Müller as "approaching," which in the Chinese translation is 依...故, "depending upon," or "relying on," or more correctly "because of one's dependence." Therefore, in this case as well as in the following passage, the context assumes quite a different signification from that given by Max Müller.
10. Max Müller here has: "A man who has approached the Prajñā-pāramitā of the Bodhisattva dwells enveloped in consciousness." But this is evidently not the reading generally adopted by the Mahāyānists, his reconstruction of the palm-leaf manuscripts is against the spirit of the Śūnyatā philosophy; besides, as was pointed out by Prof. Ryōsaburō Sakaki, of the Kyōto Imperial University, the original text does not necessarily warrant the reading of Max Müller, who as we know was more of a philologist than a Buddhist philosopher. Our Sanskrit text in the following pages gives our own reading.
11. The question is whether we regard "Prajñā-pāramitā" as the title of the Sūtra, or as designating the prefect realization of Prajñā. When we adopt the first interpretation, the mantra itself is the realization or that which leads us to the final goal. The Tibetan version, according to Prof. Yenga Teramoto, has Prajñā in the genitive as in one of the Japanese Sanskrit MSS, and not in the locative as Max Müller and our own text here have it.

The Sanskrit Text

| namaḥ sarvajñāya ||

evaṃ mayā śrutam | ekasmin samaye bhagavān rājagṛhe viharati sma gṛdhrakūṭe parvate mahatā bhikṣusaṃghena sārdhaṃ mahatā ca bodhisattvasaṃghena | tena khalu samayena bhagavān gambhīrāvasaṃbodhaṃ nāma samādhiṃ samāpannaḥ | tena ca samayenāryāvalokiteśvaro bodhisattvo mahāsattvo gambhīrāyāṃ prajñāpāramitāyāṃ caryāṃ caramāṇa evaṃ vyavalokayati sma | pañca skandhāḥ | tāṃś ca svabhāvaśūnyān vyavalokayati | athāyuṣmāñ chāriputro buddhānubhāvenāryāvalokiteśvaraṃ bodhisattvam etad avocat | yaḥ kaścit kulaputro gambhīrāyāṃ prajñāpāramitāyāṃ caryāṃ cartukāmaḥ kathaṃ śikṣitavyaḥ | evam ukta āryāvalokiteśvaro bodhisattvo mahāsattva āyuṣmantaṃ śāriputram etad avocat | yaḥ kaścic chāriputra kulaputro vā kuladuhitā vā gambhīrāyāṃ prajñāpāramitāyāṃ caryāṃ cartukāmas tenaivaṃ vyavalokitavyam | pañca skandhāḥ | tāṃś ca svabhāvaśūnyān samanupaśyati sma | rūpaṃ śūnyatā śūnyataiva rūpam | rūpān na pṛthak śūnyatā śūnyatāyā na pṛthag rūpam | yad rūpaṃ sā śūnyatā yā śūnyatā tad rūpam | evaṃ vedanāsaṃjñāsaṃskāravijñānāni ca śūnyatā | evaṃ śāriputra sarvadharmāḥ śūnyatālakṣaṇā anutpannā aniruddhā amalā na vimalā anūnā asaṃpūrṇāḥ | tasmāt tarhi śāriputra śūnyatāyāṃ na rūpam na vedanā na saṃjñā na saṃskārā na vijñānam | na cakṣur na śrotraṃ na ghrāṇaṃ na jihvā na kāyo na mano na rūpaṃ na śabdo na gandho na raso na spraṣṭavyaṃ na dharmāḥ | na cakṣur dhātur yāvan na manodhātur na dharmadhātur na manovijñānadhātuḥ ||

na vidyā nāvidyā na kṣayo yāvan na jarāmaraṇaṃ na jarāmaraṇakṣayaḥ | na duḥkhasamudayanirodhamārgā na jñānaṃ na prāptir nāprāptiḥ | tasmāc chāriputra aprāptitvena bodhisattvānāṃ prajñāpāramitām āśritya viharaty acittāvaraṇaḥ | cittāvaraṇanāstitvād atrasto viparyāsātikrānto niṣṭhanirvāṇaḥ | tryadhvavyavasthitāḥ sarvabuddhāḥ prajñāpāramitām āśrityānuttarāṃ samyaksaṃbodhim abhisaṃbuddhāḥ | tasmāj jñātavyaḥ prajñāpāramitā mahāmantro mahāvidyāmantro 'nuttaramantro 'samasamamantraḥ sarvaduḥkhapraśamanamantraḥ satyam amithyatvāt prajñāpāramitāyām ukto mantraḥ | tadyathā | gate gate pāragate pārasaṃgate bodhi svāhā ||

evaṃ śāriputra gambhīrāyāṃ prajñāpāramitāyāṃ caryāyāṃ śikṣitavyaṃ bodhisattvena | atha khalu bhagavān tasmāt samādher vyutthāyāryāvalokiteśvarasya bodhisattvasya sādhukāram adāt | sādhu sādhu kulaputra evam etat kulaputra | evam etad gambhīrāyāṃ prajñāpāramitāyāṃ caryaṃ cartavyaṃ yathā tvayā nirdiṣṭam anumodyate tathāgatair arhadbhiḥ |

idam avocad bhagavān ānandamanā āyuṣmāñ chāriputra āryāvalokiteśvaraś ca bodhisattvaḥ sā ca sarvāvatī pariṣat sadevamānuṣāsuragandharvaś ca loko bhagavato bhāṣitam abhyanandan |
|| iti prajñāpāramitāhṛdayasūtraṃ samāptam ||

— 4 —

Nāgārjuna's *Mahāyānaviṃśaka*

Yamaguchi Susumu

Introduction

The Madhyamika philosophy of Buddhism goes in China under the name of the Sānlùn School (Sānlùn zōng 三論宗 J. Sanronshū), which literally means the school of the three treatises, which are Nāgārjuna's *Madhyamika-śāstra, Dvadaśadvāra-śāstra,* and Āryadeva's *Śataka.* In Tibet there is a Buddhist school known as the Prāsaṅgika which claims to transmit the tradition of the Madhyamika philosophy as this was expounded by such later followers of Nāgārjuna as Buddhapālita and Candrakīrti. The Prāsaṅgika school has five treatises by Nāgārjuna for its doctrinal authority. They are known as "rigspahi tshogs sde" (Division of Norm-collection) and consist of (1) *Mūlamadhyamika,* (2) *Yuktiṣaṣtikā* (3) *Śūnyatāsaptati,* (4) *Vigrahavyāvartanī,* and (5) *Vaidalya.*

While it goes without saying that the fundamental ideas of the two schools, Chinese Sānlùn and the Tibetan Prāsaṅgika, are derived from Nāgārjuna's original treatise (*Kārikā*) on the Madhyamika, we can distinguish three different undercurrents of thought in the text-books of the Madhyamika school. (1) Of the five Tibetan works, the *Vigrahavyāvartanī* and the *Vaidalya* may be regarded as forming the logical wing of the school, as its central subject is a critical study of the Nyāya; (2) The *Śūnyatāsaptati* has for its content a subject-matter somewhat different from the other texts, but as it is on the whole a summary of the *Mūlamadhyamika,* it forms another branch of thought together with the *Mūlamadhyamika* and the *Dvadaśadvāra-śāstra,* which last is again a compendium of the *Śūnyatāsaptati* and the *Mūlamadhyamika;* and lastly, (3) The *Yuktiṣaṣtikā* differs not only in its subject-matter but in its tendency of thought from the rest of the Madhyamika works, and what we especially notice in this book is that it betrays an idealistic way of thinking. This is shown in the following extracts:

hbyuṅ ba che la-sogs bśad-pa ||
rnam- par ses-su yaṅ-dag ḥdu ||
de śes-pas-ni ḥbral hgyur-na ||
log-par rnam-brtag ma-yin nam || (Verse 34)

What are known as the elements, etc., are included in Vijñāna (consciousness): knowing this, would one think of the elements as separate from Vijñāna? The elements so regarded are the result of wrong discrimination.

And again in Verses 36 and 77, we have this:

> This world is said to be conditioned by ignorance; when ignorance vanishes, the world too vanishes. Being so, the world is no more than discrimination.

In the *Mahāyānaviṃśaka* whose Tibetan texts along with the Chinese version are given below, this idealistic tendency is more pronounced than in the *Yuktiṣaṣṭikā*. There is no doubt that the philosophy of the *Prajñā-pāramitā Sūtra* and the theory of *śūnyatā* as advocated by Nāgārjuna are derived from the phenomenalism of the Buddhist teaching that things (*bhāvāḥ*) have no reality of their own because of the law of conditionality. Thus naturally Nāgārjuna is ever intent everywhere in his philosophical treatises to dwell upon the ten similes in the *Prajñā-pāramitā Sūtra* illustrative of the theory of śūnyatā (emptiness), saying that all things are like dreams, visions, the moon reflected in water, and images in the mirror. The reason, however, why we see all these actualities before us in spite of Nāgārjuna's phenomenalistic interpretation of existence is, according to him, due to our ignorance which stirs up our minds to create all these dream-like existences. This absolute idealism or subjectivism which denies the reality of an external world in itself, logically leads to the Vijñānavāda point of view as held by Asaṅga and Vasubandhu. According to this teaching, *vijñāna* alone exists (*vijñaptimātra*), no reality is granted to external objects (*artha*), and even mind (*citta* or *vijñāna*) as one of such objects cannot claim any reality: in brief, apart from the comprehended (*grāhya*) there is no comprehending subject (*grāhaka*) either.

While the philosophy of Nāgārjuna is based upon the theory of *śūnyatā* as expounded in his encyclopedic commentary to the *Prajñā-pāramitā Sūtra*, it is also supported by the Avataṃsaka doctrine, the final word of which is that "the triple world is mind only"; and indeed his treatise on the ten stages (*daśabhūmi*) of Bodhisattvahood is no more than the confirmation of this psychological dictum. In this respect the *Mahāyānaviṃśaka* is quite explicit as we see in verses 6, 8-12, 17-20, 22, etc., especially in verse 10 which corresponds to the utterance of Nyorairin 如來林 Bodhisattva at Yāmadeva's Palace as described in the *Avataṃsaka*:

> "Mind is like an artist
> Variously producing the five skandhas."

Verse 17 begins with the following:

> *Mdo-las | kye rgyal-baḥi sras-dag ḥdi-lta ste | khams gsum-pa ḥdi-ni sems-tsam-mo shes ḥbyaṅ-baḥi phyir-ro*
> "As we read in the Sūtra, O sons of the Buddha, in the triple world there exists mind only."

This is in full agreement with the idea of the *Viṃśakavṛtti*, where we have this:

> *Bya byed rmi-lam gnod-pa ḥdra.* 如夢害作事.
> (It is as in a dream that evil deeds are committed.)[1]

And again verse 16 reads:

> *mṅon-sum blo-ni rmi-sogs bshin || de-yaṅ gaṅ-tshe deḥi tshe || khyod-kyis don de mi snaṅ-na || de-ni mṅon-sum ji-ltar ḥdod*
> 證智如夢中　是時如證智　是時不見塵　云何塵可證
> (Our knowledge of reality is like a dream in which things appear as if real, but there are no objective realities in dreams, and in like manner how can we prove the reality of an objective world?)

We may add that the various currents of thought to be discerned in Nāgārjuna's works above referred to including the *Mahāyānaviṃśaka* are traceable in his stupendous commentary on the *Mahāprajñā pāramitā-sūtra*. In the fifteenth volume, Nāgārjuna comments, "If all existences (*bhāvāḥ*) are real, it is impossible for mind to know them. If they exist because of their being known by mind, this is not to be called existing." In Volume Eight we have: "All existences are like a plantain-tree; all is created by mind. But when you know that things have no reality, the mind itself ceases to exist." Nāgārjuna's comments on the ten similarities explaining the theory of *śūnyatā* also testify to the idealistic tendency of his philosophy.

While lately making a comparative study of the philosophical verses of Nāgārjuna which are preserved in the Tibetan and the Chinese Tripiṭaka, I came across two versions of his *Mahāyānaviṃśaka* in the *mdo ḥgrel* of the *bstan ḥgyur*, which in Cordier's Catalogue correspond to No.

1. Ed. Adjusted from the original "It is as if in dream that evil deeds are actually committed."

17 (Tsa), 156a, 4-157 a, 5; and No. 33 (Gi), 211 b, 8-213 a. In the Chinese Tripiṭaka there is just one version of this work (Nanjō No. 1308). In the following pages all these three versions are given for comparison. The Chinese consists of three parts: the prefatory verse, the text proper, and the dedicatory: the Tibetan (Tsa) contains 23 verses like the Chinese, but each division retains the same gāthā form. Towards the end of the text the Tibetan version grows disorderly and does not conform to the Chinese order; in this latter respect however the Tibetan (Gi) version consisting of twenty verses is in better agreement with the Chinese. In the following edition of the *Mahāyānaviṃśaka*, the "Tsa" text has been used as the principal one for comparison. As I have so far no access to other Tibetan editions than the Red Peking edition brought over here by Professor Yenga Teramoto, there are some points in each of the three texts, Tibetan and Chinese, which require further elucidation. It is my earnest wish that scholars would help us to clear up all the difficulties I have left here unsettled. An English translation and notes giving reasons for various readings and corrections will appear in the next issue of *The Eastern Buddhist*. [Here, these now follow immediately.]

English Translation[2] of the *Mahāyānaviṃśaka*

Editor's note. The "Tsa" translation, used as the basis for the following, is by Paṇḍita Candrakumāra and Bhikṣu Śākhayaprabhā; the "Gi" translation is by Paṇḍita Ānanda of Kaśmir and Bhikṣu Kīrtibhūtiprajñā of Lotsāba. Square brackets imply the translator's additions to complete the sense. The footnotes give matters of philological comparison, which may be disregarded by the general reader, while notes relating substantially to content are given after the text.

Adoration to *Mañjuśrī-kumāra-bhūtā*.

(Alternative in "Gi": Adoration to the Three Treasures.)

(1) The Buddha who is undefiled and enlightened, elucidates well, being full of mercy, that which is not a word nor is to be expressed in words: therefore I adore the [Buddha's] power which is beyond thought.[3]

2. The author wishes to acknowledge his deep indebtedness to Professor D. T. Suzuki, one of the editors of *The Eastern Buddhist*, in the preparation of this translation.

3. This verse (Tsa) agrees generally with the Chinese translation. *Snan-gyur-pa* in the 3rd line is the passive form of *dṛś*, corresponding to the Chinese 宣說 as well as to *bstan* in Gi; should it not then be the causative of *dṛś*? As *blon-me-pa*, the 3rd line, in Gi, corresponds to *bsam-mi-khyab*, the 4th line, in Tsa, *blon-med* does not seem to be correct. *Rgyul-bar*, of the 3rd line, in Tsa, is my correction according to the Chinese translation 善, adverbially used here. The original reads *rgyal-ba*. 非無言 in the Chinese 3rd line does not appear in Gi. *Brjod-par bya-ba-min*, the 2nd line, Tsa, corresponds to *brjod-du med*, Gi, the original Sanskrit probably was *na vācāvācya*, and this was misread by the Chinese translator *vācā avācya*.

(2) From the absolute point of view there is no birth, here again there is no annihilation; the Buddha is like sky, so are beings; they are of one nature.[4]

(3) There is no birth on the other side, nor on this side; nirvāṇa too in its self-nature exists not. Thus when surveyed by a knowledge which knows all things, empty are the created.[5]

(4) The self-nature of all things is regarded as like a shadow; they are in substance pure, serene, non-dualistic and the same as suchness.[6]

(5) [To think of] self or of no-self is not the truth; they are discriminated by the confused; pleasure and pain are relative; so are passions and emancipation from them.[7]

(6) Transmigration in the six paths of existence, the excellence and enjoyability of the heavenly world, or the great painfulness of the purgatories. All these come from apprehending the external world [as reality].

(7) One suffers very much when there is nothing pleasurable; even when there are things to enjoy, they pass away because they are impermanent; but it is so settled that good indeed comes from good deeds.[8]

(8) Things are produced by false discrimination where there is no origination, so, when the purgatories, etc., are manifested, the erroneous are burned like a forest fire.[9]

(9) Like things created by magic, so are the deeds of sentient beings who take the external world [for reality]. The [six] paths of existence are in substance magical creations, and they exist conditionally.[10]

---

4. 随轉 (2nd line in Chinese) seems to be a wrong rendering of *ni vṛt*, which the translator read for *anu vṛt*. *De-ñid-du* (Tsa and Gi) is read in my translation as *tasmin eva*, but as the Chinese has 無性, could this have been *de-(kho-na)-ñid-du (tat-tvena)*?

5. The first line, Tsa, agrees with the Chinese, but how shall we reconcile this with *bshin-skyes-pa-yi* (*yoniśa utpannaḥ*)? *Rten-skyes* (Gi) agrees with the Chinese 緣所生 (*pratītya utpanna*): this evidently corresponds to *mya-ṅan-ḥdas* (*nirvāṇam, nirvṛta*); but in what relation do they stand to each other? Evidently *ḥdus-byas* (*saṃskṛta*) in both Tibetan texts is read by the Chinese translator as *saṃskāra* 諸行. *Tshul-rol* (first line, Tsa) is *tshul-rol* in the original text, the correction was made according to the Chinese reading.

6. *Dag*, (3rd line, Gi) is *ḥdag* in the original, but as this corresponds to *rnam-par-dag* (Tsa), *bdag* is incorrect. *Rnam-dag* (*viśuddhi*) is translated in the Chinese as 無染.

7. *Bden-pa*, (first line, Tsa) is rendered here as *satyaḥ* according to the usual method of transcription, but as it is to be regarded as corresponding to *de-ñid-du* (first line, Gi), it may be meant for *tattva*. In this case the difference between the two Tibetan texts hangs on the particle, *na*, or the privative prefix, *a*.

8. *Rga-daṅ-nad*, second line, Gi, was originally *rga-daṅ-na*? the correction is due to the Chinese translation.

9. *Rtog-pas*, first line, Tsa, was originally *rtogs-pas*, which is here corrected from the Chinese reading 妄分別.

10. Ed. Revised from "Like unto things magic-created..."

(10) As the painter painting a terrible monster is himself frightened thereby, so is the fool frightened with transmigration.[11]

(11) As a stupid child making a muddy pool is himself drowned in it, so are sentient beings drowned in the mire of false discrimination and unable to get out of it.

(12) As they regard non-existence as existence they suffer the feeling of pain. In the external world as well as in thought they are bound by the poison of false discrimination.[12]

(13) Seeing that beings are weak, one with a heart of love and wisdom is to discipline oneself for perfect enlightenment, in order to benefit them.[13]

(14) Again, if one with such [a heart] accumulates [spiritual] provisions, one attains, from the relative point of view, supreme enlightenment and is delivered from the bondage of false discrimination. Such an enlightened one is a friend of the world.

(15) When a man perceives the true meaning [of reality] as it becomes, he understands that the paths of existence are empty, and cuts asunder [the chain of] the first, middle and last.[14]

(16) Thus regarded, saṃsāra and nirvāṇa have no real substance. Passions are without any substance.[15] Such notions as the first, middle, and last are done away with when their self-nature is understood.

(17) As perception takes place in a dream which when awakened disappears; so it is with sleeping in the darkness of ignorance: when awakened, transmigrations no more obtain.[16]

(18) When things created by magic are seen as such, they have no existence; such is the nature of all things.

(19) They are all nothing but mind, they are established as phantoms; therefore a blissful or an evil existence is matured according to deeds

11. *Gśin-rje* in Gi evidently corresponds to *yakṣa*, and the original was probably *yama*.

12. The last syllable in the first line, Gi, originally read *min*, but judging from its relation to the succeeding line *min* should be *yis* as in Tsa. *Rtog* beginning the fourth line, Gi, was originally *dogs*, but in accordance with Tsa and also with the Chinese 虛妄心, *rtog* has been adopted here. *Gnod-par-byed* (*bādhayate*) must have come from *badhyate* in Tsa. As regards the third line, Gi, inasmuch as *ñam-na* is derived from *saṃśaya*, we are led to the Chinese 疑惑 (uncertainty, doubt), but how shall we understand it in the light of the third line, Tsa? Further evidence is needed to clear this up.

13. 救 (salvation) in the Chinese text corresponds to *śaraṇa*, Gi, rather than to *sāra*, Tsa. 佛 (Buddha) is the subject in the Chinese as well as in Gi.

14. In the first line of the Chinese 從 evidently corresponds to "*pratītya samutpāda*" of the first line of Tsa; against this, Gi has in the second line, *utpannajñānāḥ*: in what relation does this stand to the Chinese as well as to Tsa? Can we regard the Chinese as equivalent to *utpanna*?

15. Ed. Revised from "Passions have not any substance."

16. The second line, Tsa, originally stood as *so-sor rtog-pa snaṅ-ba-yin*, but in accordance with the Chinese and Gi, *rtog* was changed into *rtogs* and *yin* into *min*.

good or evil.[17]

(20) When the mind-wheel ceases to exist all things indeed cease to exist; thus there is no ego in the nature of all things and therefore their nature is pure indeed.

(21) When the ignorant wrapped in the darkness of ignorance conceive eternity or bliss in objects as they appear or as they are in themselves, they drift in the ocean of transmigration.

(22) Where the great ocean of birth and death is filled with waters of false discrimination, who could ever reach the other shore unless carried by the raft of the Mahāyāna?

(23) When it is rightly understood that the world arises conditioned by ignorance, where could false discrimination obtain?

Notes relating to the content

(The numeration refers to the verse numbers above)

2. That *ḥgag-pa* (2nd line) is changed into *grol-ba* in Gi is justifiable according to the idea upheld in Nāgārjuna's *Madhyamika Śāstra*, in the chapter on *nirvāṇa*, where the author refutes the view of *nirvāṇa* as non-existence (*abhāva*), destruction (*vināśa*), annihilation (*nirodha*), and so on.
5. The first line, in Tsa, is the assertion of the idea expounded in the second stanza of the *Śūnyatā-saptati* (空七十論), where we have "*bdog-med bdog-med min*, there is neither self nor no-self." To deny both egoism (*ahaṃkāra*) and non-egoism (*nirahaṃkāra*) is the fundamental idea of Nāgārjuna philosophy, which is elucidated in his *Madhyamika Śāstra*, Chapter on Ego (*ātma-parīkṣā*). The Chinese translation is in agreement with Gi but not with Tsa.
6. As the last syllable of the fourth line in Gi is lost, the sense is not quite clear, but Tsa and the Chinese (third line) suggest the following reading, "The objective world is not to be considered real."
7. The first and the second line, Gi, have again, "pain, old age, disease, and impermanency, which are not enjoyable"; this corresponds to the Chinese. But as we have in the third and the fourth line, Gi, "pleasure and pain variably mature (*vipāka*) from all kinds of karma," the latter half of this stanza differ in all three texts.
8. The missing second line, in Tsa, may have been something corresponding to the Chinese second line, which reads "the fire of passions burns."
11. Tsa generally agrees with the Chinese, especially in the first and the second line; in Gi the agreement is confined to the first line while the rest reads quite differently: "As ignorant betake themselves to pleasures, even

17. All three agree generally; in particular the Chinese 安立 in the second line is the exact rendering of Tibetan *gnas-pa*. If we follow the Chinese, *rnams* in the fourth line may be altered into *smin*.

so are all beings drowned in the mire of discrimination which is pleasing."

13. Gi reads "seeing them without shelter, the Buddha as he has a pitying heart applies himself to enlightenment for the benefit of all beings."

14. *Kun-rdsob* (*saṃvṛti*) stands in contrast to *paramārtha*; according to the latter view, there is no merit to accumulate, no provisions to store, they are all empty in essence, all is absolute quietness where we cannot speak of gain or loss. Therefore, to say that perfect enlightenment is, as in the present stanza, realizable through the accumulation of spiritual merit, is in accordance with the *saṃvṛtya* view of truth. The Chinese translation is evidently from a text considerably different in form from the Tibetan versions.

15. "The beginning, middle, and ending are laid aside,"—the idea also appears in the latter half of the twenty-fifth stanza in *Yuktiṣaṣṭikā*: "it grows from the seed of ignorance; the beginning, middle, and ending are laid aside."[18] According to Candrakīrti, "As all component things are produced from the seed of ignorance as cause, they have no existence of their own. In order to explain that they have no self-nature in themselves, Nāgārjuna says that the beginning and middle and ending are laid aside; in other words, it means that there is no production, no abiding, and no destruction."[19]

16. According to Gi, the present stanza reads: "They do not see the ego (reality) as belonging to saṃsāra and nirvāṇa. There is no defiling, no changing; there is serenity from the first, and lucidity." This corresponds to the Chinese. How did the fourth line of the preceding stanza come to be repeated here in the Tsa text? There must have been some confusion.

21. This stanza in Tsa seems to be the amalgamation of the two stanzas 16 and 17 in Gi which correspond to the Chinese 18 and 19. Gi 16 (roughly corresponding to Chinese 18, line 2, and 19, lines 3 and 4) reads: "When such thoughts as eternity, ego, and bliss are entertained in objects which have no self-nature, the night of avarice and ignorance falls and there arises the ocean of beings." Gi 17 (equivalent to Chinese 18, lines 3 and 4, and 19, line 2) has: "While there is no birth in its self-nature, worldly people discriminate that there is birth: both discrimination and sentient beings have no existence."[20]

---

18. *Rokujūshōnyoriron* 六十頌如理論 (從無明種生, 離初中後際); *ma-rig rgyu-las śiṅ-tu byuṅ, thog-ma dbus mthaḥ rnam-par spaṅs.*

19. *Ji-ltar ṅo-bo-ñid-kyis grub-pa (med-pa de-ltar bstan-paḥi phyir, thog-ma dbus mthaḥ rnam-par spaṅs, shes-bya-ba) ston-te skye-ba daṅ gnas-pa dan ḥjig-pa daṅ bral-ba shes-bya-baḥi tha-tshig-go.* (*Bstan-ḥgyur*. B. 24. 21b. 2-3.) The same thought is expressed in "*kālaparīkṣa prakaraṇaṃ*," of Nāgārjuna's *Madhyamika Śāstra: uttama— ādhama—madhyādin— ca lakṣyet.*

20. Ed. The syntax of this line has been slightly adjusted.

— 5 —

An Outline of the *Avataṃsaka Sūtra*

Beatrice Lane Suzuki

Of Mahāyāna sūtras, the *Kegon*, the *Hokke* (*Saddharma-Puṇḍarīka*) and the *Nehan* (*Nirvāṇa*) sūtras are the most outstanding, and among these the *Kegon* is important because it is considered to be the teaching given out by the Buddha Śākyamuni just after his enlightenment, and in consequence his enlightenment is made the centre or pivot of the sūtra's substance.

The sūtra is called *Avataṃsaka* in Sanskrit and in Japanese *Kegon*. The full Japanese title is *Dai-hō-kō-bu-tsu-kegon-kyō*: *dai* = great, *hō* = normative, *kō* = all-pervading, *butsu* = enlightened one, *kegon* = adorned with flowers, [*kyō* = sūtra]. The title means [in paraphrase]: "How beautiful is the Enlightened One who has grasped the great all-pervading Truth which is the normative principle of the universe."

The scope of this sūtra is very grand. On the ocean of it, like a mirror, everything is reflected and revealed. In form it is bold and grand, yet delicate and subtle. It is one of the supreme works of the world.

There are two complete translations [into Chinese], one in sixty volumes translated by Buddhabhadra (359–429 CE) of Northern India in the Eastern Jìn Dynasty (317–420 CE).[1] The Kegon sect uses this sixty-volume version. And one in eighty volumes was translated by Śikṣananda, of the Táng dynasty, 695–699.

The forty-volume sūtra translated by Prajñā in 796–797, called the *Fugengyōganbon* "Practice and Vows of Samantabhadra" corresponds to the *Gaṇḍavyūha*. This forty-volume *Kegon* (*Gaṇḍavyūha*) together with the *Jūjikyō* (*Daśabhūmika*) and other sūtras makes a complete *Avataṃsaka*. The *Gaṇḍavyūha* occupies about a fourth of the *Avataṃsaka* [though it is] is complete in itself. [Within the sūtra] it is the *Nyūhokkaibon*, i.e. the

1. Ed. Eastern Jìn Dynasty: Dōng jìn cháo 東晉朝. The author refers to the Eastern Shin Dynasty, presumably because Shin is the Japanese pronunciation for 晉/晋.

Chapter on Entering into the Universe through the Practice and Vows of Samantabhadra, and describes the pilgrimage of a youth called Sudhana in his efforts to enter the Dharmadhātu and his consultation with fifty-three good friends. It is the *Pilgrim's Progress* of Buddhism.[2]

This sūtra is not so much preached by Buddha himself, for he is for the most part silent; it is rather a dramatic description to reveal the contents of enlightenment. The Bodhisattvas and devas are active, but their activity is performed under the will of the Buddha, and the infinite varieties of activity shown are a revelation of the Buddha's power. This point must be remembered, that although he seems to be a silent participant he is in reality the true actor and preacher since all the others are performing and speaking through him. In so far as Buddha is the preacher he is Vairocana[3] the Supreme Buddha, the Dharmakāya, rather than the historical Buddha Śākyamuni. According to this sūtra, the human mind is the universe itself and identical with Buddha, and it is said that Buddha, Mind, and Beings are one and the same. This is a famous saying and expressive of Mahāyāna philosophy.

This sūtra is said to have been spoken three weeks after the Buddha's Enlightenment in a state of meditation and in the Dharmakāya form.

Samantabhadra plays a most important part. He is supposed to represent the student stage, not yet in a perfect state of supreme enlightenment. But all the preaching is really the preaching of the Dharmakāya and is enlightenment or Truth itself which in personal form is called Vairocana. Exoterically, the Buddha in enlightenment may mean the mendicant under the Bo-tree, but esoterically he is the pervading and permanent Dharmakāya; and this world is no longer an ordinary world, but the universe, Dharmadhātu, consisting of interpenetrating worlds.

The action of the sūtra takes place in seven places and there are nine assemblies. Of the seven places there are three on earth and four in heaven. Those on earth are:

1. under the Bo-tree
2. the bright palace
3. the Jetavana grove

and those in heaven are:

2. It is now being translated into English by Dr. Daisetz Teitarō Suzuki of Ōtani University, Kyōto, and Editor of *The Eastern Buddhist*. Ed. Suzuki Daisetsu's account of the *Gaṇḍavyūha*, relating it to Zen Buddhism, was published in his *Essays in Zen Buddhism Third Series*, Chapter II. These essays were originally published for the Eastern Buddhist Society by Luzac and Co in London 1927–1934 and then republished by Rider, London 1953. Suzuki Daisetsu also published other articles on the *Avataṃsaka Sūtra* in *The Eastern Buddhist*.

3. Ed. Suzuki transcribed as Vairochana, to indicate the pronunciation to readers of English.

1. the dwelling of Indra
2. the dwelling of Yama
3. Tuṣita, the dwelling of Maitreya
4. the Paranirmita [heaven].[4]

The eighth assembly is the Jetavana Grove repeated and this gives the story of Sudhana's pilgrimage, the subject of the forty-volume *Kegon* or *Gaṇḍavyūha*. The assemblies take place in range from earth to heaven, and then to earth, again beginning with Śākyamuni's enlightenment under the Bo-tree, and then ranging to the heavens showing the unimpeded movement of the Buddha's mind.

Although the first seven assemblies make Vairocana the master, each assembly has its own central personality who unfolds the brightness of his wisdom through the power of the Buddha. Of all the Bodhisattvas, Mañjuśrī and Samantabhadra are the chief ones, Mañjuśrī representing Wisdom (*prajñā*) and Samantabhadra Practice (*caryā*). These two attributes are two aspects of the Buddha's enlightenment, for the contents of the Dharmakāya, Wisdom and Practice, complete the attainment of Enlightenment. Wisdom is necessary for the first step, but Practice completes the stride, so as Samantabhadra represents Practice, the stress of this sūtra is put upon this Bodhisattva.

There are forty steps of Practice and among these are ten stages or *bhūmis*. These ten stages are significant. The chapter on them is circulated as an independent sūtra known as the *Jūjikyō* or *Daśabhūmika*. The last assembly is called the *Nyūhokkaibon* or "Entering the Dharmadhātu," and this is the chapter which also became independent bearing the title *Gaṇḍavyūha*.

The fifteenth chapter is the *Jūjuhon* on the ten States, which describes the stages of the Bodhisattva from "cherishing the first thought for enlightenment" to the attainment of full Buddhahood.

In the sixteenth chapter the pure deeds of the Bodhisattva are described. Succeeding chapters enlarge upon this theme. The twenty-fifth chapter is interesting because it preaches the doctrine of Pariṇāmana (*ekō*), the turning of merit for the salvation of others. Chapter Twenty-seven deals with the Vows of Samantabhadra. But the most illuminating chapter of all is the thirty-ninth describing the ninth assembly, "Entering into the Universe," and it is this chapter which makes up the *Gaṇḍavyūha*. It deals with belief, understanding, practice, and enlightenment, which are after all nothing but one's own mind, and this one mind enters into universality and becomes enlightenment itself.

4. Ed. Suzuki also referred to this heaven as Taketsu, but the Japanese term behind this is probably Takejizaiten 他化自在天, a place in which beings enjoy things conjured up by others for a long time.

Interpenetration is the doctrine taught in the *Kegon.* When we look at the world in the spiritual light of Vairocana Buddha, we see it full of radiance, indeed a world of pure light. Everything in this world is interpenetrating, everything is mutually conditioned and conditioning. All things are one and that one is the Supreme Reality which embraces them.

> All the Buddha-lands and all the Buddhas themselves,
> Are manifested in my own being, freely and without hindrance,
> And even at the point of a single hair a Buddha-land is perceived.
> The Buddha-lands as innumerable as particles of dust,
> Are raised from one thought cherished in the mind of the Bodhisattva of Mercy (Samantabhadra),
> Who, practising meritorious deeds in numberless kalpas, has led all beings to the Truth;
> A Buddha-land rests in every particle of dust,
> And the spirit of the Buddha like a cloud covers and protects it.
> All lands are interpenetrating in the Buddha-land,
> And they are countless in number—a phenomenon beyond our understanding:
> There is nothing that does not fill up every quarter of the universe,
> And things are inexhaustible and immeasurable and move with perfect spontaneity.
> All the Buddha-lands are embraced in one Buddha-land,
> And each one of the Buddha-lands embraces in itself all the other lands;
> But the land is neither extended nor compressed.
> One land fills up all the ten quarters of the universe,
> And in turn the universe with all its contents is embraced in one land,
> And yet the world as it is suffers no damage.
> In every particle of dust throughout the Buddha world,
> The creative power of Vairocana Buddha is perceivable;
> His voice resounds over the ocean of universal salvation,
> Wherein all beings are brought under his control.[5]

When we do not see this radiant world of the Buddha's enlightenment in which Pure World everything is interpenetrating, the Buddha feels sorrow for beings and puts forth his activity to help all these beings to attain enlightenment. The Bodhisattvas follow him and through their own practice of the six virtues of perfection (*pāramitā*) help suffering beings to attain supreme enlightenment.

5. *Avataṃsaka Sūtra*, translated by D. T. Suzuki. Ed. This has been slightly edited for possible typing slips and the removal of old English verb forms ending in "-eth" (which have no particular basis in the original). The translation was presumably available informally to Beatrice Suzuki, and hence there are no reference details.

The Buddha is our refuge, unsurpassed and peerless,
He removes the sufferings of all beings;
If they desire to see him face to face,
He appears to them like the full moon over the mountain high.[6]

Now let us consider the *Gaṇḍavyūha.*

Once Buddha dwelt at Śravasti in the grove of Jetavana in the garden of Anāthapiṇḍika. In that assembly there were five hundred Bodhisattvas headed by Samantabhadra and Mañjuśrī. All the members of the assembly were waiting for the Buddha to preach. Then he entered *samādhi* (deep meditation) and as soon as he did so the forests of Jetavana suddenly became so wide that they became filled with an inexpressible number of worlds, and many Bodhisattvas from the ten quarters came and worshipped the Buddha, composing verses of praise. Buddha issued a ray of light from between his eyebrows and illumined the Bodhisattvas and all the ten quarters and thereby the Bodhisattvas were filled with compassion to benefit all beings.

Mañjuśrī went out from the Pratisthāna to the human world going south and preached the Mahāyāna doctrine to many people. While he was staying in the city of Dhanyākara, among his audience of listeners was a handsome youth of a noble family, Sudhana. While Sudhana was listening with the desire to learn, lead, and perfect the life of a Bodhisattva, Mañjuśrī, looking over the audience, perceived the young Sudhana and knew his aspiration, so he advised him thus: "You must find a true friend to help you in your search. Go to Myōhō Mountain in the country of Shōraku and there you will find a Bhikṣu Sāgaramegha (Toku-un).[7] He will give you good advice."

Sudhana set out on his journey, visited Sāgaramegha who taught him wisely and then sent him on to another friend. In this way he was sent to one friend after another until fifty-two friends in all had been visited, and at last he came to Samantabhadra, under whose teaching he perfected his vow and entered into the Dharmadhātu (Supreme Reality).

In this story of Sudhana we can see that Samantabhadra plays the chief part as master and Mañjuśrī as the guest, and the activity of both of them is represented by the youth Sudhana who visits fifty-three good friends seeking advice and finally attains entrance to the Dharmadhātu. It is the story of Enlightenment of "entering into the universe" by means of the practice and Vows of the religious life of Samantabhadra.

6. See previous note.

7. Ed. While the name Sāgaramegha literally means "ocean cloud," the Japanese version given here means Cloud of Virtue. Myōhōsan: Wondrous Peak Mountain. *Shōraku*: possibly 勝楽 i.e. "the land of superb joy."

In regard to the good friends whom Sudhana visited, besides Mañjuśrī who appeared three times and Samantabhadra the first and the last, there were fifty in all. What kind of persons were they? If we classify them we will find that there were five Bodhisattvas, five monks, one nun, eight householders, a physician, a perfume seller, a sailor, two kings, two laymen, four laywomen three of whom were ladies and one a heavenly maiden, several children, a number of deities, a mendicant, a hermit, and two Brahmins.

In the *Gaṇḍavyūha*, we find the Mahāyāna tendency to lay stress upon lay people rather than upon monks, and among all the friends [mentioned] we find only five monks. Not all of the friends were aristocratic and wealthy. One was a perfume seller, one a sailor, and one woman a courtesan.

Sudhana during his pilgrimage was seeking outside of himself by asking help of others and he passed through many experiences mental and spiritual, but later he realized that true knowledge must come from within. The fifty-third friend was Maitreya who directed Sudhana to go to Mañjuśrī to ask about the law by which he could enter into Samantabhadra's religious life.

The last volume of the sūtra is devoted to Samantabhadra's Ten Vows and the desire to be born into Sukhāvatīvyūha (that is, Pure Land).

The Ten Vows of Samantabhadra are:

1. To worship the Buddhas;
2. To praise the Tathāgatas;
3. To make offerings to all the Buddhas;
4. To confess past sins;
5. To rejoice in the virtues and happiness of others;
6. To request Buddha to preach the Law;
7. To request Buddha to live in this world;
8. To study Buddhism in order to teach it;
9. Always to benefit all beings;
10. To turn the stock of merit [over] to others.

These vows are the basis of the Bodhisattva's life in Mahāyāna Buddhism. This last part concerning Samantabhadra's Vows has also been issued separately, and is known as the *Fugengyōganbon* ("Practice and Vows of Samantabhadra").[8]

The story of Sudhana is ultimately an epitome of the entire *Kegon* sūtra. In the background is always the Dharmakāya. Every activity depicted is really the activity of Dharmakāya. It is a sūtra of Enlightenment and emphasizes the fact that all beings can be reborn in the house of the Buddha if they obtain enlightenment. The previous portions of the *Avataṃsaka* emphasize this and the Sudhana chapter states it practically.

8. Ed. See the following chapter.

— 6 —

The Hymn on the Life and Vows of Samantabhadra

Izumi Hōkei

Introduction

The importance of the *Hymn on the Life and Vows of Samantabhadra* has been well known in Japan since early days, not only from the doctrinal point of view but as a piece of Buddhist Sanskrit literature accessible to Japanese scholars. My object in editing the Hymn is to produce a perfect Sanskrit text as far as the present source of information and the facility of obtaining the material and the scholarship of the present editor permit.[1] Jiun 慈雲 (1718–1804) and his followers were among the foremost students of the text. The one who brought it first from China was Kōbō Daishi 弘法大師 (774–835). When the late Dr. Bun'yū Nanjō was studying Sanskrit under Max Müller of Oxford, he collected according to the advice of his teacher as many original Sanskrit texts as he could at the time; among those there were the *Smaller Sukhāvatīvyūha*, *Vajracchedikā*, *Prajñāpāramitāhṛdaya*, and *Bhadracarī*. Nanjō however did not have the chance to study the *Bhadracarī*, and it was possible that his friend Kenju Kasawara was planning to take up this study himself. Dr. Kaikyoku Watanabe was the first who made a thorough investigation of the text, while he was studying in Germany (1900–1910), and the result was published in Leipzig;[2] but the pamphlet is almost inaccessible at present. All the

1. Ed. The first two sentences have been transposed. The article is taken up here for the sake of the English translation and the introductory discussion. For this reason a long list of correspondences between non-standard and classical Sanskrit terms has been omitted, and the philologically interested reader should refer to the original article both for these and for the Sanskrit text as reconstituted by Izumi.

2. *Die Bhadracarī, eine Probe buddhistisch-religiöser Lyrik untersucht und herausgegeben. Inaugural-Dissertation zur Erlangung der Doktorwürde der philosophischen Fakultät der*

problems that may be raised concerning the *Bhadracarīpraṇidhāna* are discussed in it. My partial study of the text took place in 1909 and a comparison of the different Chinese and Tibetan translations of the Hymn appeared in a Japanese magazine called *Mujintō* 無尽燈, but I was unfortunately prevented from pursuing the study any further.

This Hymn, sometimes known as an epitomized *Kegonkyō* 華嚴経, contains the essence of the Buddhist life expressing itself in the ten vows and culminating in rebirth in the Pure Land of Amitābha. It may be regarded in a way as the foreshadowing of the Pure Land doctrine.

Samantabhadra, frequently abbreviated as Bhadra, is one of the most important bodhisattvas belonging to Mahāyāna Buddhism; he symbolizes in his life, virtues and vows, everything that is required of a good, faithful follower of the Buddha.

The text has been widely circulated as an independent hymn all over the Buddhist countries, but the title varies according to the localities where it is found:

in Japan: *Bhadracarī nāma samantabhadra-praṇidhānam*
in Nepal: *Bhadracarīpraṇidhāna, or Ārya-bhadracarī(-mahā)-praṇidhāna-rāja*
in Tibet: *Ārya-samantabhadra-caryā-praṇidhāna-rāja;*[3]
as quoted in Śāntideva's *Śikṣāsamuccaya* (pp. 290, 291, 297): *Ārya-bhadra-caryā-gāthā.*[4]

Going over these different titles, we conclude that Bhadra is the abbreviation of Samantabhadra, and that *carī* stands for *caryā*. It is likely that the hymn was first written in a dialect form which was later turned into classical Sanskrit.[5]

The composition of the hymn must have taken place rather early in the history of the Mahāyāna sutras. When Buddhabhadra, in CE 418–421, translated the *Sixty-Volume Kegonkyō* in which the sutras belonging to the Kegon family are put together, he did not find this Hymn in the *Kegonkyō*, and produced it as an independent work in 420 CE under the title *Wénshūshīlìfāyuàn jīng* 文殊師利發願經 (i.e. *Mañjuśrīpraṇidhāna-sūtra*).

According to the statement in the *Chūsānzànjìjí* 出三藏記集 [Collection of Notes on the Tripiṭaka], the following was found inscribed in the Chinese translation: "The four groups of Buddhists in the foreign country generally recite this Hymn when they worship the Buddha, vowing to seek the truth of Buddhism." From this we may infer that the Hymn

Kaiser Wilhelms-Universität zu Strassburg, vorgelegt von Kaikioku Watanabe aus Tokio. Leipzig, Druck von G. Kreysing, 1912. Ed. Watanabe is the surname.

3. "Rāja" is dropped in three of the five commentaries on the Hymn.

4. At the reference in *Śikṣāsamuccaya* 291 Ārya is omitted.

5. Ed. Cf. note 1 above.

was in wide circulation in India at the time of the Chinese translator, both among the ordained and the lay followers.

In one of the esoteric sutras known as *Chéngjiú miàofăliánhuājīng wángyúqiéguānzhì yíguǐ jīng* 成就妙法蓮華經王瑜伽觀智儀軌經 the following reference is made to the Hymn:

> After making proper obeisance to the Buddha the devotee should once recite the *Samantabhadracaryāpraṇidhāna* with singleness of mind, thinking of all Buddhas and Bodhisattvas, and reflecting with a pure heart on the signification of each phrase of the *Samantabhadracaryāpraṇidhāna.*

The sūtra is concerned evidently with the honouring of the *Saddharmapuṇḍarīka Sūtra*, and yet the devotee is asked reverently to recite the Hymn in connection with it. This shows that the recitation of the Hymn formed a regular part in the Buddhist service already in the seventh century when the above-mentioned sūtra was translated into Chinese.

We read in the life of Amogha[vajra] in the *Biographies of the High Priests* completed in the Sòng dynasty (988 CE) that Amogha when a child was able to recite the *Wénshūshīlìfāyuàn jīng* after only two nights while other children were supposed to learn it by heart in one year. Amogha was one of the translators of the Hymn. No doubt it was still popularly recited among the Indian Buddhists.

Seeing that during the last two thousand years the Hymn has been treated as containing the gist of Mahāyāna Buddhism crystallizing all the merits in connection with the life of the bodhisattva, the Hymn deserves a careful study on the part of scholars.

There are three Chinese translations of this Hymn. The oldest of them is Buddhabhadra's *Mañjuśrī-praṇidhāna Sūtra* (*Wénshūshīlìfāyuàn jīng*), of which mention is made above. Compared with the Sanskrit text presented with this article,[6] Buddhabhadra's translation has less stanzas, and as to its contents we notice some disagreement in detail. Buddhabhadra's line consists of five Chinese characters instead of seven as in other cases. The translation is not quite literal, that is, it is not a word-for-word translation, but the translator seems to have a better grasp of the meaning. It is interesting to note that Buddhabhadra's title is *Mañjuśrīpraṇidhāna* and not *Samantabhadra-caryā-praṇidhāna*, by which latter title the Hymn is now better known to us. Is it possible that originally Mañjuśrī and Samantabhadra were different names for the same individual Bodhisattva as is sometimes maintained by some Chinese Buddhist exegetists? It is certain that the Hymn was known at one time in its history as *Mañjuśrīpraṇidhāna* and not as *Samantabhadra-praṇidhāna.*

The second Chinese translation was done by Amoghavajra in the reign of Dài Zōng (763–779) of the Táng dynasty under the title *Pŭxián-*

6. Ed. See note 1.

púsà-xíngyuàn zàn 普賢菩薩行願讃 [Praise of the Deeds and Vows of Fugen Bosatsu]. This agrees best with the Sanskrit.

The third one was produced by Prajñā, in the twelfth year of Zhēn Yuán (796) as the concluding Gāthās of the *Forty-Volume Kegonkyō* 四十華嚴. The work began on the fifth day of the sixth month of the twelfth year of Zhēn Yuán (796), and a complete copy was presented to the emperor on the twenty-fourth day of the second month of the fourteenth year of the same era. This version on the whole agrees with the Sanskrit.

As mentioned above, the hymn was circulated independently, when it first came to China; perhaps it was so in India too. And it was not until the *Forty-Volume Kegonkyō* was translated that the Hymn found itself incorporated in the *Kegonkyō*. Later on, however, it became detached again from the mother Sūtra, assuming its independence; in Nepal we find the Hymn circulated as such. And in Japan too it is recited and studied as not necessarily belonging to the *Kegonkyō*.

The fact that it was once taken into the body of the *Kegonkyō* is shown by the prose prologue which is found in the Nepalese text as well as in the Japanese even when it is used separately.

According to Chéngguān 澄觀 who wrote a commentary on the *Forty-Volume Kegonkyō* there was an entry in the two preceding translations, Buddhabhadra's and Amoghavajra's, to the following effect:

> In each of the two preceding translations we read that 'this is the work of Xiánjíxiáng púsà 賢吉祥菩薩 (Bhadraśrī Bodhisattva), and not a sūtra preached by the Buddha himself.' But as we know that this is the teaching of Pǔxián púsà 普賢菩薩 (Samantabhadra Bodhisattva), there is a confusion of the names [in the above entry], that is, between Pǔxián 普賢 (Samantabhadra) and Xiánshǒu 賢首 (Bhadraśrī); and again as this Hymn has generally been in circulation independently, it is probable that the ancient masters of the Tripiṭaka regarded it as not one of the sūtras preached by the Buddha himself.

It is difficult to know how Xiánshǒu 賢首 came to be confused with Pǔxián 普賢 because there seems to be a great difference between the two terms, except Bhadra [xián] which is common to them. If any confusion were possible, it might take place between Bhadracarī and Bhadraśrī. And it is likely that the hymn was known in some quarters under the title of *Bhadraśrī-praṇidhāna* instead of *Bhadracarī-praṇidhāna*, which latter being the title of our text. From this fact the hymn probably came to be known as the work of Bhadraśrī, that is, Xiánjíxiáng 賢吉祥 or Xiánshǒu 賢首. While the hymn is generally entitled *Bhadracarī-praṇidhāna* as we have already noted, we have reason to suspect that it was also known among some Mahāyānists as *Mañjuśrī-praṇidhāna*;[7] for Buddhabhadra's

7. *Mañju* is a synonym of Bhadra as they both mean "beautiful" or "lovely."

Chinese translation bears this title.

According to the view of Zōngmì 宗密 (780–841) which is recorded as a note to this passage, he thinks Bhadraśrī extracted these passages from the sūtra relating to the life and vows of the Bodhisattva and made them into a form of hymn.

The hymn that was introduced into Japan was the one brought over to China by Amoghavajra. Amoghavajra who came to China about 747 CE was a representative of the esoteric Buddhism which at the time prevailed in southern India and Ceylon. He brought a number of Sutras belonging to this school and the *Bhadracarī-praṇidhāna* was among them. It was Kūkai 空海 (i.e. Kōbō Daishi) who first brought the hymn to Japan in 806 CE; he was the disciple of Hùigǔo 慧果 and Hùigǔo transmitted the esoterism of Amoghavajra.

After Kūkai, Engyō 圓行, who was his disciple, brought two handwritten copies of the hymn (836). Eight years after Engyō, Eun 惠運 brought another copy of the hymn from China; Ennin 圓仁 was the last importer of the text from China. Hitherto the hymn had been brought by Buddhist priests of the Shingon sect, but now for the first time a priest belonging to the Japanese Tendai school carried a copy of it back to Japan. Altogether five different copies came over here from China, but the one we still have belongs to Kūkai's transmission; all the rest are lost now.

Kūkai's original copy is evidently lost, but four different copies of it are still in existence, and the oldest one dates back as far as 966. And the text in circulation at present is the one revised by Jiun who carefully collated the four different copies made from Kūkai's original copy. Jiun's revision probably dates not later than 1767, this being the year when he began to lecture on his own manuscript of the *Bhadracarī-praṇidhāna*.

An English Translation

1. All the lions of mankind in all the three divisions of time who are in the ten quarters of the universe—all these without exception, I, the pure one, salute with body, speech, and mind.

2. Making my body as numerous as particles of dust composing the earth I pay reverence to all the Buddhas, imagining in mind to be in the presence of all the Buddhas, by virtue of Bhadra's Life-of-vows.

3. Buddhas as numerous as particles of dust are sitting surrounded by the Bodhisattvas, even at the end of a particle of dust; thus I believe all the universe without exception is filled with the Buddhas.

4. And of them, with an ocean of voice in which all notes of sound are found, I praise all those Buddhas, by exalting all the virtues of these Buddhas, which are like the ocean of inexhaustible nature.

5. With the best flowers, wreaths, musical instruments, ointments, umbrellas, lamps, and incenses, I make offerings to the Buddhas.

6. With the best garments, scented wood, powdered incense in heap equal to the Meru, arrayed with all these excellent [offerings], most exquisitely I make offerings to the Buddhas.

7. This is, I believe, what is to be the best, munificent offering to the Buddhas; it is clue to my faith in the life of Bhadra that I salute and make offerings to all the Buddhas.

8. And of all the sins that may have been committed by me, due to my greed, anger, and folly, with my body, speech, and mind, I make full confession.

9. And whatever is the happiness of all beings, the Learners, the non-Learners, Pratyeka-Buddhas, Bodhisattvas, and all the Buddhas, in the ten quarters—for all that I feel sympathetic joy.

10. Those who being awakened in enlightenment are the light of the world in the ten quarters have attained non-attachment, all these I entreat to revolve the wheel that is unsurpassed.

11. Those who wish to manifest Nirvāṇa I entreat with folded hands, to stay [in this world] for a number of Kalpas equal to particles of dust making up the earth, for the benefit and happiness of all beings.

12. Whatever goodness, accumulated by me accruing from the Salutation, Offering, Confession, Sympathetic Joy, Request, Solicitation, all this I dedicate towards enlightenment.

13. May all the Buddhas of the past be revered, and those residing now in the ten quarters of the world and those of the future—may they be at ease, be fulfilled in their aspirations, and awakened to enlightenment.

14. May all the lands in the ten quarters be pure, extensive, and filled with Buddhas who went under the king of the Bodhi tree and with Bodhisattvas.

15. May all beings in the ten quarters be always happy and healthy; the benefit of righteousness be possessed by all beings; let them be blissful, and their wishes be fulfilled.

16. While practising a life of enlightenment, wherever I may be born in the paths of existence, may I remember my previous lives; in all the forms of life I may be born and pass away, but may I always lead a mendicant's life.

17. Learning after all the Buddhas, perfecting the life of Bhadra, let me always practise a pure and spotless life of morality, without breakage, without leakage.

18. With the speeches of the gods, with the speeches of the Nāgas, with the speeches of Yakṣas, Kumbhāṇḍas, and mankind—with all the speeches wherever there are speeches in the world, I will disclose the Dharma.

19. Let him who is disciplining himself in the exquisite Pāramitās never be confused in mind as regards enlightenment; from those sins that are hindering let him be thoroughly freed.

20. Let me practise in the walks of life emancipation from karma, evil passions and from the way of Māyā; like the lotus that is not stained by water, like the sun and the moon that are not attached to the sky.

21. Extinguishing all pains in the evil paths, establishing all creatures in happiness, let me practise [the life of Bhadra] for the benefit of all creatures, as far as there are lands and paths in the ten quarters.

22. Conforming to the lives of all beings, perfecting the life of enlightenment, and holding up the life of Bhadra, let me discipline myself to the very end of time.

23. May I always be associated with those who would keep company with me in the life [of Bhadra]; let us all practise one life of vows with body, speech, and mind.

24. Those well-wishing friends who are witnesses of the life of Bhadra, with them may I always be associated, and may I never grow tired of them.

25. Let me always be personally in the presence of the Buddhas, leaders surrounded by the Bodhisattvas, and let me make them munificent offerings without growing weary to the end of time.

26. Holding up the true law of all the Buddhas, making the life of enlightenment shine out, and purifying the life of Bhadra, let me discipline myself to the end of time.

27. And transmigrating through all the paths of existence I have infinitely accumulated all merit and wisdom; let me be an inexhaustible store-house, filled with all the virtues such as Supreme Wisdom, Skilful Means, Mental Concentration, and Emancipation.

28. There are lands as numerous as particles of dust at the end of a particle of dust, and in each of these lands there is an inconceivable number of Buddhas, whom I see sitting in the midst of the Bodhisattvas, while I discipline myself[8] in the life of enlightenment.

29. Thus, in all the quarters without exception, even to the hair-like passage through all the three divisions of time, there is an ocean of Buddhas, an ocean of lands, an ocean of Kalpas of [devotional] life: into all these may I enter.

30. There is one voice containing an ocean of meaning, a voice of purity uttered by all the Buddhas, which is the voice in accordance with the aspirations of all beings, this is the eloquence of the Buddha, into which may I enter.

31. And revolving the wheel of the doctrine, and by the power of the understanding, may I enter into those inexhaustible sounds and languages of the Buddhas walking in the three divisions of time.

32. Entering into all future time may I enter in an instant; and into the three divisions of time measure, at an instant point of time, may I discipline myself.

---

8. Ed. Adjusted from "I disciplining myself...."

33. May I see all the lions of mankind in the three divisions of time in an instant, and may I always enter into their realms with the power of emancipation which is like Māyā.

34. And may I manifest throughout the three divisions of time excellent lands in full array at the end of one particle of dust; thus may I enter into all the Buddha-lands in full array in the ten quarters without exception.

35. The world-lamps of the future when enlightened will revolve the wheel and show themselves in Nirvana in absolute tranquility: all those leaders may I approach.

36. By the power of the psychic faculties swiftly moving everywhere, by the power of the vehicle in every direction, by the power of deeds productive of all virtues, by the power of all-pervading good-will,

37. By the power of all-purifying merit, by the power of wisdom which is conducive to non-attachment, by the power of Transcendental Wisdom, Device, Mental Concentration; accumulating the power of enlightenment,

38. Purifying the power of Karma, crushing the power of passions, disarming the power of the evil one, may I perfect all the power of the life of Bhadra.

39. Purifying the ocean of lands, releasing the ocean of beings, reviewing the ocean of phenomena, plunging into the ocean of wisdom,

40. Purifying the ocean of deeds, fulfilling the ocean of vows, worshipping the ocean of Buddhas, may I discipline myself untiringly in the ocean of Kalpa.

41. The excellent deeds and vows of enlightenment which belong to the Buddhas of the three divisions of time, all these without exception, may I fulfill, and awake in enlightenment for the sake of the life of Bhadra.

42. There is the eldest son of all the Buddhas, whose name is Samantabhadra; to those who walk the same path as this wise one may I dedicate all the good works [of mine].

43. Purity of body, speech, and mind, purity of life, and purity of land: such is the name of Bhadra, the wise one, with such as he I wish to be equal.

44. To be thoroughly pure in the life of Bhadra, may I discipline myself in the vows of Mañjuśrī, untiringly through all the future time I wish to fulfill all the deeds without exception.

45. Let me practise all the deeds that are beyond measure, let me practise all the virtues that are beyond measure; establishing myself in the deeds that are beyond measure, let me know all their miraculous powers.

46. Only when space-limits are reached, only when the end of beings is reached, with none left, not even with a single being unsaved, only when karma and passions are exhausted, then my vows would come to an end.

47. There are innumerable lands in the ten quarters which are adorned with jewels, may I give them to the Buddhas; all the excellent happiness that belongs to the gods and men may I give to [them] for Kalpas [as

numerous as] particles of dust composing the earth.

48. Listening for once to this king of the turning-over of merit, faith will grow [in one's heart] who will seek after the supreme enlightenment, the merit thereby acquired will be the highest and most excellent of all merits.

49. One who practises the life and vows of Bhadra will be kept away from evil paths as well as from bad friends and will instantly see that Amitābha.

50. They will easily obtain whatever is profitable, they will live a worthy life, when they are born among human beings they will be welcomed; they will be like Samantabhadra himself before long.

51. When a man has committed by reason of his ignorance the five sins of immediate nature, let him recite this hymn called "the life of Bhadra," and have his sins instantly and completely extinguished.

52. He will be endowed with wisdom, beauty, and the auspicious marks, born in a [high] caste, in a [noble] family; he will not be crushed by a host of heretics and evil ones, will be revered in all the triple world.

53. He will immediately go under the Bodhi tree, king [of trees], going there he will take his seat for the welfare of beings, he will be awakened in enlightenment, revolve the wheel [of Dharma], he will entirely crush evil ones with his army.

54. When a man holds, recites, preaches this life and vows of Bhadra, the Buddha knows what maturity he will attain, have no doubt as to [his attaining] the excellent enlightenment.

55. Mañjuśrī the hero knows, so does Samantabhadra; following them in my study I apply all my good deeds [towards that end].

56. By the turning over of merit which is praised as best by the Buddhas of the past, present and future, I apply all my good deeds towards the attainment of the most excellent life of Bhadra.

57. At the time of my death, all the hindrances being cleared off, may I come in the presence of the Buddha Amitābha, and go to his land of bliss.

58. Having gone there, may all these excellent vows come up in my mind; and may I fulfill them without exception in order to benefit all beings to the full extent of the world.

59. May I be born in the assembly of the Buddhas pure and delightful, and in a most beautiful lotus, and obtain there the declaration of my future destiny in the presence of the Buddha Amitābha.

60. Having obtained the declaration of my future destiny, I will, then, transforming myself in many hundreds of *koṭīs* of forms, benefit all beings in the ten quarters, in a most liberal manner, by the power of my wisdom.

61. By whatever goodness gathered by myself by reciting this "life and vows of Bhadra" let all the pure vows of the world be fulfilled in a moment.

62. By the infinite and most excellent merit which is acquired by devoting oneself to the life of Bhadra, let the whole world sinking in the flood of calamities go to the most excellent city of Amitābha.

Part III

Hints of Laity in the Esoteric Tradition

— 7 —

Fudō the Immovable

Beatrice Lane Suzuki

I

From the earliest days of Buddhism in Japan, one of the most popular gods (or symbolical beings) known as "Vidyārājas" has been Fudō the Immovable, i.e. Fudō Myōō 不動明王, meaning Bright King Fudō (known in Sanskrit as Acala).[1] His name, and his features and attitude, as these are generally represented in paintings and sculptures, suggest the fierceness of his original character. One may think that such a terrible-looking god could represent only evil, destroying every vestige of goodness in the world. But his fearsome attitude is not directed against anything that is good and holy, but against iniquities, enemies of Buddhism, obstructors of enlightenment. He is to be feared only by those that harbour evils in their hearts, but to be warmly greeted by friends of justice, virtue, and knowledge. His inflexible courage is eternally set for the destruction of everything that will finally lead the world to ignorance and selfishness. In this work he is indefatigable. But strangely, in popular minds he has turned to be a god of worldly welfare and is worshipped as one who will grant his devotees all the material advantages that they may ask of him. Hence his extreme popularity.

Theoretically, Fudō the Immovable belongs to the Shingon sect and is one of the Five or Eight Vidyārājas, Lords of Knowledge (*Myōō* 明王).[2] He is also known as one of the "Krodharājas," Lords of Wrath (*Funnu-myōō*

---

1. Ed. Strictly speaking, with "Fudō the Immovable" Suzuki has created a reduplicated nickname, because Fudō literally means "immovable."

2. Ed. The literal meaning of *avidyā* + *rāja* is knowledge + king, and the literal meaning of *myō* + *ō* is bright + king, but bright in this case can also mean mentally bright or alert, and can be contrasted with *mumyō* 無明 (Skt. *avidyā*), the standard Buddhist term for ignorance.

忿怒明王), ten of whom are generally reckoned. But Fudō is regarded as the principal one of the Five Vidyarājas who are representatives of the Five Buddhas. According to the Shingon doctrine, a Buddha is considered to have three forms of manifestation, called "three vehicles." First, he remains in his own natural form; second, he assumes a Bodhisattva form in order to make himself accessible to human beings according to their various spiritual needs; third, he manifests himself as a Lord of Wrath to make evil-doers amenable to the teaching of the Buddhas, showing that evil is to be handled frequently in a rough, merciless manner, and that the world is not such as it ought to be, where there is so much ungodliness that is to be brought to subjection. The Five Buddhas enumerated in the cosmology of the Shingon are Vairocana (Dainichi 大日), Akṣobhya (Ashuku 阿閦), Ratnasaṃbhava (Hōshō 寳生), Amitāyus (Muryōju 無量壽) and Amoghasiddhi (Fukūjōju 不空成就); the corresponding Bodhisattvas are: Prajñā (Hannya 般若), Vajra (Kongō 金剛), Vajragarbha (Kongōzō 金剛蔵), Mañjuśrī (Monju 文殊), and Vajrayakṣa (Kongōge 金剛牙); the Five Lords of Wrath incarnating the respective Buddhas are: Acala (Fudō 不動), Trailokyavijaya (Gōsanze 降三世), Kuṇḍalī (Kundari 軍荼利), Yamāntaka (Daiitoku 大威德) and Vajrayakṣa (Kongōyasha 金剛夜叉).[3]

Strictly speaking, every Buddha is supposed to have his *krodhakāya*, wrath-body (*funnushin* 忿怒身) as well as his female counterpart (*śakti*), but the number of the known Gods of Wrath is far less than that of the Buddhas. The Gods of Wrath most popularly known are those five just mentioned, although sometimes the number goes up to ten.

The Five *vidyārājas* or *myōō* were formerly worshipped as a group, none of them being singled out as a special object of devotion. But later Fudō, the Immovable, somehow came to leave the group of five and make himself the representative of all the Wrath-manifestations of the Buddhas. The reason was partly, I believe, that he symbolizes Dainichi, the Great Sun Buddha (Biroshana 毘盧遮那, Skt. Vairocana), who is the great illuminator of the universe according to the Shingon, and the central figure of the world-system. It is through Dainichi that all existence is made possible, and that life, though filled with various defilements can be enjoyed in its purity. Fudō thus came to play such an important role in the pantheon of Buddhism. But probably the main reason was that the popular mind could not grasp all the subtleties and intricacies of the philosophy of the Shingon and simply wanted one figure of Wrath, in whom all the speculative abstraction would be symbolized and yet who could appeal to the imagination of the Japanese; for they abhor too intensified and seemingly

3. Amoghasiddhi Buddha seems to have just one name as bodhisattva and as *krodharāja*, both being called Vajrayakṣa. But in Japanese, his Bodhisattva name is Kongōge (meaning "*vajra*-tooth") and his Rāja name is Kongōyakusha which is the combination of Vajra and Yakṣa, a demigod.

grotesque personifications of anger, revenge, and punishment. As we may recognize in all the Fudō pictures and sculptures, there is something in them that rather kindly attracts us to the god, he is not so repellent or too awe-inspiring, even in his most intense passion, as are the other Lords of Wrath. Perhaps, in spite of his immovable graveness, his form is that of an undeveloped child, suggesting his innocent and cherubic character which is appealing. His original vow (*honzei* 本誓, Skt. *samaya*), as every spiritual being is supposed according to the Shingon doctrine to have made some kind of oath which justifies his reason of appearance in the world, is to remove all possible obstacles lying in the progressive course of Buddhism. United with his personality, this vow must have helped to lift him up to his present position among the gods of Buddhism in Japan.

II

To paint or sculpture Fudō, the immovable God of Wrath, one has to observe the rules that are set forth in the books devoted to his worship. Since the introduction of the symbolic Shingon sect into China in 716 CE and Japan in 816 CE, a special class of Buddhist literature known as the Guhyakalpa (*Himitsugiki* 秘密儀軌) has developed, comprising several hundreds of volumes in its Chinese edition. They principally describe all the Buddhas, Bodhisattvas, *vidyārājas*, *devas*, *yakṣas*, etc., that belong to the iconography of the Shingon; they are a veritable encyclopedia of this field of Buddhist study, and around them there has grown an immense library of commentaries, notes, illustrations and documents to be secretly transmitted. These "Books of Mystic Rituals" are not confined to the mere descriptions of the various objects of Buddhist worship, but give all the necessary information as to how to make them religious offerings, how to produce their images and portraits, when and where they are to be worshipped, and so forth. It is really astounding to see how deeply and sometimes how fantastically the human imagination can work out this phase of mystic symbolism. Shingon ritualism is quite an absorbing study for those who are interested in occultism generally. To show how Fudō is to be depicted, I quote from one of the Kalpa Books dealing with his worship.

Paint Acala the Messenger[4] on good silk;[5] he has a red garment worn across the body, his skirt too is red. One braid of his hair hangs down over his left ear. He looks somewhat squintingly with his left eye. A rope

4. His title is sometimes "messenger," sometimes "lord of knowledge," and sometimes simply "the honourable." In this may be traced various stages of the historical development of the god.

5. This is not always required. To make the prayer efficacious for the suppression of evil-doings the devotee may paint the god with his own blood on a cloth taken from a grave. It is sometimes recommended to paint him on any good cloth.

Figure 7.1 Fudō according to the Mystic Rites of Acala the Messenger.

is in his left hand, and a sword upright in his right. The top of the sword resembles a lotus-flower,[6] and on its handle there is a jewelled decoration. He sits on a rock made of precious stones. His eyebrows are lifted, and his eyes expressing anger are such as to frighten all sentient beings. The colour of his body is red and yellow.

Having thus painted the god, the devotee is told to take the picture to the bank of a river or to the seashore where he should be enshrined according to the established formula. Hence his association in Japan, popularly, with waterfalls and springs. This suggests that he was formerly a water-god.

The book from which the above is quoted is called *The Mystic Rites of the Dhāraṇi of Acala the Messenger* (*Fudōshisha darani himitsuhō* 不動使者陀羅尼秘密法). In the same book a little further down, however, we have a somewhat different description of the god. He is here reddish-yellow, wearing a blue garment across the body, but with a red skirt. His left braid is the colour of a black cloud. The features are boyish. A *vajra*, Indra's thunderbolt, is in his right hand and a rope in his left. From both ends of his mouth, his tusks are slightly visible. His angry eyes are red. Enveloped in flames he sits on a hill of stone. In this description, flames symbolize the burning of passions, and the stone on which he is made to sit points to his adamantine will. In the *Trisamaya-acala-kalpa* (*Chirisan-*

6. In none of his pictures I have so far come across is this observed. See the illustrations.

Figure 7.2 a) Another form of Fudō described in the Mystic Rites; b) Fudō in the Acala Kalpa; c) Fudō with sword in left hand and rope in right hand, sitting on a lotus-flower; d) Fudō with four faces and four arms.

mayafudōsonbō 底哩三昧耶不動尊法)[7] the god is supposed to wear a skirt of the colour of red earth and sits on a lotus-flower. In another place he holds a *vajra*, not a sword, in his right hand and a sacred staff in his left.

7. There are two versions of this book, one in three volumes and the other in one volume.

The eyes are somewhat reddish and his whole person is enveloped in flames.

These representations, though more or less different in detail, are essentially alike. Quite another form of the god is described in the *Book of Rites Concerning the Ten Gods of Wrath* (*Jūdaifunnumyōōgiki* 十大忿怒明王儀軌):

> He has a squinting eye, boyish features, six arms, and three faces, each of which has three eyes, and wears boyish personal ornaments. The front face is smiling; the right face is yellowish with the tongue sticking out, the colour of which is bloody; the left face is white, has an angry expression, uttering the sound 'hum.' The colour of the body is blue, the feet rest on a lotus-flower and on the hill of precious stone. He stands in a dancer's attitude and is able to keep away all evil ones. The entire person wrapped in flames has, like the sun, a circle of rays about it. The first right hand has a sword, the second a *vajra*, the third an arrow. Of the left hands, the first holds a rope with the thumb standing, the second the *Prajñāpāramitā-Sūtra*, and the third a bow. The god wears a Buddha crown which is the symbol of Akṣobhya Buddha.

There are some other forms of the god Fudō somewhat differing from the foregoing ones, but I will not go into details here. Suffice it to state in a general way that he assumes different features according to the different purposes for which his help is invoked. For instance, when he is requested to suppress an enemy, his body is to be painted yellow with four faces and four arms. Sharp tusks are protruding from the mouth, and his expression of anger is most intense; he is wrapped in burning flames, and his posture is such as to make one think that he is going to devour at once an entire army of the enemy.

In most of his modern pictures or images we see flames enveloping his whole body, which is blue; and the seat on which he sits or stands is not always decorated with gems, it is merely a huge block of stone, or a sort of tiled pedestal.[8] His forehead has in most cases some wrinkles in the form of waves, which is in accord with the description of the *Vairocana Sūtra* (*Dainichikyō* 大日経).

III

The meaning of all these various symbols is explained as follows in the introductory part of the *Trisamaya-acala-kalpa* (the three-volume version): There is a deep significance in his being one-eyed,[9] for this is the symbol of the utmost ugliness and compels Acala to think of his own

8. This tallies with *The Rites of the Ten Gods* as well as with Vajrapāṇi's description of the god in the *Sūtra on the Baptism of Light* (*Kongōshukōmyōkanjōkyō* 金剛手光明灌頂經).

9. In the foregoing descriptions, squintingly; and in some images both eyes look alike.

shortcomings and defects which stand in such contrast to the noble, perfect, and superior features of the Buddha. Furthermore, this ugliness tends to frighten away evil beings. The seven knots on the top of his head signify the seven branches of Bodhi (wisdom). One braid of hair hanging down his left shoulder typifies his merciful heart, which is sensitive to the sufferings of all lowly situated and much neglected beings. The sword in his right hand is meant to wage war against evils in the same way as a worldly warrior fights against the enemy. The rope in his left hand is to bind those devils whose unruly spirits have to be kept under control by the Buddha's restraining hands. The rock on which he sits is the symbol of his character, that is, the immovability of his will. Like the mountain pacifying the tumultuous waves of the giant ocean, the rock represents the eternal calmness of his mind. It also signifies spiritual treasure as the mine conceals in its bosom precious metals and stones. The fire enveloping the deity typifies the burning up of all the impurities that are attached to the human heart.

Another interpretation of Fudō appears in the *Commentary on the Vairocana Sūtra* by Yīxíng:

> This god has in a long past attained his Buddhahood upon the lotus-pedestal of Vairocana; but owing to his original vow he now manifests himself in his early imperfect form which he had at the first awakening of his great heart. Becoming the Tathāgata's servant and messenger, he is engaged in various menial works. He holds a sharp sword and a rope in his hands, this being in obedience to the Tathāgata's impassioned commands to destroy all evil spirits. The rope represents the four practical methods of inducing [people to the Dharma]—methods that are contrived through the thought of enlightenment (*bodaishin* 菩提心, *bodhicitta*). The rope will ensnare the unruly ones and keep them in check. The sharp sword of wisdom is to cut off the interminable life of karma possessed by unruly spirits in order to make them obtain a great transcendental existence. When the karma-seed of life is removed, all idle windy talk will come to a final end. Therefore, the god tightly closes his mouth. The reason why he sees with one eye only is to show that when the Tathāgata looks about with his eye of sameness there is not a sentient being who is to be saved.[10] Therefore, in whatever work this god is engaged, his whole object is to accomplish that work. His firm position on the pile of huge stones signifies the immovable spirit with which he works for the strengthening of the pure thought of enlightenment.[11]

10. In another place this is understood as meaning the uniqueness of the Buddha's spiritual eye-sight, which is one, and not two, nor three.

11. Ed. *Commentary on the Sūtra on Vairocana's Attainment of Buddhahood* (*Daibirushana-jōbutsukyōshō* 大毘盧遮那成佛經疏), see *Taishō Daizōkyō* Vol. 39, 633b.

Fudō the Immovable is in fact the incarnation of obedience, faithfulness, and loyalty. He becomes messenger to Vairocana, for he wishes to perform for him the servile duties of transmitting the august orders and messages of his lordship. As he is commanded, he goes among the poor as well as the noble, he makes no discrimination, and his only anxiety is to execute all the offices, whether good or bad, entrusted to him by Vairocana. He therefore symbolizes the slave and all his good qualities. The knots of hair hanging on the left side of his head denote the number of generations of the master whom he has served. The lotus-flower[12] on his head is the vehicle on which he will convey his master to the other shore of life eternal, that is, to the Pure Land. In his menial capacity he will most faithfully serve his worshippers who are at the same time his masters. The reason that his left eye looks differently from the right, is because this is usually noticeable among the servile class. In the *Trisamaya-acala-kalpa* (the one volume version) we are advised:

> to make an offering to this holy one with a part of our own food and drink. As his original vow is to give himself up to loving kindness, he is willing to serve all those who hold and recite his mantras (or magic phrases, which are given at the end of this article); his desire is to enslave himself as we may see from his one-eyed form. He accepts our left-over food and will be sure to protect us, if we thus remember him at each meal, against the evil demons including Vinayaka [that is, Ganeṣa], and remove for us whatever obstacles or difficulties we may be suffering.

The following story is told of the God Immovable in Yīxíng's *Commentary on the Vairocana Sutra* (Chapter "On the Removal of Obstacles"): When the Tathāgata received illumination, all sentient beings in the universe came to greet him with the exception of the great lord of the heavens, Maheśvara, who was too proud to come and greet the Buddha. Thereupon, Acala was despatched to summon him to the earth. But the lord of the heavens surrounded himself, though quite unbecoming to his dignity, with all sorts of filthy substances, so that nobody would dare approach him; for, however proficient one may be in magic arts, filth is supposed to be the most efficient means of disenchantment. Acala was not to be disheartened. All the filth was immediately devoured and done away with. The lord however refused seven times to listen to the protest of Acala, saying that he was the supreme master of the heavens and had no cause to yield to his request. But the latter proved himself to be more

12. This lotus-flower does not seem to be mentioned anywhere in the Kalpas relating to the worship of this god, but in most of the images we see in Japan there is the flower on his head. *Cf.* illustrations here reproduced from various sources. Ed. The author gives no details for the provenance of her illustrations, but they would have been widely available, for example as iconic depictions (*miei*) which can be had at temples.

Figure 7.3 Fudō trampling on Iśvara and his consort.

than a match for the haughty lord; for he firmly set his left foot upon the half-moon on the forehead of the lord himself, while his right foot was placed on that of the lordly consort. They both expired under the pressure, but in the meantime they realized the significance of the holy doctrine as discovered by the Buddha and were promised their future attainment of Buddhahood. This explains the meaning of certain pictures of Fudō in which he is depicted as stamping on two figures, male and female. It also reminds us of the Hindu god Śiva.

Fudō is sometimes identified with Ucchuṣma-Vidyārāja (Ususama Myōō 烏樞沙摩明王) who is the god of filthy places and seen generally enshrined over the entrance-door to a lavatory in Japanese Buddhist temples. That Fudō devoured all the filthy substances with which the lord of the heavens surrounded himself, may have caused this confusion (or might it be identification?). There are many instances in the iconography of the Shingon where the functions of the gods, buddhas, bodhisattvas and others seem to overlap one another, indicating that the Shingon pantheon was not the growth of one day or the production of one mind, but that various elements, including the popular superstitions of the different nations where they were once honoured, were somewhat indiscriminately adopted to fill up the cosmological plants of the Shingon philosophy.

IV

Fudō is commonly found attended by two figures and less frequently by eight. But his attendants are said sometimes to be as many as thirty-six or forty-eight. In the case of the two attendants, the one standing on his left, a young boy, is called Kiṃkara, and the other to the right who looks like a malicious demon is Ceṭaka. According to *The Mystic Rites Concerning the Eight Boy-Attendants to the Holy Lord of the Immovable* (*Shōmudōsonhachidaidōjiki* 聖無動尊八大童子軌), Kiṃkara is a boy of about fifteen years and wears a lotus-crown. His body is white. His hands are folded together and between the forefingers and the thumbs he holds a *vajra* crosswise. He wears a celestial garment as well as a Buddhist robe. The other boy, Ceṭaka, has a red lotus colour, and his hair is tied in five knots. In his left hand there is a *vajra* and in his right a *vajra* staff. As he cherishes anger and evil thoughts, he does not wear a Buddhist robe but a celestial garment only which hangs about his neck and shoulders. But in most of the popular pictures Kiṃkara holds a lotus-flower. He represents wisdom whereas Ceṭaka means bliss.

Fudō the Immovable sometimes appears in the form of a sword entwined by a dragon or snake whose mouth bites the triangular point of it. This is known as Kurikara Fudō 倶利迦羅不動 and is supposed to be the symbolical representation of the god. But there is apparently a

Figure 7.4 Fudō with his two attendants.

confusion here, for Kurikara who is the king of the Nāgas or dragons and whose Sanskrit name seems to be Kūlika, is one of the eight attendants and is probably to be identified with Anavataptanāgarāja (Anokudatsuryūō 阿耨達龍王).

There are many variations of Fudō partly because various legends are connected with his life, and partly because the artist or devotee is free to have a figure of the god as he has conceived him in a vision or otherwise. Still another cause of variation, and a strong one, is his extreme popularity.

This god, as was mentioned before, is associated with the waterfall, and is generally carved in a rock nearby.[13] The devotee himself stands in the flowing water as a token of purification, while devoutly offering his prayers to the flame-enveloped deity. In Tokyo, there are many Buddhist temples dedicated to Fudō, and one of the most famous is that at Fukagawa on the south side of the river Sumida. In the midst of the cold season, many earnest followers of the god, men and women, can be seen bathing themselves in the water-falls which have been artificially constructed there for the purpose. Prayers thus offered during the cold season are considered to be particularly efficacious. In former days these bathers were all naked, but the authorities do not permit this now.

In the neighbourhood of Tokyo, Narita is most noted, where thousands of the devotees pay their respects to Fudō yearly, making bounteous offerings both in money and in kind so that not only the town itself prospers but the temple-keepers are able to maintain a fine library, a school, and other organs of public utility.

Almost all the temples in Japan issue what is known as an *o-fuda* 御札, an "honourable tablet (or slip of paper)," or an *o-mamori*, 御守, an "honourable guard," of various kinds. This is generally a piece of paper (or sometimes a wooden board) oblong and varying in size ordinarily from about 1 x 3 to about 7 x 15 inches, on which is printed the image of a Buddha or a Bodhisattva, or of one of the gods, but frequently a Sanskrit character or phrase, or some words of prayer which have been offered on behalf of the devotee. This *o-mamori* is supposed to have the power to ward off evil spirits if a man carries it about him or pastes it up on the entrance-door of his residence or on the wall. Some *o-mamori* or *o-fuda* will even keep burglars away from one's home, some will protect the silkworm from an epidemic, while others may ensure the safe delivery of a child. These are only a few of the things promised by the Buddhist god, or rather by the priests.

The general masses of people nowadays do not understand the full signification of Fudō worship. They go to his temple merely because he is a Buddhist god and as such is naively supposed to grant them anything

13. Ed. A very common position is just *above* the waterfall.

Figure 7.5 A form of Fudō preserved at the temple Miidera, at the foot of Mt. Hiei.

Figure 7.6 Another form of Fudō preserved at Miidera, at the foot of Mt. Hiei.

they may be in need of. For instance, they may ask of him to win in races and games, or to be fortunate in their commercial enterprises, especially when they involve much risk and speculation, or to be free from accidents in travel, or to pass successfully the entrance examinations to school or colleges, or to be exonerated from military duties. But, judging from the general tendencies of his character, he seems to be especially efficient in removing all kinds of obstacles which lie in the way of one's undertakings, religious or otherwise. His qualification is more negative than positive. This is natural; for the very fact that a supreme, perfect being had to incarnate himself in this fierce, abnormal, disquieting form proves the extraordinary character of the god. His other title is "The Great Destroyer of Hindrances." When the worshipper has thoroughly succeeded in identifying himself with the god, we are told, his fire will consume all the worlds and make them one mass of flame shining like seven suns; his mouth will devour like that of the great horse the multitudinosity of things; and not the least chance will be left for any evil spirit to work mischief. Thus, he is to be invoked particularly when there are difficulties or obstructions to overcome, that is to say, when an epidemic is to be checked, or a drought to be broken, or an enemy to be annihilated, or a building to be insured against fire, storm, earthquake, etc. For the latter purpose, however, there is a specific ritual to be performed. Fudō then appears in a form somewhat different from the popular one. The Fudō ritual that takes place at a Shingon temple is quite an elaborate performance, and on some important occasions the ritual is not to be disturbed by any outsiders.

There are innumerable pictures and images in stone or wood or clay of Fudō, the Immovable God, enshrined and worshipped by his devotees all over Japan. Among them the most noteworthy paintings, artistically considered, are the "Aka-Fudō" (Red Fudō) of Myōō-in, at Kōyasan, the "Ki-Fudō" (Yellow Fudō) of Manju-in near Kyōto, and Fudō of Seiren-in in Kyōto. Of the sculptures one may mention two as most highly appreciated by art critics, the one at Shinnō-in, Kōyasan, and the other at Kyōōgokokuji, Kyōto.[14] Particularly notable is the "Aka-Fudō" of Kōyasan,[15] of which one of the official art advisers to the Department of Education says:

> Whoever comes to Kōyasan, this is the first thing to which he ought to pay homage. We say this, because it is the spiritual creation of an artistic genius inspired really by a burning faith. As the whole body is coloured

14. Ed. Kyōōgokokuji is a more elaborate name for Tōji. For further description, see Beatrice Lane Suzuki's *Buddhist Temples of Kyōto and Kamakura* (Eastern Buddhist Voices, No. 4), Sheffield 2013.

15. Ed. Shown as a frontispiece to the issue of *The Eastern Buddhist* from which this article was drawn.

Figure 7.7 The form taken by the noted Yellow Fudō.

red it is popularly known as "Aka-Fudō." To paint the adamantine spirit-body in red as seated enveloped in flames, is probably what everybody could conceive of, and yet it was what nobody ever attempted to do except for the present artist. The reddened body is delineated with strong lines boldly drawn like a rude steel cord; and the red robes are painted with large flower designs while the drapery-folds are shaded with gold pigment. Such technique is something we rarely have since Fujiwara and is powerful enough to depict the unapproachable dignity of the Myōō. The attendant-boys are simply and concisely done, their freedom from elaborate decorations is quite appropriate here. The picture is like a great pyramid towering far above in the arts of mystic Buddhism.

VI

The three mantras used in the invocation of Fudō the Immovable are classified according to the number of syllables which each contains (in Sanskrit in the *Siddham* style[16]): short, middling, and unabridged.

16. Ed. Unfortunately the script could not be reproduced here; if necessary, see the original publication.

The short one is:

Namaḥ samantavajrāṇāṃ hāṃ!
I.e. "Adoration to the All-Vajra! Ham!"

The middling one is:

Namaḥ samantavajrāṇāṃ chaṇḍamahāroṣaṇa sphāṭaya hūṃ traṭ hāṃ māṃ.

I.e. "Adoration to the All-Vajra! O the Terrible One! O the Great Wrathful One! Destroy! Hum! Trat! Ham! Mam!"

The fullest, unabridged one runs thus:

Namaḥ sarva-tathāgatebhyo viṣvamukhebhyaḥ sarvathā traṭ chaṇḍamahāroṣaṇa khaṃ khāhi khāhi sarvavighnaṃ hūṃ traṭ hāṃ māṃ.

I.e. "Adoration everywhere to all the Tathāgatas, to the All-faced Ones in all places! Trat! O the Terrible One! O the Wrathful One! Kham! Destroy, destroy every obstruction! Hum! Trat! Ham! Mam!"

When Fudō is represented by characters alone, "Ham-mam" or "Tram" may stand for him. His *o-fuda* is often found to be nothing but one of these Sanskrit characters written in the *siddham* style.[17]

17. The writer wishes to acknowledge her indebtedness in the preparation of this article to Professor D. T. Suzuki for his supply of the original materials and to Professor Izumi for his transcription of the mantras.

— 8 —

Ceremonies for Disciples on Mount Kōya

Beatrice Lane Suzuki

At Kōya-san (Mt. Kōya), the headquarters of the Shingon Sect, there is a Shingon Ritsu (i.e. Vinaya) temple where certain ceremonies take place which are available both to priests and laymen.[1] This temple is Entsūritsuji, popularly called Shinbessho,[2] the head of which, Rev. Keiho Tamayama, is noted for his strict and austere life, his learning and his kindness. These ceremonies comprise the Bosatsukai, the Sanzenbutsumyō, and the Ango.[3] When the Sanzenbutsumyō (Homage to the

1. As these ceremonies are given at other temples, slight variations in the text are to be found. This translation follows the text as in use at Kōya-san. I wish to thank Rev. Shōken Akizuki of Kōya-san for his help in making this translation. Ed. It should be noted that the idea, or the report, that these ceremonies were open to lay persons (some eighty years ago) cannot be confirmed by present enquiries (cf. Introduction above).

2. Ed. The following information was provided by Elizabeth Tinsley. Shinbessho 真別処 is a temple used as a training centre for monks doing their initial training or *shugyō* 修行 which is known as *Shido kegyō* 四度加行. The temple's formal, original name is Entsūritsuji 円通律寺 and as this name suggests it is a place where the precepts are strictly observed. Today attendance in this temple is permitted only to a very limited number of persons, giving a very strict, retreat-like experience, and women are only allowed there for receiving precepts. Since the temple is situated at one remove from the other temples on Kōya-san, its quietness is conducive to *shugyō*. The main object of reverence (*go-honzon*) is an image of Śākyamuni Buddha with the status of an Important Cultural Property. The temple was first established in the Heian Period by a disciple of Kūkai.

3. Ed. Bosatsukai 菩薩戒, i.e. the Bodhisattva Precepts. Conceptually, *bosatsukai* may be considered to transcend the distinction between monk and lay. However, in the case of the Ango 安居 ceremony for the commencement of the traditional retreat at the start of the rainy season, we have to remember that this arises in principle because, long ago in India, the homeless monks were permitted a settled retreat

Three Thousand Buddhas) is given, it serves as an introduction to the Bosatsukai, in which case it takes place in the morning and the Bosatsukai in the afternoon. The Bosatsukai is often given without the Sanzenbutsumyō. The Sanzenbutsumyō ritual consists of the calling aloud by the priest of the names and the *dhāraṇis* of Three Hundred Buddhas representing the Three Thousand Buddhas. As each name is called, the participants in the ceremony repeat the name of the Buddha and make a low bow on their hands and knees. All these ceremonies are held in the Śākyamuni Hall of the Shinbessho.

I

Bosatsukai (Bodhisattva-Śīla)

The Ceremony of Taking the Bodhisattva Precepts

The participants in the ceremony are:

Wajō 和尚, the abbot;
Kyōju 教授, a priest representing the Bodhisattva Maitreya;
Shōja 小者,[4] a priest representing the Bodhisattva Mañjuśrī;
Shōmyō 証明,[5] i.e. priests acting as witnesses;
Jusha 受者, the candidates for receiving the Precepts.

The Precepts are received by the Jusha from the Wajō, the Kyōju assists him, the Shōja (or Komashi) transmits, and the priests are witnesses. When all are seated before the altar, facing the statue or picture of Śākyamuni, the Wajō invokes the help of all the Buddhas and Bodhisattvas and makes a declaration of the purpose of the ceremony as follows:

> The purpose of Śākyamuni our founder in coming here to this world and attaining enlightenment was to teach and guide sentient beings. If anyone has faith in his teaching, then he is first instructed in the Precepts. A week after the Buddha's enlightenment he taught the *Kegonkyō* (*Avataṃsaka sūtra*), the first part of which is called the *Bonmōkyō* (*Brahmajāla sūtra*), which states that all sentient beings must observe the Buddha's Precepts. He who is instructed in the Precepts can then join the order of all the Buddhas and be called a son of the Buddha. After living eighty years the Buddha preached *Nehangyō* (*Nirvāṇa sūtra*), which teaches that if a being wishes to realize his Buddhahood and attain Parinirvāṇa, he

during the great rains. Even so, Beatrice Suzuki reports that it was open to lay persons by special permission of the abbot (see below).

4. Ed. The original had "Komashi" but current information is that *shōja* would be expected here, for one who assists the *kyōju* in some of the ritual actions.

5. Ed. *Shōmyōnin* 証明人 is reportedly more common.

must practise the holy Precepts with all his heart.

When the time of the Buddha's Nirvāṇa approached, in the quiet midnight, he taught the *Yuikyōgyō*,[6] which states that if there are no holy Precepts all goodness and merit cannot exist. If a being observes these Precepts he can perfect all the meditations and the wisdom of Nirvāṇa. So we see that the Buddha told us of the importance of the Precepts both at the beginning and at the end of his life. Buddha taught at various places and he preached differently according to the scene and the understanding of his hearers, as we can see by reading the different sutras spoken by him. But in respect to these Precepts there is no difference in regard to place and time.

In the Precepts we find the teaching of the Buddha as spoken by himself without the addition of anything by Bodhisattvas and Śrāvakas, which are found in other sutras. After the Buddha tried for forty years to improve the minds of his followers, he preached the *Hokekyō* (*Saddharma -Puṇḍarīka*, "Lotus Sūtra"[7]), in which he was able to perfect his real purpose in coming to this world. Sharihotsu (Śāriputra) could understand it; that day he became a real son of the Buddha. The Buddha was pleased and remarked that his most cherished wish was satisfied. The real purpose of the Buddha in coming to this world is to teach these Precepts. Although sentient beings have Buddhahood (latently), it cannot be realized by them on account of their delusions and ignorance. To realize true Buddhahood is to keep the Precepts.

There are two ways to receive the Precepts, the general and the special; the former is for all collectively, but the latter is to one alone of the special spiritual ranks. If the Precepts are taught to all then Sanjujōkai is given as we find at the beginning of the Bosatsukai and it is the same for laymen as for great *bhikṣus*. But if the candidate has not yet taken refuge in the Triple Jewel he must do so first. There are four kinds of Triple Jewel, *ittai*, *ritai*, *kesō*, and *juji*. The main purpose for taking refuge in the four kinds of Jewel is to observe these Precepts and to obtain the Dharma of wisdom and the Sangha of the three activities, i.e., the uniformity of the activities.

To observe the Precepts one must take refuge in the Triple Jewel[8] of *ittai*

6. Ed. *Yuikyōgyō* 遺教經, i.e. the *Sūtra of the Last Sermons* [of the Buddha]. Suzuki referred to this a little vaguely as "the teaching of the Precepts."

7. Ed. The original article had "Lotus Gospel."

8. The Triple Jewel (*Triratna*) is the Refuge formula:

   I take my refuge in the Buddha.
   I take my refuge in the Dharma (Teaching).
   I take my refuge in the Sangha (Order).

and of *ritai* and then his behaviour becomes like the wise.[9]

The object of practising the Precepts is to stop sufferings and troubles among sentient beings and to encourage them to have faith in the Truth. The formula of taking refuge in this way is expressed thus:

1. Not to do evil;
2. To seek enlightenment;
3. To do good to others.

The mind which is ready to stop bad actions and to practise good toward others comes from the self-consciousness of being one with the Buddha and beings and the resolution to save all sentient beings. The real saving is to make all sentient beings realize their own nature, i.e. Buddhahood. When we realize the truth that all sentient beings have Buddhahood, we cannot be satisfied to leave them in the miserable state of unenlightenment. Unenlightened beings transmigrate in the ocean of birth and death, through delusion committing bad actions. There must be an intimate relation between them and ourselves, so we can look upon all men as our father and all women as our mother—which indeed they must have been in former existences. How then can we help but lead them out of their lives of illusion and make them realize their Buddhahood?

The Śrāvaka and the Pratyekabuddha can perfectly realize the two forms: "Not to do evil" and "To seek enlightenment"; but the third formula of the refuge most characteristic of the Mahāyāna Bodhisattva, "To have a compassionate heart to others," cannot be so well realized by them.

There must be mutual help between great compassion and great wisdom. On account of their wisdom, Bodhisattvas are free from delusions in their worldly life, while because of their compassion they do not desire Nirvana for themselves, and they vow not to enter Nirvana until all other beings have realized Buddhahood. In the mind of the Bodhisattva there is no distinction between himself and others.

The ultimate state of Bodhicitta (the desire for enlightenment) is to try not to let anyone remain in an unenlightened state through the help of the Bodhisattva's two great minds, i.e. seeking the realization of their enlightenment and seeking the salvation of others. Buddha's mind is great compassion and this is the essence of all the Tathāgatas.

---

9. In *ittai* we can see the three aspects of Buddhism in one. In *ritai* we can see the three activities in Shinnyo (*tathatā*) apportioned to the Triple Jewel. In *kesō* we see the three Bodies (*kāya*) of the Buddha; the six Pāramitās represent the Dharma and wise persons the Sangha. In *juji* we see the Buddha's image remaining after his Nirvāṇa, the sūtras are the Dharma and the present believers are the Sangha. All the sayings of the Buddha can be included in the Precepts (*śīla*), meditation (*dhyāna*) and Wisdom (*prajñā*), the Precepts coming first.

> The receiver of the Precepts must make the vows fully conscious of this great mind of compassion. Enlightenment and compassion are really one, but what is more fundamental is compassion; therefore you who vow to observe the Precepts ought to exercise yourselves in the practice of a great compassionate heart.

Now comes the taking of the Three Refuges as follows:

1. I [mentioning the candidate's own name] in this bodily existence to the end of future time, take refuge in the Buddha, the most honoured of all men.
2. I take refuge in the most honoured Dharma, which is free from desires.
3. I take refuge in the Brotherhood, most honoured of all beings.

(These refuges are repeated three times.)

Then the Jusha (candidate for the Precepts) says,

> After this, I take the Buddha as my teacher and I will not take anyone else for a teacher. I only pray, O Triple Jewel, compassionately accept me.

Here incense is offered by the Jusha who bows three times.
The Jusha now expresses the formula of Awakening Bodhicitta:

> As I have awakened the desire for enlightenment, I wish to benefit all beings and I vow to practise the Six Pāramitās[10] for the sake of attaining realization. All the Bodhisattva and the Brotherhood will be my witnesses and help me to attain final realization and to benefit all sentient beings. O worthy priests, listen to me!

The Kyōju asks the Wajō to give the Precepts. The Jusha burns incense and bows three times. The Jusha says:

> I wish to have the Precepts given by you. On account of your compassionate heart, you will not regard this as a trouble.

The Wajō answers:

> Yes, I will give the Precepts. I am, however, only a transmitter, and the real giver of the Precepts is Śākyamuni himself, and his presence will be asked together with four other holy ones, Mañjuśrī, Maitreya, and other Buddhas and Bodhisattvas of the ten directions.[11]

The Wajō burns incense and the Jusha bows three times.

---

10. They are: *dāna* (giving), *śīla* (morality), *kṣānti* (forbearance, patience), *vīrya* (energy), *dhyāna* (meditation), *prajñā* (wisdom).
11. The Ten Directions are, North, South, East, West, North-East, North-West, South-East, South-West, Up and Down.

Wajō:

You ask Śākyamuni to be your Wajō.

The Jusha repeats after the Wajō:

I [giving own name] ask the fully enlightened Śākyamuni to be my Wajō at this Bosatsukai. I can receive the Bosatsukai and depend upon him on account of his great compassion.

Wajō:

Now ask Mañjuśrī to be your Shōju (transmitter).

Jusha:

Now I am going to receive the Bosatsu Precepts and Mañjuśrī is asked to be my transmitter. Out of compassion, out of compassion, out of compassion. (Bows.)

Wajō:

Now invite Maitreya.

Jusha:

Now I ask Maitreya to come here as Kyōju (helper). "Out of compassion, out of compassion, out of compassion." (Bows.)

Wajō:

Now invite all the Buddhas as Shōmyō (witnesses).

Jusha:

I ask all the Buddhas in the ten directions to come here as witnesses. Out of compassion, out of compassion, out of compassion. (Bows.)

Wajō:

Now invite the Bodhisattvas.

Jusha:

I ask all the Bodhisattvas to come here as companions. Out of compassion, out of compassion, out of compassion. (Bows.)

Wajō:

We have asked the five unseen teachers to be here, with their great compassion. Śākyamuni becomes your Wajō while Mañjuśrī and Maitreya standing on each side certify to the determination of your religious mind, and the Bodhisattvas of all the ten directions are also present. Now before these teachers confess your sins from the beginning of time, purify your body, so it may become a suitable vessel for the Precepts.

Although pure in your nature, you transmigrate on account of your delusion, and for this reason you are called an unenlightened being. When you can return to your real nature giving up the false, then you can be a Buddha. Since the moon of the real nature has been covered with the dirt of delusion, the differences come out in the three worlds and many births take place. The sins committed by greed, anger, and ignorance cannot be enumerated, but we can destroy those sins which you confess and repent with all your heart, so make an earnest confession.

Jusha (repeats after the Wajō):

All the evil things which I have committed in my past lives were done out of ignorance and I ask to be cleansed of these sins and impurities. They are all due to greed, anger, and ignorance which I have cherished since ancient times, and they have been practised through my body, speech, and mind. Now, without exception, I make full confession of them and repent of them resolving not to commit them after this to the end of future time.

Wajō:

To what family do you belong?

The Jusha answers.

Wajō:

Have you committed any of the seven sins?

The Jusha answers.

Wajō:

O Triple Jewel be witness with your confession and cause your sins to depart.

Wajō:

Are you now a Bodhisattva fit to receive the Precepts?

Jusha:

Yes.

Wajō:

Have you awakened the desire for enlightenment (bodhicitta)?

Jusha:

Yes.

Wajō:

The Precepts consist of three forms. The first are the Precepts of morality which destroy evil conduct belonging to the Brotherhood; the second are the Precepts regarding general morality; and the third are those which promote benevolence toward all beings. All these Precepts are intended to destroy all that is evil and to bestow benefits to all. The first reveals the Dharmakāya, the second the Saṃbhogakāya, and the third the perfect Nirmāṇakāya. When you practise these Precepts, the result will be the perfection of the Three Bodies (*trikāya*).[12]

These Precepts have been observed by all Bodhisattvas of the past, and Bodhisattvas of the present are observing them, and Bodhisattvas of the future will observe them, and now you are also asked to do so until the end of all your lives. Will you indeed observe the Precepts?

Jusha:

I will.

Wajō:

The first vow has now been made. With all your heart, do you vow to keep the Precepts?

Jusha:

I do.

Wajō:

The second vow has been made. Accomplish now the endless efficacy of the Precepts by making the vow for the third time. You can accomplish it when you declare your vow to abide by the Precepts. At every moment of your practice you will improve until you can come to the Buddha's state of mind. Listen to me and accomplish it. Again, do you vow to keep the Precepts?

Jusha:

I do.

Wajō:

I ask all the Buddhas, Bodhisattvas and priests to witness this ceremony now taking place at this temple.

This is a rare event to receive these Precepts from the Buddha. Thinking of this holy opportunity you must redouble your efforts to carry out your resolutions. When such an event as this took place in the time of the Buddha all other spiritual worlds were aware of it. In the same way this present happy event is sure to have response in other worlds, and all

12. *Trikāya*, the three bodies of the Buddha: *Dharmakāya*, the final reality, *Saṃbhogakāya*, enjoyment, and *Nirmāṇakāya*, form.

the Buddhas and Bodhisattvas will give you spiritual power to observe the Precepts.

Now I give the Precepts to you.

The Jusha answers to each: I will.

1. Not to kill any living thing wilfully throughout all your lives. Will you observe this Precept?
2. Not to steal throughout all your lives. Will you observe this Precept?
3. Not to commit adultery throughout all your lives. Will you observe this Precept?
4. Not to lie throughout all your lives. Will you observe this Precept?
5. Not to drink[13] spirituous liquors throughout all your lives. Will you observe this Precept?
6. Not to deliberately criticize and blame others for their faults. Will you observe this Precept?[14]
7. Not to praise yourself or to blame others throughout all your lives. Will you observe this Precept?
8. Not to grudge giving to others as for example your possessions, time, and teaching others, throughout all your lives. Will you observe this Precept?
9. Not to get angry in either speech or action throughout all your lives. Will you observe this Precept?
10. Not to desecrate the Triple Jewel throughout all your lives. Will you observe this Precept?

Wajō:

These are the ten most important Precepts and you must observe them at all cost until the end of future time. There are other Precepts which you should strive to practise. They are:

1. Do not despise your teacher;
2. Do not drink wine;
3. Do not eat meat, because a Bodhisattva is to save sentient beings not to destroy them;
4. Not to eat the five strong vegetables of the onion family;
5. Not to commit incendiarism;
6. Not to use ornaments and perfumes and visit places of amusement;
7. Not to sleep on luxurious beds;
8. Not to eat after noon time.

Will you strive to practise these Precepts also?

---

13. Ed. The original had "not to sell" which was probably a misunderstanding.
14. Ed. The original article only numbered the first two precepts, and omitted this item in error.

Jusha:

I will.

Now the Wajō speaks and the Jusha repeats after him.

Now I have received the Precepts with all the merits accruing from their observance. I wish to turn this merit so that it may be distributed among all beings. If they have not freed themselves, let them be freed. If they have not obtained enjoyment in the Dharma, let them enjoy it. If they have not awakened the thought of enjoyment, let them awaken it. If they have not destroyed evil thoughts and promoted good deeds, let them do so now. If they have not become Buddhas, let them quickly attain to Buddhahood. All these merits I wish to extend all over the world, and after my death together with all beings I wish to be born in that Buddha land, where, listening to the Dharma, I may come to the realization of it, and obtaining great spiritual power go over all the worlds in the ten quarters, listening all the time to the Mahāyāna doctrines as preached by all the Buddhas. Again, with the merit obtained in receiving the Precepts, I wish that all beings from this time forth may be released from this body of transmigration and released from this inferior body which suffers all kinds of bondage and infirmity and become great spiritual teachers for all beings. I wish that if any beings hear my name they will awaken in themselves a heart for enlightenment, and that if any beings see my body, they will cease from evil and devote themselves to good. I wish that those who listen to my name will obtain great wisdom and those who know my mind will at once attain to the path of Buddhahood.

I pray that this merit will extend everywhere so that not only we, but all other beings may attain to the path of Buddhahood.
I turn this merit to the universe and to the highest Truth. (*The bell is struck.*)
I call the name of Śākyamuni. (*The bell is struck.*)
I call upon the Kuyōjō-dhāraṇi. (*The bell is struck.*)
I revere the Eternal Triple Jewel and all other Jewels. (*The bell is struck.*)
I take refuge in Mahāvairocana. (*The bell is struck.*)
I wish that the flowers, incense, and lights offered by me at this ceremony today may be eternal offerings to the Triple Jewel and that I and all others may attain equally to the Highest Enlightenment. (*The bell is struck.*)

Wajō:

I call upon the name of Śākyamuni, upon the title of the *Bonmōkyō* (*Brahmajāla sūtra*), upon the name of the Bodhisattva Avalokiteśvara, and upon the Dhāraṇi called Kuyōjō (Pure Offering) bowing to the Triple Jewel which abides forever. I bow to the Triple Jewel in all quarters, I

> bow to Vairocana Buddha and to Śākyamuni Buddha. I offer the incense, the flowers and the candle lights to the Triple Jewel which extends indefinitely, which lasts indefinitely throughout all our lives; and let everyone, myself, and others attain to enlightenment that realizes the very highest.

The Wajō bows three times to the Buddha, to the witnesses; then all bow and leave the Hall.

In connection with the Bosatsukai, the Vows of Bodhi are [now] given as found in the *Bodhicaryāvatāra* by Śāntideva (See Hastings' *Encyclopedia of Religion and Ethics*, article on Bodhisattva).

1. The sin accumulated in my former existences, accumulated in all creatures, is infinite and omnipotent. By what power can it be conquered if not by the thought of

Bodhi, by the desire to become a Buddha for the salvation of men? This totally disinterested desire is infinitely sacred. It covers a multitude of sins. It assures happiness during the round of existences. It is a pledge of the supreme happiness of the Buddhas for oneself and one's neighbour. All honour to the Buddhas whom everybody quite naturally loves and who have as their sole aim the salvation of men!

2. I worship the Buddhas and the Bodhisattvas in view of undertaking the vow of Bodhi (*vandana*). Possessing nothing, by reason of my sins, how can I render unto them the worship (*pūjā*) which is their due? I beg them to accept this whole universe which I offer them in thought. But I am wrong. I do possess something, I give myself unreservedly, by pure affection, to the Buddhas and to their sons, the divine Bodhisattvas. I am their slave and, as such, have no more danger to fear. Of all dangers the greatest is that which comes from my sins. I know how harmful these sins are, I deplore them, I acknowledge them. I see and you see them as they are, pardon them!

3. But enough of myself. Let me belong entirely to the Buddhas and to creatures. I rejoice in the good actions, which among ordinary men for a time prevent evil re-births. I rejoice in the deliverance gained by the arhats. I delight in the state of Buddha and Bodhisattva, possessed by the Protector of the world (*puṇyānumodanā*). I entreat the Buddhas to preach the Law for the salvation of the world (*adhyeṣanā*). I entreat them to delay their entrance into Nirvāṇa (*yācanā*). All the merits acquired by my worship of the Buddhas, my taking of refuge, my confession of sins, etc., I apply to the good of creatures and to the attainment of the Bodhi. I wish to be bread for those who are hungry, drink for those who are thirsty (*pariṇāmana*). I give myself all that I am and shall be in my future existences to creatures (*ātmabhavaparityaga*). In the same dispositions as those in which the former Buddhas were when they undertook the vow of Bodhi, and just as they carried out the obligations of future Buddhas,

practising in their order the perfect virtues in these dispositions, I conceive the thought of Bodhi for the salvation of the world, so also I shall practise in their order my obligations (*cittotpāda*, or vow, *praṇidhi*).

Now one is a seed of a Buddha.

The Ritual consists of

1. Daily confession of sins with its preliminaries of adoration and worship;
2. Acquiescence or rejoicing in good; and
3. Prayer with a view to securing the preaching of the Law and delaying the entrance of the saints into Nirvāṇa.

The application of merits and the vow complete the ritual.

II

The Ango Ceremony

This ceremony takes place on or near the sixteenth of July.[15] It is primarily for the benefit of priests, but earnest laymen and laywomen approved by the abbot are permitted to take part in it.[16]

The line of participants forms and the priests and lay disciples walk around the chapel and then kneel at the door. The bell strikes and the participants chant the following:

Now we overcome the evil influences of Māra,[17]
And all delusions are dispelled;
Hearing the bell strike on this open ground
Monks come together.
Anyone wishing to hear the doctrine
And to pass over the ocean of birth and death,
On hearing the fine sound of the bell,
Come here like a cloud to attend this meeting.
(*The bell strikes.*)

All enter the chapel and kneel facing the altar on which stands the statue

15. Ed. The literal meaning of the term *ango* 安居 is "peaceful dwelling" (translating Sanskrit *vārṣika*), and it refers to the sheltered retreat for which the historical Buddha gave permission to his monks during the rainy season, when it was impractical to meditate in the rain-sodden forests. This momentous concession led to lay patronage for the establishment of *vihāras* and thus to settled monasteries in Buddhism. There really is a rainy season in Japan, round about July, but nevertheless the opening ceremony for the retreat has taken on a symbolic quality because there is now settled accommodation anyway.

16. Ed. On the matter of lay participation, which is currently not permitted, cf. notes 1-3 above.

17. The Evil One.

of Śākyamuni. The abbot is sitting in his chair within the inner circle.

Chanting:

As we have observed the Precepts, we are pure like the full moon;
Our bodily actions and our speech are pure without blemish.
All present are harmonious and friendly,
So we can take part in this ceremony together.
(*The bell strikes.*)

Three young priests rise and place vessels of hot and cold water before the altar; the first priest washes and wipes his hands and the others do the same.

Chanting:

The holy water of eight merits[18] purifies from all defilements;
As we wash our hands, our minds become pure,
Observing all the precepts without fail,
We hope that all sentient beings will be saved.

While the chanting goes on, the three young priests pass among the congregation carrying a pitcher and pour a little cold water over their hands and pass a towel for drying them, and then the same process is done with hot water while the chanting continues.

Now as we have washed in hot water and all defilements are removed;
Our Dharmakāya is perfected and also the five virtues.[19]
The Wisdom of Prajñā[20] comes to us in its full activity and our emancipation is complete.
All sentient beings share in this and there is absolute communication throughout the Dharmadhātu.[21]

The abbot tells the reasons for the ceremony, that it contributes merit

18. The Eight Good Qualities received by laymen who take the Precepts according to the *Jūzenkaikyō* are: 1) Not to enter Hell; 2) Not to become a *gaki* (hungry ghost); 3) Not to become an animal; 4) Not to become an *asura* (fighting demon); 5) Always to be born into the human world and to hear the doctrine; 6) To be born in the Kāmadhātu Heaven; 7) To be born in the Brahma Heaven, asking the Buddha to preach the Law; 8) To obtain Enlightenment.

19. The five virtues to be obtained by a Bodhisattva abiding in Samādhi are: 1) To be re-born into a good existence; 2) To be re-born into a noble family; 3) To be re-born with excellent sense organs; 4) To be re-born as a male; 5) To be re-born with the remembrance of past lives.

20. Prajñā-Wisdom.

21. Dharmadhātu (Hōkai) sometimes means Shinnyo (Truth, Substance) and sometimes it refers to all things and beings in the universe. In this case, it refers to the latter. Ed. *Shinnyo* 真如 (corresponding to Sanskrit *tathatā*) is usually translated as suchness, but admittedly there is a nuance of "truth-ness" or "being-like-reality" in this Sino-Japanese term.

to the Emperor, teachers, and parents; blesses the participants; gives freedom from evil karma; and states that all sentient beings in the universe can be born in the Buddha's land and obtain Buddhahood.

The three priests take up two boxes containing small sticks.

Chanting:

The Bodhisattvas and holy priests
And unenlightened beings are harmonious:
As we purify these sticks with fragrant water
We wish to save all beings through the merit of this ceremony.

The chief attendant priest with two others come to all the participants to present them with the sticks which are received on their folded hands. While they are being received all are kneeling and the following is chanted:

The stick is the symbol of the Vajra[22] which is hard as the diamond, free and emancipated.
It is difficult to meet and receive it,
But now we, as well as all sentient beings, can have it to our great happiness,
And all other sentient beings join us.

The sticks one after the other are returned to the boxes.

Chanting:

Having become purified, we receive the stick;
Having perfected Purity, we return the stick.
Without any transgression we cherish gladness of heart and impartiality firmly,
And we wish that all other beings may do likewise.
As we become pure like the full moon,
We attend this ceremony with pure minds,
And all our actions of body and speech become pure too.
All who are present here can participate in this ceremony.

The chief attendant priest approaches the Abbot and asks him to teach the Precepts to all. The Abbot rises in preparation. The attendant priests throw flowers before the altar.

Chanting:

Throwing flowers and arranging ornaments the light shines clear;
Scattering holy flowers in all the ten directions they become a curtain.

Hymn by the Vice-abbot:

---

22. Vajra means hard and brilliant like a diamond, used as a symbol for hardness. It also means a religious object (Tibetan, *dorje*) which is used by a priest in ceremony, especially in the Shingon sect.

So we make offering to all the Tathāgatas
We bow down to all the Buddhas
To the Dharma and the Sangha.
We explain the Precepts taught by the Buddha
In this way, we make the right Dharma remain in the world forever.
Upāli[23] remains at the head and the others are witnesses;
Now we explain the most important meaning of the Precepts,
And all wise men listen to it.

Incense is offered.

The incense from morality together with Meditation and Emancipation,
And also the light of wisdom like clouds invade our entire universe.
All are offered to the Buddhas of the ten directions.[24]
And everyone who sees and hears are so affected that they may attain Nirvana.

The Vice-abbot chants:

We live in the world but with our thoughts as broad as the sky.
We are like the lotus flower which rises from the dirty water, but is never stained.
Far purer than the lotus, we can rise above everything.
We offer our respect to the highest one.

Chanting by all:

The first happiness is that the Buddha came to this world;
The second is that we can attain peace by hearing the Truth and practising it;
The third is that all members are harmonious and free from disturbance;
The last is that all sentient beings get rid of pain and enjoy peace and happiness.
We take refuge in Śākyamuni Buddha,
We take refuge in Daishi Henjō Kongō.[25]
(*The last two lines are recited three times.*)
We take refuge in the Buddha and wish that all other sentient beings may awaken their thought to the highest truth, in order to realize the great Way. (*All bow.*)
We take refuge in the Dharma and desire that all other beings will do so also, that they may enter into the treasury of the Sūtra and have as

23. Upāli: one of the Buddha's disciples.
24. The Ten Directions are, North, South, East, West, North-East, North-West, South-East, South-West, Up and Down.
25. Daishi Henjō Kongō is a name for Kōbō Daishi. Daishi = great teacher, Henjō = universal illumination, Kongō = hard like a diamond.

deep knowledge as the ocean. (*All bow.*)

We take refuge in the Sangha and wish that all other sentient beings will do the same, and we hope for harmony among all the participants of this ceremony with no hindrances whatever. (*All bow.*)

The participants in the ceremony face each other, two by two, kneeling and one recites:

We are able to perform Ango in this place;
We do not cause suffering to rise, but should it do so we shall expel it;
If anyone is sick, we shall nurse him,
We are provided with medicine and have sufficient food and drink.
And Kōya is settled as our domicile.
With great earnestness on the sixteenth day of July,
We priests perform this ceremony of Ango.
People everywhere will be our helpers,
And one will be appointed as our manager.
And another as nurse for the sick.
Whatever is to be done in the way of repairs will be duly executed,
I shall remain in this place all the summer.

The second participant answers:

O Bikya. (It is so.)

The first one responds:

Sadho. (Well done.)

Then the second participant kneeling with folded hands, recites:

Listen, holy monks now performing this ceremony, I also perform it.

On this day, I ask you to tell of all things seen, heard and doubted to all the attendants, especially the elder ones.

May all these attendants and elder ones have compassion upon me and show me what wrong I have done and so pity and benefit me. You having compassion upon me, let me repent.

Tell me, what you have observed of me as the precepts require.

The first participant answers:

O Bikya. (It is so.)

The second participant replies:

Sadho. (Well done.)

All bow before the Buddha and then, walking with folded hands encircle the inside of the Chapel, offer incense before the Buddha, and leave the Hall.

Part IV

Revisiting Masters of the Nenbutsu

— 9 —

The Pure Land Doctrine in Shōkū's "Plain Wood" Nenbutsu

Sugihira Shizutoshi

I

Introduction

It seems to us that there is a universal miscomprehension in the West concerning the nature of Pure Land Buddhism, interpreting it as a kind of salvation doctrine in its Christian form. Strictly speaking, the word salvation is not appropriate for the work Pure Land Buddhism proposes to effect. It may be more proper to call it a form of self-enlightenment; because it is not a doctrine which teaches us deliverance from sin and its consequences. On the other hand, it teaches us how to get free from the bondage of birth and death and attain peace of mind by exhausting our own will-power which originates from egoism. It is true that the Pure Land doctrine disapproves of self-power (*jiriki* 自力) and upholds other-power (*tariki* 他力), but we must remember that the words "self" and "other" here are not used in their relative sense; that is to say, when the Pure Land followers speak of self-power they refer by it to a relative world, while by other-power is meant a realm where there is no more relativity, for in the realm of other-power there is no distinction between given and giving, between received and receiving. It is where transcendental unity prevails.

The Pure Land doctrine emphasizes the signification of our sin. It holds that we are sinful mortals suffering the pain of birth and death from time immemorial, wandering through the six paths of existence, because we know no clue whatever as to the way to escape from transmigration. But the Pure Land follower's conception of sin is different from that of Christians. We are sinful not because we have transgressed the laws of God who is the creator, but because we are ignorant of the truth, *tathatā*, or suchness of things. As the result, all that we do is evil, not only such deeds as are generally considered evil, but also even such as are recognized as good by men of the world. As this existence dualistically conceived is sin as the result of our ignorance of truth, so our existence itself, according to the Pure Land believers, is something to be abandoned as the creation of self-power. When this abandonment is effected, we are reborn to a world of higher order where we are united with the Buddha.

The foundation of Pure Land doctrine is laid upon the Forty-Eight Vows of Amida who vowed them in order to lead all sentient beings to his own Pure Land where they all can attain Buddhahood. To make the vows effective, he contemplated for five aeons, practised austerities for endless aeons and finally attained Buddhahood; and thereby all sentient beings are now assured as to their rebirth into the Land of Purity which is under his government. This land is situated in the western quarter beyond hundreds of thousands of millions of lands, where his believers are reborn to attain Buddhahood. To effect the rebirth into Amida's Land of Purity, what is required of believers is simply to recite the name of the Buddha [i.e. Amida Buddha].[1] This may sound quite easy—this reciting of the Buddha's name; but in fact this is just as hard as that which is experienced by followers of Zen, for example, who endeavour to attain *satori* after so many years of self-discipline. Self-power asserts itself in spite of the desperate attempt which devotees of Nenbutsu put forward in order to be taken into the Land of Amida. Self-power is such an obstinate instinct in all of us, that to uproot it more than our will-power is needed. When this will-power comes to an end, we throw ourselves at the feet of Buddha who will now pick us up in his boat of salvation to cross the ocean of birth and death. Let me remark here that Amitābha Buddha and his Land are not to be conceived of as belonging to a world of relations. This being the case, the salvation offered by the Pure Land doctrine is not to be identified with that of Christianity. If we could say so, the Christian salvation still is on this side of existence where dualism prevails, whereas that of the Pure Land is in a realm of the absolute, that is, of *tariki* in its transcendental sense. Masters of the Pure Land doctrine have tried in various ways to bring forth this characteristic point in the doctrine of *tariki* salvation. In the following we have the document known as "Shiraki no Nenbutsu" 白木の念仏 or "Plain-wood Nenbutsu," which was written by Shōkū 証空 (1177–1247), founder of the Seizan

1. Ed. Both the author, Sugihira, and Shōkū himself, when referring to (the) Buddha, in fact mean Amida Buddha. Since "Buddha" is not a proper name but an epithet or title, the definite article has usually been added.

branch of the Pure Land Sect, and which will help us to understand what is really meant by *tariki* salvation.

II

The Plain-wood Nenbutsu (text by Shōkū)

Those of the self-power apply some paints to the Nenbutsu. Some colour it with the enlightenment of Mahāyāna doctrine, some with profound learning, some with the observance of morality, some with tranquillization of body and mind. Some are exulted to be assured of their rebirth in the Pure Land, because they have practised the Nenbutsu tinged with contemplation or morality; while others feel dejected over their inability of being reborn there, because their Nenbutsu is not coloured with any paint. Both the exultation and the dejection are delusions which come from reliance on self-power.

The Nenbutsu which, according to the *Larger Sukhāvatīvyūha Sūtra*, will last for one hundred years after the disappearance of the Right Law, and the Nenbutsu which the *Meditation Sūtra* prescribes for the three inferior grades of beings, is the plain-wood Nenbutsu, devoid of all paints. "Believing with serene thought" in the Original Vow of Amida was understood by Zendō to mean "repeating the name of Amida ten times," and this is no other than to return to a plain-wood state of mind.

The lowest grade of being so called in the *Meditation Sūtra* means an ordinary mortal with no merit, worldly or unwordly. In him there is no paint whatever with which to colour the Nenbutsu. Is he not moreover a being who is oppressed with the agony of death not knowing what to do, as he has lost all his control over his speech, body, and thought? He has been a wicked man through his life, so he has acquired no merit on which he can specially rely. Now at this last moment he is harassed with the pangs of death, and has no time to think of ceasing from evils and practising virtues, nor can he be mindful of enlightenment taught by the various schools of Buddhism. In this state of mind he cannot think of erecting a pagoda or a statue, nor has he time to think of abandoning the life of a householder and of worldly enjoyments. He is indeed the most wicked of all beings. He knows of no means whereby to save himself.

A teacher may try to awaken him to the faith, hoping that he will comprehend the meaning of other-power or that he will meditate on the mystery of the Buddha's name. But neither of these hopes avails, since the pangs of death harass him to the extreme and his mental powers are gradually leaving him. The teacher may now take up another form of teaching, that is, the recitation of the Buddha's name, telling him to call out the name of Amida aloud even if he fails to fix his mind on Amida. Thereupon, the man utters the name of Amida ten times, though his mind is in a state of perfect confusion. Each utterance then cancels his sins of eighty thousand millions of kalpas, and he will get the favour of seeing the "Golden Lotus like the Sun." In this state, he has no special wish to be enlightened, nor is he tainted with any paint of contemplation or morality. And yet he will be reborn in the Pure Land by virtue of uttering the Buddha's name in a plain-wood state of mind, while he knows of no contrivance other than following the advice of the teacher. This is likened to a child learning how to write with its hand guided by another; the child has no claim for the writing. So is the practice of the Nenbutsu of the lowest grade of being. Guided by the teacher and embraced by the merciful heart of Amida, this simple utterance of His name enables the sinner to be reborn in the Pure Land.

The Original Vow of Amida is the Vow and Work whereby He practised austerities for the sake of those who are heavily burdened with the five deadly sins. Therefore, it is in the plain-wood Nenbutsu which is uttered [at the time of death] when one's mental powers are exhausted, that one finds Amida's Vow contemplated for five kalpas and His merit accumulated for endless ages all livingly active. This Nenbutsu of one thought holds in it all the birth and death of endless duration, and accomplishes in one utterance all the discipline of countless eons.

Again the Nenbutsu which, according to the *Larger Sukhāvatīvyūha Sūtra*, will continue after the disappearance of the Three Treasures,[2] is also the plain-wood Nenbutsu. The reason is: Sūtras, Śāstras, and Vinayas, Hīnayāna as well as Mahāyāna, being all stowed away in the palace of Nāgas, the Three Treasures will no more be seen in this world. Then in this Jambudvīpa,[3] there will be nothing left but ignorant beings and their evils, and the word "good" will be unknown. With the disappearance of the Vinaya texts in which the moral life is taught, where should we go for instruction to stop our evil-doings and to practise good deeds? When the Sūtra which teaches us how to cherish the desire after enlightenment has already disappeared among us, to which Sūtra should we look for enlightenment? As there is no one who knows this truth, there is no way to learn it. Therefore, the sole reality that will be still abiding this world, will be the plain-wood Nenbutsu, containing the Buddha's name in six characters,[4] devoid of all sorts of colouring, contemplative or moral. It is said in this Sūtra that those who then hear and recite the name shall all be reborn in the Pure Land. That they are all reborn there by reciting the name once or for ten times, means that those beings who are outside of Buddhism are able to be reborn there simply by virtue of the Buddha's name recited in a plain-wood way.

2. The Buddha, the Dharma, and the Sangha.
3. Ed. The ordinary world inhabited by human beings, in ancient Indian cosmology.
4. Namu-amida-butsu consists of six Chinese characters: 南無阿弥陀仏.

Some may say that we of this age are by far superior to those beings who may be living in the last days of Buddhism, because we are still in possession of Sūtras and Śāstras, Hīnayāna as well as Mahāyāna. But being of imperfect nature we have nothing superior to those who come when the Three Treasures are gone. Though Buddhism may still be prevalent at present, our nature is so imperfect that we have no power sufficient to practise the three kinds of discipline.[5] Though there are Sūtras and Śāstras, Hīnayana as well as Mahāyāna, we have not enough ardour to study them assiduously. Such imperfect beings as we are have no desire to be enlightened, are born in vain in these days of Buddhism. If this is the case when the Three Treasures are gone, we may say that the matter cannot be improved. But we are living now in the time when Buddhism is still flourishing, and that we have no desire to observe morality and practise meditation and wisdom, shows that we are imperfect and not at all in the way of enlightenment. Amida's Vow-power is thoroughly perfected when it comes upon us, so benighted. That is why we cannot be too grateful for the plain-wood Nenbutsu. On our part we are lacking in faith and work, and our thoughts succeeding one another are full of folly. Delusions growing out of our false attachment and perverseness are growing stronger every day and evil karma and evil passions are assailing us night and day. The Nenbutsu that comes from such a defiled being may be regarded as not different from an act of evil passion, and it is not even coloured with any virtue, contemplative or moral; but in the Buddha's name once recited, all the virtues of all the Buddhas are concentrated, and on that account the mind-water is not muddied and the supreme virtue is produced. The Namu-amida-butsu which is recited simply in the belief that by the recitation our rebirth in the Pure Land is assured, without any effort on our part and [being] thoroughly absorbed in this thought, is the Nenbutsu required in the Original Vow of Amida. This is what I call the plain-wood Nenbutsu. [End of text by Shōkū]

III

Exposition of Shōkū and "the Plain-wood Nenbutsu"

Those who are interested in the growth of Pure Land Buddhism in Japan cannot afford to ignore the name of Shōkū. He was one of the most prominent disciples of Hōnen, the founder of the Nenbutsu Sect of Buddhism, and finally became himself the founder of the Seizan 西山 Branch of the Nenbutsu Sect. He had many noted disciples and his spiritual influence was great. Ippen 一遍, the founder of the Ji Sect (Ji-shū 時宗) which is also a branch of the Nenbutsu school, draws his inspirations

5. The observance of morality, tranquillization of body and mind, and profound learning.

from the teaching of Shōkū.

The "Plain-wood Nenbutsu" here translated is a brief but excellent statement concerning the doctrine of Nenbutsu. It is said that he wrote this discourse with the purpose of making his doctrine intelligible even to the unlettered. In spite of its plain wording it expounds in a most remarkable manner the profound significance of the doctrine, and its value is not limited to the unlettered. It is composed of two parts. The first paragraph which is brief makes reference to the Nenbutsu of the *jiriki* follower, which Shōkū designates as coloured, meaning that it is not free from *jiriki* pigments. In the second and the following paragraphs he compares the pure and colourless Nenbutsu of the *tariki* follower to a piece of wood untouched, unsoiled by the dirt of relativity and dualism. According to Shōkū, the only way in which we become united with the Buddha is to awaken in us a state of consciousness in which Nenbutsu is recited colourlessly.

IV

The Difference Between *Tariki* and *Jiriki*

Self-power (*jiriki* 自力) and other-power (*tariki* 他力) are technical terms whereby the Pure Land believers express the philosophy of their religious experiences, and they advise us to give up *jiriki* and take to *tariki*. The interpretation of these two terms, *jiriki* and *tariki*, varies according to the different teachers of the Pure Land doctrine, resulting in the evolution of the different schools. I confine myself here to the exposition of Shōkū's point of view in regard to self-power and other-power.

According to him, the difference does not lie in the outward behaviour but the inner consciousness of the believers. He says:

> Suppose there are two persons reciting Nenbutsu before the Buddha. As far as their outward appearances go, they are the same, but [innerly] there is a wide difference; the one is the *tariki* follower while the other the *jiriki*.
>
> The *jiriki* follower sincerely wants to have the desire to be reborn in the Pure Land and asks the Buddha surely to implant that desire in him. As he thinks that, when his desire is sincere and his distrust of worldly life is by no means feeble, the Buddha will not fail to receive him in the Pure Land, so he feels encouraged about the nearness of his rebirth when his believing heart grows stronger; but he feels discouraged as if his rebirth were a most distant fact if his mind is full of delusions and becomes ungovernable. Apparently he is an earnest seeker of religious faith, but really he is further away from the Vow of Amida. As he tries to work out his rebirth by his own efforts, he is further away from the Mercy of the Buddha.

> But it is not so with the *tariki* follower. The more capable he finds himself of stopping evil thoughts and desiring for his rebirth in the Pure Land, the more keenly he is awakened to the sense of gratitude for the Buddha's Vow and discipline. If the Buddha's Vow-power nourished in meditation for five kalpas were not the devotee's own desire and discipline for rebirth, I would no more cherish the hope of rebirth; but as is the case, I feel so grateful for the fact that our own desire and discipline for rebirth had already been fulfilled on the part of the Buddha. This being so, his Nenbutsu may continue night and day, there is nothing of *jiriki* Nenbutsu in him. Each Nenbutsu as it is recited fulfils the merit of *tariki*.[6]

Here we see the difference between *tariki* and *jiriki*: the *jiriki* follower is uncertain of his rebirth and endeavours to work it out by destroying his evil passions, while the *tariki* follower is convinced of his rebirth and all his evil passions are converted into opportunities of feeling grateful towards the Buddha. What then is the cause of this difference? The *jiriki* consciousness is that he is strong enough to destroy his evil passions all by himself, while the *tariki* follower feels that he is too weak to cope successfully with his own sins.

V

Human Nature

Is our nature really too feeble to destroy evil thoughts and passions and to practise works good enough for a rebirth in the Pure Land?

Good works may be grouped under two heads, contemplation (*jōzen* 定善) and morality (*sanzen* 散善). Contemplation keeps the mind collected so that nothing of evil thought would ever creep into it. Morality stops evil doings and practises good deeds with utmost vigilance.

> [Shōkū says] But we are not able to practise contemplation. When we try, we soon grow confused being attacked by various delusive thoughts. When we endeavour to meditate on the sublime views of the Pure Land, worldly affairs are sure to upset us. When we try to meditate on the excellent features of the Buddha, our minds are perturbed by the six senses. Our ears seem to be listening to the teaching of Buddhism, but innerly we have arrogance and evil thoughts more tempestuous than the ocean. In our mouth we speak of the emptiness of things, but in our heart egotism towers higher than a mountain.
>
> Nor can we practise morality. When we wish to practise it, evil deeds are multiplied and nothing good is accomplished. We are not filial to parents, nor are we truthful to our elders. Though our heads are shaven and our bodies are wrapped in the monkish robe, our actual life is far from being in accord with the rules of discipline. As there are very few true

6. *Jutsujō* 述誠.

> followers of Buddhism who are faithfully observing all the disciplines, to whom should we go for instruction even when we desire so? As there is no serious wish for Mahāyāna enlightenment, we find ourselves to be mere seekers of fame and profit instead of doing seriously what is good. Even though there is a touch of good intention, it is like writing on water; waves of greed and anger are too high, no traces of goodness are left.[7]

Jiriki followers are ignorant not only of human nature but of the Buddha. The Buddha is conceived by them as one who keeps himself away from them and to whom they do not stand in an intimate relationship; for this reason they want to win the Buddha over to their side by their own efforts. On the other hand, *tariki* followers know their own impotence to attain Buddhahood by performing any good work, and they realize how closely Buddha is related to them.

Shōkū illustrates this close relation between the Buddha and *tariki* followers in these three respects: "Intimate," "Near" and "Helpful." Shōkū says:

> First, by "intimate" relation I mean that the Buddha's virtues in his threefold activity pertaining to body, speech, and thought, are not separable from our evil deeds which will be committed with our threefold activity pertaining to body, speech, and thought, because the Buddha is an Unobstructable Light which constitutes the essence of Buddhahood and to which he attained in order to bring all sentient beings under his protection, no matter how imperfect and ignorant they may be. Hence it is said that, when we recite his name, he hears us; when we worship him, he sees us; when we think of him, he knows it. This means that when we trust in him without troubling ourselves about how good or how bad our hearts are, the Buddha hears our recitation, sees us worshipping him, and knows us thinking of him, and he is sure all these deeds are decidedly leading us to rebirth in the Pure Land. This is why Zendō says that Buddha's threefold activity (pertaining to body, speech, and thought) is inseparable from our threefold activity (pertaining to body, speech, and thought).
>
> Secondly, by "near" relation I mean that we can see the Buddha when we long to see him, because when this "intimate" relationship between the Buddha and ourselves has reached its height, he knows all about our threefold activity pertaining to body, speech, and thought, and at the same time we come to know the Buddha's threefold activity pertaining to body, speech, and thought. It is also due to this relation that the Buddha appears to us in a dream or at the time of death.
>
> Thirdly, by "helpful" relation I mean that the above-mentioned two relations between the Buddha and ourselves are effected by other-power (*tariki*). As Zendō says, "All sentient beings who recite his name shall get rid of all their sins for which they have to suffer through countless kalpas. When their lives draw near to the end, the Buddha and his holy

7. *Nyoingosho* 如院御書.

> retinue come to welcome them, and all their evil deeds and karma relations would offer no hindrance whatever. This is what we call helpful relation." The sentence, "All sentient beings who recite his name shall get rid of all their sins for which they have to suffer through countless kalpas," explains the "intimate" relation effected by *tariki*, and the following sentence, "when their lives draw near to the end...would offer no hindrance whatever," explains the "near" relation effected by *tariki*. Therefore, this "helpful" relation expresses other-power (*tariki*) by which the above-mentioned two relations are effected.
>
> When we understand this, our recitation of his name which is according to the "intimate" relation between the Buddha and ourselves cancels all our sins for which we have to suffer through countless kalpas. Actuated by this cancellation of sins, we shall surely come to tremble at evils and abandon them altogether, never allowing ourselves to be influenced by them. Again, our seeing of the Buddha which is the "near" relation perfects the highest virtue. Impelled by this virtue, we rejoice at the good we have done, and our hearts are bent more than ever on practising good. This is what is meant by the so-called "helpful" relation.[8]

In this manner the Buddha is closely related to all sentient beings. Why is this so? Because Amida, while he was in his Bodhisattva-hood, vowed that all sentient beings should be reborn in his Pure Land, through the merit of good works carried out by himself; and finally through this merit he attained enlightenment, proving that all sentient beings' rebirth in the Pure Land has thus become an accomplished fact. Therefore, when we believe in his Vows he enters into our hearts thereby attaining his enlightenment, and at the same time assuring our own rebirth. This being the case, we should not keep the Buddha away from us but feel embraced by the Buddha believing that the Buddha's Vows and works are the cause of our own rebirth.

VI

Rebirth and the Nenbutsu

Our rebirth in the Pure Land is assured when we have the faith that the Buddha embraces all sentient beings who do not know how to escape transmigration. This must not be regarded, however, as a kind of creed; because it is not a dogma but an experience. Therefore Shōkū says:

> Even though we may understand what *tariki* is or recite the Buddha's name, we are not yet to be called *tariki* believers, if we think that our understanding of *tariki* or our recitation of the Buddha's name is all by ourselves. We are called true *tariki* believers, only when we have an actual experience of unification with the Buddha and recite his name.[9]

---

8. Shōkū's letter to Yoritsune.
9. *Tahitsushō* 他筆抄.

It is not we but Amida who awakens us to this unification and occupies our being by entering into ourselves.

> When we were *jiriki* believers, we had to run after the Buddha asking him to save us; but when we become *tariki*, we realize that Amida has been running after us all the time. Only because we did not know this, we had to transmigrate.[10]

Shōkū thinks that this is why the *Meditation Sūtra* teaches that even the gravest sinner is reborn in the Pure Land by reciting the Nenbutsu at the moment of his death.

> [This] is not due to his understanding of this truth, but due to the following fact, that harassed by the death-agony and though not realising how, putting a stop to the *jiriki* thought of running after the Buddha, he utters Namu-amida-butsu, which is thus naturally in harmony with the *tariki* thought of Nenbutsu.[11]

Shōkū also thinks[12] that this is why the *Larger Sukhāvatīvyūha Sūtra* teaches that the Nenbutsu will last for one hundred years after the disappearance of the Right Law and that those who will then hear and recite the Nenbutsu will be able to be reborn in the Pure Land. That they are assured to be reborn there is not due to their merit but to their having nothing but the Buddha's name. As there is nothing but the Nenbutsu, the recitation naturally makes the mind of the devotee become concentrated in the Nenbutsu itself, and it is by the strength of this concentration that they are reborn in the Pure Land.

Thus our rebirth is not the thing which is worked out by our own efforts but the thing which is assured to us at the moment when our mind is united with Amida's by abandoning our self-thought which necessarily issues from egoistic impulses. The same can be said of the Nenbutsu, because our saying it is not the work of *jiriki* which seeks salvation through the Nenbutsu, but because it is recited out of the simple naïve belief in the assurance given by the Buddha for our rebirth in the Pure Land. This is what is meant by the Nenbutsu not requiring any "colouring" of good works. Shōkū compares the Nenbutsu to the virginity of plain wood.

VII

Spiritual Rest

When our rebirth in the Pure Land is thus assured by the Nenbutsu which is given in the Original Vow of Amida, there is a state of spiritual

10. *Jutsujō* 述誠.

11. *Jutsujō* 述誠.

12. As in the "Plain-wood Nenbutsu."

rest in which we have the feeling that the Buddha is always present with us. So we have:

> Even though your nights are passed in sleep, you are active with Amida in accumulating various virtues. Even though your days are spent busy in worldly matters, you are enjoying with Amida the perfect serenity of his inmost realization.[13]

It is a state of mind full of joy and exultation in the assurance of one's rebirth in the Pure Land, though one is imperfect and too feeble to do anything good. According to Shōkū:

> Even though your nature is imperfect, you need not be mortified; for there is Amida's Vow which embraces such inferior souls. Even though your meritorious work is small, you need not doubt your rebirth in the Pure Land; for in the Sūtra it is said, 'If you should have repeated my name, say, ten times, and if you should not be reborn in my Pure Land, I might not obtain the perfect enlightenment.'[14]

With this spiritual rest one comes back to the world where rules of morality are observed.

> As far as the *jiriki* rules our heart, all our doings are false; but when *jiriki* is replaced by *tariki*, all that we do is true.[15] [And:] As soon as we realize our weakness in doing good, real goodness is performed. For it is born of *tariki*.[16]

Shōkū strongly warns against those who misunderstand Amida's saving power of the wicked, for they are apt to grow all the more addicted to the commission of evil deeds. He says:

> You should not imagine that you may commit crime just because it is taught that Amida loves even a grave sinner. It is on the part of the Buddha that he will save grave sinners, and not on the part of sinners. Nor are you to think that the repeated recitation of the Buddha's name is to no purpose, as according to the Sūtra our rebirth is already assured by saying the Nenbutsu once for all. Just because of the Buddha's assurance sinners such as you are embraced in his love, so you are to grieve over your evil deeds and recite the name of the Buddha as frequently as you can.[17]

In brief, Shōkū's doctrine of *tariki* is to find our spiritual rest where we become united to the Buddha by believing his Vows and Works, by realising our utter inability to achieve our own salvation without the Buddha's mercy working within ourselves; it is in this state of mind that

13. *Chinkanyōjin* 鎮勧要心. Ed. Original showed as *Chinkwanyōjin*, with old forms of characters.
14. *Chinkanyōjin* 鎮勧要心.
15. *Jutsujō* 述誠.
16. *Jutsujō* 述誠.
17. *Nyoingosho* 如院御書.

we come back to this world and practise whatever good works we can according to our own individual capacities.

VIII

The Nenbutsu by Other Pure Land Masters

What corresponds to this "Plain-wood Nenbutsu" of Shōkū is the "Independent Nenbutsu" of Hōnen, his master and the father of Pure Land Buddhism in Japan. It runs thus:

> Set the Nenbutsu on its own legs, as is given in the Original Vow. Do not seek assistance in any other work. Those who seek assistance in any other work shall be reborn in the outskirts of the Pure Land. To seek assistance in any other work means to seek assistance in wisdom, to seek assistance in morality, to seek assistance in the wish for enlightenment, and to seek assistance in charity. Therefore, let a good man practise the Nenbutsu as he is, let a bad man practise the Nenbutsu as he is; just to practise the Nenbutsu according to his inborn nature is what I mean by the Nenbutsu not seeking assistance in any other work.[18]

Again, the "Plain-wood Nenbutsu" corresponds to Shinran's Nenbutsu which he defines as "not being a special deed of merit or of goodness." Shinran was Shōkū's fellow-disciple and the founder of the Shin Sect. We read in his *Tannishō* VIII:

> The Nenbutsu is neither a deed of merit nor one of goodness, as is practised by the believers. It is not a deed of merit because it is not that which should be practised by our self-efforts. It is not a deed of goodness because it is not that which should be practised by our self-efforts. It is solely due to other-power; therefore, it is not a deed of merit nor one of goodness, as is practised by the believers.

Shinran in another place defines the Nenbutsu as "irrational," that is, beyond logical calculation. "The master (Shinran) said in regard to the Nenbutsu that its reason is where it transcends all reasonings because it is inexpressible, indefinable, and inconceivable."[19] In one of his letters, Shinran says:

> Reasoning is contrivance, contrivance is on the side of devotees which means self-power, and it is called reasoning. As other-power lies where the Original Vow is believed and rebirth in the Pure Land is assured, there is no reasoning whatever in this. Therefore, it is called "Irrational."[20]

Ippen, the founder of the Ji Sect, who was inspired by Shōkū's teach-

---

18. *Wagotōroku* 我語登録.
19. Ed. Tannishō, Section 10.
20. Ed. This is to be found in *Shinran Shōnin ketsumyaku monjū* 親鸞聖人血脈文集.

ing, treats the Nenbutsu in a similar manner. He says:

> Do not give a foundation to the Nenbutsu. What enables you to be reborn in the Pure Land is neither your deed of goodness, nor your way of saying it, nor your way of acting, nor your mental attitude towards it; just say Namu-amida-butsu. It is enough.[21]

All these statements by the masters of Pure Land Buddhism—the "Independent" Nenbutsu, the "Irrational" Nenbutsu, the Nenbutsu "not being of any special deed of merit nor of goodness," the Nenbutsu "without any foundation," and the "Plain-wood" Nenbutsu—they all aim at attaining one and the same end which is our union with the Buddha. Here we naturally come back to Hōnen's "One Sheet Document" which was given as the last message to Genchi, one of his disciples. It runs thus:

> The Nenbutsu is not the practice of meditation on the Buddha nor the invocation of the Buddha's name which is practised as the result of study and understanding as to the meaning of the Nenbutsu. It is just to recite the name of Amida, without doubting that this will issue in the rebirth of the believer in the Pure Land. Just this, and no other consideration is needed.

Just to recite Namu-amida-butsu, without doubting that this will issue in the rebirth of the believer in the Pure Land—this is the secret of Pure Land Buddhism by which its followers are enabled to free themselves from the bondage of birth and death.

21. His *Sayings*, i.e. *Ippen goroku* 一遍語録.

— 10 —

Myōe's Critique of Hōnen

Bandō Shōjun

I

Soon after the death of Hōnen Shōnin 法然上人 (1133–1212) which occurred on January 25th, 1212, Myōe Shōnin 明恵上人 (1173–1232) successively published two books severely criticizing Hōnen's great writing on the significance of the Nembutsu practice, the *Senchaku hongan nenbutsu shū* 選択本願念仏集 (abbreviated hereafter as *Senjakushū* 選択集).[1] These were *Ikkō senjushū senchakushū no naka ni oite ja o kudaku rin* 於一向專修宗選択集中摧邪輪 (abbreviated hereafter as *Zaijarin*[2] 摧邪輪) and *Zaijarinshōgonki*[3] 摧邪輪荘厳記 (abbreviated hereafter as *Shōgonki* 荘厳記), published on November 23rd, 1212 and June 22nd, 1213 respectively. In view of the many repercussions Myōe's works caused in the contemporary philosophical world and thereafter, it would be worthwhile to consider the ideological encounter of these two eminent Buddhist sages against the background of the Kamakura Period, in which they were near contemporaries.

Hōnen succeeded in achieving independence from the established Buddhist sects with his clear-cut teaching of salvation through single-minded invocation of the Name of Amida, thus establishing for the first time in the history of Japanese Buddhism an independent Pure Land sect; and this bold step began the new Kamakura Buddhist reform movement with all its far-reaching consequences. The spiritual influence exercised by Hōnen

1. Ed. In the Jōdo School the abbreviated title of this key work by Hōnen is *Senchakushū* but in Shin Buddhist circles it is pronounced *Senjakushū*.
2. Ed. Alternatively *Saijarin*.
3. Ed. Alternatively *Saijarinshōgonki*.

is clearly reflected in the reactions of contemporary Buddhist leaders of both old and new factions. This is attested to in their writings, sayings, and diaries. If the founding of the Tendai and Shingon Schools by Saichō and Kūkai at the beginning of the Heian Period (794–1192) is called the first attempt at religious reformation imposed from above, that is, from the Imperial Household of the Emperor Kanmu, Hōnen's founding of the Pure Land School toward the end of the Heian Period might well be called a second religious reformation, which this time represented and responded to the aspirations of the lower levels of society. This marked the most significant point in the history of Japanese Buddhism, the emergence of what is now known as the Kamakura new Buddhism. The fact that its influence not only inspired the common people but also extended to the established Buddhist sects may be compared to the Reformation movement inaugurated by Luther and Calvin in 16th century Europe and the subsequent Counter-Reformation which arose within the Catholic world.

Among the violent reactions, both political and doctrinal, of the traditional Buddhist circles on Mt. Hiei and at Nara against Hōnen's reformative attempts the most remarkable in the Nara Buddhist camp were those of Jōkei 貞慶 (Gedatsu Shōnin 解脱上人, 1155–1213) and Kōben 高弁 (Myōe Shōnin).[4] Jōkei, as the leader in Nara, appealed to the emperor to have Hōnen's teaching banned. Myōe, being in a position equal in influence to that of Jōkei, lost no time in publishing two books criticising the doctrines expounded in Hōnen's *Senjakushū*. He took these measures immediately, and not by way of political maneuvering but by philosophical and doctrinal argument.

An outstanding feature of Myōe's criticism of Hōnen was that he did not merely denounce superficial moral transgressions which Hōnen's followers may have committed, but penetrated much deeper, focusing his criticism on Hōnen's teaching itself. It presented a challenge hardly to be dismissed lightly by Pure Land circles since it was a positive argument posed by an authentic Buddhist master with years of hard-gained experience encompassing the three aspects of precepts, meditation, and wisdom. This accounts for the fact that these two works by Myōe have been the centre of frequent scholarly disputes and controversies until the present day.

Historically, Saichō's establishment of the Tendai School on Mt. Hiei at the beginning of the Heian Period can be seen as expressing his rejection of the degenerated Nara Buddhism. He sought thereby to initiate a disciplinary reform for Mahāyāna practicers based upon the precepts in the *Fànwǎn jīng* 梵網経 (the *Brahmajāla-sūtra*[5]), and thus disavowed the whole

4. Ed. The older form of the second character will also be found: 明惠上人.

5. Ed. The original publication has *Mahāyāna Brahmajāla Sūtra*: see list of texts for precise indications.

existing monastic structure which was based on Hīnayāna-type ordination. Hōnen's founding of the Pure Land School can also be seen as a dialectical unity of Nara and Heian Buddhism: he regarded the Nenbutsu as consummating all other religious practices, while Heian Buddhism had already passed its zenith and had lost sight of its early reformative zeal.

The *Senjakushū*, Hōnen's declaration of religious independence, fell prey to the rigorous criticism of Myōe's *Zaijarin* and *Shōgonki* after Hōnen's demise, so he himself had no chance to respond to it. The task of attempting to reconcile the thought of these two sages was thus left to posterity.

Besides Myōe's works, other writings criticizing the *Senjakushū* are known to have been published from both Mt. Hiei and Nara. Not a few writings by Hōnen's followers refuting those criticisms also appeared. Of these works, the most systematic and thoroughgoing is Shinran's *Kyōgyōshinshō* 教行信証 (*Teaching, Practice, Faith and Realizing* [*of the Pure Land*]), which is deeply sympathetic with Hōnen's own motives. The viewpoint that Shinran's *Kyōgyōshinshō* and *Gutokushō* 愚禿鈔 (*The Writing of a Bald-headed Ignoramus*) were motivated by Myōe's criticisms is nowadays widely accepted. In the following, let us look into Myōe's life and the philosophical background and character of his two works mentioned above.

II

The life-span of Myōe Shōnin of Toganoo 栂尾 was sixty years and so, while not approaching Shinran's ninety, exceeded the average life-span of the age in which he lived, and in view of the quantity and quality of his work his life was undoubtedly one of the most rich and productive of his times. Born in Arita county of Kii Province (present day Wakayama Prefecture, south of Ōsaka), he lost both his mother and father at the age of eight. He subsequently entered Jingoji Temple 神護寺 at Takao 高雄, northwest of Kyōto, through the good offices of his uncle, Jōgaku-bō Gyōji 上覚房行慈, who was a disciple of Mongaku 文覚, and was initiated into the Buddhist teaching. He was officially ordained at the age of sixteen at Tōdaiji Temple 東大寺 in Nara. At Sonshō-in 尊勝院, one of the sub-temples of Tōdaiji, he is said to have studied the *Abhidharmakośa* under the tutelage of Rinkan-bō Shōsen 林観房聖詮, scholar of the Kegon (*Avataṃsaka*) School, and familiarized himself with such Buddhist writings as the *Yuikyōgyō* 遺教経, the *Sūtra of Buddha's Last Sermon.* At nineteen he was anointed in the Kongōkai (*vajradhātu*) ritual by Rimyō-bō Kōzen 理明坊興然. From about this time Myōe is said to have frequently seen auspicious visions during practice of the *dhyāna* (meditation) called "Butsugenhō" 仏眼法 (the Method of Buddha's Insight)[6] before the

6. Ed. The literal meaning of *butsugen* is "Buddha eye."

Tantric image of Butsugen-Butsumo-Son 仏眼仏母尊 belonging to the Taizōkai (*garbhadhātu*).[7] Thereafter, Myōe's learning and practice centered around the *Avataṃsaka-sūtra* and Tantric literature, and was based on strict observance of precepts and frequent practice of various kinds of meditation. His sphere of activity ranged from Takao, Makinoo, and Toganoo in Kyōto to his several hermitages in Arita, Kii prefecture, with occasional visits to Nara.

Myōe's habit of elaborately recording visions he experienced is one of the conspicuous traits of his religious character. His *Yumenoki* 夢之記 or *Record of Dreams*, kept for nearly forty years from his nineteenth to fifty-eighth year (1191–1230), is seemingly indicative of an inherent inclination to fall easily into *samādhi* and also of his serious reverence for such spiritual experiences. Such a proclivity no doubt constitutes one of the most precious gifts of his religious personality and stamps him as a mystic visionary.

Interesting in this connection is that Hōnen himself, the object of Myōe's criticism, is also believed to have been richly gifted with this quality. Hōnen, according to traditional Jōdo sect sources, is credited with a work known as the *Mukanshōsōki* 夢感聖相記 (*A Record Perceiving Holy Appearances in a Dream*), which was recorded on May 2nd, 1198, the same year in which he published the *Senjakushū*. Therein he vividly depicts a mysterious encounter with Shàndǎo of Táng China while in a Nembutsu *samādhi*:

> I (Hōnen) kept up the practice of reciting Nembutsu for many years, never discarding it for even one day. In a dream one night, I saw a great mountain range stretching far north and south with its ridge extremely high. Along the western slope of that mountain-range, a great river flowed southward from its source in the north. Its banks, spreading widely on either side, were seemingly boundless. Rich foliage grew luxuriantly all along its length without diminishing. Soaring I reached a spot halfway up a nearby hill. As I was commanding a view of the distant range to the west, a drift of purple cloud floated in the air before me about 50 feet above the earth. No sooner had I considered this to be an auspicious sign, indicating that someone somewhere was about to be born in the Pure Land, than that cloud came to hover above me. Looking up, I saw a number of birds, peacocks, parrots, and the like emerging from out of it to descend upon the riverbank and sport about. These birds, without brilliance of their own yet gloriously resplendent, flew back into the cloud. Nothing could have seemed more wondrous to me. Soon the cloud sped to the north, covering the mountain and the river. I again surmised that it must have gone to receive a Pure Land aspirant residing

7. Ed. I.e. the womb mandala.

> to the east of that mountain-range. Then in a moment, the cloud, coming over me once again, grew steadily larger until finally it covered the entire universe. A high priest emerged from the cloud suspended in the air before me. Thereupon, as I reverently paid homage and gazed up at his holy countenance, I found the upper half of his body that of an ordinary priest, whereas the lower half was that of a golden Buddha. I put my palms together in reverence, bowed my head, and asked, "Reverend Sir, may I ask you who you are?" "I am Shàndǎo of the Táng period," he replied. Again I asked, "Our ages are far apart; tell me what brings you here?" He replied, "I consider it extraordinary that you are engaged in spreading the way of the single-minded practice of Nembutsu. Thus I have come to testify on its behalf." Then I asked, "Are you sure that those who exclusively practice the Nembutsu are all to attain rebirth?" The dream ended before he answered. Even now, long after the dream, that holy appearance seems present before me.[8]

In addition to this, Seikan-bō Genchi 勢観房源智, one of Hōnen's main disciples, published a work entitled *Sanmaihottokuki* 三昧発得記 ("A Record of Receiving Samādhi Revelation"), which he edited from his master Hōnen's notes. This might be called Hōnen's version of *Yumenoki*, for it is the record of his dreams for six years (his 66th to 74th years), that is, from 1198 to 1204. Since Myōe had already been recording his dreams since 1191, it thus turns out that Hōnen and Myōe were keeping records of their visions concurrently.

It is well known that Hōnen thought very highly of the virtue of *samādhi* in a religious personality. In his *Senjakushū* there is a passage which reads:

> Question: In the tradition of Pure Land Buddhism there are a number of distinguished masters such as Jiácái of Hóng fǎ Temple[9] and Címǐn. Why do you not depend upon those masters and rely on Master Shàndǎo alone?
>
> Answer: Indeed, those masters relied on the teaching of the Pure Land, but they did not embody the quality of *samādhi*. Master Shàndǎo embodied the virtue of *samādhi*. His attainment of it is evident.

This obviously refers to the story related by Shàndǎo himself at the end of his *Commentary on the Meditation Sūtra*, about the monk who appeared nightly in his dreams and directed him to write the commentary.

8. I have included this record in spite of the fact that scholars now generally believe it to have been written after Hōnen's death by one of his disciples in order to show Hōnen's similarity with the Chinese Pure Land patriarch, Shàndǎo, who also had such visions. I feel however that it is fully in keeping with the overall character of Hōnen's religious personality as seen in his writings.

9. Ed. Hóngfǎ sì 弘法寺.

No wonder then that Myōe took a deep interest in Hōnen, who not only held Shàndǎo, an adept in *samādhi*, in deep reverence, but who himself possessed a similar proclivity. Consequently it is difficult to think of the spiritual encounter between Myōe and Hōnen as a mere coincidence.

Although this proclivity toward absorption in *samādhi* must have been, to some extent, inherent in Myōe's nature, he still consciously searched for the method of meditation best suited to him among a number of traditional *samādhi* techniques. He experimented with a wide range of methods, such as the Butsugenhō, the meditation with Butsugen-Butsumo-Son as the object; the meditation according to the *Engakukyō* 円覚経 (*Sūtra of Perfect Enlightenment*), which he practiced at his Rennyadai 練若台 hermitage in Sekisui-in 石水院 (temple at Toganoo); the *Shinnyokan* 真如観, or the meditation on Suchness (*bhūta tathatā*) based upon the teaching of the *Awakening of Faith in the Mahāyāna*; the *Gosōjōshinkan* 五相成身観 (fivefold meditation to achieve the body of Mahāvairocana Buddha) of Shingon Buddhism; and the *Bukkōkan* 仏光観 or meditation on Buddha's emanating light, based upon the *Avataṃsaka* commentary by Lǐ Tōngxuán 李通玄. This reminds us that Myōe was not merely a scholar of Kegon philosophy but a practicing Buddhist ever bent on training himself by various methods of meditation. In other words, while he initiated a simultaneous practice of *Avataṃsaka* and Tantric doctrines in which both teachings were beautifully harmonized into a coherent personality, he was also a *Brahmacārin* (person of pure conduct) to the letter, celibate, strict in observing all precepts, and constantly devoting himself to the practice of meditation. His vigilance, his repugnance of fame, and his inner aspiration for the anchoretic life are already in evidence in his early years.

When Myōe was thirty-three, while he was secluded in a hermitage in Kii prefecture contemplating his long cherished pilgrimage to India, the birthplace of Śākyamuni Buddha, he received a letter from his master Jōgaku in Kyōto requesting him to return to Takao. Myōe declined his master's request:

> With the fruit of learning and practice so hard to attain, my only thought now is to risk all in travel through desolate deserts and among green peaks, while keeping the Buddha's name in mind, or the title of a sūtra, or even one mantra. I have not a single thought of associating with other people...

In his irresistible yearning for the native land of Śākyamuni Buddha, and with certain actualities of his daily life temporarily frustrating fulfillment of his practice, he twice made plans for travelling to India, relying upon such records as Xuánzàng's *Travels to the Western Countries*. Yet he gave up his plans when the wife of his patron Yuasa Munemitsu drew two inauspicious oracles from the Daimyōjin 大明神 of the Kasuga

Shrine. This may be said to show the ethnic character of his belief.[10]

This passage in his *Record of Dreams* clearly reveals Myōe's criticism of the state of Nara Buddhism, his disillusionment, and his aspiration for Enlightenment:

> Ever since my distant childhood, my constant thought was to seek the Dharma. After coming of age, when I took to the study of various teachings, exoteric as well as esoteric, I heard only voices clamouring for position and fame. I found friends as well as teachers engrossed in fleeting matters, oblivious of the truth of the teaching. I felt forsaken by my karmic link to Buddhist practice. I could not help but be deeply disheartened.

Therefore his attempt to lead an anchoretic life in remote Kii province[11] was not mere escapism, but a necessity in order for him to maintain his meditational practice in solitude. It was in the nature of a new renunciation for him. Symptoms of his sensitivity and vigilance in matters of fame are seen in some rather humorous inscriptions he made at the end of a commentary he copied in his youth at Sonshō-in Temple in Nara: "This is a book owned by Jōben [his priestly name at the time], the meanest outcast within this temple; Myōe-bō, a piece of smashed tile from the temple roof; a toilet-cleaner priest." And, "This is a book owned by the outcast priest Jōben, the meanest beggar monk in the whole of Japan, who will never become a bishop or archbishop, not in this life nor in eternity." The title *hinin* 非人 (outcast) was also used by him when he later wrote *Zaijarin* at the age of forty; in the colophon he signed his name with this title. This reminds us of Shinran's "Gutoku" (Baldheaded Ignoramus), the term of self-reference he began to use after he was sent into exile. Such extreme humility is perhaps common to all the great Buddhist figures.

The famous painting of Myōe's solitary figure deeply absorbed in *samādhi* in the branches of a tree in the forests of Takao free from worldly pleasures and fame, is preserved in the temple Kōzanji, and is an extraordinary image of a religious seeker.[12]

His resolution in cutting off his right earlobe before the image of Butsugen-Butsumo-son at his Kii hermitage to spur himself to greater concentration might strike the modern mind as a somewhat gruesome

10. Ed. By referring to the "ethnic" character of Myōe's belief, Bandō is emphasizing that the famous Kasuga Shrine at Nara is couched in the Shintō tradition, although in mediaeval times the symbiosis of Buddhist and Shintō conceptions was intense.
11. Ed. The original text has "prefecture" but Kii does not figure in the modern system of prefectures.
12. Ed. This frequently reproduced painting was published in the original colours as a frontispiece to *The Eastern Buddhist* Vol VII, 1 (New Series) 1974. Here we show a detail, in that the interlaced tree branches are slightly reduced.

Figure 10.1 Myōe's solitary figure deeply absorbed in *samādhi* in the branches of a tree in the forests of Takao free from worldly pleasures and fame.

sacrifice, but in view of his motive, it is, at the same time, indicative of his firmly rooted resolution to avoid all fleshly temptation by disfiguring his own handsome countenance.

In the reply to his master Jōgaku quoted above, Myōe stated, "My only thought now is to risk all in travel through desolate deserts and among green peaks..." Despite his genuine aspiration to visit India, a tinge of melancholy, perhaps prompted by a kind of death wish, appears to shroud his words. On the other hand, it may be said that his task of seeking Enlightenment was never unrelated to the matter of life and death. Later, when he was received by the brotherhood of monks at Toganoo and became engaged in educating disciples there, he had come to positively accept the thought of death and had thoroughly sublimated it in his meditation-oriented daily life. This may be seen in his words recorded in the *Kyakuhaimōki* 却廃妄記 ("Notes To Avoid Falling into Oblivion") by Jakue-bō Chōen 寂恵房長円, his foremost disciple:

> Constantly keep in mind that if someone were going to be beheaded, you would be prepared to take his place; then everything, your study included, will succeed. Once the Mind of Enlightenment has awakened in the process of your following the Way of the Buddha, you will be free from any concern over your body and mind.

III

It is clearly coincidental that the publication of Myōe's *Zaijarin* came right after Hōnen's death. At the end of the *Senjakushū* Hōnen says:

> I have been requested by the Lord Kenjitsu Hakuriku 兼実博陸 (Fujiwara Kanezane 藤原兼実) to write this work. I cannot decline. I have therefore presumed to collect important passages on the Nembutsu teaching and have, moreover, pointed out its essential meaning. Only wishing to do his bidding with respect, I did not reflect on my own unworthiness. I now see it was the height of presumption on my part. It is only hoped that once you have graciously glanced at this writing you will hide it in some cavity in the wall and not leave it before the window, to keep slanderers of the Dharma from falling into the evil paths.

Thus it was not Hōnen's intention to have the *Senjakushū* published immediately. At first, he allowed only a limited number of his most trusted disciples to copy it. Everything, its Chinese literary style included, indicates that it could not have been meant for the general public. Although opinions vary as to the time of its completion, it is almost certain that it was written after Hōnen was sixty-six years old. Its first publication is believed to have been in September, 1212, a little more than six months after his death on January 25th.

Since Myōe finished writing *Zaijarin* on November 23rd of the same year, we cannot but be deeply impressed by the astonishing rapidity with which he wrote this large three-volume book in reply to Hōnen's work.

In the first volume of *Zaijarin* Myōe writes: "When I examined several different editions of your book, I found that all of them had this character." This tells us that, already, Myōe had in his hands several editions of the *Senjakushū*, and was giving the work an unusually scrupulous reading. And it was not long, on June 22nd of the following year, before he published a second volume, entitled *Zaijarinshōgonki*, which is a continuation of the first book. These two works reveal how seriously the forty year old Myōe concentrated himself on the criticism of Hōnen's work, and what astoundingly rich resources of scholarship and insight he had accumulated. It is therefore understandable that in the *Record of Dreams* there should be an entry in which he records seeing Hōnen in a dream.

With the maturing of his character and the ripening of his scholarly attainments, the eremitically inclined Myōe finally and with reluctance complied with his master's request and took up residence at Toganoo. He founded in the neighbourhood a convent called Zenmyōji 善妙寺 for the education of nuns, and became engaged in many social activities. According to the collection of his sayings recorded by one of his disciples, Myōe used to caution his followers against finding fault with others:

> Why think and speak of other people's shortcomings, and expose their shameful secrets, disregarding the possibility of causing them life-long disgrace? If somebody is to blame, he himself is at fault; whereas if somebody else makes an issue of this fault, it becomes his own... Bear in mind not to speak of such things. However hard it may be to repress your urge to speak out, shut it up deep in your mind, and make sure that you hold your tongue. If it must be said, then admonish him openly to his face.

He also taught:

> It is when one is lacking in virtue oneself that one tends to find fault with others. As the ancients used to say, "*toku*" 徳 (virtue) is "*toku*" 得 (something one gains). It resides in one who loves it. Whoever tends to find fault with others only betrays his own faults and in him no virtue resides.

In another source, he is quoted as saying:

> A legend has it that the Venerable Ānanda's sister, who was a nun, fell into hell because she became angry with the Venerable Kāśyapa. Since this holds true for each individual at present too, if anybody gets angry with a monk, it produces *karma* destining him for hell. However, people nowadays, myself included, are deluded into thinking that such a small thing will never be counted as sinful, and so remain unrepentant. How shameful!

From these statements, we learn that Myōe was ever on his guard against the poisonous nature of anger and speaking ill of others. How, then, are we to judge the violent harangues in his *Zaijarin* and *Shōgonki* against Hōnen's *Senjakushū*?

IV

In summation, Myōe, a strict observer of the Buddhist precepts, led an anchoretic life that centered around meditative practice away from the world; he guarded against the allurements of fame and the transgressions of his own words, thoughts, and actions. What, then, brought this retiring man to write books of such violent criticism against Hōnen, a man he had ever held in high respect? Myōe is said to have confided to Jakue-bō Chōen, one of his main disciples, "I always feel sad about unreasonable matters. So did I feel when I wrote *Zaijarin.*" (*Kyakuhaimōki*, part II). This reminds us of the state of mind he was in when as a youth he felt compelled to leave the temples of Nara behind and enter the mountains of Kii. The circumstances which prompted him to write *Zaijarin* were, as he himself relates at the outset, as follows. In the autumn of 1212 at a certain place in Kyōto, while giving a lecture on a sūtra, Myōe incidentally criticized *Senjakushū*, mentioning two errors: 1) Its rejection of the Mind of Enlightenment, and 2) Its comparison of the Path of the Holy (those who seek Enlightenment through their own efforts) to that of robbers. Hearing of this, the Nembutsu followers among the congregation that day were offended and a dispute ensued. After that, hearing rumors that the Nembutsu followers might come to storm his residence at any moment for a doctrinal confrontation, he began to write down the main points of his convictions as a memorandum. This proved to be the basis of *Zaijarin.*

In the first volume of *Zaijarin*, Myōe tries to clarify his contentions through questions and answers. There is a passage where he refers to his reason for writing the book:

> Question: Even if you regard it (Hōnen's viewpoint) as false, as long as you do not hold such a view yourself, you will be free from falsehood. Why is it then that you have taken the trouble of writing this book to refute it?
>
> Answer: As is stated in the text of the precepts in the *Fànwǎn jīng*: "When a Bodhisattva sees a non-Buddhist or an evil man, and hears from him even one word abusing the Buddha, he feels as if his heart were pierced by three hundred spearheads." So is it with this case. Hearing the various false statements made in that book, anyone with a heart would feel as if it were pierced. Anyone who does not feel like that and lets the matter pass, clearly has no real aspiration in the Dharma.

It is obvious that Myōe believed Hōnen's contentions set forth in *Senjakushū* to be erroneous, a slandering of Buddhism. This feeling was something he could not merely suffer and remain silent about. He had to speak out in full consideration that Hōnen had already passed away and that there was a good possibility that the future social influence of his thought might be enormous. *Zaijarin* was completed by Myōe within a very short space of time. Behind the gentle expression, "I feel sad at unreasonable matters," which Myōe uttered to Chōen in his later years, at this time he no doubt felt an unbearable anguish. What was it Hōnen preached that would lead Myōe to accuse him of "slandering the Buddha" and "holding false views"?

V

The *Shōgonki*, published about seven months after *Zaijarin*, further develops Myōe's criticism of *Senjakushū*. Myōe mentions altogether sixteen errors thirteen in the former work and three in the latter—contained in *Senjakushū*. Of the sixteen, the first five mentioned are concerned with the problem of *bodhicitta* (the Mind of Enlightenment).

In the *Kōfukujisōjō*[13] 興福寺奏状 (*A Document of Protest submitted to the Imperial Court by Kōfukuji*), the draft of which was prepared by Jōkei, the head abbot of Kōfukuji, in October 1205, nine errors in the Nembutsu school are mentioned. But these nine points are merely addressed to the external aspects of Hōnen's teaching, and it is noteworthy that none of them makes an issue of *bodhicitta*. While Jōkei's name is seen in the list of those present at the discussion meeting held at the Shōrin-in 勝林院 at Ōhara in 1186, the historicity of this meeting is generally held in doubt. And though it is nevertheless probable that Jōkei met Hōnen on other occasions besides this meeting, his actual knowledge of the Nembutsu teaching seems to have been limited at the time he drew up the draft of the *Sōjō* to the behaviour of some Nembutsu followers, and, of course, to hearsay, partly because it was written prior to the publication of *Senjakushū*. Jōkei and Myōe have a number of traits in common. They both occupied leading positions in Nara Buddhist circles; both were very strict in observing the precepts, in avoiding fame, and both had anchoretic dispositions (Jōkei secluded himself in Kasagi 笠置, and Myōe at Takao and Kii); both possessed scholarly and virtuous characters and literary talent, worshiped Shintō deities, and were known as aspirants for Maitreya's Tuṣita Heaven. Myōe, however, undoubtedly excelled Jōkei in the firmness of conviction and strength of his insistence that developing the Mind of Enlightenment should be the essence and *sine qua non* of a Buddhist follower. Myōe's two writings mentioned above prove this beyond doubt.

On the one hand, *Zaijarin* was a book severely criticizing Hōnen, who, Myōe believed, had neglected *bodhicitta*; on the other hand, it was a the-

13. Ed. The transliteration of this famous temple name as Kōbukuji (in the original publication) must be regarded as misleading.

sis elaborating Myōe's own broadly viewed understanding of *bodhicitta*. Anyone who reads it will agree that *Zaijarin* is a work of profound scholarship, requiring long years of meditation and study, and that it could never have been hurriedly compiled only for the purpose of controversy. All the appropriate quotations in it, drawn from innumerable sources, are enough to persuade the reader that, although no more than a few months were needed to complete this book, it is based upon decades of research.

After the sixth of the errors *Zaijarin* mentions, several points appear which are similar to those contained among the nine faults outlined in the *Kōfukujisōjō*. For example, critical reference to the "Sesshu fusha mandara"[14] 摂取不捨曼荼羅 (*Maṇḍala* embracing all and forsaking none) current at the time, which symbolizes Amida's light illuminating only the Nembutsu followers, can be found in both. It can be concluded from this, I think, that at the time this *maṇḍala* was widely used among Nembutsu followers. However, while the points of interest shown in the *Sōjō* are mainly centered around institutional matters and social phenomena, Myōe's, as was manifested in his *Zaijarin*, largely concentrated on doctrinal matters. This is natural enough in view of the character of *Zaijarin*, which deploys detailed argument.

The *Shōgonki* may be characterized as a supplement to *Zaijarin*, in which additions and some development of argument are made. That their publications were separated by only seven months indicates that Myōe's sense of justice had not quite been satisfied by writing *Zaijarin*. This gains support from the number of scathing remarks that appear, the last thing we would expect from this usually gentle and reserved man. Some examples from the former work:

> My great ambition lies in one thing alone—to make you throw away this *Senjakushū*.
>
> By making such false statements, you have driven all your followers to dwell in this greatly mistaken view. You are a vile robber destroying the Buddhas' Pure Lands.
>
> By your false statements, you have caused your followers to discard their *bodhicitta*. Are you not a messenger of the devil?
>
> I am now convinced that you are a heinous robber belonging to the Pure Land school. You should not use the title of the son of the Buddha. How could you be entitled free access to the temple precincts? You are a sinner, a reproach to Shàndǎo. How could you be a member of his family?
>
> The practice of Nembutsu cannot be established apart from *bodhicitta*. Thus, by slandering both the practices of the Holy Path and the Pure Land Path, you yourself have attained neither of them. You therefore should

14. Ed. The Japanese transliteration *mandara* for *maṇḍala* arises, in the transcription of titles, because there is no independent letter "l" in that language.

> know that you are to be called "one who is absolutely empty-handed." The wise *brahmacārins* (those whose conduct is pure) should never live together in the same place with you. Among right causes for birth (in the Pure Land), *bodhicitta* must be regarded as the primary path. Nembutsu and other practices may vary according to the practicer. Yet, by your regarding *bodhicitta* as lacking full consummation and of small benefit, and the Nembutsu as consummate and of great virtue, you are trying to make heaven earth and earth heaven. How perverted your thinking is!

Such vehemence is kept up unabated in the second work:

> The culprit who has caused the modern decline of the Dharma is none other than you!
>
> Since you have not understood the essential significance of all such matters, you should call the *maṇḍala* of your making the "*maṇḍala* of no understanding." From now onward, it should never be called a "*maṇḍala* embracing all and forsaking none."
>
> You should not say, "Our school is reproached," but "Our heretical school is reproached."
>
> That somebody within the Buddha Dharma should give rise to misbehavior owing to the practice of miscellaneous adulterated works related to the three branches of learning (precept, meditation, and wisdom) is an ominous event. Such a person destroys the Dharma of the Buddhas attained during incalculable past time, hundreds of thousands of *kalpas*, as though a worm within the body of a lion were to consume the lion's flesh itself. You are possessed of no other abilities. You have the appearance of righteousness outside, while harboring evil inside. You are indeed the very object of the healing powers of the Buddha's truthful mind. You are a hindrance to birth (in the Pure Land). While you may be possessed of some virtues, you hold in your mind a great heretical view, and thus deceive all you encounter. What I am going to refute now is none other than this great error of yours.

These terse, passionate accusations may be taken as summarizing other extensive arguments Myōe deploys elsewhere. Together with his more elaborate and richly documented argumentation, even a casual glance over them will suffice to show the general orientation of Myōe's argument.

VI

Of the sixteen errors pointed out at the beginning of the *Shōgonki*, Myōe calls the first ten "great," and the remaining six "small." According to him, the first may be divided into two kinds: 1) the error of rejecting *bodhicitta*, and 2) the error of comparing those of the Holy Path to robbers. He further divides the first of these into five parts, and develops his arguments extensively. Hōnen rejected *bodhicitta*, counting it simply as one of many miscellaneous practices subordinate to the primary practice of Nembutsu; Myōe denounced this, saying that Hōnen regarded *bodhicitta*, which is by nature devoid of substance, as being substantive, which would be no different from the non-Buddhist view of a creator-god as substance. He defended in detail the absolute necessity of *bodhicitta* in the Way of the Buddha. These arguments seem to be largely concerned with the semantics of *bodhicitta*. Myōe, after Hōnen's death, makes use almost exclusively of quotations from *Senjakushū* in carrying out his discussions. That was inevitable inasmuch as it was no longer possible for Myōe to get Hōnen's personal responses to his challenges; but it also meant that Myōe, as he subjected Hōnen's definition of *bodhicitta* to rigorous criticism, almost totally neglected the subtle emphasis permeating that definition. Myōe relentlessly pursued his cross-examination of Hōnen's idea of *bodhicitta*, and passed the judgment that Hōnen's acceptance of *shōmyō* 称名 (the vocal utterance of Amida's Name) at the expense of the spiritual factor (*bodhicitta*) was tantamount to expecting a fruit to grow without planting a seed. He further denounced Hōnen for decreeing in his *Senjakushū* that *bodhicitta* is short of ultimacy and of little merit, while *shōmyō* is paramount and greatly beneficial. This, he says, is an inversion of the truth. He also declares that it is unreasonable to recommend single-minded repetition of Nembutsu to all sentient beings without regard for their different idiosyncracies. He even brings in the verdict that Hōnen should never be called a disciple of the Buddha as long as he rejects or makes light of *bodhicitta*, in spite of the fact, as testified to by various sūtras, that it was so cherished by the Buddha himself.

Regarding this discrepancy in their views of *bodhicitta*, we should take into consideration not only their own definitions of it, but their basic motivations as well. Hōnen adopted Nembutsu as the sole way through which all sentient beings, young and old, men and women, might equally be delivered. With this basic motivation, he systematized his personal beliefs and expressed them in his *Senjakushū*. Although the idea of *bodhicitta* was given a position among the other sundry practices, it does not necessarily follow, I think, that Hōnen, who was acclaimed by his contemporaries for his wisdom and scholarship, failed to grasp the essential significance of *bodhicitta*. As the essence of the Buddha Way it could hardly be discarded. This leads us to suppose that the reason Hōnen viewed *bodhicitta* as one of the sundry practices which he rejected must have stemmed from a belief that *bodhicitta* could not be generated by the practicer's self-effort.

Myōe, on the other hand, flatly rejects the idea of *bodhicitta* conceived only as the initial springing up of the Mind of Enlightenment, and adheres uncompromisingly to the formal conception of it as thoroughly permeating the entire Buddha Way. Even the Nembutsu that Hōnen regarded as a practice ensuring absolute non-retrogression is judged by Myōe to be only a means to the attainment of *samādhi* or deep contemplative state. Myōe consistently maintains that the practice of Nembutsu could be consummated solely by *bodhicitta* and that *bodhicitta* in turn would by no means interfere with the practice of Nembutsu. *Senjakushū*, not written for the purpose of elucidating the meaning of *bodhicitta*, does not contain any specific passage related to it. Yet the following words, ascribed to Hōnen by Shinkū 信空 one of his disciples, might be taken as representing Hōnen's teaching to the disciples closely attending him:

> Once Shōnin (Hōnen) stated: Many are the teachers who have expounded the Pure Land teaching. All of them have equally recommended *bodhicitta* and designated the contemplation of the Buddha as an authentic practice. It was Shàndǎo alone who, putting aside *bodhicitta*, decided that contemplation of the Buddha was subsidiary to the utterance of Amida's Name. People of this age can never expect to attain birth (in the Pure Land) unless they rely upon Shàndǎo's thought. (*Wagotōroku* 和語灯録 5)

This is indeed in perfect accordance with what he says on this same point in *Senjakushū*. Especially to be noted here is his expression: "People of this age." This reveals, I think, that the structure of Hōnen's religious thought was based neither on a supposition of the accumulation of learning and discipline, nor on some ideal image of what a Buddhist should be, but geared to the actual status quo of the majority of the unenlightened. Since Hōnen's basic standpoint was least taken into account in the *Zaijarin*, where Myōe's criticism of Hōnen's *Senjakushū* was made solely on general Buddhist principles, the task of clarifying Hōnen's innermost intention and basic standpoint was naturally relegated to his spiritual successors. Today, few would deny that among the numerous writings defending Hōnen's cause, the most systematic and important *apologia* are found in Shinran's works such as *Kyōgyōshinshō* and *Gutokushō* (*The Writing of a Baldheaded Ignoramus*). They are written from Hōnen's own religious standpoint and make up a persuasive reply to Myōe's sweeping critical dialectic. Although Shinran himself nowhere states explicitly that these works were written in defence of Hōnen, they are generally considered to represent just such a defence.

Both *Kyōgyōshinshō* and *Gutokushō*, written in classical Chinese which could be read only by the intellectuals, emphasize and elaborate that the faith of the individual accorded by Amida's Other Power is nothing but the great *bodhicitta*.

Shinran seems to have intended that his main work should be published in Kyōto, and not the Kantō 関東 (the eastern provinces), so that its appearance would achieve maximum effect in the traditional Buddhist circles at Nara and Mt. Hiei.

A special foreword is attached to the third volume of *Kyōgyōshinshō* in which Shinran deals with the significance of *bodhicitta* in Pure Land Buddhism in relation to the Triple Mind (sincerity, faith, and aspiration for birth in the Pure Land), and with the true meaning of being a Buddhist disciple. When all these factors are taken into account, we are made to realize the central role the defending and clarifying of his master's teaching played in Shinran's life.

Furthermore, in Shinran's *Shōzōmatsuwasan* 正像末和讃 (*Hymns on the Three Periods after the Buddha's Demise*), we find successive references to the unenlightened man's difficulty of generating *bodhicitta* by his own self-effort, a standpoint strongly suggestive of Hōnen's own. At the beginning of each of the two volumes of *Gutokushō*, Shinran confesses to "being inwardly ignorant and outwardly wise," which is reminiscent of the accusation Myōe directed against Hōnen toward the end of *Shōgonki*, when he declared him to be outwardly righteous and inwardly false. Shinran's words must have derived from this source. Though most of Shinran's writings are highly confessional, they may also be characterized as an open response not only to the traditional schools advocating the Holy Path, as represented by Myōe and Jōkei, but to the question posed by the age in which he lived, and by later history as well.

Whereas *Zaijarin* and *Shōgonki* explicitly singled out Hōnen as Myōe's opponent, Shinran's *Kyōgyōshinshō* and *Gutokushō* were addressed to no single individual. This in itself seems to suggest that his response was made in full awareness that Myōe had challenged Hōnen with radical questions of universal significance, valid throughout the entire history of Buddhism and transcending both the individual and his age.

— 11 —

Ippen Shōnin and the Nenbutsu

Yanagi Sōetsu

I

Ippen Shōnin (1239–1289),[1] founder of the Ji Sect of Japanese Pure Land Buddhism, lived during the latter half of the Kamakura period, at a time when Dōgen (1200–1253) and Nichiren (1222–1282) were active, and Shinran (1173–1262), in ripe old age, was still living as well. During this same period the European Middle Ages also saw a remarkable occurrence of many great religious saints, men such as St. Francis (1182–1226), St. Thomas Aquinas (1226–1272), and Meister Eckhart (1266–1329).

The first great Buddhist figure Japan produced was Prince Shōtoku (574–622). Saichō (767–822) and Kūkai (774–835), the Japanese Tendai and Shingon sect founders respectively, were men of the Heian period. In the following Fujiwara period, the greatest names are those of Jie (912–985) and Eshin (942–1017). These men have become great pillars of Japanese Buddhism. But it is the Kamakura period that was unquestionably the outstanding age in Japanese religious history. Perhaps it may even be said that the Buddhism prior to it was a preparation undergone for the cause of generating Kamakura Buddhism. The founders of both the Rinzai and Sōtō Zen sects, the Jōdo and Jōdo Shin sects of Pure Land

1. Translator's note. This article initially appeared in the periodical *Shinron* 新論 (Aug. 1955), and was later included in volume 4 (*Namu-amida-butsu—Ippen Shōnin*) of the author's collected works on religion (Tokyo, 1960). Readers unfamiliar with general Pure Land terminology are directed to the comprehensive glossary included in Suzuki Daisetz's translation of Shinran's *Kyōgyōshinshō* (Kyōto, 1973). Shōnin 上人 is an honorific title applied in Japan to eminent Buddhist priests, sometimes translated as saint, e.g. Saint Hōnen.

Buddhism, and the Nichiren sect all appeared during this age. The Ji sect, which begins with Ippen Shōnin, was the last of the Kamakura sects to emerge.

This great and varied religious flowering left in its wake a brilliant cultural as well as religious effulgence. A time of such a number of individual sects and schools has seldom been seen in any age, whether in the East or West. It was ushered in, in great part, by Hōnen (1133–1212), the celebrated founder of the Jōdo sect.

The Court Buddhism, the Buddhism of the upper classes, the Buddhism of the samurai class in general, Buddhism as a pacifier and preserver of the state—which which had hitherto prospered, was, through the Nenbutsu school whose foundations were laid by Hōnen, greatly broadened and made to permeate down through the levels of society until it reached the common people.

Declaring that he would "rely solely on Shàndǎo" (Jap. Zendō, 613–681), Hōnen built his entire teaching on the foundation of the Táng dynasty Pure Land patriarch Shàndǎo's *Commentary on the Meditation Sūtra* (*Guānjīngshù*). But he took a Nenbutsu teaching that until now had had nothing more than an ancillary function in several Buddhist sects, and raised it to the status of an independent sect, calling it the Jōdo, or Pure Land sect. His scriptural authority was the Three Pure Land sūtras, the *Larger Sūtra of Eternal Life, the Meditation Sūtra*, and the *Amida Sūtra*; the object of his worship, Amida Nyorai, the incarnation of great compassion (*karuṇā*). He taught that the calling of Amida's Name (*myōgō*) was the act that assured one's rebirth in the Pure Land. This is called the "other-power" teaching, for it rejects self-power and places all trust in Amida Buddha. It is also known as the Nenbutsu teaching, because it stresses single-minded repetition of the six characters of Amida's Name.[2] And since this involves nothing more than the calling out of the six characters *Na-mu-a-mi-da-butsu* 南無阿弥陀仏, it is referred to as the "easy path" as well. Developed for the needs of the common people, Hōnen's Jōdo teaching may be considered a Buddhism for ordinary lay men and women.

Various branches are discernible in the sects and schools of Japanese Buddhism, but among them the one that appears to be most Japanese in character of all, and the one that can be said to be truly indigenous to Japan, is Hōnen's Jōdo sect. The Jōdo sect reveres Hōnen as its founder and regards his great *Senjakuhongannenbutsushū* as its chief scripture. From Hōnen, a number of outstanding disciples followed, their lines later branching off further into several distinguishable streams.

2. Translator's note. In Pure Land Buddhism the *six syllable* (or character) Name (*myōgō*), i.e. the Name of Amida Buddha, refers to the words *Namu-amida-butsu*. Although in Pure Land tradition the Nenbutsu has more than one connotation, in the present essay it refers to invoking the Name, "*Namu-amida-butsu*."

Hōnen

↓	↓	↓	↓	↓	↓
Shōkō	Chōsai	Kōsai	Ryūkan	Shōkū	Shinran
1162–1238	1184–1228	1163–1247	1148–1227	1177–1247	1173–1262
Founder of Chinzei branch	Amida's Original Prayer includes practices other than Nenbutsu	Once-calling principle	Many-callings principle	Founder of Seizan branch	Shin sect founder
				↓	
				Shōtatsu (n.d.)	
				↓	
				Ippen (1239–1289)	
				Ji sect founder	

Among these, those lines which have continued to the present day are the Chinzei and Seizan branches of the Jōdo sect, the Jōdo Shin sect, and the Ji sect. As the first two belong to the same Jōdo sect, we may say that the present Japanese Pure Land school is divided into three major bodies: the Jōdo, Jōdo Shin, and Ji sects. To discuss the teachings of these sects, it is imperative to give an account of Hōnen, Shinran, and Ippen, their respective founders.

While the transition from Hōnen to Shinran is well documented, hardly anyone has devoted himself to the matter of Ippen. Since I feel this to be manifestly unjust, I wish in the following pages to draw as much attention as possible to Ippen's unique position in the Japanese Pure Land tradition.

As the above chart shows, Ippen is Hōnen's great-grandson in the Dharma. Having inherited his teaching directly from Shōkū's disciple Shōtatsu, it is clear that the Nenbutsu of the Ji sect evolved from the Seizan branch of the Jōdo sect.[3]

Ippen was born the first year of the Enō period (1239) and died the second year of Shōō (1289), making him at fifty the most short-lived of the great Kamakura priests. His relatively brief life is thought to have

3. While he was studying under Shōtatsu, his fellow disciples included a monk named Ken'i, who later expounded the so-called "Fukakusa principle" of Nenbutsu, and who had a close association with Ippen.

resulted from the severe physical trials he underwent during his religious practice and constant pilgrimage throughout the country.

He was born in Iyo, modern Ehime prefecture, on the island of Shikoku, and died on the seacoast of Hyōgo, near the modern port of Kobe. According to the *Rokujōengi*, which relates Ippen's life,[4] his family name was Ochi Kōno, and his childhood name was Michihisa. He was first drawn to Buddhism at the age of ten when death took his mother from him. It was this same sorrow that brought the youthful Hōnen, Dōgen, and Shinran to contemplate the transience of life. For each of them entrance into a life of preaching and salvation was associated with deep personal loss.

Ippen's religious practice was based on the Pure Land teaching he had learned from his teachers Kedai and Shōtatsu during the twelve years he studied under them on the island of Kyūshū. His priestly name was Chishin.[5] When he was twenty-five, upon receiving news of his father's death, he returned once again to his home in Iyo. The following seven years were difficult ones. Then, one day, seeing a spinning top revolve to a stop, he came to understand the true nature of transmigration and realized for the first time the meaning of life and death—as his biographer puts it, "he grasped the Buddha Dharma's meaning." He was thirty-three years old.

He made a pilgrimage to far-off Zenkōji in present Nagano prefecture, where he procured a painting depicting Shàndǎo's parable of the Two Streams and White Path.[6] Upon returning to the seclusion of his native Kubono, he hung the painting in an alcove of his dwelling. One day, suddenly realizing its true meaning, he expressed his understanding in a verse:

> Amida's awakening ten *kalpas* in the past [was for the sake of those] in the sentient world; In one instant of thought rebirth in Amida's land is achieved. [When we realize that] ten *kalpas* and one instant are not two, we realize the unborn; [When we realize that] Amida's Land and the sentient world are identical, we sit ourselves down among the Bodhisattvas' great assemblage.

In 1275, in his thirty-seventh year, he began a country-wide pilgrimage that was to continue for sixteen years. As a bodhisattva-act which he hoped would lead people to Buddhahood, he distributed to those he met small paper amulets bearing the words "*Namu-amida-butsu*." Their number is said to have reached a total of 251,724.

---

4. Translator's note. *Rokujōengi* 六条縁起 is one of the most celebrated of all Japanese horizontal picture scrolls (*emakimono*); also known as the *Ippenhijirie* (Pictures of the wandering priest Ippen), painted by En'i 円伊 with a text by Shōkai 聖戒, one of Ippen's disciples.

5. Kedai 華台; Shōtatsu 聖達; Chishin 智真.

6. Translator's note. This is found in Shàndǎo's *Commentary on the Meditation Sūtra* and is translated in full in the *Eastern Buddhist* (original series) Vol. III, No. 4 (1925, 288–290).

The three Japanese Pure Land patriarchs Hōnen, Shinran, and Ippen had distinctively different modes of life. Hōnen, as a priest, lived in Buddhist temples and observed the Buddhist precepts, leading a life of purity as an example to his followers. Shinran, who said he was "neither priest nor layman," shunned temple life and dwelled in the world. Ippen renounced both the temple life and the worldly life, giving up everything to Amida's Name as a *sutehijiri*, a homeless wandering priest who rejects the world and all things in it. The very manner of their different styles of life became the respective foundations which engendered the Jōdo, Jōdo Shin, and Ji sects. Together, their combined strengths built the great edifice of Japanese Pure Land Buddhism.

That being so, why is it the Ji sect alone has been passed over by the world? One reason may be found in the uncompromising declaration of Ippen himself: "My teaching is for my lifetime only." This gains additional support from the fact that he burned all his writings just before his death, leaving behind nothing but the six syllables, *Namu-amida-butsu*. Other factors could be mentioned: the wandering lives led by generations of Ji sect priests after the example of their founder, which prevented them from taking up fixed residence in one temple; the pressure applied by the Tokugawa shogunate to prohibit such wandering priests, which resulted in a decrease in the number of temples and in the vitality of the priests who dwelled in them.

But the day must come when the profundity of Ippen's teaching will be recognized. Any discussion of the Japanese Nenbutsu teaching must not be limited to Hōnen and Shinran alone.

II

What standpoint among the many diverse schools of Far Eastern Buddhism does the Pure Land teaching occupy? It has many different subdivisions, but they all invariably go back to the common concept of non-duality. In fact, it is the variations in their conception of the nature of non-duality which may be said to constitute the differences between all the sects and schools of Buddhism. It is like a high mountain peak whose summit is a single spire but whose paths of ascent are diverse. Different as well are the aspects which characterize their routes. There will, moreover, be easy paths and difficult paths, gradual ascents and sudden ones, eastern approaches and western approaches. At any rate, this is one manner of considering sectarian differences.

Still, as I said, the object is the advaitistic summit.[7] Buddhism speaks

7. Ed. Advaita: The Sanskrit term for non-duality. While the concept is deeply embedded in Mahāyāna Buddhism (as *funi* 不二) the Sanskrit term only became current in Japan in modern times and thus illustrates the extended chronological perspective from which the author explains the teaching of Ippen.

of Emptiness, Suchness, and Self-identity, and the Middle Way. It is attempting to express by such concepts the countenance of non-duality. And this is not mere speculation, for Buddhism seeks the realm of non-duality in the matters of everyday life itself. Expressions such as "unrestrictedness" and "total freedom" attempt to convey the essential functioning of non-duality. When man attains to this freedom he experiences a profound and unparalleled sense of joy and thankfulness. Realization of this non-duality is "entrance into enlightenment," "seeing Buddha," "right awakening."

Generally, there may be said to be two paths to the realization of non-duality, wisdom (*prajñā*) and love or compassion (*karuṇā*), and they are dependent on a person's character and circumstances. "Wisdom" refers to *prajñā* and "love" to *karuṇā*. These may also be described as intellectual and emotional or affective characteristics. They are merely guides used for convenience and are in no way disparate or contradictory. They represent nothing more than overall tendencies.

Buddhism has been divided into the path of the holy man or saint, and the path of the Pure Land, the former being the path of wisdom, and the latter that of compassion. The Pure Land teaching—the teaching of Nenbutsu—in general attempts to reach the summit of non-duality by following the latter path. Hence it is a course that does not stop until one has given oneself totally to Amida Buddha, who may be termed the incarnation of great compassion.

Why is it that the holy path is equated with *jiriki*, self-power, and the Pure Land path with *tariki*, other-power? Because in the former, one's reliance on one's own wisdom is predominant, and in the latter, one entrusts everything to another power in recognition of one's own incapacity. This has been illustrated by comparing the former to a person walking a land route using the power of his own legs, and the latter to a person who reaches his destination by ship, entrusting himself to the power of the wind. Why, then, the need for two ways? Because some men are endowed with native ability, and some are not. Intelligent men and ignorant men, strong men and weak, these are differences that grow out of men's characters and environments, and they must be accepted as such.

But it is the vow of the Buddha to save all sentient beings, not the chosen few alone. The weak and ignorant are not equal to the way of self-power. In the degenerate world of the latter-day Dharma[8] another way arose, by which it was possible for the common man to gain salvation as well. He cannot be saved on the strength of his intellect or wisdom. He must be taken up by the power of love or compassion. The Pure Land

8. Translator's note. The *Latter-day Dharma* (*mappō* 末法) is the last of the three periods of gradual decline following the Buddha's decease; at the end of this period the Buddha is said to have predicted the total disappearance of Buddhism.

teaching is one which can effect his deliverance. Hōnen's great contribution was to elucidate this teaching especially for the ordinary people of his time. Shinran and Ippen later carried it to consummation. What then is this Pure Land teaching? For it to prove beneficial to all men, it must above all not be too difficult. A truly "easy" path must possess a *tariki* (other-power) character. The most definite expression of such an easy way appeared in the practice of Nenbutsu.

The word Nenbutsu means to "hold the Buddha in mind." Generally, this has taken two forms, contemplative Nenbutsu and Nenbutsu as vocal utterance. The former is a mental recollecting of the Buddha in one's mind; the latter the pronouncing of the Nenbutsu formula, or, as this is called in Japanese, *shōmyō*. Nenbutsu *shōmyō* means to repeat orally the six syllables, *Na-mu-a-mi-da-bu(tsu)*. It is the easiest possible Nenbutsu practice. Although the doctrines of the Jōdo, Shin, and Ji sects may differ in other respects, they are identical in placing their main emphasis on vocal Nenbutsu; for it was their desire in this simple religious act to perfect a practice that would enable ordinary people to attain rebirth in the Pure Land. Such is the Pure Land, or other-power, teaching.

The scriptural basis for their doctrine was found mainly in the eighteenth of the forty-eight vows set forth in the *Larger Sūtra of Eternal Life*:

> Even if I were to attain Buddhahood, if the sentient beings of the ten quarters of this world who desire in true faith to be born in the Pure Land were to repeat the Nenbutsu for even a few times, and yet not gain that rebirth, then would I not attain Supreme Enlightenment.

"I" is Dharmākara Bodhisattva, the name assumed by Amida Tathāgata during his disciplinary stage prior to attaining Buddhahood. Amida is his name upon attaining right awakening or enlightenment and becoming a Buddha. The important point in the above passage is that which advocates the practice of the vocal recitation (*shōmyō*) or *Namu-amida-butsu* as the way of salvation for sentient beings—an "easy way" expressly provided for those of inferior endowment, who have only to pronounce the words. For them, there could be no more welcome teaching. Hōnen repeats over and over: Simply pronounce it. How is it that the wonderful result of rebirth in the Pure Land is achieved from such an utterance?

"*Namu*" means to take refuge, *Amida* means infinite life, and *Butsu*, Buddha, an enlightened one. Infinite life is also expressed as infinite light, though infinite does not refer to any measurable length of time, for it does not belong to the province of dualistic longs and shorts, large and small.

The pronouncing of "*Namu-amida-butsu*" signifies two things: *Namu* is "taking refuge," the complete and utter relinquishing of self; and this involves trusting oneself to Amida Buddha because one cannot hope to attain salvation on one's own.

Hōnen called himself "Hōnen of the ten evil deeds." Shinran spoke of himself as a "*gutoku*," or bald-headed ignoramus. "A man of humble capacity" was Ippen's term of self-reference. Without this realization of one's own ordinariness and lack of ability, there can be no refuge or genuine faith in the other-power. Total, unreserved awareness that one is an ordinary, unenlightened man permits no traces of self-power. For the ordinary man, there is literally nothing else to do but to give himself up totally to the other-power. This "refuge" thus indicates a pure faith unadulterated by reasoning or traces of self-power.

The word "just" in Hōnen's advice "just pronounce it" contains profound religious meaning in itself, for unless the Nenbutsu is indeed just pronounced it cannot be said to be devoid of self. The instant all traces of self are gone, the pronouncer touches the supreme truth. At this infinitesimal point of time he becomes one with the infinite. So when Hōnen says "just pronounce it," he is speaking of a Nenbutsu that does not abide in the shadow of self-power. He called all other religious practices "auxiliary practices," as opposed to the pure and undefiled Nenbutsu itself. One of Hōnen's disciples, Shōkū, referred to it as a Nenbutsu of "plain wood" (*shiraki* 白木). It ceases to be a Nenbutsu that "I" pronounce.

Shinran said that the Nenbutsu possessed "meaningless meaning." We read in one of Ippen's Buddhist sermons, "Because they are sensible people, Shàndǎo called those who abandon argumentation and repeat the Nenbutsu single-mindedly, the best among men."[9] Only a Nenbutsu that does not abide in self is able to receive the other-power in its totality. To utter such a Nenbutsu is to enter the realm of the Pure Land.

A *myōkōnin*[10] named Tahara no Osono was once repeating the Nenbutsu over and over as was her usual practice, when someone came up and began to mock her: "Are you mouthing those empty Nenbutsu again?" Osono is said to have made the following reply in sincere gratitude:

> If the Nenbutsu of someone like me were to accrue some merit, what would happen then? You teach me that the Nenbutsu is "empty" ... I hadn't heard a "good friend" was in the neighborhood.[11]

"Empty Nenbutsu"—that is the beginning and the end of the Pure Land Nenbutsu teaching, which began with Hōnen and was brought to maturity in Shinran. Let us now turn and examine the course it took in the life and teaching of Ippen Shōnin.

---

9. Translator's note. This and all other quotations not otherwise identified are from Ippen's Buddhist sermons, the *Ippengoroku* 一遍語録.

10. Translator's note. The term *myōkōnin* 妙好人 (lit. wondrous good men) refers to especially devout Pure Land believers who practice the Nenbutsu in single-minded faith.

11. Translator's note. *Good friend—zenchishiki* 善知識, a general term referring to one who helps another achieve religious progress.

III

The budding of the religious mind begins early, in the insecurity man experiences on observation of the world's relentless flux. This may be stated in other terms as the desire for some constant within this flux. If the feeling of insecurity increases, self-reflection and a persisting concern over one's own actions will arise. Why am I so filled with envy and contentiousness? Why so seized by deceit and pride? On reflection, these anxieties are seen to come from man's confrontation with life and death, and from a division of self and other. Yet for the ordinary man, freedom from his evil karma is totally impossible. In which case, where can he turn? The Nenbutsu practice advocated by Hōnen represents a way to resolve this problem. In his work *Senjakushū*, Hōnen writes:

> Whenever you call out (the Name of) the Buddha, the Buddha hears you forthwith. If you constantly bow in reverence to the Buddha, the Buddha sees you. ... If sentient beings desire to see the Buddha, the Buddha immediately appears before them in answer to their thought.

These words are essentially similar to those of Jesus: "Seek and you shall find, knock and it shall be opened unto you."

When you pronounce the Name of the Buddha, the Buddha hears your voice—this is the salutary message of Hōnen's teaching. With the calling of the Name man is able to attain the joy of encountering the Buddha and having all anxieties dispelled. That is why Pure Land Buddhism speaks of it as "the act that definitely assures rebirth in the Pure Land" (*shōjō no gō* 正定の業). Hōnen's teaching of salvation was one that led from man to Buddha.

But with the passage of time Nenbutsu thought acquired an even greater maturity. On the foundation laid by Hōnen, Shinran erected the great pillars of his own Nenbutsu thought. Nenbutsu means to contemplate the Buddha, to entrust oneself to the Buddha. If so, then the calling of Nenbutsu does not, and moreover cannot, be dependent on one's own power. Rather than saying that man contemplates the Buddha, Shinran taught that, essentially, it is the Buddha that thinks of man: from being a practice that goes "from man to Buddha," Nenbutsu must mature into an act that proceeds from Buddha to man. In Shinran's own often repeated words, " 'Take refuge' [Namu] is the royal command of Amida's Original Vow summoning sentient beings." Pronouncing of the word "Namu" (take refuge), rather than meaning one is giving oneself to the Buddha, signifies the Buddha's summons to man: Take refuge in me. And it is only after hearing this call that man truly takes refuge. Without Amida Buddha's infinitely compassionate Prayer, there would be no way for ordinary people to be saved. According to Shinran, everything depends on the functioning of the Buddha, who makes his appeal to all sentient beings. For Hōnen, it was from the devotee to the Buddha; for Shinran, this process was reversed.

What, then, was Ippen's teaching? In holding that man supplicates to the Buddha, or that the Buddha beckons to man, there remains a basic man-Buddha dualism. Even when salvation is defined as the mutual interpenetration of the two, the words "man" and "Buddha" are still separate. If we make out the Buddhist Dharma to be the non-dualistic view, then it is desirable for us to seek a more profound standpoint. The Name (the pronouncing of the Nenbutsu), which is able to eliminate this duality, contains within it man's actual rebirth in the Pure Land. So instead of man contemplating Buddha or Buddha contemplating man, one must attain the realm where Nenbutsu is just Nenbutsu, and nothing else. We may consider the following quotations from Ippen as the last word on Nenbutsu teaching. A purer statement could not be made. "At the instant of each calling of the Name, the Nenbutsu recites the Nenbutsu." In the same way, the hearing of the Name is not man's hearing, neither is it the Buddha making man hear it. "The Name hears the Name; there is nothing to be heard apart from the Name... You must know it as the Name that does not allow of other thoughts." For Ippen, the words "*Namu-amida-butsu*" do not indicate the interpenetration of man who gives himself with the word "*Namu*," and the Buddha who receives him with the words "*Amida-butsu*." "*Namu*" and "*Amida-butsu*" are self-identical, and the meaning of the Name lies hidden in what is prior to its separation into two words. Consequently, rebirth cannot be said to exist apart from this un-bifurcated state. "It is simply that '*Namu-amida-butsu*' gains rebirth..." "Originally, the Name itself is the rebirth." Ippen's profundity lies in pointing out that it is not man's birth in the Pure Land but the birth of the Name. In the Name, not even the shadows of the two words "Buddha" and "man" leave any trace. This is what he means when he speaks of the Name being single and solitary. Over the pillars set in place by Shinran, Ippen thus placed the ridgepole and roofing, bringing to completion the great Nenbutsu edifice of Japanese Pure Land Buddhism.

One can also trace the transition from Hōnen to Shinran to Ippen in their respective interpretations of the word *Na-mu* (in Japanese, *kimyō* 帰命). Hōnen took them as meaning that man entrusts (*ki*) his life (*myō*) to the Buddha. Shinran regarded "*Namu*" as the Buddha directing (*myō*) man to entrust (*ki*) himself to Buddha. For Ippen, it meant to entrust or return oneself (*ki*) to the non-dualistic life-source (*myō*) that is prior to division into man and Buddha.

A similar development appears in their concepts of merit-transference (*ekō* 回向). The words *shishin ekō* 至心回向, which appear in the *Sūtra of Eternal Life*, were generally thought to refer to man transferring the merit he had accumulated in religious practice to the Buddha. That is how Hōnen understood it. But Shinran went against the normal interpretation and dared to understand it as merit-transference made by the absolute mind (*shishin*) of Amida, viewing all from the standpoint of Amida Buddha. It was of course his personal religious experience which led him to read it in this way. Pure Land thought thus achieved another forward step, with the act of merit-transference advancing into that of "no merit-transference" (*fuekō* 不回向). If the transference is from man, traces of self-power must be said to remain. But if everything comes from the side of the Buddha, then for man it is not transference of merit. This interpretation shows Shinran's desire to encompass everything within the working of Amida's other-power.

But is this indeed the final, deepest significance in merit-transference? In the Buddha's act of merit-transference to man there still remains a distinction between man and Buddha. Both man and Buddha must be taken up within the dynamic working of merit-transference, which has been described as knowable "only between Buddha and Buddha," or as a "communication between one Buddha and another." The words of Ippen quoted previously about "Nenbutsu doing Nenbutsu" constitute perhaps the ultimate response. He says:

> Though you put your mind into the Name, you must not put the Name into your mind.
> Though you are ruled by the Name, you must not influence the Name.
> ... The Name does not depend upon meaning; it is a Dharma independent of man's mind.
> There is no meaning in the Name of Amida. *Namu-amida-butsu.*[12]

Therefore,

> You may regard as gibberish all words other than Nenbutsu.
> Do not be preoccupied with knowledge about the Nenbutsu.
> Apart from this present *Namu-amida-butsu* do not cherish any distinction of before and after.[13]

Here, thoughts about merit-transference versus no merit-transference vanish, leaving only the aspect of merit-transference transferring its merit and Buddha face to face with Buddha.

Therefore, the "*Namu*" of the *ki* and the "*Amida Butsu*" that is the Dharma truth (*hō*) which is his refuge, are originally one. In a work entitled the *Kongōhōkaihiketsushō*[14] we read: "Within the Nenbutsu there is

12. Ed. These lines represent three separate sayings.

13. Ed. These lines also represent separate sayings.

14. Translator's note. *Kongōhōkaihiketsushō* 金剛法戒秘決章—a work dating from the mid-Kamakura period, attributed in later times to Hōnen, but this is doubtful.

never devotee and Dharma. What is there to call a practiser? What to call Dharma?" The concept of oneness of *ki* and *hō* is the philosophic principle of the Pure Land school. The Chinzei branch of the Jōdo sect, the Shin sect, and the Ji sect all succeeded to this tradition. Ippen says: "Since *ki* and *hō* are the non-dual Name, apart from *Namu-amida-butsu* neither subject nor object has any place to turn."

In the *Anjinketsujōshō*,[15] we find: "Though we pronounce *Namu-amida-butsu*, we do not thereby draw nearer the Buddha-body; the virtue of enlightenment as the oneness of *ki* and *hō* appears in the act of sentient beings reciting the Nenbutsu." "Returning to the *Namu-amida-butsu* of the *ki-hō* oneness, is called Nenbutsu *samādhi*."

When he speaks of the "oneness" of *ki* and *hō*, he is of course referring to the teaching of non-duality.

IV

All Nenbutsu schools advocate the pronouncing of the Name. Prior to the establishment of the distinct and separate sects of Japanese Pure Land Buddhism, the Nenbutsu was included among the practices of various sects in China and Japan. From early times, for example, the so-called *jōgyōsanmai* 常行三昧, the "*samādhi* of constant practice," was a prominent discipline, the "constant practice" referred to being that of Nenbutsu. After all, what is wanted is Nenbutsu in the normal activities of daily life, rising with Nenbutsu and retiring at day's end with Nenbutsu as well. This is a reason some Nenbutsu followers make it a practice to intone a constant Nenbutsu, up to tens of thousands of times each day. There is a Jōdo sect temple in Kyōto known popularly as the "Hyakumanben" ("One Million Nenbutsu Repetitions"), which shows the inseparable role the actual practice of Nenbutsu has played in the Japanese Pure Land schools. In this temple[16] there is a great rosary (also called Hyakumanben). Devotees sit around in a large circle and take a section of the rosary and pass the beads through their hands, reciting the Nenbutsu as they count them off one by one. In the Pure Land tradition such practices are called *tanenbutsu* 多念仏, many Nenbutsu callings, in which large numbers of repetitions are preferred. It was one of Hōnen's disci-

15. Translator's note. *Anjinketsujōshō* 安心決定鈔. A work which contains one of the clearest expositions of the other-power teaching, and which has been very influential in the Shin sect especially. It has been attributed to Ken'i, one of Ippen's fellow disciples.

16. Ed. The name of this Jōdo temple is Chionji 知恩寺. It should not be confused with Chion'in, also in Kyōto and of greater importance for the Jōdo school. Hyakumanben 百万遍 is the name given to the main crossroads at the location of Kyōto University. Note that the character for *-ben* is the same as the *-pen* in the name of Ippen, which literally means "one time."

ples, Ryūkan Risshi, who made the principle of many repetitions a matter of Pure Land doctrine.

But it is not that there is merit or virtue in great amounts of Nenbutsu. *Tanenbutsu* means nothing more than this: if one spends all one's time in Nenbutsu, it leads naturally to many repetitions. Hence even a single repetition, if it is uttered in sincerity and purity, in accord with ultimate reality, is an assurance of rebirth in the Pure Land. Even the Pure Land sūtras speak of repeating the Nenbutsu "up to ten" times, and "down to" one time. The idea thus developed of a "mind pacified" (*anjin* 安心) through "faith" being more profound than Nenbutsu as "practice." This notion is known as the *ichinengi* 一念義 or "principle of one calling." It derives from another of Hōnen's disciples, Kōsai, and expresses even the uselessness of many Nenbutsu repetitions.

But this view was expelled from the Jōdo sect as heretical; and understandably so, for the idea that a single calling of Nenbutsu is enough is hardly in keeping with the orthodox Jōdo position of a more or less continual Nenbutsu. Naturally, Hōnen, the founder of the sect, advocated many repetitions in terms of practice. He said: "Of the practices for Pure Land rebirth, Nenbutsu is foremost."

Shinran, however, put greater emphasis on "faith" than on "practice," and held that the practice for attaining rebirth in the Pure Land was rooted in the devotee's faith. Hence he valued the *quality* of the single repetition over the *quantity* of many. The story, which first appeared in Shinran's 13th-century "biography," the *Godenshō*, in which Shinran's master Hōnen is said to have upheld the position of faith over that of practice, is surely historically inaccurate. Pure Land tradition distinguishes two general branches of Pure Land teaching, one which emphasizes Nenbutsu practice (*kigyōha* 起行派), and one which stresses faith (*anjinha* 安心派). The Jōdo sect belongs to the former group, and the Shin sect to the latter.

Therefore, in the Shin sect the pronouncing of the Name, rather than being regarded as an act bringing about rebirth, came to be interpreted as a Nenbutsu of "thanksgiving" (*hōsha* 報謝). This is a reason for the dispute between advocates of one calling and advocates of many callings that arose within the sect from an early period. Hōnen's attitude with regard to the question was characteristically equitable and moderate:

> If one pronounces the Nenbutsu carelessly because of the teaching that one attains rebirth in the Pure Land by one calling of the Name or by ten callings of the Name, one's faith will hinder one's practice. If one feels uncertain about the efficacy of only one calling because of the teaching to recite the Nenbutsu continuously without let-up, one's practice of the Nenbutsu will hinder one's faith. Believe, trusting in the efficacy of one calling, and then continue that practice throughout your life.

Viewing the Nenbutsu horizontally, we have the Jōdo sect's *practice*; viewing it vertically, we have the Shin sect's faith. What is the Ji sect's standpoint regarding these two?

Ippen is no different from Shinran in the belief that a single Nenbutsu calling can assure Pure Land rebirth. But this "one calling" is not a numerical frequency. "One calling" is something that must come into play at each and every calling. Therefore, there is a continuity of such "one callings." And this is not a matter of many callings for their own sake, nor many callings intended as recompense or thanksgiving. It is a series of single callings that arise newly and freshly at every new moment. Hence, for Ippen there were numerically neither one calling nor many callings.

He said that "for the Name there is no reckoning of one calling or ten callings." Since it is a quantity-less Nenbutsu, why give rise to distinctions of one and many? One calling in itself is many callings, and vice versa.

The Jōdo sect leans predominantly to the side of many callings, placing importance on the continuity of the Nenbutsu. On the other hand, the Shin sect inclines toward the idea of one calling, with all other additional callings coming to signify merely an act of thanksgiving. The Ji sect looked to a Nenbutsu beyond numerical distinctions, and thus eliminated the contradiction between one and many callings. "There should not be any distinction of before and after apart from the *Namu-amida-butsu* of this very moment," is how Ippen puts it. "Distinctions," of course, also refers to those between one calling, many callings, and thanksgiving.[17] The Nenbutsu must be pure and unalloyed.

Two opposing ideas concerning man's rebirth in the Pure Land exist in the Pure Land tradition, the notions of *rinjūraigō* 臨終来迎 (also termed simply *raigō*) and *heizeigōjō* 平生業成 (also expressed as *furaigō*, that is, no *raigō*). The Jōdo sect is generally identified with the former concept, which holds that one is welcomed into the Pure Land by the coming of Amida and his attendant Bodhisattvas at the time of one's death. The latter concept, associated with the Shin sect, teaches that the act effecting Pure Land rebirth is something which can be perfected in this life without waiting for the next.

The idea of deathbed salvation has its original source in the Three Pure Land sūtras, one of which, the *Amida Sūtra*, states simply:

> that person, when about to die, will see Amida Buddha and his Bodhisattva host appear before him. And immediately after his death, with his mind undisturbed, he can be reborn into the Pure Land of Amida Buddha.

It is not difficult to imagine the ardor with which Pure Land followers

17. Ed. This sentence has been slightly rephrased.

embraced this idea. Its humanistic appeal was enhanced especially by the imaginative depictions of Buddhist painters such as Eshin (Genshin). Paintings attributed to him such as the Yamagoe Amida, the Coming of the 25 Bodhisattvas, and the widely esteemed Coming of the Three Honored Ones, give fine expression to the devoted faith of these followers. In a sense, birth in the Pure Land has the meaning of being received by Amida Buddha. Therefore, if we visit temples of the Jōdo sect, we find that the central figure of worship, Amida Buddha, is depicted coming toward us to welcome us into the Pure Land. Hōnen said:

> Since Amida's original prayer vows to save all sinful sentient beings through the calling of the Name, when we simply pronounce the Nenbutsu in singleminded faith, there is no doubt that the coming of Amida Buddha will follow as a natural matter of course.

There being no rebirth without Amida's coming, the Jōdo sect has always held pictorial representations of this "welcome" in particular esteem. But in the Shin sect this belief died out. The reason, as I stated before, is that the Shin sect teaches *heizeigōjō* (rebirth attained in daily life), that is, Pure Land rebirth may be assured prior to death, that the work of rebirth may be consummated in one's everyday life in this world. Why should Pure Land rebirth be attainable only at death? If one is able to establish true faith during one's lifetime, then the assurance of rebirth is attained. Therefore, if one can attain to "one thought" or "one calling" (*ichinen* 一念) of faith, one has no need to look to the coming of Amida at the time of death. This is the Shin sect's idea of *furaigō* (literally, "not-coming"), that is, not depending on Amida's deathbed welcome. The Shin priest Zonkaku (1290–1373) writes in his work *Jōdoshin'yōshō* 浄土真要鈔 that:

> The principle of *heizeigōjō* held by followers of Shinran does not emphasize the hope of Amida and the Bodhisattvas coming to lead us to the Pure Land at death. It teaches their "not-coming," and is not wedded to the principle of "coming." *Heizeigōjō* applies only to those who encounter the Dharma during their earthly life.
>
> And if one were to encounter the Dharma at the point of death, then one would attain rebirth at that moment. We do not say that it occurs during this life. We do not say that it occurs upon death. We say simply that when true faith is attained, rebirth is forthwith determined. Thus we say that rebirth is attained at the same time as faith (*sokutokuōjō* 即得往生).

In Shin sect temples one therefore does not find enshrined the figure of Amida coming to welcome devotees into the Pure Land. In the alteration of view regarding Pure Land rebirth from *rinjūraigō* to *heizeigōjō* we trace the path that goes from the Jōdo sect to the Shin sect. Yet the transition from "coming" to "no coming" can be said to follow in the same channel as the change from many callings to one calling, from merit-transference to no merit-transference. "No coming" does not leave the realm of dualistic thought any more than coming does. Once again, was not Ippen the one who brought this conflict to a final stop?

The Jōdo sect formulated a view of Pure Land rebirth centered at the time of death. The Shin sect's view had to do with this life. The Ji sect saw through to the basic core of Pure Land rebirth in its view of time of death-*qua*-this life, preaching that there is no time of death that is apart from this present life; that each moment is in fact the time of death; that the coming of Amida and the Bodhisattvas occurs within this life. In a word, wherever the Nenbutsu is called, there is the continual coming of the Buddha. Thus death occurs in this life and the coming of the Buddha takes place at each moment. This gives a new touch of life to the view of Amida's welcoming visitation at death that the Shin sect had forgotten, and still encompasses the idea of death and rebirth in this present life that the Jōdo sect overlooked. Or, as Ippen tells us,

> Apart from this present Nenbutsu there is no time-of-death Nenbutsu; it is "time of death" within this present life.
>
> The reciting of the Nenbutsu is itself the site of Amida's coming. Know truly that the reciting of the Nenbutsu is the coming of the Buddha, and you have gained absolute assurance of his coming.
>
> In *Namu-amida-butsu* there is neither time of death nor this life. ... This present instant of Nenbutsu calling is established as the time of death. Each such instant is therefore the time of death. Each such instant is Pure Land rebirth.

The teachings of non-transference of merit (*fuekō*) or Amida's not-coming (*furaigō*) cannot be said to have fully sounded the non-dualistic Buddhist Dharma. Nenbutsu has no relation to temporal distinctions. "This present Nenbutsu" does not allow of before or after. Therefore, in Nenbutsu the difference between this life and time of death, between coming and not coming, disappears.

Hōnen saw Pure Land rebirth chiefly in terms of the moment of death, and Shinran saw it in this life, in a single Nenbutsu uttered in true faith. But it was Ippen who came to understand Pure Land rebirth in terms of this life *qua* time of death united in the calling of the Name.

V

Prior to the Japanese Nenbutsu sects no way had existed that fully actualized the universal prayer to provide salvation for all sentient beings. In the various sects belonging to the Holy Path teaching, enlightenment was limited to the select few able to perform the austere practices. The development of the other-power sects opened the doors of the Buddha's teaching to the lesser mortals hitherto shut out.

In fact, the merit of the Pure Land teaching is primarily that it was able to equalize the differences that exist between people. Sexual distinction was swept into the background. Even women, who were said to be especially sinful, were promised expressly the salutary possibility of rebirth. Even the lowest class of courtesan could claim its benefits. Differences of social rank were done away with, as were those of wealth and poverty. The common people were welcomed together with royalty and nobility. The appearance of the Nenbutsu teaching meant that each and every person was accorded the chance of attaining Pure Land rebirth. It did not matter whether one was a monk or a layman, wise or dull-witted. In fact, it preached that the total illiterate would be taken up in the Buddha's compassion even more cordially. Nor did it balk, as previous Buddhist teachings had, at the contrast separating the good and the evil. On the contrary, it declared distinctly that evil men were the true object of Amida's teaching. For the calling of Nenbutsu, therefore, it makes no difference whether or not one observes the Buddhist precepts. It matters not if one is a criminal, though of course this does not mean to condone evil. Amida's compassion is first and foremost a favor or "gift" accorded to all men through the power of his vow. For the sake of the ordinary man, the other-power renders all things totally and wonderfully incomprehensible.

On this point of the grace or "favor" imparted by the Buddha (*button* 仏恩), Pure Land teachers did nothing more than simply encourage the exclusive recitation of the Nenbutsu. Still, such Nenbutsu practice must be based on faith. No, faith is given even greater weight than practice. As I stated on a previous page, this is in effect the doctrinal shift that we find from Hōnen to Shinran. The great fifteenth-century Shin priest Rennyo, who succeeded to Shinran's teaching, said, "You can wrap yourself up in Nenbutsu-callings seven or eight layers deep, but if you don't attain faith, rebirth is impossible."

All religion is based on faith. With the attainment of faith one is assured of drawing near to the Buddha: without it, one grows remote from him. That is why faith is said to be the root of practice. The Shin school continually stresses this point.

In one sense, I do not think this view is mistaken. On the other hand, is an other-power teaching unburdened by distinctions of men's good and evil, wisdom and lack of wisdom, justified in making the line between faith and lack of faith a matter of established doctrine? Are the doors of salvation closed to those suffering people who are unable to attain to faith? Is not faith too a power that is limited to a select group? Are the blessings of Pure Land rebirth not accorded to those without faith?

This very question is the ultimate one that must confront anyone who would establish a Nenbutsu teaching. It was Ippen who felt compelled to give it its most profound answer. Not only did he eliminate the distinction between good and evil, wise and dull-witted, in the face of Pure Land rebirth, he swept away differences of faith and lack of faith to boot. Latent here was the opportunity by which the other-power teaching was to progress from the Shin sect to the Ji sect. During his wandering throughout the country distributing his Buddhist charms, Ippen once encountered a priest of one of the disciplinary schools. He held out a charm, saying, "Establish faith, repeat the Name, and accept this charm." The priest refused it, saying, "It would be wrong for me to accept it, for I have no faith in the 'one calling' ... that I do not is something that lies beyond my power." The priest's reply was made in all sincerity. He was not equivocating. How can one honestly continue to persuade non-believers to have faith? Is it not meaningless to distribute charms to those without faith? That night, deeply troubled by such thoughts, Ippen stopped at Kumano Shrine, where Kumano Myōjin was enshrined. The Myōjin was widely believed to be the incarnation of Amida temporarily manifesting himself in the form of a Japanese *kami*. Ippen shut himself up in the shrine and prayed for some resolution to his problems. After he had fallen asleep, the Myōjin appeared to him in a dream and gave him the instruction:

> O wandering priest, engaged in spreading the all-pervading Nenbutsu. Why do you go about it in such a worthless way? It is not through your efforts that sentient beings are enabled to attain rebirth. Their rebirth by means of Nenbutsu is something that was determined ten *kalpas* ago through Amida Buddha's enlightenment. You should distribute your charms without differentiating between the faithful and the faithless, the pure and the impure.

Ippen's great joy made him shout out, "From this moment I have relinquished forever the self-satisfaction of self-power." Man's rebirth in the Pure Land was decided once and for all at the very instant Amida attained to supreme enlightenment ten *kalpas* in the past. Man does not reach the Pure Land by his own power, nor can he make others attain it. Neither is rebirth such that it can be influenced by mental distinctions such as faith and non-faith, pure and impure. Were rebirth possible through man's own power, faith and purity as well would be unnecessary. Rebirth was consummated with Amida's enlightenment long ago. Man's faith is not needed to support it. So how can distinctions of good and evil, faith and lack of faith disturb Amida's original prayer? Ippen says,

> A person who wearies of this world and wishes to abandon it and joyfully

> seek the Pure Land should not trouble over faith or lack of it, purity or impurity, sinfulness or goodness. He must simply recite *Namu-amida-butsu* in the joy of having chanced to hear of the wondrous Name of Amida.

Not to trouble over faith or lack of it, is the other-power teaching's final astonishing statement. Was it not for these very people without faith, just as they are, that Amida created his way of salvation? Pure Land rebirth is something that was accomplished with Amida's enlightenment and is not governed by anything within man's limited capability. To say that rebirth is impossible without faith fails to know fully the power of Amida Buddha. The profundity of Ippen's religious experience finally went beyond faith and lack of faith, and there discerned the full promise of Pure Land rebirth.

VI

In the *Myōgishingyōshū* 明義進行集, a treatise on the Jōdo sect's doctrine and practice, the following quotation from Hōnen is recorded.

> At first, in addition to doing the Nenbutsu, I too used to read the *Amida Sūtra* three times a day, once according to the Táng pronunciation, once according to the Wǔ pronunciation, and once according to the Japanese reading. But since in effect this sūtra preaches just to pronounce the Nenbutsu, I have now ceased the practice of sūtra-reading, and devote myself single-mindedly to the Nenbutsu.

The *Amida Sūtra* instructs, "Keep and maintain Amida's Name single-mindedly and without wavering." Are we to be remiss in our practice of Nenbutsu for the sake of benefits sought in sūtra readings? Is not the practitioner of single-minded Nenbutsu the true Nenbutsu devotee? This led Hōnen and his followers to the practice of a "continual" Nenbutsu recited from morning till night.

In the letters of Shinran's wife Eshinni a similar story is related of Shinran. Shinran embarked on a plan to recite for the benefit of sentient beings the entire text of the three Pure Land sūtras one thousand times. Then, recalling that there was nothing lacking in the Name by itself, he ceased reading the sūtras and returned to single-minded Nenbutsu practice. Later, however, when he was once feverishly ill, he is said to have babbled off what seemed words from the sūtras. After the fever had run its course and he was told what had transpired, he is said to have been deeply ashamed and to have reproved himself for conceiving he should need anything other than his faith in the Nenbutsu. To do away with even sūtra-readings and concentrate exclusively on pronouncing the Name is the way of the Nenbutsu school.

Yet in order to preach about this Nenbutsu school both Hōnen and

Shinran left behind them tens of thousands of written words; Hōnen has his *Senjakuhongan nenbutsushū*, and Shinran the *Kyōgyōshinshō*. Both works employ a great many quotations from scriptural sources, and marshal logic and rhetoric for the purpose of elucidating the other-power doctrine. Why did they bequeath such voluminous literary legacies? Actually, it was simply to explain the incomprehensible mystery contained in the Name. It should be noted too that the followers of the Jōdo and Shin sects revere as their basic religious texts the above works of their respective founders.

Yet, are not these works merely in the interest of the six syllables of the Name? No. Such verbal abundance is but a shadow before the Nenbutsu. The Nenbutsu should not, in the interests of any "other words," become a shadow of itself. When Ippen realized his death was approaching, he took all the religious writings in his possession as well as works he himself had written in the course of his life, and committed them to the fire. To his disciples in their profound sorrow, he spoke the brief instruction, "The religious teaching of my entire lifetime has been reduced to *Namu-amida-butsu*."

There the essence of the Pure Land teaching emerges in its entirety: to leave nothing at all behind and set the Name alone in bold relief. There can be nothing lacking if only we have the Name. The countless volumes spawned by the Pure Land tradition in China and Japan teach nothing beyond the pronouncing of the six syllables, *Namu-amida-butsu*. The Ji sect thus has no scripture for its followers to place their reliance on. For them it is the six syllables and the six syllables alone. No scripture could surpass that.

Although it is true some of Ippen's sayings have been handed down to us, they are merely the record his disciples later set to writing as they remembered it. For Ippen himself, the six syllables themselves filled all needs. Or, it would be better to say that they alone were truly valid. Nothing else could surpass them. No other words must be allowed to defile them or reduce their purity. In order to increase the efficacy of Nenbutsu to the utmost, one should use the least possible number of other words, for they are all superfluous. Amida's Name alone and nothing but the Name! Has any other Pure Land teacher raised the Name to such heights? Drawing from his predecessors Hōnen and Shinran, Ippen gave the finishing touch to the Pure Land teaching. According to his recorded sayings, the *Ippengoroku*:

> Someone asked Ippen if he had made any decision about what should be done after his death. Ippen replied, "After me, make non-succession the way of succession. ... I mean my 'succession' is the Nenbutsu-calling of all sentient beings. *Namu-amida-butsu*."

Ippen is said to have once met the Zen master Hattō Kokushi (Kakushin,

1207–1298), the founder of the Fuke sect of Japanese Zen. Kakushin asked him to say something about the meaning of the words, "the arising of thought is in itself realization." Ippen responded with a poem:

> When the Name is recited
> There is no Buddha, no self,
> Only the voice of
> *Namu-amida-butsu.*

"You haven't reached it yet," Kakushin said, meaning that he thought Ippen still lacked full awakening. Ippen answered him with another verse:

> When the Name is recited,
> There is no Buddha, no self.
> *Namu-amida-butsu,*
> *Namu-amida-butsu.*

When he heard this, Kakushin awarded Ippen his seal of approval as a Zen master.

Other-power, self-power, Pure Land teaching, Zen teaching—we see here again the truth of non-duality. Ippen elevated the path of Nenbutsu to its ultimate summit.

(Translated by Norman Waddell)

— 12 —

Shinran and his Song on Amida Buddha

Beatrice Lane Suzuki

I

Introduction[1]

The Songs of Shinran Shōnin were written by him in praise of the Buddha Amitābha [Japanese: Amida] and also of certain sūtras and of the patriarchs of the Shin sect: Nāgārjuna,[2] Vasubandhu,[3] Donran,[4] Dōshaku,[5] Zendō,[6] Genshin,[7] and Genkū.[8] In the Japanese language they are called

1. Ed. This short account of Shinran was originally placed after the "Song in Praise of Amitābha Buddha" which follows below. Some characters have been added for the convenience of students; however others will be found in the Character List for Historical Persons.
2. Nāgārjuna (J. Ryūju) lived during the second or third centuries CE. He was a great Buddhist scholar and several sects claim him as their founder. Ed. Nāgārjuna, Vasubandhu (and Asaṅga) were Indian, and the alternative names shown are Japanese readings only.
3. Vasubandhu (J. Seshin), 450 CE. With his brother Asaṅga he founded the Yogācāra school of Buddhist philosophy.
4. Donran (Chinese: Tánluán), 476–542 CE. His chief work is "Commentary on Vasubandhu's Discourse on the Pure Land." Ed. The Chinese characters for this and various other names will be found in the Character List for Historical Persons. Donran/Tánluán also composed the *Zàn amítuófó jì* 讃阿彌陀佛偈 J. *Sanamidabutsuge* on which Shinran's *wasan* is based.
5. Dōshaku (Chinese: Dàochuò), 562–645 CE. The author of *Treatise on Peace and Joy*.
6. Zendō (Chinese: Shàndǎo) died 681 CE. He left several important works on the Pure Land teaching, the chief of which is a commentary on the *Meditation Sūtra* (*Kangyō*).
7. Genshin, 942–1017 CE. First Japanese patriarch of the Pure Land school.
8. Genkū (Hōnen Shōnin), 1133–1212 CE. Japanese founder of the Pure Land (Jōdo) sect.

wasan, and this word is generally translated as "hymn" or "psalm," but as these terms have too Christian a flavour, I have preferred the simple word "songs"—which indeed they are.[9]

Shōnin means "sage" or "holy man," and is sometimes translated as "Saint." Most students of Japanese Buddhism are familiar with the life of Shinran Shōnin. But for those who are not, I shall relate it most briefly.

He was born near Kyōto in 1173 CE, and although there is some historical doubt as to his parentage and early life, he is said to have been the son of Lord Hino Arinori. He lost his parents while very young and was brought up by his uncle. When he was only nine years old he became a priest of the Tendai School, given the name Hannen, and thereafter spent twenty years in the life of a Buddhist priest at the temple of Enryakuji on Mt. Hiei near Kyōto, where he assiduously devoted himself to the study of Buddhist philosophy. But owing to spiritual dissatisfaction he joined Hōnen Shōnin's circle and learned his doctrine of salvation through faith in Amida.

This doctrine Shinran developed still further, for while Hōnen believed in the merit of good works[10] and the recital of the Nenbutsu, Shinran believed in faith alone and established his doctrine entirely upon it. He devoted his life to preaching and teaching his doctrine. He died quietly in Kyōto in 1262.

In the *Wasan* we can find the essential points of his doctrine.

The name Amida, Amitābha in Sanskrit, signifies infinite Light, and it is the first axiom of Shin [Buddhism] that Amida sends out his light to illuminate this world. So wherever we see beauty, holiness, compassion or love manifested in this world of ignorance and illusion, we can know that it is because Amida's light is shining through the darkness.

Amitābha is Light in space while Amitāyus, another name for Amida, is Life in time, so Amida is the Master of Space and Time and through him we transcend both.

An important point not only in Shin but in all Mahāyāna Buddhism is that salvation is universal; there are no beings on whom the light does not shine; all may awake to enlightenment. This being the fact, Shinran appeals to us to take refuge in the True Light which is Amitābha.

---

9. The *Wasan* have been translated twice into English; in 1922 by Mr. Oshima of Ryūkoku College, published by the West Honganji; and in 1921 by S. Yamabe and L. Adams Beck in "The Wisdom of the East" series. The former is very literal but sometimes not quite accurate and the latter, although beautiful in literary style, also contains inaccuracies. Herewith a new translation is made of the first thirty-two stanzas composing the first set of songs in praise of Amitābha. There are several sets of *Wasan*, but this set which may be called *The Praises of Amida* puts forth succinctly Shinran's doctrine in its first thirty-two stanzas, the remaining sixteen stanzas being devoted to a description of the Pure Land.

10. Ed. The idea that Hōnen believed in the value of merit arising from good works is disputable.

But how are we to take refuge through faith in Amida's power to save? To get this faith is not so easy as one might think and is claimed by teachers of Shin. There has to be a strong effort to obtain it. So in the end it may be as difficult as the efforts of Self-Power sect believers.

To obtain this faith corresponds to conversion among the Christians. According to Shinran's own explanation, the experience should be sudden, ōchō 横超 as he called it. Ōchō means "to leap crosswise" and may be contrasted to Zen's "straightforward leap." Both Zen and Shin belong to what is known as the "abrupt school." The progress made in the understanding of the truth is not gradual, not going from step to step as is done in logic but it is a leap over the gap. You come to the end of your journey, you halt and are at a loss how to make a further advance as there is before you a gaping abyss. Zen jumps straight forward while Shin jumps crosswise. The line of Zen suggests continuous extension and according to Shin is not quite a leap in its proper sense. What Shin accomplishes is really discontinuous, proving that the deed springs from the "other power"[11] which is Amida.

This is similar to what the Christian philosopher Søren Kierkegaard[12] calls the Leap and the Instant. In his *Philosophical Fragments* he says, "And now the Instant! Such an instant has a peculiar character. It is short indeed and temporal, as every instant is fleeting, as every instant is, gone like all instants, the following instant, and yet it is decisive, and yet it is full of eternity. Such an instant must have a special name, let us call it the *fullness of time*."[13] Shin would call it the fullness of faith.

And again Kierkegaard says, "Religious faith is not to be reached by any approximations of proof and probability but only by a leap."

The *Wasan* also tell us that the Light can dissolve the bondage of karma, and that not only is the darkness of ignorance broken but that joy is given to all beings through Amida's compassion.

Another important point of Shin doctrine to be met with is that those who see the Light and trust to it are, by means of their firm faith, bound for the Pure Land, there to be enlightened and attain Buddhahood.

What is the Pure Land? It is made by the will of Dharmākara who

---

11. "Other power": Shin makes the distinction between *tariki* 他力 and *jiriki* 自力. *Jiriki* means "self-power," i.e. depending on one's own virtues for rebirth in the Pure Land, while *tariki*, literally "other power," is to put oneself in a state of complete passivity and losing self altogether in the other, i.e. Amida. Zen according to Shin is *jiriki* and Shin is pure *tariki*.

12. Søren Kierkegaard, religious philosopher of Denmark, born 1813, died 1855. He had through his writings a great influence on many modern philosophers and religionists.

13. Walter Lowrie, *Kierkegaard*, 312. Ed. Walter Lowrie (1868–1959) wrote several works on Kierkegaard, but Suzuki was probably referring to Lowrie's biography of the Danish theologian which appeared in 1938.

vowed not to attain to enlightenment unless through him all the worlds became enlightened.[14]

The mysterious Pure Land is built and adorned by his Original Vow, and to be born there, self-will must be renounced, and those who enter must have faith spring up in their hearts.

We have just seen that beings will be enlightened and attain Buddhahood in the Pure Land. To attain Buddhahood is a characteristic of Mahāyāna Buddhism. According to Mahāyāna, all sentient beings have the Buddha-nature and therefore must manifest a progressive development toward Buddhahood. In the so-called *jiriki* 自力 or "self-power" school of Buddhism such as Shingon or Zen, enlightenment or realization of Buddhahood can take place generally only after long preparation in this life, but in Shin it can be consummated only in the Pure Land after death in this world, and unlike Zen, true enlightenment can never take place in this world. Beings can enter the Pure Land on the ground that they are the Buddha's sons. The Pure Land is not to be regarded as a material paradise but as a positive Nirvana. Shinran calls the Pure Land Nirvana past all understanding where we labour for the salvation of all sentient beings.

The Pure Land is conceived of not only as a land of happiness and peace but as a field of enlightenment for the practice of *gensō ekō* 還相回向 ("returning to this world") in order to help sentient beings.

In one of the *Wasan* we read that after the Bodhisattvas in the Pure Land have learned how to teach all beings, they will come again to this world to enlighten them. From this we see that Paradise or the Pure Land is a place or condition or consciousness of activity, and not of negative rest.

Trust and faith in Amida is all-important in Shin Buddhism. In the doctrine of the Southern School, merit is stressed, but in Shin, merit is entirely cast aside. Good works are not necessary for salvation, instead we must throw ourselves upon the mercy of the compassionate Buddha, and by means of our faith in him, we have his assurance of salvation, for in the eighteenth of his forty-eight vows, he declared that if sentient beings have faith and, wishing to be reborn in his land, repeat his name and yet should not be reborn, then he would forfeit his own great enlightenment.

Shinran laid the greatest stress upon faith rather than, like Hōnen, on the repetition of the Name (Nenbutsu). In fact Shinran's Buddhism was a last break with ritualism; for him, it is not necessary to take time and energy for the practice of the Nenbutsu, simply turning in faith to Amida is quite enough.

Among the twenty-two stanzas of the "Songs of the Pure Land" based upon the *Larger Sukhāvatīvyūha Sūtra*,[15] the fourth stanza reads thus:

---

14. This is called "The Original Vow."

15. *Sukhāvatīvyūha Sūtra*: translated into Chinese by Saṃghavarman (J. Kōsōgai) in 252 CE.

The idea of the Tathāgata's appearance in this world
Was to disclose the truth of Amida's Original Vow
Which is however both as difficult to encounter and understand
As the appearance of the *udumbara* flower.[16]

This is another leading tenet of the Shin school of Buddhism. In the *Shōshinge*[17] Shinran states that the reason Śākyamuni was revealed to this world was solely in order to proclaim the Vow of Amitābha.

In the *Amitāyurdhyāna Sūtra*[18] it is Śākyamuni who explains to the Queen Vaidehī the teaching of Amida and the Pure Land. As Song No. 8 expresses it,

> Men were ripe for hearing the Pure Land doctrine which advises them to give up self-reliance and dependence upon merit and instead to desire to be established in the faith and power of compassionate Amitābha.

Besides faith in Amida men must express gratitude and in Shin the Nenbutsu is used only as an expression of gratitude or of praise. A number of Shinran's songs extol the virtue of praising the Name of Amida and give assurance that the Name will guard all who use it with a heart of faith and that if they remember Amida they are sure to see him and be saved.

So we see that the Songs of Shinran express poetically and emotionally most of his religious views and we can understand that they are greatly prized by the followers of the Shin sect.

II

Shinran's Song in Praise of Amitābha

1. Since the attainment of Buddhahood by Amitābha
   Ten kalpas[19] have now passed away;
   The Light radiating from the Dharmakāya[20] has no limits:
   It illuminates the world's blindness and darkness.
2. The Light of His wisdom is measureless,
   All conditional forms without exception
   Are enveloped in the dawning Light;
   Therefore take refuge in the True Light.

---

16. Udumbara flower: the *ficus glomerata*, a fig tree supposed to bloom once in three thousand years.
17. *Shōshinge* is a poem written by Shinran which summarizes the Shin faith. In this poem we find what is missing from the *Wasan*, namely the teaching that laymen and priests and saints are alike before Amida, and that even the wicked if they turn to Amida in faith can be saved and all their sins forgiven.
18. *Amitāyurdhyāna Sūtra*: [Ed. said to have been] translated into Chinese by Kālayaśas (J. Kyōryōyasha) in the first half of the fourth century.
19. Kalpa: a long period of time.
20. Dharmakāya: generally translated "Law-Body." The highest reality of personality.

3. Amida's Light is like a wheel radiating without bounds.
   The Buddha[21] declared that all things illumined by His[22] Light
   Are freed from all forms of being and not-being.
   Take refuge in the One who is universally enlightened.
4. The clouds of Light have, like space, no hindrances;
   All that have obstructions are not impeded by them;
   There is no one who is not embraced in His Soft Light:
   Take refuge in Him who is beyond thought.
5. Nothing can be compared to His Pure Light;
   The result of encountering this Light
   Destroys all karma bondage:
   So take refuge in Him who is the Ultimate Haven.
6. Amida Buddha's illuminating Light is above all,
   So he is called the Sovereign Buddha of Flaming Light,
   The darkness of the three evil paths[23] is opened:
   Take refuge in the Great Arhat.[24]
7. The radiance of His Light of Truth surpasses all,
   So He is called the Buddha of Pure Light:
   Those who are embraced in the Light
   Are cleansed from the dirt of karma and attain enlightenment.
8. However far His Light illumines, love penetrates.
   The joy of faith is attained,
   So we are told.
   Take refuge in the Great One who gives comfort.
9. He is known as the Buddha of the Light of Prajñā[25]
   Because He dispels the darkness of ignorance;
   The Buddhas and the beings of the Three Vehicles[26]
   All join in praising Him.
10. As there is a constant flow of Light,
   He is known as the Buddha of Increase;
   Because of perceiving the power of light with uninterrupted faith,
   We are born into the Pure Land.
11. As the Buddha of Light knows naught of measurement,
   He is known as the Buddha of Miraculous Light:

---

21. The Buddha, i.e. here, Śākyamuni.
22. His, i.e. Amida's.
23. Three evil paths: the hungry ghosts, the animal world, and hell.
24. Arhat: one of the ten titles of the Buddha, he who is worthy of respect.
25. *Prajñā*: transcendental knowledge or source of all knowledge.
26. Three Vehicles: 1. The Bodhisattva, being of enlightenment, 2. *Pratyekabuddha*, solitary Buddha, and 3. *Śrāvaka*, hearer.

All other Buddhas praise the Ōjō[27]
And the virtues of Buddha Amida are extolled.

12. As His Wondrous Light transcends form and description,
He is known as the Buddha of Inexpressible Light;
His Light has the power to enlighten all beings:
So he is praised by all the Buddhas.

13. As His Light surpasses that of the Sun and the Moon,
He is known as the Sun-and-Moon-Surpassing Light;
Śākyamuni could not praise Him enough:
Take refuge in the One who is peerless.

14. At the first discourse given by Amida
The holy multitudes were beyond calculation;
Those who wish to go to the Pure Land
Should take refuge in the Buddha who commands great numbers.

15. The numberless great Bodhisattvas in the Land of Bliss
After one birth more will become Buddhas;
When they have taken refuge in the virtues of Fugen[28]
They will come back to this world in order to teach beings.

16. For the sake of all beings in the ten quarters[29]
They gather up all the Dharma-treasures[30] of Tathāgatahood,[31]
And to save them lead them to the Original Vow.[32]
Take refuge in the Ocean of the Great Heart.

17. Together with Kannon[33] and Seishi,[34]
He illumines the world with the Light of Mercy;
Leading all those in ripe condition for the Dharma,
He knows no time for rest.[35]

18. Those who reach the Land of Purity and Happiness,

---

27. *Ōjō*: literally "to go and be born," i.e. assurance of rebirth in the Pure Land.
28. Fugen: the Bodhisattva Samantabhadra, one of the most important figures of Mahāyāna, engaged in the work of salvation.
29. Ten quarters: the eight points of the compass *plus* the nadir and the zenith.
30. Dharma-treasures: virtues or values.
31. Tathāgata(hood): "One who thus comes," a title for a Buddha.
32. Original Vow: *purvapranidhāna* in Sanskrit is the expression of the will of love Amida cherishes for all beings.
33. Kannon: Avalokiteśvara Bodhisattva standing to the left of Amida represents Mercy.
34. Seishi: Mahāsthāmaprapta Bodhisattva standing to the right of Amida represents Wisdom.
35. Ed. Suzuki takes this whole stanza to refer to Amida "together with" Kannon and Seishi and, though the original is grammatically ambiguous, this seems more plausible than turning Amida's two companions into independent agents, as has also been translated.

When they return to this world of five defilements,[36]
Like Buddha Śākyamuni work without cessation
For the welfare of all beings.

19. The miraculous power and self-mastery
Enjoyed by them is beyond calculation,
They have accumulated virtues beyond thought:
Take refuge in the Honoured One who is peerless.

20. Śrāvakas[37] and Bodhisattvas in the Land of Happiness,
Men and gods all radiant in Prajñā,
In form and appearance are equally majestic;
But, different names are given in different worlds.[38]

21. They are incomparably perfect in features,
Exquisite in bodily form, their equals cannot be found;
Appearing from the Void,[39] yet they have infinite form;
Take refuge in the Power to whom all beings are equal.

22. Those who aspire to the land of Happiness
Must abide "in the group of perfect faith"[40]
None are to be found there who long for wrong or unsettled faith,
And they are praised by all the Buddhas.[41]

23. When all beings in every condition within the ten quarters,
Endowed with all excellent virtues,
Hearing the name of Amida with sincerity of heart,
Attain faith; how they will rejoice at what they hear!

24. "Because of my Vow if they should not be born [in the Pure Land]
I will not attain enlightenment."
When the right moment for faith arises, joy is instantly felt,
And rebirth is definitely confirmed, once for all.

25. The Buddha Land of Happiness with everything belonging to it

---

36. Five Defilements: *pañca kaṣāya* in Sanskrit. Defilement relating to age, philosophical insight, morality, physical existence, and life-length.

37. *Śrāvakas*: Literally "hearers," contrasted to Bodhisattvas; roughly put, the hearers are followers of Hīnayāna and Bodhisattvas belong to Mahāyāna.

38. Ed. The translation has been slightly adjusted here. The underlying text says that these various beings are named in accordance with the varying directions, i.e. worlds in the ten directions other than that of Amida in the west.

39. Void: *śūnyatā* in Sanskrit. The Mahāyāna system is based on this idea. The term is quite frequently misunderstood. Ed. This is not surprising, because the Sanskrit term means empti-*ness* and the suffix indicating a quality (of things) is not transported into Buddhist Sino-Japanese. The meaning for Shinran, as translated here, appears to reflect an ontic origin, however this may be a misunderstanding, for "voidness" is anti-ontic.

40. Group of perfect faith: group of Buddhists who are definitely assured of their attainment of Buddhahood.

41. Ed. The Ryūkoku translation (cf. Introduction above) completes the stanza as "Hence Buddhas praise Him," i.e. Amida, which may be more appropriate.

Is the product of the power of Dharmākara.[42]
There is nothing compared to it above or below the heavens:
Take refuge in the Great Mind-Power.

26. The splendid views of the Land of Happiness
Śākyamuni with all his unobstructed wisdom declared
To be really beyond all expression;
Take refuge in the Buddha whose glory is beyond description.

27. Rebirth [in the Pure Land] for all the periods of time[43]
Not only is assured for beings of this world
But for all in the Buddha-lands of the ten quarters:
Their number is indeed measureless, numberless, and incalculable.

28. Those beings who hearing the Holy Name of Amitābha Buddha
Feel joyous and adore him,
Will be given treasures of merit
And benefits great and incomparable.[44]

29. Although the great chiliocosm may be filled with flames,
Yet he who hears the Holy Name of the Buddha,
Always in accord with steadfastness,
Will freely pass [to the Pure Land].

30. Amida's mysterious limitless Power
Is praised by innumerable Buddhas;
From the Buddha-lands in the East
As many as the sands of the Ganges, numberless Bodhisattvas come.[45]

31. From the Buddha-lands in the remaining nine quarters.
Come the Bodhisattvas to see him;
Śākyamuni the Tathāgata composing songs
Praises his virtues infinite.

32. All the countless Bodhisattvas of the ten quarters
In order to plant the root of merit
Pay homage to the Bhagavat and praise him in song:
Let all beings take refuge in Him.

[The present translation ends here. As noted above, a further sixteen stanzas are focused mainly on a description of the Pure Land of Amida Buddha.]

---

42. Dharmākara: The name assumed by Amida while still in the stage of Bodhisattva-hood.

43. Periods of time: Past, present, and future.

44. Ed. Suzuki provides no equivalent for the concept of *ichinen* 一念 which should give: "...great and incomparable merits in one thought..." This "one thought" may be presumed to refer here to the first utterance of the *nenbutsu* in true faith (note the occurrence of the same element *nen*) but *ichinen* also has a wider pedigree in Mahāyāna Buddhist thought, and suggests the instantaneous contemporaneity of all phenomena and/or of all aspects of liberation.

45. Ed. Corrected from "Buddhas" in accordance with the original.

— 13 —

On Steadfast Holding to the Name

Kakunyo Shōnin

(The Introduction and the Translation are Anonymous.)

I

Prefatory Notes

This short treatise known as the *Shūjishō* 執持抄 is a compilation by Kakunyo of Shinran's sayings on Shin teaching. In the title, *shūji* has the literal meaning of "steadily holding to" or "holding on" while *shō* means "treatise."[1] At the time of Kakunyo (1270–1351), who was the great-grandson of Shinran, divergent views prevailed concerning the interpretation of the doctrine of Rebirth by Nembutsu. Wishing to hold up against the prevailing heterodoxies the view which he learned as orthodox from his predecessors, he selected five topics, on four of which the founder's views are quoted while on the remaining one the compiler expresses himself. These selections were given to [the monk] Ganchi, of the province of Hitachi, at whose request in fact they were selected. The author wants to see all his readers hold on faithfully to the founder's teaching as stated in this tract. Hence the [fuller] title "Tract on Steadily Holding to the Faith as held by the Holy Master of the Honganji," that is, by Shinran Shōnin.

The following notes will be found helpful for a better understanding of the text. According to the Jōdo teaching, the Buddha accompanied by a host of Bodhisattvas comes to greet his devotees to the Land of Purity and Happiness when they are about to pass away. Therefore, thoughts they may cherish at "the last moment" of death have a deciding influence over their future course of existence. If they cherish wrong thoughts

1. Ed. The syntax of these opening sentences has been redrawn. The implication is that of holding fast to the name of Amida, hence the expanded English title.

they are bound for hell, but if they have the right kind of thoughts they will surely see the holy host appearing among the purple-coloured clouds to take them up to Heaven. This is the belief entertained by followers of the Jiriki (self-power) school. Those of the Tariki (other-power) school, on the other hand, hold that what is most efficient as the cause of rebirth in the Pure Land is to have the right thought if only just for once in their "ordinary hours," that is, while they are actively living, which ensures their joining the "order of steadfastness." When this joining takes place, they are assured of rebirth in the Pure Land, hence of enlightenment, no matter what thoughts they may have at the last hour of death. We can, according to them, never be sure of our thoughts while we are at the point of death, for we may die in agony with no time for recollection and mental adjustment. What conditions the rebirth is not the thought we may happen to hold at the last moment of death, but the right one awakened in our ordinary moments of life. This means that the rebirth is a matter of faith and not of merit accumulated by good works. Have a faith thoroughly established in the Original Vow of Amida and he will see to it that we are reborn in his Pure Land when this earthly life comes to an end. But as long as we rely on the merit of good deeds performed by our "self-power," which is always found [to be] limited in every way, we can never be sure of attaining our object. Work cannot in its nature be "the efficient cause" of rebirth in Amida's Land. "The efficient cause" comes from Amida, and without our being supplied with it by his grace, we are left helpless in our aspirations. The Name: "Namu-amida-butsu" is "the efficient cause" supplied by Amida for our rebirth in his Land; therefore, by cultivating faith in him and calling his Name, the devotees are ushered into the "order of steadfastness," whereby they have the assurance of rebirth or Nirvana. (In the Jōdo teaching generally, Nirvana is used in the sense of enlightenment. Rebirth and Nirvana and Enlightenment are synonyms.)

The idea of merit-transference, we must know, is really at the bottom of the whole system of thought which makes up the teaching of Shin as distinguished from the Jōdo. All the merit Amida has accumulated for innumerable aeons by his good and unselfish deeds is vowed by him to be transferred to all sentient beings so that the latter, however evil-minded and crime-committing and deficient in true wisdom, will be thereby directed towards the Pure Land. If they were to rely upon their own resources, they would never be delivered from the whirlpool of birth-and-death because they are by nature too limited in knowledge and virtue to achieve their own final emancipation. Amida as Eternal Life and Infinite Light turns all his wisdom and love and virtue towards all sentient beings and causes them to look up to him and awaken a faith in their hearts which assures them of being reborn into his Land of Purity. The whole mechanism of rebirth, or salvation to use Christian terminology, is set to work when the devotee utters even for once from the very depths of his being—that is, moved by the other-power of Amida, the miraculous phrase "Namu-amida-butsu," which vibrates with Amida's transcendental wisdom and all-embracing love.

II

The Text

1

The Holy Master of the Honganji said:

The Welcoming Buddha[2] is meant for those who believe in Rebirth by Works, because they are devotees of self-power. To wait for the Last Moment, to rely upon the Welcoming Buddha—this is said of those who believe in Rebirth by virtue of Works. As to those devotees [of other-power] who cherish a true believing heart, they abide with the Order of Steadfastness,[3] because of [Amida's] all-embracing Light from which no beings are excluded. And as they abide with the Order of Steadfastness, they are sure of Nirvana. There is no need for them to wait for the Last Moment, nor for the Welcoming Buddha: this is the idea of the Eighteenth Vow.[4] To wait for the Last Moment, to rely upon the Welcoming Buddha—this is the idea of the Nineteenth Vow[5] in which Rebirth by Works is promised.

---

2. This refers to the Jōdo belief as stated in the Prefatory Notes that the Buddha with a host of Bodhisattvas appears before the devotee when he is at the point of death, in order to welcome him to the Land of Purity and Happiness.

3. This is the stage where the faith is firmly established with no possible regression. It is reached while in this life and is the assurance of Rebirth in the Pure Land when the present span of life comes to an end. In the *Wasan* we read:
   Any one who obtains the true believing heart
   Instantly abides with the Order of Steadfastness [in this life],
   If he is thus qualified to abide in the condition of no-retrogression
   He is firmly assured of attaining Nirvana [in the Pure Land].

4. The Eighteenth Vow is as follows:

   "If after my obtaining Buddhahood all beings in the ten quarters should not desire in sincerity and trustfulness to be born in my country, and if they should not be born [Ed. in the Pure Land] by only thinking of me for ten times, except those who have committed the five grave offences and those who are abusive of the true Dharma, may I not attain the Highest Enlightenment."

5. The Nineteenth Vow is as follows:

   "If after my obtaining Buddhahood all beings in the ten quarters awakening their thoughts to enlightenment and practising all deeds of merit should cherish the desire in sincerity to be born in my country and if I should not, surrounded by a large company, appear before them at the time of their death, may I not attain the Highest Enlightenment."

2

Further he said:

This self who is unable to distinguish right from wrong, good from evil, who has no claim even for little deeds of love and compassion, yet is willing just for name and gain to pose as a teacher—[how shameful!]. What is of the foremost importance for one who wishes to be reborn in the Pure Land is a believing heart—and all other things are of no concern whatever. Rebirth is the greatest event of life and is not a matter for the ordinary man to achieve himself; it is altogether to be left in the hands of Amida. Not only we ignorant beings but even Bodhisattvas, including Maitreya of one more birth, cannot measure the incomprehensible wisdom of the Buddha. How can we then of little wisdom measure it? I repeat most emphatically that [the matter of Rebirth] is to be entirely left with Amida's Vow. [Those who take to this view] are known as the Other-power devotees in whom the awakening of a believing heart has taken place.

Therefore, as regards myself I have no idea as to my destiny whether I am bound for the Pure Land or for hell. According to my late master (that is, Hōnen Shōnin, of Kurodani), "You just follow me wherever I may be." This being what I have been told by him, I am ready to go wherever he is bound for—even be it for hell. If I did not happen to see my good master in this life, I, ignorant as I am, may not know where else to go but to hell. But being instructed by the holy master I have been enabled to hear Amida's Original Vow and to understand the reason of His all-embracing Light from which no beings are excluded. Thus to be detached from birth-and-death—which is difficult, and to be assured of Rebirth in the Pure Land—which is also difficult: this is most certainly not due to my power. Even if my holy master deceived me as to trusting in Amida's Buddha-wisdom and reciting the Nembutsu—which might really be the deed for hell but which he made me think to be the efficient cause of my Rebirth in the Pure Land, and even if I should thereby fall into hell, I would have no regret whatever.

The reason is: if there were no chance at all for me to see my clear-sighted master, my destination would decidedly have been no other place than the evil path. But if I, deceived by my good master, should fall into the evil path, I would not be all by myself; I would have my master with me. My destination after all may be hell, but inasmuch as I have made up my mind to follow my late holy master wherever he is bound for, whether it be for a good existence or for an evil one, I have no choice of my own.

[Comments Kakunyo] "This is the attitude of mind assured by the other-power devotee who has given up the self-power faith."

3

Further, he said:

The monk of Kōmyōji (that is, Zendō[6]) comments on the significance of the Eighteenth Vow dealing with Rebirth[7] through the Nenbutsu[8] as is given in the *Daimuryōjukyō*.[9] "There are no beings, good or bad, who are reborn [in the Pure Land] without riding on Amida-Buddha's Great Vow which functions as the most efficient agency [for the event of Rebirth]." The idea is: however good a man may be, he is incapable, with all his deeds of goodness, of effecting his Rebirth in Amida's Land of Recompense, much less so with bad men. Except for the three (or four) evil paths of existence, where else can their evil deeds bear fruit? How can these be the cause of Rebirth in the Land of Recompense? Being so, good deeds are of no effect and evil deeds of no hindrance [as regards the Rebirth]. Even the Rebirth of good men is impossible without being helped by Amida's specific Vow issuing from His great love and compassion which is not at all of this world.

As regards the Rebirth of bad men, they have really no reason to hope for the Land of Recompense which is ruled by the Buddha of Recompense [that is, Amida]. But in order to demonstrate the incomprehensible power of Buddha-wisdom, Amida meditated on the matter for five long kalpas and practised a life [of love and compassion] for an infinite number of kalpas for the sake of evil-minded beings, who have no other abode than the six paths of existence[10] or the four forms of birth,[11] and who thus for ever have no opportunity whatever for emancipation. As His Vow is thus specifically meant for them, they need not feel humiliated because of their evil karma.

Therefore, unless you lose yourself in your reverential trust in Amida's Buddha-wisdom, how can your evil nature which is in you be the cause of your Rebirth in the Pure Land? The most certain thing is that, influenced

---

6. He was a great advocate of the Pure Land doctrine in the Táng dynasty and was chosen by Shinran as one of the seven great fathers of Shin Buddhism. Ed. The reference is to the Chinese Shàndǎo 善導 (613–681) whose name is pronounced Zendō in Japanese. Shàndǎo resided at a temple called Guāngmíngsì 光明寺 which is read Kōmyōji in Japanese.

7. Ōjō 往生. This literally means "to go and be born."

8. Nenbutsu 念仏 literally means "thinking of the Buddha," that is, of Amida. In this case it is to pronounce the Name of Amida, i.e., to recite "Namu-amida-butsu," believing in the efficacy of his Original Vow.

9. *Daimuryōjukyō* 大無量寿経, that is, the *Larger Sukhāvatīvyūha-sūtra*.

10. The six paths of existence are: hells, the world of hungry ghosts, the animal world, the world of fighting demons, the human world, and heavens.

11. The four forms of birth are: those born from a womb, the egg-born, the moisture-born, and those that come into existence through transformation.

by various evil conditions such as the ten evil deeds[12] [especially the first four of them], the five grave offences,[13] or acts committed against the Dharma, you are to sink into the three evil paths or to suffer the eight kinds of calamity.[14] Being so, how can [evil karma] be of any other use?

Thus we see that as good is not the seed of Rebirth in the Land of Bliss it is not needed for this purpose; so with evil, as aforesaid [it is no hindrance to our Rebirth in the Pure Land]. That we are good or bad is due to our nature [as beings of this world]; and as to the other world there is no hope whatever in us except for our taking refuge in the Other-power. For this reason, Zendō's commentary reads: the Rebirth in the Pure Land of beings good or bad finds its efficient cause in Amida's Great Vow. "That there is no Rebirth without the Vow efficiently working"—this means that there is nothing surpassing Amida's Great Vow [as the efficient cause of Rebirth].

4

Further, he said:

We talk about cause and condition in regard to the Light and Name. According to the Twelfth[15] of the Forty-eight Vows made by Amida, He vowed that His Light might be boundless. This is meant to embrace all beings who are the Nembutsu devotees. This Vow is fulfilled and His Light which knows no hindrance anywhere now illuminates all the worlds numberless as atoms in the ten quarters, shining ever on the evil passions and evil deeds of all beings. When, coming in contact with this Light which serves as the condition [of Rebirth] for them, they feel the darkness of Ignorance gradually fading in them and are ready to see the seed of good karma germinate, they hear the Name which is the efficient

12. The ten evil deeds are: destroying life, theft, adultery, lying, talking nonsense, speaking evil of others, being double-tongued, greed, anger, and irrationality. The first four of these are especially grave, so they are called *shijū* 四重, "four grave," or *pārājika* (J. *harai* 波羅夷), meaning "four heinous evil deeds."

13. The five grave offences are: patricide, matricide, arhat-murdering, causing dissension in the Brotherhood, and causing the Buddha's body to bleed.

14. The eight kinds of calamity are: (1) to be born in Hells; (2) in the animal world; (3) in the world of hungry ghosts—these three paths of existence are called "the three evil paths" wherein one cannot hear the Dharma on account of severe pains and sufferings; (4) to be born in the Heaven of Longevity; (5) to be born in the Uttarakuru—both of these are worlds wherein one can enjoy much pleasure and longevity, but because of these sensual pleasures he has no chance to hear the Dharma; (6) to be blind, deaf, and dumb; (7) to be secularly wise; (8) to be born before the birth of and after the death of Buddha Śākyamuni.

15. The Twelfth Vow is as follows: "If after my obtaining Buddhahood my light should be limited and not be able at least to illumine hundreds of thousands of *koṭis* of Buddha-countries, may I not attain the Highest Enlightenment."

cause of Rebirth in the Land of Recompense as is stated in the Eighteenth Vow which deals with Rebirth through the Nembutsu. We know by this that the holding of the Name is not of self-power but solely due to the energising effect of the Light. Therefore, we read that the Light as condition prepares the ground for the Name as [a] cause [for it] to germinate.

This is the reason why the master (Zendō) declares that "By virtue of the Light and the Name, Amida embraces all beings when their believing heart is awakened and they seek for Rebirth." "Their believing heart is awakened and they seek for Rebirth"—by this it is meant that the Light and the Name are like the parents who are bent on bringing up their child; but so long as there is no child to issue, there are no parents claiming the name; it is only when there is a child that they deserve the name of father and mother. In a similar way the Light is likened to motherhood and the Name to fatherhood, but there must be a seed of believing heart which comes out of them destined for Rebirth in the Land of Recompense. So, when a believing heart is awakened and Rebirth in the Pure Land is desired, the Name is recited and the Light embraces the devotee. If there were no devotees who would awaken a believing heart in the Name, Amida with His Vow to embrace all beings without a single exception would have to remain helpless. If Amida did not make His Vow to embrace all beings without a single exception, how could His devotees see their desire for Rebirth in the Pure Land fulfilled? For this reason [we have this chain of dependence completed]: The Original Vow and the Name, the Name and the Original Vow, the Original Vow and the devotee, the devotee and the Original Vow.

We read in the *Kyōgyōshinshō* compiled by the Holy Master of the Honganji in which the author comments [on the idea expounded here]: "if not for the Name as a kindhearted father, the generating cause is wanting; if not for the Light as a loving mother, the condition for birth is insufficient: the Light as mother and the Name as father are, however, external conditions while the functioning consciousness [or the mind] with the true right faith is the inner cause: and when the inner cause and the external conditions are properly united, the devotee attains the true body worthy of the Land of Recompense."

To illustrate this by analogy: when the sun is up only halfway around Mt. Sumeru, the other side of the mountain is well illuminated, but this side is still in the dark. When it approaches this side southwardly coming around from the other side, the night is dispersed. It is evident that the morning dawns with the sun rising. People generally imagine that the morning first dawns and then the sun rises—which is quite contrary to the statement I have just made. As the illumining rays of the sunlight of Amida-Buddha prevail, the darkness of the long night of Ignorance[16]

16. *Mumyō* 無明 (Skt. *avidyā*).

is dispelled, whereby we take hold of the gem of the Name which is the efficient cause of Rebirth in the Land of Happiness.

5

My statement is:

Do not feel humiliated because of your being poorly endowed, for the Buddha is great love, knowing how to save inferior beings. Do not cherish any doubt [as to Rebirth] because of your tendency to be remiss in reciting the Nembutsu, for in the sūtra we have a passage[17] beginning with "Even with one thought..." the Buddha speaks no falsehood, and how can the Original Vow fail? That the Name is known as the right definite act [of Rebirth] is because when one relies upon the incomprehensible power of the Buddha, the work for Rebirth is definitely completed. If even when a man recites the Name through the power of Amida's Original Vow his Rebirth were a matter of indefinite uncertainty, the Name could not be known as the right definite act [of Rebirth].[18] [But that the Name is the efficient cause of Rebirth is illustrated in my own case. For] I [as an other-power devotee] am already the one who firmly holds on to the Name as is given in the Original Vow; and it is now only left to me to rejoice at the completion of the work for Rebirth. It goes without saying, therefore, that my Rebirth is assured even if I do not again recite the Name at the time of my death.

As I observe, there are infinite varieties of karma which determine conditions of all beings; and so are their conditions of death: some die of disease, some die under the sword, some die drowned in water, some die burned by fire, some die while in sleep, some die from intoxication; these are all due to their past karma and there is no escape for them. When they meet death in these various ways, it is quite possible for them to cherish a wrong thought for which they were not prepared; how could they as ordinary mortals at that moment awaken the right thought of reciting the Name or the desire of being reborn in the Pure Land? If what they expected to take place all along in their ordinary moments fails, their hope for Rebirth will entirely be nullified. The attainment of Rebirth is therefore to be settled by One Thought[19] which they can hold

17. The passage is found in the *Larger Sukhāvatīvyūha-sūtra*, which runs as follows: "All sentient beings, upon hearing the Name [of Amida], would awaken a believing heart, even with one thought and rejoice in it. [Amida], with all the sincerity of heart, has transferred [all his own merit on all beings], wherefore those who desire to be reborn in his country would instantly be assured of their Rebirth and abide in the condition of no-retrogression, barring only those who have committed the five deadly sins and those who have abused the Good Law."

18. Ed. Syntax adjusted.

19. "One Thought" is a momentous term in the philosophy of Shin and Jōdo. Its San-

in their ordinary moments. If their minds are in a state of uncertainty in their ordinary moments, Rebirth will be impossible for them. When in accordance with the words of a good master they awaken in their ordinary moments One Thought of trust in Amida, let this be regarded as the last moment, the end of this world, for them.

[How is it that the holding of the Name, "Namu-amida-butsu"[20] is the efficient cause of Rebirth?] Namu means "to trust," and to trust [in Amida] is for the sake of attaining Rebirth, it is also the desire [for Rebirth]. Further, as this desire is possible because of the truth that every deed and every good [performed by Amida] is transformed into the efficient cause of Rebirth for His devotees, it again means merit-transference.[21] When the trusting heart on the part of the devotee and its object of trust which is the Buddha-wisdom of Amida are in correspondence, all deeds of devotion practised by Amida while in His stage of discipleship and all meritorious virtues resulting therefrom are in the most exhaustive manner absorbed in the Name, which thus becomes for all beings in the ten quarters the efficient cause of their Rebirth. Hence [Zendō's] comment: "Amida is no other than the Act," [that is, the Name is the efficient cause of Rebirth].

When a murderous deed is committed, this is surely a sufficient cause for the offender to go to hell; he may not repeat such a deed at his last moment; but as long as his karma committed in his ordinary moments

---

skrit original is *eka-kṣaṇa* meaning "one instant" or "one moment." As we say in English "quick as thought" or "quick as a flash," "one thought" represents in terms of time the shortest possible duration, which is to say, one instant. The one instant of faith-establishment is the moment when Amida's Eternal Life cuts crosswise the flow of birth-and-death, or when his Infinite Light flashes into the darkening succession of love and hate which is experienced by our relative consciousness. This event takes place in "one thought" and is never repeated, and therefore is known here as "the last moment," "the end of this world," and I would say, it is even the coming into the presence of Amida. This moment of "One Thought" is the one in our life most deeply impregnated with meaning, and for that reason must come to us in our "ordinary moments of life" and not wait for "the last moment" in its relative sense.

20. "Namu-amida-butsu" 南無阿弥陀仏 arises from the transliteration of the Sanskrit, *namo 'mitābhāya buddhāya. Namo* or *Namas* (=*namu*) means "adoration" or "salutation," and *amitābhāya buddhāya* means "to the Buddha of Infinite Light." So "adoration (or salutation) to the Buddha of Infinite Light" is the meaning of "Namu-amida-butsu." But in Shin the full form of "Namu-amida-butsu" is regarded as the Name of the Buddha Amida, because Amida perfected his Name as "Namu-amida-butsu" as embodying his great Vow which expresses his love for all sentient beings. Amida-butsu 阿弥陀仏 causes us to trust (= *namu* 南無) Him as our saviour. "Namu" and "Amidabutsu" are therefore essentially inseparable, being two phases of his saving power. The idea of "Namu-amida-butsu" is not "Ask and you shall be given," but "to be caused to ask and be given."

21. That is, *ekō* 回向 (Skt. *pariṇāmana*).

is active, hell is the certain destination for him. It is the same with the Nembutsu: if a man believing in the Original Vow recites the Nembutsu, he should know that his Rebirth at that moment becomes a matter of utmost certainty.

Postscript: According to the postscript, this was written in 1326 when the author was fifty-seven years old, and copied for Ganchi-bō[22] of Hida Province in 1340 when his age was seventy-one. He adds that all this is meant for the benefit of all beings.

22. Ed. I.e. the monk Ganchi.

— 14 —

Rennyo the Restorer

Kaneko Daiei

Part I

The life of Rennyo[1]

The great work which Rennyo Shōnin (1415–1499) achieved during his lifetime was the restoration of Shinshū.[2] Through it he brought the Shin teaching to the people, a mission he undertook not only to bring prosperity to the Honganji lineage, but also to spread the spirit of the Founder, Shinran Shōnin (1173–1262), throughout the land. It is for this reason that he is revered as the reincarnation of the Founder.

The motive for his revival of Shin goes back to an episode in childhood. Born in 1415 (Ōei 22) February 25th, during the reign of Emperor Shōkō, his father Zonnyo Shōnin (1396–1457) was the seventh abbot of the Honganji lineage. The name of his mother, though, is not recorded.[3]

1. This is a translation of the first section of Kaneko Daiei's "Renshi no chūkō," the eighth chapter of his *Shinshū no kyōgi to sono rekishi* (Shin Doctrine and Its History), 1915, compiled in his Collected Works, supplementary volume 3, 311–317. We wish to thank Kaneko Hiroshi Sensei for permission to publish it here [Ed. i.e. in *The Eastern Buddhist*]. We also wish to thank Kaji Yōichi for editing the translation. Annotation has been provided by the translator except when denoted "Ed."
2. Ed. Shinshū: Shin-shū, the Shin denomination, Shin Buddhism.
3. As one editor notes, that his mother's name is not recorded—surprising to us, perhaps—may in fact reflect the prevailing custom of the time. Rennyo's mother was apparently forced to leave upon the marriage of his father to a woman of social standing, which his mother, a commoner, was not. The loss of his mother had a significant impact on his life, and may in part explain his strong sympathy for the ordinary people.

The *Rennyoshōninitokuki*,[4] or "The Legacy of Rennyo Shōnin," says:

> On the 8th day, twelfth month, Ōei 27 [1420], his mother summoned him to her and divulged to the six-year-old her never-revealed wish for his future: that he see to the revival of the lineage [to which he was rightful heir]. This she conveyed in the warmest of tones. Shortly after this, she left the temple and was never heard from again.[5]

These words of instruction were etched into the heart of the child and later became the source of inspiration for the great work he would achieve in his lifetime.

It was not until he was fifteen that Rennyo first grasped the significance of his mother's words. The *Legacy* says:

> It was in his fifteenth year that he first took the revival of Shin to heart. It grieved him to think how past generations had let the teaching waste away, and his thoughts dwelt constantly on how he would in his lifetime bring the lineage of the Founder to the attention of people everywhere and thus revive the school.[6]

What first fueled his efforts was the decline of the Honganji. In a society increasingly under Ashikaga rule, a period when Buddhism held no sway among religions in general, it was not surprising that the fortunes of the Honganji declined. To make matters worse, from the time of the third abbot Kakunyo (1270-1351) the school seems to have lost the call; fossilizing around rituals, the tradition slowly began to deteriorate. Seeing these things with his own eyes Rennyo became acutely aware of the mission that lay ahead of him.

The years of religious study were fraught with difficulties for Rennyo. First and foremost he had to eke out an existence for himself. The *Rennyoshōningoichidaikikigaki*, or "Record of Sayings from Rennyo's Life,"[7] tells us there were times when "he had nothing to eat for two or

4. The *Rennyoshōninitokuki*, or *Itokuki* (hereafter cited as the *Legacy*), is one of the earliest biographies of Rennyo. Published during the early Tokugawa period, in 1674, its highly literary narrative spawned numerous other Rennyo biographies, such as the Katata Honpukuji related *Rennyoshōningyōjōki* (1716). It remained standard Shin-shū reading material up until the nineteenth century, and was included in the *Shinshū hōyō* (Nishi Hongwanji, 1765) and the *Shinshū kana shōgyō* (Higashi Honganji, 1812), the forerunner of the *Shinshū shōgyō zensho* (1941). It has now been eclipsed from Shinshū awareness, in part because it is no longer included in the *Shinshū seiten* used by followers. For a recent version, see Mori Ryūkichi et al., eds., *Shinshū shiryō shūsei*, 11 (1983), 791–802.

5. *Shinshū shiryō shūsei*, 11, 791–792. For an English study, see also Minor L. Rogers and Ann T. Rogers, *Rennyo, the Second Founder of Shin Buddhism* (Berkeley: Asian Humanities Press, 1991), 47–48, a good source of information on Rennyo.

6. *Shinshū shiryō shūsei*, 11, 792.

7. A representative collection of sayings by Rennyo compiled from early historical documents, this work has long enjoyed a vogue among Shin followers for the in-

three days," times when "the only things he had to wear were scraps of paper," times when "he had to pack up all the children to take them somewhere [they could get fed]." Indeed, "many a sad story was woven out of these dire circumstances." As we can well imagine, the life he led had little to celebrate.

> For him to pursue studies, so as not to waste money on lamp oil he would get some burnt wood[8] [to use as a source of light] before he would begin reading the sacred teachings; at other times he would wait till the moonlight was bright enough before he would begin to read the scriptures.

It was literally through reading by the light of fireflies[9] that he achieved what he did.

The second difficulty he faced was the lack of a proper teacher. Ever since his seventeenth year when he was ordained, he had the desire to study. Teachers were available from other lineages, but the problem was there was none who could instruct him in the finer points of Shin doctrine, and so he had to teach himself. He read the *Kyōgyōshinshō*[10] diligently, thumbing through it so often he managed to rub a hole in the cover, and tried to understand its meaning by going through the explanations set down by Kakunyo and others as well as the various sacred teachings.

Third among his difficulties were the immediate circumstances [of the Honganji]. The *Legacy* says:

> At that time, only a few understood the distinctive [doctrine] of our lineage and there was only a vague sense of it being different from those of other establishments and schools. As a result, [it made him] always uneasy around people and inclined to shun the world. Even when reading through the sacred teachings, he would do so furtively, away from the prying eyes of others; at times, just to examine a few pages, he would use the lantern light spilling through a crack in the wall; at other times, on clear nights when the moon had ascended the blue expanse of sky, he would peruse a manuscript and apply himself to the master's commentary.[11]

---

sights it provides into Rennyo's life and thought. It was included in the 1765 *Shinshū hōyō* and the 1812 *Shinshū kana shōgyō*. It is also available in the *Shinshū seiten* and in *Taishō daizōkyō*, Vol. 83. Numerous studies have been done on it since the Tokugawa period, and there are several English translations by various parties.

8. *Kyōnokuroki*, literally, "black wood from the city," refers to blackened firewood from a bonfire.

9. A reference to the story of Chēyìn 車胤 (J. Sha'in) in the *Chin Annals* who had to struggle to get an education, even reading by the light of fireflies at night. The allusion appears in the *Itokuki*, at *Shinshū shiryō shūsei*, 11, 792. The use of literary references from Chinese classics would indicate the high literacy level of the composers, as well as that of the audience for whom it was intended.

10. The popular title of Shinran's main work, written in *kanbun*, or classical Chinese.

11. *Shinshū shiryō shūsei*, 11, 792.

We can gather from this account that Rennyo's education [in Shin doctrine] took place away from the eyes of others. In the account handed down, it is said he took this course of action to avoid conflict with the ways and doctrines of other sects and lineages, but his actions can well be explained in large part by his complicated domestic situation.[12]

In these trying circumstances he underwent spiritual training and sought to live a religious life; turning his thoughts inwardly, as a matter of course he arrived at an understanding of the awakening of faith that *tariki*, or other power, brings about;[13] directing his thoughts to the external world, he realized that the fundamental cause for the break-down of the [Shin] tradition was the failure to spread its doctrine. What seems to have driven this awareness home were his first tours of the northeastern regions. In the fifth month of Bunnan 4 (1447), Rennyo, then in his 33rd year, went to the Kantō (eastern) area, and in the first month of Hōtoku (1449), to the Hokuriku (northern) area. The purpose of these journeys was of course propagation, combined with a pilgrimage to sites sacred to the memory of Shinran. But what Rennyo must have discovered with his own eyes and ears was that the followers were largely ignorant of the Founder's basic message; instead, mistaken interpretations and superstitions were rampant, these to an alarming degree. The lifeblood of a religion lies in the beliefs it inculcates in its followers. Yet he witnessed that the beliefs they held drew them ever deeper into evil paths. The question loomed how to put the tradition back on its feet again. This became a pressing concern for Rennyo, and so with the wish to restore the Shin tradition he came into the cause to which he would devote his entire life.

To compare Rennyo with Kakunyo, Kakunyo's contribution was the clarification of the Shin doctrinal principles vis-à-vis the Jōdo-shū, the Pure Land Buddhist sect founded by Hōnen (1133–1212). By contrast, Rennyo addressed the ordinary people of those days and regarded propagating the Shin teaching amongst them as his life mission. The kind of people Rennyo focussed on were the ones who had suffered the misfortune of being displaced by the wars that ravaged the land and had no homes to return to. And so when Rennyo speaks of the impermanence of human life, as he often does in his *Ofumi*, or "Letters,"[14] this is not merely

12. Rennyo's father's marriage created a politically charged atmosphere on the home front. Years later Rennyo's stepmother would seek to make her own son the next head of the Honganji lineage.

13. *Tariki shinjin* points to the essential Shin experience: achieving the one moment of faithful mind mediated by the working of other power, that is, the Vow of Amida Buddha.

14. The *Ofumi* fall into two categories: the official collection and the *jōgai*, or unofficial, collection. The official collection represents a selection made by his sons, and comprises 80 letters in five fascicles. They figure in certain official ceremonies where

the rhetoric of Buddhist propagation. He was speaking to people who lived in a world of constant danger; one skirmish with a raiding party could turn the scene into a battlefield seething with warriors; for them, indeed, there was no guarantee they would survive till the end of the day. The sentiments Rennyo expressed in his letters were thus directed to those who found themselves in this critical situation. To these people who had nowhere to turn, Rennyo instructed them to take to heart the promise of Amida's Vow; this was the wish he held for them.

In Chōroku 1 (1457), Rennyo, in his 43rd year, succeeded to the eighth abbotship of the Honganji lineage after the demise of his father. Rennyo's stepmother sought to have her own son Ōgen (1433–1503) succeed the abbotship, but Rennyo's uncle Shōmitsu-in Sen'yū (1412–1460) made a decision he felt clearly reflected the wishes of the deceased and appointed Rennyo the next abbot. After this, Rennyo was in an even better position to devote himself to the restoration of Shin.

The magnitude of the project being what it was, it was only to be expected he would meet with strong oppression from other schools and lineages. The persecutions and at times outright confrontations this brought on involved Rennyo in one struggle after another, with the result there was nowhere he could take haven permanently, and throughout his life he was forced to move constantly from place to place. His life may thus be divided into the following periods:

1465, the razing of the Honganji in Kyōto;
1471, the establishment of Yoshizaki;
1475, the propagation in Settsu and Kawachi;
1480, the establishment of the main temple at Yamashina; and
1496, the establishment of Ōsaka.

The burning of the Ōtani Honganji took place in the first month of Kanshō 6 (1465), when Rennyo was in his 51st year. This misdeed was perpetrated by monastics on Mount Hiei who justified their attack on the grounds that the Mugekō-ryū, or Unimpeded Light Lineage, as the Shin followers called themselves, had spoken disparagingly of the various other dharma teachings and schools, and had belittled other gods and buddhas by their words and deeds. The monastics of Mount Hiei regarded the Honganji as the instigator of these dissidents and so vented their anger on them in this way.

But the monastics had other, more palpable reasons to find displeasure with this Pure Land school. Rennyo had emerged as a powerful contender successfully proselytizing the people of the Kinai [region]. This

they are read aloud by the *dōshi* who leads the service. The unofficial collection comprises an almost equal number, and has gone largely unstudied. Ed. Translations may be found in Minor and Ann Rogers' *Rennyo. The Second Founder of Shin Buddhism,* Berkeley 1991.

was highlighted by his conducting a large scale memorial service for Shinran on the 200th anniversary of his death in Kanshō 2 (1461). It was this event combined with other factors that made for envy on Mount Hiei, and so precipitated the violence. The loss of the Honganji in Kyōto forced Rennyo to move to Ōtsu in neighboring Ōmi province (present Shiga prefecture). The province is where Rennyo would make his first loyal follower, Zenjū (Dōsai, 1399–1488) of Kanagamori, and it was here that the Shin teachings would come to hold sway over the people.[15]

In Ōnin 2 (1468), in his 54th year, he again made a tour of the northeastern regions, returning the following year to Ōtsu, where he established the Kenshōji, a temple south of Miidera that would house an image of Shinran.

In a letter he writes: "There shall be no disparaging the various dharma teachings and schools. All of them are the Buddha's exposition, and as long as a person practices in accordance with them, there is sure to be benefit."[16] Here, taking a lesson from the destruction of the Honganji, Rennyo seeks to admonish any indiscreet elements among his following.

The establishment of Yoshizaki took place in Bunmei 3 (1471), when Rennyo was in his 57th year. In one of his letters he writes:

> Around the beginning of the fourth month of the third year of Bunmei, I just slipped away, without any settled plan, from our place near Miidera's southern branch temple at Ōtsu, in the Shiga district of Ōmi province, and travelled through various parts of Echizen and Kaga. Then, as this site—Yoshizaki,[17] in the Hosorogi district of [Echizen] province—was particularly appealing, we made a clearing on the mountain, which for many years had been the habitat of wild beasts, and beginning on the 27th day of the seventh month, we put up a building that might be called a temple.[18]

This letter alludes to the fact that, after the destruction of the Ōtani Honganji, Rennyo went into seclusion for a period in Ōmi province, but that continued pressure by Mount Hiei monastics forced his remove to the northern regions. When the *bōsha*, or priest's quarters, were being built in Yoshizaki, Rennyo's propagation activities in Echizen, Kaga and Etchū attracted crowds of followers. The work at Yoshizaki was speeded along by the deep alliance Rennyo made with military governor Asakura Toshikage. The situation being what it was, the temple was built on a moun-

15. Kanagamori is on the eastern shore of Lake Biwa. Rennyo also had loyal followings on the western shore, at temples such as the Katata Honpukuji in Ōtsu.

16. See Rogers and Rogers, 176.

17. Yoshizaki is on the northern edge of present Fukui prefecture. Closely associated with Rennyo's name, a waka praising the Shiogoshi pines in Yoshizaki attributed to Saigyō in Bashō's *Oku no hosomichi* (1694) is claimed by Shin followers to be Rennyo's.

18. Rogers and Rogers, 71, 157.

tainous site in Yoshizaki. The four years that Rennyo spent at Yoshizaki were significant, for during that time he laid the groundwork for the Shin religion in the Hokuriku area that prospers to this day. The years he lived and proselytized in Yoshizaki were not without complications. It was within the sphere of influence of the heterodox practices such as the *hijihōmon*, or secret teachings, and so on, flourishing in nearby Echizen. Moreover, the followers of the Takada-ha, one of the ten denominations of Shin, had an ongoing feud with those belonging to the Honganji, and there were rabble-rousers who sought to work it to their political advantage. Other centers, such as the Hyōsenji and Hōgenji, functioned as mini-Mount Hieis in wielding secular power.

Rennyo stood in the midst of this. To defuse the situation, he set down regulations that were to be followed religiously by his followers: he admonished them, while speaking out against heterodoxies within Shin, not to speak disparagingly of the various other schools; he cautioned them not to draw undue attention to themselves; for a period he even forbid assemblies at Yoshizaki, saying this was a place of religious practice, not a place to jockey for political advantage.

As regards his Letters, this was the period in which he produced the most; that is, the forty items in *Letters* I.1 to IV.10 were all written during this four-year period. In these letters Rennyo set down *okite*, or regulations, which prescribed how followers were to behave with regard to other sects and in society; in them he also set down explanations of the true meaning of the Shin doctrine in terms that the followers could relate to, as well as instructions for daily religious life. In Bunmei 5 (1473) he issued a woodblock edition of Shinran's *Shōshinge* and *Sanjōwasan*,[19] a significant event as it set the form for the services Shin followers would conduct morning and evening from that time on.

However, on the 28th day of the third month in the following year, Bunmei 6 (1474), at six p.m., a fire broke out at lodgings near the south gate that grew out of control and eventually burned down the entire Yoshizaki complex. The story of how Honkō-bō Ryōken gave his life to save the copy of Shinran's manuscript goes back to this time.[20] The following month, Rennyo moved to temporary quarters, and then went on a pilgrimage to nearby provinces, before returning to Yoshizaki once

19. *Shōshinge*, or "Song of True Faith," and *Sanjōwasan*, the collection of Shinran's hymns in Japanese. In part, they present in verse form the spiritual lineage of Jōdo Shinshū as conceived by Shinran. Rennyo's printing of these works gave tangible form to the Shin religious life, as they were chanted during the daily service by Shin followers. The next great spurt in Shin printing activity would not be until some two hundred years later, in the early Tokugawa period, when the stabilization of society made the publishing of Buddhist books possible, around the Genroku period, 1688–1703.

20. The story is that Ryōken died in the burning building, protecting one of Shinran's writings from the flames.

again. When military governor Togashi Masachika and Shimotsuma Hōgen fanned the embers of the lingering feud between Takada-ha and Honganji followers into a full-blown disturbance, Rennyo gave up all plans to rebuild at Yoshizaki, and in the eighth month of Bunmei 7 (1475) left for good. It was an inevitable decision.

Leaving Yoshizaki, he went by boat to Obama, in Wakasa province (Fukui), and then by way of Tanba (Kyōto) and Settsu (Hyōgo) entered Kawachi province (Ōsaka), where he established the Kōzenji temple at Deguchi in Matsuda ward. After this, for the next two or three years he sojourned in Settsu (Hyōgo), Kawachi, and Izumi (Ōsaka), founding temples and preaching. Among the temples he established are the Kōzenji in Deguchi, Kawachi province, installing his grandson Kōjun[21] (1474–1497) as resident minister; the Kyōgyōji in Miyata, Settsu province; the Shinshō-in in Kai-no-ura, Izumi (Ōsaka), with Shinshōji Jōson as resident minister. While he established temples and preached wherever he went, he never failed to appoint someone to the stewardship of the temple after he retired from the position—a shrewd policy on the part of Rennyo to preserve the Shin teaching.

In the first month of Bunmei 9 (1477), Zenjū of Kanagamori proposed the main temple be built at Yamashina, in the Uji ward of Yamashiro province.[22] At the beginning of the following year, Rennyo went to inspect the site and agreed to the plan. Building a thatched hut, he made it his provisional living quarters. The construction work was begun in Bunmei 11 (1479) and continued until the eighth month of year 12 of the same era, when the Founder's Hall was completed. Next, the Main Hall was begun, and finished in Bunmei 14 (1482). Thus it was not until eighteen years after the destruction of the Ōtani Honganji that Rennyo at last was able to rebuild the main temple. It is recorded that the Main Hall was 3-*ken* square and the Image Hall was 5-*ken* square.[23] One can well imagine the joy Rennyo and his disciples felt when the halls were finally built. In another sense, we could also say that he had laid the groundwork for these halls by his eighteen years of roving and preaching.

Having earlier handed over the responsibilities for the temple to his eldest son Junnyo (1442–1483) in Ōnin 2 (1468), with the latter's death in 1483 Rennyo was obliged to resume the ministership of the temple once again. In Entoku 1 (1489), Rennyo, in his 75th year, handed over the position to his eighth child, Jitsunyo (1458–1525), and himself opted for

21. The son of Rennyo's eldest daughter Nyokei (1446–1471). Here we see an example of Rennyo's practice of placing his children and grandchildren in strategic temples, thus extending his temporal influence and ensuring the stability of his lineage in future generations. This program was enhanced by the fact Rennyo had twenty-eight children, the last of which was fathered in his eighties.

22. Yamashina is located in a long valley between Kyōto city and Lake Biwa.

23. One *ken* is about six feet.

retirement under the name of Shinshō-in. At that time he said: "As for me, at last I can retire from this world to immerse myself in the leisurely study of the Buddha-dharma."

In the ninth month of Meiō 5 (1496), when Rennyo was in his 82nd year, construction of the *bōsha*, or priest's quarters, was begun at Ōsaka in Settsu province, and late in life he allowed himself to be moved there. Around the summer of Meiō 7 (1498), however, he began to feel ill, and sensing the time had come when he would never rise from bed again, he urged others to consummate their faith:

> This was all he longed for, morning and evening: "May there be a decisive settling of faith for everyone while I am still alive." Although this does indeed depend on the fruits of one's own past good deeds, there was never a moment when it was not on his mind.[24]

In the second month of Meiō 8 (1499) he returned to Yamashina. Though gravely ill, he spoke to his family and disciples, urging them to always remember their gratitude to the Buddha and the Founder, and to be respectful of the unseen forces of Buddha-dharma in one's life. Then on the 25th day of the third month he passed from this world.

For his words and deeds see the *Rennyoshōningoichidaikikigaki* [A Record of Sayings from Rennyo's Life], and for an account of his achievements the *Rennyoshōninitokuki* [The Legacy of Rennyo Shōnin]. The former was recorded by his son Rengo (1468–1543) and his disciple Kūzen and others, and compiled by his son Jitsugo (1492–1584). The latter is a selection made by Rengo and recorded by Jitsugo. For those interested in Rennyo, these two works are a must.

Part II

The hallmark of Rennyo's teaching[25]

There is a one-volume commentary that Rennyo wrote on Shinran's *Shōshinge* ("Song of True Faith") called *Shōshingetaii*,[26] which he com-

24. Rogers and Rogers, 240; adapted.

25. This is a translation of part two of "Renshi no chūkō" [Rennyo the Restorer], in the author's *Shinshū no kyōgi to sono rekishi* [Shinshū doctrine and its history], in the third supplementary volume of his Collected Works, 317–322. We wish to thank Kaji Yōichi for editing the translation and Kaneko Hiroshi Sensei for permission to publish it here [Ed. i.e. in *The Eastern Buddhist*]. Subsection titles and annotation have been supplied by the translator.

26. *Shōshingetaii*. For a translation, see Kenneth K. Tanaka, trans., "A Translation of Rennyo Shōnin's *Shōshingetaii*: A Commentary on Shinran Shōnin's *Verses on True Shinjin*," in *The Rennyo Shōnin Reader* (Kyōto: The Institute of Jōdo Shinshū Studies and The Honganji International Center, 1998), 91–109.

posed at the request of Zenjū.[27] The best record of the message he propagated, however, is not in this document, but in his *Ofumi*, or *Letters*.[28] These letters contain the very breath with which he spread the Dharma. Compiled into their present form by his grandson Ennyo Kō'nyū, the entire set comprises five collections of eighty letters. The first four collections contain fifty-eight letters selected mainly from the Yoshizaki period to the Ōsaka period. Written to followers, all of them are clearly dated. The remaining twenty-two letters, these undated, are words of instruction cast in lucid terms on the theme of *tariki anjin*, the peace of mind effected by other power. In addition to the *Letters*, there is the *Ryōgemon*, a declaration Rennyo made to deal with dissident elements at Yoshizaki. This also enables us to learn of some of the essential points that Rennyo stressed in his propagation.

Holding to Amida

When we look at the message he sought to spread in his Letters, it is of course no different in spirit from that of our Founder, Shinran Shōnin. It is also evident that the style of propagation he used owes much to Kakunyo Shōnin. But there is one innovation he makes that we cannot fail to notice and that is his emphasis on *nenji no gi*, or "holding to Amida." Rennyo urges we hold to Amida when we say the Name of the Buddha and implore [him] to save us in the life to come. This places *anjin*, or "peace of mind," at the hub of the Shin teaching. In *Goichidaikikikigaki* it says,

> [Shinran] Shōnin taught that *tanomu ichinen* or the act of "imploring with singleness of thought" is the essential key [to salvation]. As a result this so-called act of imploring was accepted perfunctorily by all succeeding generations [of Shin leaders], but they never enlightened us as to what object this act of imploring was to be directed. Fortunately for us, our honored leader of two generations past Rennyo composed numerous letters during his lifetime that clarified that our putting aside useless practices and seeking salvation in the life to come was already consummated in the act of imploring Amida with singleness of thought. This is one reason he is known as Rennyo the Restorer.[29]

27. Zenjū (1399–1488), also known as Dōsai, was a loyal supporter who rallied followers for Rennyo. In some accounts he is given a key role in the success of Rennyo's propagation efforts in the Kinai region.

28. For an English translation of the official collection of the *Letters*, see Rogers and Rogers, *Rennyo. The Second Founder of Shin Buddhism* (Berkeley 1991). There is also an unofficial collection called *Jōgai ofumi* that has gone largely unstudied.

29. *Goichidaikikikigaki* presents considerable difficulties for the modern reader unfamiliar with the grammar and lexicon of the time. For a rough translation of this particular passage (No. 188), see Yamamoto Kōshō, trans., *The Words of St. Rennyo: Complete Translations of the Rennyoshōnin goichidaikikikigaki and the Anjinketsujōshō* (Ube City, Yamaguchiken: Karinbunko, 1968), 68–69.

Further, in the *Itokuki* it says,

> To take refuge in one moment [of focused practice and faith] (*ichinen kimyō no kotowari*) is a veritable truth which we have endeavored to achieve since the time of our Founder Shinran Shōnin, but it was not [until Rennyo] that it was couched in terms of our "holding to Amida" (*nenji no gi*) in that one moment of invocation.[30]

These passages lead us to conclude that *nenji no gi*, or holding to Amida in that one moment [of practice and faith], is the crowning achievement of Rennyo's efforts to propagate Shin and can truly be said to be the hallmark of his teaching. It goes without saying that *shinjin*, or "the awakening of faith," is axial to the Shin teaching. This awakening of faith is to accept without a shred of doubt the Name derived from the Original Vow. The word *shinjin* does nothing for us as long as it remains mere letters on the page. But when we come into contact with the dynamic Will giving expression to that word, we have no choice but to take refuge with singleness of heart (*isshin kimyō*).

To point out what *kimyō*, or "taking refuge," means, Shinran in marginalia defines it as "to put your trust in [him], to implore [him]"; that is, what he calls *shinjin* would have to mean imploring Amida with singleness of heart. However, we can look to Shinran only so far for a clarification. It was due to Rennyo's efforts that this basic notion underwent a further development and came to be expressed in the only way he could conceive: as the imploring of Amida with singleness of thought. That is, it is Amida who should be the object of our imploring.

It is due especially to Rennyo that the formulation to implore the Buddha, saying, "Amida, save me in the life to come," came to earn the high regard it did. Through the development of *nenji no gi*, or holding [to Amida] in one thought, the fundamental qualities of *tariki shinjin*, or the awakening of faith generated by Other Power, were clarified to a further degree. As we embrace this hallmark of Rennyo's teaching, we should deeply appreciate the implications it holds for us.

The unity of seeker and Dharma

If we gave thought to the matter, we would find that the self we think we know is only apparitional; the real self is something we know nothing of. For this reason, we float through life in a dream; we deceive ourselves, thinking it our fate to paddle about, never reaching solid ground. Clinging to wife and child out of attachment to dear life, we strive to extend our life as long as possible. We add to the larder our aspersions to wis-

30. *Rennyoshōninitokuki* is a sixteenth century biography of Rennyo; for an annotated translation of the first chapter, where this citation appears, see "The Legacy of Rennyo Shōnin: *Rennyoshōninitokuki*," Part 1, in *Eastern Buddhist* XXXI, 2 (1998).

dom and good; we want to believe that we harbour deep in ourselves the light of inner convictions to see us through bad times.

But religion challenges our notions, saying: *Be yourself, throw down that mask, reflect on who you really are.* For those who truly wish to live, this is what must be done: admit the vanity of your knowledge and deeds, and confront the darkness and ignorance of your own soul. Own up to the fact that in an ever-changing world we are merely life forms that bear within ourselves the terrible seed of our own demise. When it comes our time to confont this ultimate source of despair, there is no turning to wife or children or worldly possessions for consolation. At this final impasse we learn the truth that man, born alone, dies alone.

Forced to face the darkness of our own soul, there is one thing this miserable portrait of self elicits from us: the desire to be saved. With our entire being focused toward that one purpose we implore the powers that be, "Buddha, save me," and we stand ready to give everything—all our worldly possessions—if only the Buddha would "Save me in the life to come."

Rennyo taught that "with the thought of holding fast to the sleeve of this Buddha Amida, we [should] entrust ourselves [to him] to save us"[31]—words describing a direct encounter [with the Buddha]. Answering our thought of "Buddha, save me" is the Buddha's immediate assurance, "Count on me to save you." In Shinran's words,

> For within the one thought-moment of taking refuge—NAMU—there is aspiration for birth and directing of virtue. This, then, is the thought that Amida Tathāgata directs to ordinary beings.[32]

The cry of "Buddha, help me" of one in distress issues spontaneously when one comes in direct contact with Other Power. Our cry for help and the Buddha's promise to save us may seem worlds apart, but that is only when things are seen at a remove, in the way scholars view matters when absorbed in the study of religious concepts. A truly religious sentiment stirs the moment the life of the soul awakens unto itself. This event occurs when the seeker's cry of "Save me" is in complete rapport with the salvific Buddha's "I'm coming." Our call for help is the other side of the loving thoughts the Buddha directs toward us. Rennyo thus spoke constantly of the unity of seeker and Dharma (*kihō ittai*),[33] and of

31. *Letters* II-13; trans. Rogers and Rogers, 189–190.

32. *Letters* V-5; trans. Rogers and Rogers, 245.

33. *Kihō ittai* is a term from the *Anjinketsujōshō*, a work by an unknown hand. Although it is undated, it is thought to postdate Shinran since he never cites the work. The *Anjinketsujōshō* is important to Rennyo and he frequently mentions it in his *Letters*. In 1708, however, a Shinshū *shūgaku* scholar named Ekū discussed it as a Seizan-ha work. This compromized its centrality as a Shinshū work and it has since been ushered to the sidelines until its fate is decided. For a translation, see Dennis Hirota, trans., "On Attaining the Settled Mind: *Anjinketsujōshō*," in *The Eastern Buddhist*

the unity of the Buddha and ordinary beings (*butsubon ittai*).

Further, he advocated that the expression of our will to be saved by imploring Amida seen in the words "Buddha, save me," is concomitant with the expression of the Buddha's will to save us, seen in "Call on me." Therefore, Rennyo would say that the Buddha's saying, "Call on me and surely you will be saved," is not issued as a condition of salvation, but rather that it is an expression of the Will of that salvific force. The phrase "Count on me" entirely expresses the intent with which the true Buddha issues the vow [to save all beings].

This [intent of the vow] is the summation of the entire life force of the Tathāgata Buddha.[34] When the intent of the vow emerges in the world space of an ordinary being, it takes the form of the single thought of "Save me." Whether we are speaking of Tathāgata Buddha or ordinary beings, the life force that energizes them is one and the same. When we call on this selfsame life force, the ripples of our pleas reach the other side; when we implore to be saved, the salvific force gushes forth [as if from the very ground on which we stand].[35] It is here that we have proof that Namu Amidabutsu is nothing other than the unity of seeker and Dharma (*kihō ittai*).

The act of taking refuge

In this connection, Rennyo always advocated *nenji no gi*, or holding to Amida, in terms of understanding Namu Amidabutsu. One key emphasis in his teaching was, "Realizing faith means...understanding what NAMU-AMIDA-BUTSU is."[36] Thus, he relied on Shàndǎo's explanation of the six-character Name (NA-MU-A-MI-DA-BUTSU),[37] but interpreted it rather freely. To wit,

> In our tradition the meaning of settled mind is wholly expressed by six characters, NA-MU-A-MI-DA-BUTSU. That is, when we take refuge (NAMU), Amida Buddha immediately saves us. The two characters NA-MU mean "taking refuge." "Taking refuge" signifies the mind of sentient

23/22 (1990), 106–121, and 24/1 (1991), 81–96.

34. Ed. The combination of Tathāgata (thus come one) and Buddha (enlightened one) is unusual but is presumably meant to emphasize the transcendental nature of the Buddha in this and subsequent contexts.

35. The influence of Soga Ryōjin (1875–1971) on the author is particularly evident in this passage, where the imagery of spiritual energy gushing forth from the ground is used. It derives from the earthsprung bodhisattva in the Lotus Sutra that Soga also noticed in Nichiren. Soga has a long early study on Nichiren; see volume two of his Collected Works.

36. *Letters* 5-5; trans. Rogers and Rogers, 245.

37. Ed. "*Butsu*" may look like two syllables when transliterated, but it is theoretically one syllable; the final *u* is hardly pronounced, leaving *buts*, and in the context of the *nenbutsu* it is contracted to *bu*.

> beings who abandon the sundry practices and steadfastly entrust themselves to Amida Buddha to save them, [bringing them to buddhahood] in the afterlife. [The four characters A-MI-DA-BUTSU] express the mind of Amida Tathāgata who, fully knowing sentient beings, saves them without exception. Accordingly, since Amida Buddha saves beings who entrust themselves—NAMU—we know that the import of the six characters NA-MU-A-MI-DA-BUTSU is precisely that all of us sentient beings are equally saved. Hence our realization of Other-Power faith is itself expressed by the six characters NA-MU-A-MI-DA-BUTSU. We should recognize, therefore, that all the scriptures have the sole intent of bringing us to entrust ourselves to the six characters NA-MU-A-MI-DA-BUTSU.[38]

From this example alone, we can see that Rennyo put emphasis especially on the two characters NA-MU of the six-character Name. [The act of taking refuge signified by] the two characters NA-MU thus lies at the heart of *nenji no gi*, or holding to Amida.

Scholars have long since discussed this aspect of Rennyo's message in terms of [a progression from] (A) *niji-soku-shiji* ("two equals four characters"), to (B) *niji-soku-rokuji* ("two equals six characters"), and finally to (C) *rokuji-soku-rokuji* ("six equals six characters"). In the seeker's one thought of taking refuge, the conditions for Amida's Buddhahood are brought to fulfillment (two equals four). Accordingly, the seeker's thought of NA-MU is not simply NA-MU, but the entire Namu Amidabutsu turned over to the seeker by the Tathāgata Buddha (two equals six). [In the end,] the seeker and the Dharma are one in Namu Amidabutsu (six equals six).

The summons of the Tathāgata

Namu Amidabutsu is thus the true source of our strength; it is the true intent of the vow made by the Tathāgata Buddha.

> Amida Tathāgata has declared that he will unfailingly save those sentient beings who single-heartedly rely on him—ordinary beings in the last age and people like ourselves, burdened with evil karma, however deep the evil may be.[39]

This passage is revealing of Rennyo's understanding of the Eighteenth Vow; it also highlights his thinking on the significance of the six-character Name.

The summons of the Tathāgata calls to us, its resonance rising up through the depths of the soul to reach the very ground on which we stand. The voice may be so faint as to be barely audible, and though its roots are strong and run deep, it is possible for a person to pay it no heed. On the other hand, it is possible that the summons we want to

38. *Letters* V. 9; trans., Rogers and Rogers, 249; slightly adapted.

39. *Letters* IV. 9; trans., Rogers and Rogers, 234.

ignore is a strong one. In that case, we are only deceiving ourselves if we pass our lives turning a deaf ear to that inner call. Or, rather, it is *because* we hear the call of Amida's summons that we are stricken with remorse that our life full of bad karma makes it impossible to leave off the spurious life we are now living [to start anew].

However, if, hearing that call (*monshin*), we open ourselves to that summons, this is none other than the emergence of that one thought of imploring the Buddha to save us. It is rare that salvation comes knocking on our door. Yet, this marks the determination of our birth in the Pure Land by the salvific force of the Buddha. This is the proof of future birth in the midst of our activities in ordinary life (*heizei gōjō*), and we need not wait in anticipation for the Buddha to appear to us in a vision on our deathbed (*raigō*). As a consequence Rennyo taught,

> The nenbutsu, saying the Name of the Buddha, should then be understood as the nenbutsu of grateful return for Amida's benevolence, through which the Tathāgata has established our birth.[40]

Correcting odd notions

This simple and uncomplicated message worked like magic to slake the spiritual thirst of people then. The truth is, though, Rennyo also had to expend much effort to correct the odd notions (*igi*) and popular misunderstandings of that age. In his *Letters* we find references to odd notions such as the settled mind of ten *kalpas* (*jū-kō anjin*), secret practices requiring no buddha worship (*ogamazu hiji*), relying on your teacher to work out your salvation (*zenchishiki danomi*), joining the community sheerly for one's own benefit (*ichiyaku hōmon*),[41] chanting as the true cause of salvation (*shōmyō shōin*), believing that the amount of donation is determinative of salvation (*sebutsu danomi*), and so on. To deal with them he would point out just exactly how they are mistaken, or he would set down in writing how these views are absurd and should be thrown out.

It seems that these odd notions were a transference of the doctrine of human perfectibility (*shōdōmon*) to Shin doctrine. Joining the community sheerly for one's own benefit (*ichiyaku hōmon*) would seem to be one such example. Others represent the influx of variant streams of Pure Land Buddhism into Shin Buddhism. Chanting as the true cause of salvation (*shōmyō shōin*) is an example. In those days, the final voicing while facing the west was thought to hold great merit for the dying practitioner and was popular not only in the Jōdo-shū but also in certain Shin circles where chanting the nenbutsu in this setting was thought to be determinative of salvation. Further, during his travels in Kaga and

40. *Letters* V. 10; trans. Rogers and Rogers, 249.

41. Ed. There may be alternatives in the translation of this particular point.

Echigo (present day Ishikawa and Niigata prefectures) the most prevalent of such groups he encountered in the community were those who followed secret practices (*hiji*). All of the various odd notions can be said to derive from the followers of such secret practices. Rennyo had to deal with them severely and declared,

> [These] are certainly not the Buddha-dharma; they are deplorable, outer [non-Buddhist] teachings. Relying on them is futile; it creates karma through which one sinks for a long time into the hell of incessant pain.[42]

Regulations

In addition, in his *Letters*, he set down *okite*, or special regulations, that he had to institute on certain occasions. One such case is known as the *Rokujō no ofumi*, or Six Item Letter.

> Item: Do not make light of shrines.
> Item: Do not make light of the buddhas, bodhisattvas, or temples [enshrining deities].
> Item: Do not slander other sects or other teachings.
> Item: Do not slight the provincial military governors or local land stewards.
> Item: The interpretation of the Buddha-dharma in this province is wrong; therefore, turn to the right teaching.
> Item: Other-Power faith as established in our tradition must be decisively settled deep in our hearts and minds.[43]

In the final two items Rennyo urges the correct pursuit of *shinjin* and cautions that *anjin*, or settled mind, will be realized only after unorthodox notions have been dispensed with. He comments further on the fourth item, saying,

> [In regard to the provincial military governors and local land stewards] deal carefully with fixed yearly tributes and payments to officials and, besides that, take [the principles of] humanity and justice as fundamental.[44]

This he issued as an injunction to those who called themselves Buddhists yet whose behavior went beyond normative social bounds. The third item was intended as a warning to undisciplined elements who, while taking up the shield of dedicated nenbutsu practice, made light of the gods and buddhas of other traditions. There are in any age those who will fail to act discreetly in the religious setting, but their numbers swell especially during times of social disturbance and war. As can well be imagined, the unruly elements of his community who transgressed in

42. *Letters* II. 14; trans. Rogers and Rogers, 190–191.

43. *Letters* III. 10; trans. Rogers and Rogers, 209.

44. *Letters* III. 10; trans. Rogers and Rogers, 211.

word and deed were numerous, and it was no easy matter for Rennyo to keep them in line.

It is only natural that these regulations set down at a certain time and place should be adopted as perennial guidelines for the Shin tradition. Rennyo not only formulated rules of conduct for followers in society at large, he was also constantly concerned with how individual followers interacted with one another and advised them accordingly. Numerous entries in *Goichidaikikikigaki* contain examples of such advice. As we let his words serve as mottos for daily life and as we pursue lives of self-reflection, we should be inspired by the legacy of Rennyo who himself stood in awe of the invisible working [of the Buddha] in life.

(Translated by Wayne S. Yokoyama)

— 15 —

Asahara Saichi the Myōkōnin

Satō Taira

This contribution was first published in *The Eastern Buddhist* in 1985 and for this edition a small number of revisions have been made by the author himself.[1]

I

In the introduction of Japanese spirituality to the West, the greatest emphasis has been placed on the dynamic figures of the Zen sect. With their enigmatic words and forceful actions they have made interesting figures of study, a study aided by the vast collection of Zen literature and mystical writings, and by the highly visible profile maintained by the Zen sect throughout Japanese history. Japan has, however, another tradition of deep spirituality, one which represents in many ways an antithesis to the Zen approach. This is the Shin Buddhist tradition of the *myōkōnin* 妙好人, the "wondrous, good people." Writings on them in English have been largely confined to a few articles by D. T. Suzuki, who says:

> They are distinguished generally by their good-heartedness, unworldliness, piousness, and lastly by their illiteracy, that is, their not being learned in the lore of their religion and not being at all argumentative about what they believe... they are not intellectually demonstrative, they just go on practising what they have innerly experienced. When they express themselves at all, they are unaffected, their words come directly from their innermost hearts and refer directly to the truth of their faith.[2]

1. The article was adapted from "*Myōkōnin Asahara Saichi no nyūshin ni kansuru ichikō-satsu: Toku ni sono oya to no kankei o megutte*" (The Spiritual Awakening of the Myōkōnin Asahara Saichi: With Emphasis on Saichi's Relation to His Parents), in *Shinran Kyōgaku*, Volume 39 (November 1981), 56–71. The translation for the first edition was made by Thomas Kirchner (cf. Original Publication Details below).

2. D. T. Suzuki, *A Miscellany on the Shin Teaching of Buddhism*, Kyōto (Shinshū Ōtaniha Shūmusho) 1949, 71.

The simplicity and illiteracy of the *myōkōnin* meant, of course, that they seldom attained positions of religious leadership and rarely left records of their spiritual insights. Even within the Shin sect their position has been largely peripheral. Writings on them began to reach the general public only with the work of D. T. Suzuki, who viewed the *myōkōnin* as representing one of the purest forms of Japanese spirituality.[3]

Biographies and other such works did exist prior to this. Such late Edo Period (1603–1867) publications as the *Biographies of Myōkōnin* and *Further Biographies of Myōkōnin*[4] record the words and deeds of some 150 *myōkōnin*, men and women alike, who lived during that era. Other biographies appeared later, principally in the form of booklets devoted to a particular *myōkōnin*, such as *The Record of the Way of Life of Shōma* (*Shōma Arinomama no Ki*).

These works were compiled by Shin priests on the basis of interviews and secondary reports; they invariably take the form of narratives in the third person, with the compiler's own commentary and interpretation comprising the greater part of the text. This makes it hard to achieve any kind of contact with the living personalities of the *myōkōnin* themselves.

For this reason the diaries of Asahara Saichi 浅原才市 (1850–1932) are of particular value, providing a record of the spiritual insights of one deep in this tradition. Saichi was a woodworker who lived in the town of Kobama in Iwami Province, present-day Shimane Prefecture. He was a shipwright until his early fifties, when he changed trades and became a maker of *geta* (Japanese wooden clogs), a job he continued until his death at 83.[5]

As Saichi sat carving his *geta* he would note down verses on shavings and scraps of wood (see illustrations). They are artless expressions of his inner, spiritual life; his very lack of erudition made them, if anything, all the more direct and alive. As these verses accumulated Saichi copied them into grade school notebooks, and they eventually comprised quite a large collection. Entered over a period of seventeen years, from the

3. See D. T. Suzuki, *Japanese Spirituality*, translated by Norman Waddell (Tokyo: Japan Society for the Promotion of Science, 1972). At the beginning of his chapter on Saichi, Dr. Suzuki writes, "I first heard of *Myōkonin* Saichi from Professor Nishitani Keiji almost two years ago [in 1943]. ... Upon reading [his poems] I felt that Japanese spiritual insight was here manifested in its pure form" (p. 177).

4. The former work, *Myōkōnin den* (Biographies of Myōkōnin), compiled by Kōsei and Sōjun, and edited by the latter, was published in 5 volumes between 1842 and 1858. *Myōkōnin den zokuhen* (Further Biographies *Myōkōnin*), was compiled and edited by Zō-ō, and published in 1850.

5. Ages given in this article are based on the old Japanese system of calculation, in which the first year of life is counted as age one, and the New Year marks the common birthday of everyone in the country. Thus all ages are one or sometimes two years higher than under the Western system.

Figure 15.1 Asahara Saichi.

spring of 1915 until his death early in 1932, they are estimated to number upward of ten thousand. Over 3,500 of these poems were edited by D. T. Suzuki in *The Collected Poems of Myōkōnin Asahara Saichi.*[6] Another 1,600 are found in the two-volume collection *The Poems of Myōkōnin Saichi* edited by Kusunoki Kyō.[7] The Suzuki and Kusunoki editions account for over 5,000 of Saichi's poems, even taking into consideration the duplication of one notebook (notebook 7 in Kusunoki's second volume reproduces notebook 27 of the Suzuki edition). The remaining poems were in some thirty other notebooks in the possession of the Teramoto family, which were unfortunately lost during the Tokyo air raids of World War II. Another ten notebooks or so remain unpublished to date for various reasons. We may estimate, then, that for the period represented by these notebooks, Saichi was composing verses at an average rate of two a day.

Important biographical information on Saichi is provided in Teramoto Edatsu's *My Memories of Asahara Saichi.*[8] This is an account written by the intimate friend who first introduced Saichi to the world.

6. D. T. Suzuki, ed., *Myōkōnin Asahara Saichi Shū* (The Collected Poems of Myokonin Asahara Saichi) (Tokyo: Shunjūsha, 1968); hereafter referred to as Suzuki, ed., *Collected Poems.*

7. Kusunoki Kyō, ed., *Myōkōnin Saichi no Uta* (The Poems of Myokonin Saichi), two volumes (Kyōto: Hōzōkan, 1949, 1977); hereafter referred to as Kusunoki, ed., *Poems.*

8. Teramoto Edatsu, *Asahara Saichi-ō o Kataru* (My Memories of Asahara Saichi) (Tokyo: Chiyoda Jogakuen, 1952); referred to hereafter as Teramoto, *Memories.*

Figure 15.2 Poem by Saichi pencilled on a wood-shaving.

This work has until now been the sole source of information on the awakening of faith in Saichi. Because much of it was written nearly 20 years after his death, however, it inevitably contains various errors and embellishments. A valuable source of cross-reference and additional information has been found in the records of Nehanji,[9] the family temple of the Asahara household. Much of this material has been used here to fill in details regarding Saichi's life and spiritual development.

This essay examines Saichi's relationship with his parents on the basis of the above documents, in an attempt to reveal something of the process through which Saichi became a *myōkōnin*. Due, perhaps, to the influence of the pietistic Edo period biographies, *myōkōnin* spirituality has often been stereotyped as a kind of natural religious genius, a product of unusual moral rectitude, or even the result of their very lack of education. Saichi's life, however, demonstrates that the *myōkōnin* must, like all people, endure the trials and tribulations of this world; this should help

9. A Shin sect temple originally located in the town of Ida, Shimane Prefecture, but moved in 1975 to the city of Gōtsu in the same prefecture due to Ida's decline in population.

correct the misunderstanding that the *myōkōnin* had an inborn capacity to perceive the spiritual dimensions of life.

As an introduction to the religious experience of Saichi, I would first like to give a brief overview of the concept of spiritual development as viewed by Shinran Shōnin (1173–1262), the founder of the Shin Buddhist sect. For Shinran, the path to pure spirituality involves a three-step process of deepening reflection,[10] by which the practiser attains to the world of "faith alone."[11]

As described in Shinran's chief work, the *Kyōgyōshinshō*, sincere aspiration begins with the awakening of religious consciousness and the desire for the attainment of Buddhahood through the power of Amida's Name. At the first stage, this takes the form of an ethical, moral desire to practice good and cultivate virtue. Here the practice of *nenbutsu* is viewed as one ethical discipline among many, on the same level as all acts of moral good.

Poem on woodshaving

Dō de kō de no
Omoni o torare.
Omoni torarete
Raku raku to.

The heavy burden of pondering
this-and-that
Has been lifted from me.
Released from the heavy burden,
I live free and at ease.

Poem pencilled on wood

Namu Amida morōte
Tonaeru nenbutsu wa,
Ichimi no jihi ga riyaku nari.
Hōsha no nenbutsu kore
kara deru zo. Go-on ureshi ya,
Namu Amida Butsu.

Chanting "*Namu Amida*,"
The *nenbutsu* I have been given;
The benefit is the taste of

10. See the *sangan tennyū* 三願転入 section of the *Kyōgyōshinshō*; *Shinshū Shōgyō Zensho*, Vol. II (Kyōto: Ōyagi Kōbundō, 1958), 165-66; hereafter referred to as SSZ.

11. Faith alone: *yuishin* 唯信, i.e. absolute faith in the Original Vow of Amida Buddha. The Original Vow is the 18th of Amida's vows listed in the *Larger Sūtra of Eternal Life*, in which Amida pledges not to attain Buddhahood until he has first saved all beings. The implication of this in Shin thought is that, since Amida has in fact attained Buddhahood, consequently all beings are already saved; faith is the complete awakening to this fact.

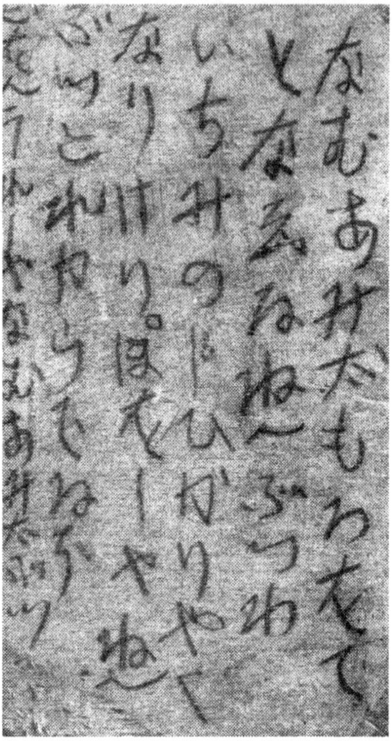

Figure 15.3 Poem by Saichi pencilled on wood.

all-embracing compassion.
The *nenbutsu* of gratitude flows
forth from this!
Such kindness fills me with joy—
Namu Amida Butsu!

Next comes the stage of single-minded *nenbutsu*, practiced as the ground of all virtue and the source of all ethical activities, the supreme good transcending all others. With sole concentration on the *nenbutsu*, the religious fervor of the practicer reaches a peak.

Shinran, however, criticizes this approach to *nenbutsu*, saying, "These people seek salvation through the power of the Original Vow with minds still bound by moral concepts of good and evil. Such single-mindedness is rooted in self-power."[12] Elsewhere he says, "Faith cannot appear in those who take the auspicious Name of the Original Vow to be their own root of good."[13] The phrase "still bound by moral concepts of good and evil" means that one holds with the principle of linear cause and effect, believing that pleasure results from good and pain from evil. This way of thinking has yet to transcend the realm of ethical discrimination. "Those

12. SSZ, Vol. II, *Kyōgyōshinshō*, 158.

13. SSZ, Vol. II, *Kyōgyōshinshō*, 165.

who take the auspicious Name of the Original Vow to be their own root of good" are not yet free from the attachment to "self-power" found at the base of man's ethical strivings. Here the ethical mind takes what is purely religious, the *nenbutsu* pledged in the Original Vow, and attempts to appropriate it as a personal technique for the attainment of salvation. The practiser still holds to self-power and has yet to attain the pure heart of faith imparted by the Original Vow. The final stage on Shinran's path is attained when the practiser has left behind the predilection to self-power underlying his ethical strivings and enters the world of true faith, trusting his birth in the Pure Land entirely to the *nenbutsu* given us in the Original Vow. At this stage, the believer awakens to the fact that the Buddha's salvation has always been his. With this realization, the *nenbutsu* is transformed from an ethical practice to an expression of gratitude for the compassion of Amida. This is the purity of faith manifested in the spirituality of the *myōkōnin.*

Regarding the *myōkōnin*, Shinran writes in his *Gāthas on the Two Gates of Entering and Leaving the Pure Land*:

> An ordinary person, filled with passions, comes to be embraced through relying on the power of the Buddha's vow ... such faith, extremely rare, is that of the *myōkōnin*, the most excellent of beings.[14]

Shinran, here as in all his writings, puts primary emphasis on "faith alone." This is especially evident when the quotation above is compared with the sūtra and commentary passages which inspired it. The *Meditation Sūtra*, one of the three Pure Land Sūtras, likens the practiser of the *nenbutsu* to a white lotus flower, the symbol of enlightenment.[15] In his *Commentary on the Meditation Sūtra*, Shàndăo (613–681) praises the practiser of the *nenbutsu* as a *myōkōnin*, *myōkō* referring to the "wonderfully beautiful" lotus flower and *nin* to the "person" who practises.[16] In both the *sūtra* and the commentary emphasis is placed on the practice of *nenbutsu*. In contrast, Shinran considers faith in the *nenbutsu*, not its practice, to be of greatest importance. The *myōkōnin* is thus the person of pure faith. This dimension of "faith alone" is also evident in the following passage from the *Tannishō*: "For me, Shinran, there is no other choice except to put faith in the words of my good teacher Hōnen, who told me, 'Just say the *nenbutsu* and you will be saved by Amida.'"[17] This Shin Buddhist emphasis on faith in the *nenbutsu* alone provided, I believe, the single necessary factor for the appearance of the *myōkōnin*, a phenomenon not seen in other schools of Pure Land Buddhism.

14. SSZ, Vol. II, *Nyūshutsunimonge*, 484.
15. SSZ, Vol. I (1957), *Kanmuryōjukyō*, 66.
16. SSZ, Vol. I, *Kangyōsho*, 558.
17. SSZ, Vol. II, *Tannishō* 2, 774.

II

Saichi was born in the small village of Kobama on the Japan Sea coast. His childhood was not to be a peaceful one. According to Teramoto Edatsu's *My Memories of Asahara Saichi*, in 1860, when Saichi was 11 years old, the Asahara household was broken apart by the departure of Saichi's father Yoshirō, who entered a small Buddhist hermitage near the cemetery of Anrakuji Temple in the same village. His subsequent lifestyle was to have a great influence on Saichi's development. Dwelling in poverty and solitude, he embarked on a path of world renunciation he was to continue for the rest of his life. He supported himself by selling flowers gathered in the fields and by helping at nearby Nehanji Temple; with his tattered robe and straw sandals, he was looked down upon as a beggar-monk by the townspeople.

Saichi's father's decision to leave home does not appear to have been altogether sudden or unexpected. He had been ordained at Nehanji at the age of six, receiving the Buddhist name Saikyō, and had lived there as an acolyte until he was 18. During his years as a householder he maintained his ties with that temple as a lay assistant, most likely shaven-headed. Evidence suggests that he always preferred the religious life to the secular; even his marriage seems to have been prompted mostly by his filial duty to continue the Asahara family line.[18]

It is said in *My Memories of Asahara Saichi* that, after Saikyō's departure, his wife returned to her parents' home taking Saichi along with her. She remarried soon after to a man of the same village named Yamamoto Wahei, and it was arranged for Saichi to become a carpenter's apprentice at the home of his paternal grandmother, the Kondō family. Thus Saichi was left homeless and virtually an orphan from a very young age, although ironically both parents continued to live their separate lives in the same village. In this unhappy state of affairs, Saichi completed his apprenticeship and began to work in a shipyard.

As Saichi commenced his career as an ordinary member of society, the otherworldly presence of his father Saikyō must have been a constant source of tension for him. It may well have been in blind reaction to his father's way of life that Saichi began seeking diversion in such pursuits as gambling.

Just as in Shinran's above-mentioned outline of spiritual development, Saichi's awakening to the Buddhist teachings began with the stirrings of moral consciousness. While he was in his early twenties and employed

18. Based on Teramoto, *Memories*, plus much new information found in the records of Nehanji. See the author's article, "Myokonin Asahara Saichi no chichioya Saikyō ni tsuite" (On the *Myokonin* Saichi's Father), in the *Journal of Indian and Buddhist Studies*, Vol. 33, No. 2 (March 1985).

as a carpenter at the Tsunozu shipyards in San'in, Saichi was arrested on a gambling charge. According to Teramoto Edatsu's account, the young police officer in charge of the case gave him such a severe reprimand that he swore he would make an effort to become a responsible citizen. In an earnest attempt to keep his promise, he started making the rounds of the Buddhist temples in the area, where he would quietly listen to sermons.

The self-reflection brought on by his arrest resulted in a complete turnabout in the direction of Saichi's life. Until then he had been driven by the pursuit of self-centered desires—what Buddhists call the three evil paths. Once awakened to his moral responsibility, however, he vowed to "become a human being,"[19] and quickly abandoned his former ways to seek a life of moral virtue. By turning to the Buddhist teachings in his search for inner peace, Saichi's decision reflects the influence, if only subconsciously, of his father Saikyō, who at the price of renouncing the world had finally won peace of mind.

In his search for moral truth, Saichi had now progressed beyond the stage of blind reaction evidenced by his earlier gambling activities. He still remained, though, in fundamental opposition to the religious world view of Saikyō. Resting in the Buddha's compassion, Saikyō could renounce the world from a position transcending the duality of good and evil. Saichi, still bound by moral considerations, could only regard the transcendent world view of his father as wholly antagonistic to every ethical and humanistic value he held. To those whose way of thinking is confined to the ethical perspective, the transcendence of ethics can only appear as the denial of ethics. Such individuals regard themselves to be righteous by virtue of their own moral efforts. For Saichi, then, the more earnestly he searched for truth on the conscious level, the more peaked his defiance to his father's religious outlook became.

Saichi, now twenty-five, took a wife named Setsu and settled in Kobama, though his job as a shipmaker entailed frequent trips to other areas. The new household may have offered Saichi an opportunity to start anew, after the bitter experiences of childhood. Thinking it the pious thing to do, he decided to invite his father to live with him and his wife. According to Teramoto, Saichi pleaded with his father to give up the solitary life he had been leading and to join their new household. From Saichi's ethical point of view, this was the highest virtue to which he could aspire in his relationship with his aged parent. The offer did not sit well with Saikyō, though, who flatly refused to consider it. He spent the rest of his life in the shack-like abode he was accustomed to, and never ventured to live in the home of his son.

19. As related by Kusunoki in his postscript to *Poems*, Vol. I, 243.

This episode was crucial for both of these truth seekers; had Saikyō assented, the situation would have been ruinous to both their religious careers. Saikyō refused to let Saichi be complacent with the mere ethical level of existence. The childhood affection that Saichi felt for his father had to be rejected once and for all, along with his conceptions of filial duty. It was such sternness that enabled Saichi's later religious faith to flower.

His father continued to live the same beggar-like existence day after day. In a poem Saichi wrote after faith had awakened in him, he recollects the period and expresses the humiliation he felt at that time:

> Saichi's heart is the heart of a demon,
> Saichi's heart is a great serpent.
> You hoped Father would hurry and die.
> You fool, you fool, you utter fool!
> How wretched I am!
> How wretched!
> *Namu Amida Butsu,*
> *Namu Amida Butsu.*[20]

On January 3, 1891, Saikyō passed away at the age of 83. Saichi was 45 at the time. Their confrontation remained unresolved even as Saikyō breathed his last. Nevertheless, his death must have had a profound influence on Saichi's feelings regarding their relationship. When the object of contention vanishes, the thoughts that gave rise to the contention lose their foundation, and all that remains is the ego which underlay them. No longer distracted by his father's physical presence, Saichi was forced to consider the true condition of his own spirit. Saichi later wrote:

> Father's only bequest:
> *Namu Amida Butsu.*[21]

From this it is clear that, impressed in Saichi's mind, the figure of his father had merged with the formless *Namu Amida Butsu.*

III

With his father's death, Saichi's desire for enlightenment was inflamed. Having realized the futility of attempting to cultivate merit through moral deeds, Saichi's final hope was "Father's only bequest: *Namu Amida Butsu.*" Saichi was left with a deep consciousness of guilt by his realization of the resentment he felt toward his father, resentment occasioned by his own frustrated attempts at ethical self power, and expressed in his wish

20. Teramoto, *Memories*, 91.

21. Teramoto, *Memories*, 32. The original notebook containing the poem from which these words came has been lost.

that "Father would hurry and die." In this state of desperation, he was equally conscious of the *nenbutsu* as the sole, absolute means to salvation.

Spurred by his guilt, Saichi embarked on the exclusive practice of the Name. For a time, he confined himself to the *Nenbutsu Samādhi* Hall of Gokurakuji, the village's Jōdo sect temple, where he applied himself assiduously to the constant repetition of the Name. Strict religious observance marked his daily life as well. He never failed to perform morning and evening devotions, he attended sermons regularly at local temples, and he even helped with temple affairs. This was the life he led from the time of his father's death until the establishment of his own faith some fifteen years later.

This rigorous devotion was the actualization of a tendency latent in Saichi for quite some time. In the only extant poem of his earlier years, written when he was 31, Saichi says:

> What have I learned in these thirty-one years?
> Only a lot of monkey-wisdom.
> Giving up my monkey-scheming,
> I just recite *Namu Amida Butsu.*[22]

The moral element here is still strong, with *nenbutsu* viewed as a method of ethical training—little of the joy that fills his later verses can be seen.

Saichi had engaged in other devotional activities as well. At the age of thirty-three he made a three-month pilgrimage to Kinki, Hokuriku, and Shinano to visit the historic sites sacred to Shinran Shōnin. Two years later, in 1880, he took the confirmation ceremony[23] at the Honganji headquarters in Kyōto, receiving the Buddhist name Shaku Shūso. Saichi's wife Setsu also underwent this ceremony in 1891, receiving the name of Shakuni Kōryū.

Saichi's renewed devotion after the death of Saikyō gives some idea of the sincerity with which he sought to live up to the legacy bestowed upon him: "Father's only bequest: *Namu Amida Butsu.*" Even in the fastness of his stern religious life, however, Saichi's life was not free of incident. Following the common Japanese custom, a husband for Saichi's only daughter Saki was adopted into the household to ensure the continuance of the Asahara family name, and to provide support for Saichi and his wife in their final years. This marriage ended in failure, however, as did another to a second adopted husband. Saki finally left the household and married a third time to a man named Umeki Unosuke, with whom she emigrated to Korea in 1902.[24] Left without guarantee of

22. Found in the records of Nehanji. This poem appears to have been transcribed by someone other than Saichi, as it is not in his hand.

23. Ed. This probably refers to *kikyōshiki.*

24. This information found in the Asahara family records, preserved at the Yunotsu town hall.

Figure 15.4 Asahara Saichi in group at the temple Anrakuji.

support in old age, Saichi's position was quite insecure. It appears to be about this time that he left the physically demanding work of shipbuilding and turned to *geta*-making, a more sedentary occupation which he could continue throughout old age.[25] It was probably also about this time that he began receiving frequent instruction from the priest of Anrakuji, Umeda Kenkyō, who was to be his teacher for the rest of Saichi's life.

In the midst of a collapsing world, his personal efforts frustrated, Saichi continued in his earnest search for salvation. His sole guide was the legacy left him by his father, the realization of *Namu Amida Butsu*. In his search, even his relationship with his wife provided no escape from the utter loneliness he felt:

> How wretched this heart, this devil's heart!
> Her heart, too, is a devil's heart.
> A wretched lot we are,
> Snarling at each other every time we meet.
> Sure proof I am in hell! How wretched I am!
> *Namu Amida Butsu, Namu Amida Butsu.*[26]

Long years of struggle, of "snarling at each other every time we meet," must have passed before Saichi could express the humility revealed in the last two lines of this poem, written after his attainment of faith.

In the desperation of his search at this time, it is said that Saichi

25. See the author's article, "Asahara Saichi no tegami" (A Study of a Newly-discovered Letter by the *Myōkōnin* Saichi), in *Shunjū*, No. 261 (September 1984), 11–15.

26. Teramoto, *Memories*, 104–105.

reached such an impasse that at one point he nailed his home altar shut, declaring, "The difficulty of Amida's message is too much for me."[27]

When Saichi was fifty-nine his mother Sugi passed away. As best we can tell, Saichi's attainment of faith occurred when he was approaching sixty, hence these two events roughly concur. There is no direct evidence linking Saichi's attainment with his mother's death, but he was undoubtedly deeply affected by the event. In a poem from one of his later journals he writes:

> Father, age 84, borne away to the Pure Land.
> Mother, age 83, borne away to the Pure Land.
> Should I get there too one day,
> We three, parents and child together, will rescue all beings.
> Such kindness fills me with joy! *Namu Amida Butsu.*[28]

Saichi's realization that he had been compassionately embraced by Amida Buddha (referred to as Oyasama, literally meaning "parent") coincides with the final severing of his ties with his parents. It is intriguing to speculate on the exact content of Saichi's first notebook, now lost, for it would shed much light on the earliest phase of Saichi's religious transformation. All that is known about it is that it was a plain school notebook, entitled "The First Notebook of a Layman's Joy in the Dharma" (*Daiichi Hōetsuchō Ubasoku*). Fortunately, at least some of its contents are known to us through quotations found in the Teramoto book. Judging from those entries, the poems are not as polished as those of his later years, but they vividly convey to us Saichi's state of mind around the time that he embarked on his journey into the world of faith. Among the entries is a poem of unusual length and humility, of which this is one part:

> Numberless the ranks of evil men
> Yet of all people in the world
> My heart is the worst of all.
> Though I may not have actually said it in words,
> In my heart I wished my father dead.
> I wondered why he didn't die.
> It's amazing the earth hasn't yet cracked open under me,
> This mass of monstrously evil karma. ...[29]

A sorrowful tone of confession is detected in these lines. Saichi had accepted his father's bequest, *Namu Amida Butsu*, and made efforts to practise it single-mindedly, but he had failed to realize that his desire to see his father dead implicated him spiritually in the crime of patricide.

---

27. An anecdote related to the author by Yamamoto Ine, a native of Saichi's village.
28. Teramoto, *Memories*, 19. Saichi himself gives the age of his father's death as 84; more accurately, as stated earlier, his father died at age 83.
29. Teramoto, *Memories*, 22–23.

Till then his attachments to self-power had confined him to the ignorance of ego-centered discrimination, and he remained unaware of his own profound guilt. Without the light that sunders the shroud of ignorance, he could never realize that he was "this mass of monstrously evil karma."

When and from where did this light issue? It had always been present. The light shining upon Saichi was the *Namu Amida Butsu* into which he had poured his life. With the penetration of the light of Dharma, the light of Other Power, into the core of his existence, Saichi was made aware of the monstrously evil karma of one who had wished the death of his own father. With this insight into the true nature of his helplessness, he realized the futility of his reliance on self-power, enabling the absolute compassion of Other Power to come forth. Thus his encounter with Other Power came at the same time as his encounter with his true self. Or rather, in the moment of encounter, both Self and Other Power were fully discovered.

The Japanese word for encounter is *deai* 出会い. It literally means "to come out" (*de*) and "to meet" (*ai*). It aptly expresses the nuance that "meeting" can only occur with "coming out" (*ekstasis*), in the sense that true encounter can occur only when one has come out of the world one is the center of. We encounter the true man or the true Dharma only when we leave our self-centered discriminations, our conceptualizations of "self" and "Dharma."

Thus in the true encounter with self, ego-centered duality is left behind and the self becomes self-as-it-is. At the moment of full realization of self-as-it-is, the separation between self and Dharma disappears.

"Meeting" (*ai*) also carries the connotation of a moving together into unity; the encounter with self is the absolute unification of that self which has transcended the duality of ego consciousness. In the encounter of this self with Dharma, the primordial unity of self and Dharma is realized. In this lies the existential actualization of "the identity of opposites" (*coincidentia oppositorum*) and "the self-identity of absolute contradiction" of which the philosophers speak.

This encounter with self brought Saichi to the realization of his "monstrously evil karma." In Shin this is the realization of "the evil man who entrusts himself to Other Power,"[30] a term which implies a turning away from the self-centered performance of good to complete dependence on Other Power. Saichi writes:

> In Other Power
> There is no self-power, no Other Power.

30. From *Tannishō* 3; SSZ, Vol. II, 775. The full context of this phrase is: "The essential intent with which [Amida] made the Vow...was the attainment of Buddhahood by the person of evil; hence the evil person who entrusts himself to Other Power is precisely [the one possessed of] the true cause for birth" (Hirota trans., *Tannishō. A Primer*, Kyōto: Ryūkoku University, 1982, 61).

All is Other Power: *Namu Amida Butsu.*[31]

"Other Power" in the first line is Saichi's experience of absolute Other Power. In the second line, he alludes to the relative, dualized "Other Power" that stands opposed to "self-power." The true experience of Other Power is of the absolute Other Power that transcends our conceptual thinking—in this there is no discrimination between self and other. "The evil man who entrusts himself to Other Power" discovers his true self in the midst of Other Power, as expressed in the last line, "All is Other Power."

Upon the realization of his true nature as "this mass of monstrously evil karma," Saichi earnestly sought refuge in Other Power. A pure faith in the great compassionate heart of Amida was born in him.

The Parent (Amida) and myself are joined in spirit.
Of course we're joined: self and Other Power are one [in *Namu Amida Butsu*].
We often hear about unity,
But there's no unity as perfect as this.[32]
Nothing is as intimate as Parent and child;
Your spirit and my spirit are together as one.
Namu Amida Butsu has become my soul.[33]
Parent's mind and child's mind,
Between them there is no restraint.
Namu Amida Butsu is both Parent's "Come!" and child's "Yes!"[34]
In all the world there is but one Parent, one child;
Parent and child in *Namu Amida Butsu.*
Reciting *nenbutsu* full of joy.[35]

The number of Saichi's poems celebrating the "parent-child" relationship ("Parent," of course, referring to Amida, and "child" to Saichi) is too great to count. When we become aware of the absolute compassion of Amida Buddha, a compassion which forgives and accepts even that which we would be afraid to show our own flesh-and-blood parents, then we become truly as children and achieve the realm of peace of the Compassionate Parent.

But this parent-child unity is not the unity of one who has never experienced separation. Saichi's realization of himself as a great sinner, one who "wished his father dead," is not the realization of one who has yet to leave his relationship of childish reliance on his parents. It is possible only from a position of full independence.

---

31. Suzuki, ed., *Collected Poems*, 174.
32. Kusunoki, ed., *Poems*, Vol. I, 132–133.
33. Kusunoki, ed., *Poems*, Vol. I, 93.
34. Suzuki, ed., *Collected Poems*, 71.
35. Suzuki, ed., *Collected Poems*, 449.

IV

Through his confrontation with his parents, Saichi severed his natural relationship with them and found himself absolutely alone. In that state he encountered the Parent of Great Compassion. The unity expressed in the poem above is, therefore, a unity which has been re-attained after a passage through separation, possible only after a complete severance has taken place. There is a poem which expresses this well:

> The Name of the Parent cuts too well,
> Too sharp to feel is the Parent's *Name.*
> Not conscious of the borderline between "*Namu*" and "*Amida Butsu*"—
> Such is the sharpness of the six-syllable Name.
> Self and Other Power are one, through the kindness and compassion of the Parent.
> To this does Saichi surrender.[36]

This poem brings to mind a line from one of Shàndǎo's hymns: "Like a keen sword is the Name of Amida: With one recitation all evil is removed."[37] It is likely that Saichi had just heard a sermon on this phrase when he wrote the verse above. Yet there is in his understanding something unique, profound, and subtle. The keen blade of *Namu Amida Butsu* cuts so well that one is unaware that the cut has been made. The cut here is between "*Namu*" and "*Amida Butsu,*" that is, between the self which supplicates and the object of supplication.

Saichi writes, "Not conscious of the borderline between '*Namu*' and '*Amida Butsu*'," meaning that these two have been severed with one stroke; "*Namu,*" the self, and "*Amida Butsu,*" Other Power, have been cut in two. In this act, what has actually been cut is the discriminating intellect which stood between "*Namu*" and "*Amida Butsu*" trying somehow to force them together: The keen edge of the Name has cut off the attachments of the rationalizing mind to its own self-power. With this severed, "*Namu*" is just "*Namu*" and "*Amida Butsu*" is just "*Amida Butsu,*" and herein lies the realization of the absolute "*Namu Amida Butsu*" where both self (*Namu*) and Other Power (*Amida Butsu*) are one, and at the same time both independent and just as they are. This is the true experience of faith in Shin Buddhism, where self and Other Power are united in the transcendence of attachments to the discriminating mind.

This absolute *Namu Amida Butsu* appears with the cutting off of the world of discrimination by *Namu Amida Butsu.* This is the realm of absolute reality expressed in the line, "Not conscious of the borderline between '*Namu*' and '*Amida Butsu*'." Praising this transcendent realm with the words, "Such is the sharpness of the six-syllable Name,"

36. Suzuki, ed., *Collected Poems*, 303.

37. SSZ, Vol. I, *Hanjusan*, 688.

Saichi then returns everything to Amida: "Self is Other Power, through the kindness and compassion of the Parent."

The first statement can be viewed as an exclamation from the world of non-duality, and the second as Saichi's appraisal of this experience after returning to ordinary consciousness. At the moment of his return to the everyday realm of separation, Saichi sees the limited nature of the self before the infinity of Other Power. Saichi's very return to self thus gives rise to a pure faith absolutely passive to Other Power. Making *geta* in this state of faith, Saichi finds his ordinary life imbued with the workings of the non-dual *Namu Amida Butsu.*

Saichi's frequent use of the expression "The oneness of self and Other Power—*Namu Amida Butsu*" is probably due to the influence of the book Letters (*Ofumi*) by the Shin Buddhist priest Rennyo (1415–1499). Saichi studied this volume every day, absorbing its teachings as he held it in his left hand and traced each line with the index finger of his right. Sometimes he noted in the margin, "These words are also for me." In Saichi's copy of this work the pages are rubbed thin where his finger traced along the paper, and a large hole is worn where his left thumb touched the cover. In the seventh letter of the third section of this book the following passage appears: "The two syllables '*Na-mu*' refer to the self which believes in Amida Buddha. The four syllables '*A-mi-da-bu*[*tsu*]' refer to the Other Power of Amida Nyorai which saves all sentient beings. '*Namu Amida Butsu* as the oneness of self and Other Power' signifies this meaning."[38] Considering Saichi's devoted study of this work, it is only natural that it would exert a profound influence on his poetic expression. This is evidenced in the following verse:

> I want to be friends with Rennyo-sama;
> If we aren't friends the loss is mine.
> If we get along and I can hear his teachings,
> Then I will know the turning point between self-power and Other Power.
> With self-power abandoned and Other Power accepted, *Namu* is me and *Amida* is the Parent.
> The oneness of self and Other Power—*Namu Amida Butsu. Namu Amida Butsu* is Parent and child.[39]

Here the expression "Parent and child" is used, but this does not refer to a relationship which has yet to experience separation. Expressions such as "no-mind," "non-discrimination," and "the mind of a child" are used to represent the experience of pure spirituality, but these must not be taken to indicate a non-differentiated, formless state. The infantile unity of parent and child needs once to be cut in the pain of separation, and with complete separation comes the moment of true unity.

38. SSZ, Vol. III (1941), *Ofumi*, 461.

39. Suzuki, ed., *Collected Poems*, 309.

The unity of emotional dependence before separation is simply another expression of the self-centered world view constructed by the intellect. This type of ego-centered world view inevitably comes to an impasse, and when this impasse reaches its extremity the dependency of the pre-separated state is finally cut off. Herein is achieved the faith of true independence, an independence rooted not in self but in absolute dependence on Other Power.

True faith is the non-discriminating faith attained in the transcendence of the dualism of self-power. Saichi's unity of parent and child is a unity which has passed through the tribulations inherent in the ordinary parent-child relationship, a unity born of a non-dual mind which accepts with simple faith the compassion of the Buddha. In this purity of faith the mind attached to self-centered discrimination is cut off, and one finds unity with Amida and all of existence. To merely remain in the parent-child state of undifferentiated unity is never to escape the primitive religious realm of mythical union, a realm thoroughly transcended by the *myōkōnin.*

I would like to conclude with a poem of Saichi's which aptly sums up his religious experience.

Suffering in heart, are you doubtful of Amida's compassion?
That would truly be a great misunderstanding.
The suffering of this evil man becomes a great treasure.
Please understand the point of this teaching.
Namu Amida Butsu is truly mysterious.
What is mysterious is that
Sea, mountains, food, lumber for building houses,
And everything else related to the life of an ordinary man,
All these are an embodiment of *Namu Amida Butsu.*[40]
Everyone, please understand this well.
This is the compassion of the Parent.
Such kindness fills me with joy!
Namu Amida Butsu, Namu Amida Butsu!
The Tathāgata possesses a truly mysterious power:
The means to turn Saichi into a Buddha.
Namu Amida Butsu, Namu Amida Butsu.[41]

40. For Saichi the term "*Namu Amida Butsu*" takes on diverse meanings. In this case it refers to his experience of Amida Buddha as Dharma-in-itself.

41. Suzuki, ed., *Collected Poems*, 298–299.

— 16 —

The Rite of Reception into Jōdo Shinshū

Dan Bornstein

The text below is an overview of the rite for the reception of new members into the Ōtani branch of Jōdo Shinshū (Jōdo Shinshū Ōtani-ha), followed by translations of the sections marked with an asterisk. This rite is known as the *Kikyōshiki.* Where applicable the translation follows the *Service Book* of the Higashi Honganji (Shinshū Ōtani-ha) of the North America District. The word *gāthā* means "verses" in Sanskrit, and is used here to correspond to its Japanese transliteration *ge*, as in *Shōshinge.*

Order of the Ceremony

1. Opening words (*kaishiki no kotoba*)
2. The Jōdo Shinshū Gāthā* (*Shinshū Shūka*)—sung in unison
3. Recitation of the Three Refuges formula—taking refuge in the Three Treasures*: Buddha, Dharma, Sangha (*san-kie-mon*)
4. Rite of tonsure (*kamisori*)
5. Congratulation on official initiation as a disciple (*shikkō no kotoba*)
6. Conferral of Dharma name (*hōmyō dentatsu*)
7. Personal vow of the disciple* (*chikai no kotoba*) (in case of more than one participant, the vow text is chosen and read aloud by one member of the group, while the rest read the same text silently)
8. Routine liturgy (*gongyō*):
   a) Recitation of *Shōshinge* (The Gāthā of the Nenbutsu of True Awakening)
   b) *Nenbutsu* (Pronouncing the Name of Amida Buddha)

c) *Wasan* (Hymn of Praise for Amida Buddha, composed by Shinran Shōnin)
d) *Ekō* (vow of propagating the truth of Buddha's teaching and striving toward awakening).
[The three latter three elements are also referred to collectively as *Dōbō Hōsan* (The Companions' Reverential Praise)]

9. Sermon (*hōwa*)
10. Gāthā of Gratitude* (*Ondoku-san*)—sung in unison
11. Closing words (*heishiki no kotoba*)

Translations

Shinshū Shūka[1]

With a heartful reverence for the Dharma
deep appreciation beyond compare.
Through listening intently I found a way
to become genuinely compassionate.

True awakening from ignorance
brings incomparable joy.
Reciting the Nembutsu,
I approach each day in mindfulness.

Taking Refuge in the Three Treasures (*san-kie-mon* 三帰依文)

It is rare to be bestowed with human form, and now I have already been bestowed with it. It is rare to hear of the teaching of the Buddha, and now I have already heard of it. If I should not save myself during this existence, in what further existence could I do so? The multitude of human beings should join together and reverentially take refuge in the Three Treasures with the utmost sincerity of heart.

I reverentially take refuge in the Buddha. May I, together with all living beings, apprehend the Great Way and awaken the ultimate mindfulness.

I reverentially take refuge in the Dharma. May I, together with all living beings, gain profound access to the storehouse of sacred scriptures and attain ocean-like wisdom.[2]

I reverentially take refuge in the Sangha. May I, together with all living beings, be included in the brotherhood of those who are guided toward perfect freedom.

---

1. *Service Book*, 80.
2. Lit. may my wisdom become ocean-like.

The Dharma—unsurpassed, unfathomable, indescribable—is rarely met with even in the course of one billion aeons. I have now managed to see, hear, and be entrusted with it. May I have the privilege of perceiving the true significance of the Tathāgata [*Nyorai*].

Personal vow of the disciple (example)[3]

I have now, before the image of our school's founder, Shinran Shōnin, undergone the ceremony of confirmation and received a Dharma name, being my appellation as a disciple of the Buddha.

I now stand firm in a new self-awareness as a disciple of Shinshū, and begin to lead a life of faith in the Original Vow and of pronouncing the *Nembutsu*.

Hereafter, I shall make the morning and evening service the foundation of my daily life, and strive to visit temples or the Main Temple of Shinshū (Higashi Honganji) and regularly attend the sermons.

Date of the ceremony
Name of head priest of the conducting temple[4]
Name of the disciple:
Dharma name with the prefix Shaku (for men) or Shakuni (for women)

Ondoku-san[5]

I vow to express my gratitude for
the Great Compassion that embraces me continuously,
until my body turns to dust.

I vow to express my appreciation for
the wonderful lessons of my Dharma teachers,
until my bodily form is shattered.

---

3. This is the actual text used at a recent *Kikyōshiki*. The reference to the image of Shinran arises because the ceremony was held at Higashi Honganji, head temple in Kyōto, where the image is located. A text without this reference is used at other locations.
4. If not at the Honganji.
5. Service Book, 82–83. The text is given twice with alternative melodies.

Synoptic List of Text Titles

This is a consolidated list of texts which are directly referred to in the present volume. These include not only underlying Buddhist scriptures but also commentaries and further texts by various thinkers and teachers, whether Indian, Chinese or Japanese. As far as Japanese Buddhists are concerned, the normative texts of Buddhist tradition are those of the Chinese Buddhist Canon. This includes material with parallels to the Theravāda Canon, the major texts of Mahāyāna Buddhism, and much else besides which originated either in India or in China. Later writings by Japanese exponents such as Hōnen, Shinran, Rennyo and others also took on an authoritative aura of their own and are therefore also included here.

Japanese writers, whether ancient or modern, were usually thinking of older Buddhist texts in a Chinese form, which may not be exactly the same as a corresponding Sanskrit or Pāli text, if indeed there is one. But it had also become fashionable in modern scholarship to use Sanskrit titles as a kind of *lingua franca*, even to the extent of reconstituting or in effect inventing such titles retrospectively (cf. the "Conventions on Names, Titles and Scripts" at the beginning of this volume).

The Japanese authors of the various articles in this volume took quite varied decisions about how to refer to ancient Buddhist texts. The titles are sometimes translated, sometimes provided with the original Chinese characters, sometimes abbreviated, and so on. In the early twentieth century it was still early days in the global presentation of Buddhist thought, so there was obviously a certain amount of experimentation and out of respect to the authors, references in the various articles have been left basically as they were. However, where confusion might arise, clarifications have been added in square brackets or in footnotes. Moreover, one important reform has been carried out in that Pāli and Sanskrit transliterations have been standardized in accordance with modern practice.

The main purpose of this integrated list of texts is to facilitate cross-checking. The cross-references first point to the main entry in Japanese pronunciation, even for Chinese texts, and there the main variants in the relevant languages will be found.[1] In a few cases Sanskrit or even Pāli titles remain as the main entry by default. Since many variations in English are just alternative attempts at translation, made in those early days, they are not all repeated in the main entries.

The listing of Sanskrit titles in the main entries does indicate that there are corresponding Sanskrit texts, but even so it should be remembered that such titles are often generic, referring to various manuscripts of varying length. They do not identify a specific original text for any particular Chinese version. In cases where an identification is particularly imprecise, or was even simply invented retrospectively, a Sanskrit form will only be shown in square brackets.

When no Chinese pronunciation is given the implication is that, although a suitably educated Chinese person could imagine a Chinese pronunciation for the title, the text is a Japanese text or a Japanese composition in classical Chinese (Japanese *kanbun*).

There is a general problem about separating the component elements of Chinese and Japanese titles in transcription, because in the original languages no such separations are made. As in some other languages, the characters just follow on without interruption. The following conventions are adopted here. Endings in Japanese titles such as *-ron* (treatise), *-kyō* (sūtra), *-ge* (verses) or *-san* (hymn) are normally thought of, when spoken aloud, as being an integral part of the title, and so are not separated. In the case of Chinese however some endings such as *lùn* (treatise) and *jīng* (sūtra) are separated as a concession to wide usage. Again, although there is no such practice in the original languages, Sanskrit endings such as *-nikāya*, *-śastra* and *-sūtra* are hyphenated for the reader's convenience. These conventions will sometimes help students to understand Japanese titles more easily, some of which may seem a little daunting.

Sino-Japanese characters shown in brackets are alternative forms for the same characters. In general, older forms such as 佛 and 經 (for Buddha and sūtra) are shown for texts found in the printed Chinese canon. The simplified forms for these (仏 and 経) may occur when variations in other characters also need to be shown, e.g. 阿彌陀經（阿弥陀経). But, in reverse, Hannyashingyō 般若心經 is not also shown as 般若心経. Alter-

1. This corresponds to the method for multilingual lists devised by the present editor in Christoph Kleine, Li Xuetao and Michael Pye (eds.), *A Multilingual Dictionary of Chinese Buddhism. Mehrsprachiges Wörterbuch des chinesischen Buddhismus* (with Appendix and Corrections), iudicium-Verlag (for: Haus der japanischen Kultur (EKŌ), Düsseldorf), 1999. In that case the "home language" is Chinese, but here it is Japanese.

natives for single characters are sometimes shown within a title, as in 攝(摂)阿毘達磨義論, to avoid repeating the whole. Character forms for texts by Japanese authors are updated, e.g. Kangyōhiketsushū 観経秘訣集 (originally 觀經秘訣集). Minor typographical variations which predate modern Japanese are very numerous, but are disregarded here. It would also have been a distraction to insert the modern simplified characters of mainland China as further alternatives, but the official *pīnyīn* has been adopted as the norm for the *transliteration* of Chinese.

In sum, the pattern for the main entries is as follows:

Romanized Japanese/characters/romanized Chinese (for Chinese texts)
Title in English (by ...author's name...)
Correct Sanskrit form of title if any (if Pāli, indicated as P.)
[non-standard, presumed or invented Sanskrit; or comment thereon]
[other non-standard or abbreviated form, comment, etc.]

In cross-references any definite articles at the beginning of English titles have been omitted.

Abidatsumashutara 阿毘達磨修多羅 Āpídámó xīudūolúo
[Abhidharma Sūtra]
[known only from citations in the Shōdaijōron]

Abidatsumakusharon 阿毘達磨倶舎論 Āpídámójùshě lùn
Abhidharmakośa (by Vasubandhu)

Abhidhammattha-saṅgaha (P)
Treatise on the Essential Meaning of the Abhidhamma
(by Anuruddha)
[Equivalent to Shōabidatsumagiron 攝(摂)阿毘達磨義論 Shèāpídámóyí lùn]

Abhidharma Sūtra > Abidatsumashutara
Abhidharmakośa > *Abidatsumakusharon*

Amidakyō 阿彌陀經 (阿弥陀経) Āmítuó jīng
Amida Sūtra
Sukhāvatīvyūha-sūtra
[N.B. In Sanskrit this sūtra bears the same name as the "larger" one]
[Smaller Sukhāvatīvyūha-sūtra]
[Amitāyus Sūtra; this title may also refer to the Muryōjukyō]

Amida Sūtra > Amidakyō

Amidawasan 阿彌陀和讃 (阿弥陀和讃)
The Praises of Amida (by Shinran)

Amitāyurdhyāna-sūtra > Kanmuryōjukyō
Amitāyus Sūtra > Amidakyō and/or Muryōjukyō
Āmítuó jīng > Amidakyō

Anjinketsujōshō 安心決定鈔
Settled Mind and Determined Mind in Summary
(Anonymous Shin Buddhist text; has been attributed to Ken'i)

Āpídámó xīudūolúo > Abidatsumashutara
Avataṃsaka-sūtra > Kegonkyō

Bhadracarī > Bhadracarīpraṇidhāna

Bhadracarīpraṇidhāna
Life and Vows of Samantabhadra
cf. Fugenbosatusgyōgansan
[Bhadracarī]
[Bhadracarī nāma samantabhadra-praṇidhānam]
[Bhadracarīpraṇidhāna, or Ārya-bhadracarī (-mahā)-praṇidhāna-rāja]
[Ārya-samantabhadra-caryā-praṇidhāna-rāja]
[Ārya-bhadra-caryā-gāthā]
[Hymn on the Life and Vows of Samantabhadra]
[Cf. Mañjuśrīpraṇidhāna—possible identification]

Biographies of Eminent Monks > Kōsōden
Biographies of the High Priests > Kōsōden
Biographies of Myōkōnin > Myōkōninden

Bodhicaryāvatāra
The Embodiment of the Way of Enlightenment (by Śāntideva)

Bonmōkyō 梵網經 Fànwǎn jīng
Brahmā's Net Sūtra
[Brahmajāla Sūtra]

Book of Five Chapters > Godanshō
Book of Rites Concerning the Ten Gods of Wrath > Jūdaifunnumyōōgiki
Bōrě jīng > Hannyakyō
Bōrě xīngjīng > Hannyashingyō
Books of Mystic Rituals > Himitsugiki
Books of Secret Rites > Himitsugiki
Brahmajāla Sūtra > Bonmōkyō
Brahmā's Net Sūtra > Bonmōkyō
Bùdòngshǐzhě tuóluóní mìmìfǎ > Fudōshisha darani himitsuhō

Cardinal Meaning of [Shinran's] Verses on True Faith > Shōshingetaii
Cautions and Recommendations to be kept in Mind > Chinkan'yōjin
Chapter on Entering the World of Dharma > Nyūhokkaibon
Chapter on the Secret of Diamond-Treasure Precepts > Kongōhōkaihiketsushō
Chapter on the Ten Stages > Jūjihon
Chéngjiúmiàofǎliánhuājīngwángyúqiéguānzhìyíguǐ jīng > Jōjumyōhōrengekyōōyuga-kanchigikikyō

Chinkan'yōjin 鎮勧用心
Cautions and Recommendations to be kept in Mind (by Shōkū)

Chirisanmayafudōsonbō 底哩三昧耶不動尊法 Dīlǐsānmèiyé bùdòngzūnfǎ
Threefold *samādhi* for the *kalpa* of Fudōson
[Trisamaya-acala-kalpa]

Chūron 中論 Zhōng lùn
Middle Treatise
[i.e. a commentary on the "Middle Stanzas," verses by Nāgārjuna, referred to in Sanskrit as Madhyamakakārikā, or on the basis of Tibetan sources as Mūlamadhyamika or Mūlamadhyamakakārikā, the latter being rendered Konponchūronge in Japanese]
[Madhyamika-śāstra: (if, then correctly Madhyamaka-śāstra, may refer either to Chūron (not in Sanskrit) or to Prasannapadā, a similar, later commentary by Candrakīrti]

Chūsānzànjìjí > Shutsusanzōkishū
Collection for Clarification of Meaning and Advancement of Practice > Myōgishingyōshū
Collection of Notes on the Tripiṭaka > Shutsusanzōkishū
Commentary on the Sūtra on Vairocana's Attainment of Buddhahood > Daibirushanajōbutsukyōshō
Commentary on the Sūtra on Visualising [the Buddha of] Immeasurable Life > Kanmuryōjukyōsho
Commentary on the Twenty Verses > Viṃśakavṛtti
Comment on the Essentials of the Pure Land > Jōdoshin'yōshō

Dàbōrě bōluómìduō jīng > Daihannyakyō
Dàchéng qǐxìn lùn > Daijōkishinron

Daibirushanajōbutsukyōshō 大毘盧遮那成佛經疏 Dàpílúzhēnàchéngfójīngshū
Commentary on the Sūtra on Vairocana's Attainment of Buddhahood (by Yīxíng)

Daibirushanajōbutsushinbenkajikyō > Dainichikyō
Daihannyaharamitakyō > Daihannyakyō

Daihannyakyō 大般若經 Dàbōrě jīng
Great Prajñā Sūtra
Great Wisdom Sūtra
[Full title: Dàbōrě bōluómìduō jīng 大般若波羅蜜多經 Daihannyaharamitakyō]
[Mahāprajñāpāramitā-sūtra]

Daihatsunehangyō 大般涅槃經 Dàbōnièpán jīng
The Great Parinirvāṇa Sūtra
[Mahāparinirvāṇa-sūtra]
[cf. Pāli: Mahāparinibbāna-sutta]

Daijōkishinron 大乘起信論 (大乗起信論) Dàshèng qǐxìn lùn (or Dàchéng qǐxìn lùn)
Awakening of Faith in the Mahāyāna

Daikyō > Daimuryōjukyō

Daimuryōjukyō 大無量壽經 (大無量寿経) Dàwúliàngshòu jīng
Larger Sūtra on Unlimited Life
[I.e. on the Buddha of Unlimited Life-span, Amitāyus. Also Larger Amitāyus, Larger Sūtra of Infinite Life, Larger Sūtra on the Buddha of Eternal Life, The Larger Sūtra, etc. English titles for this sūtra are often imprecise and vary when drawn from Chinese or Sanskrit respectively.]
Sukhāvatīvyūha-sūtra
[The Sanskrit title has the divergent meaning of "Sūtra on the Adornment of the Land of Bliss." For a different sūtra with the same Sanskrit name, see Amidakyō.]

Dainichikyō 大日經
Mahāvairocana Sūtra
[Full title: Daibirushanajōbutsushinbenkajikyō 大毘盧遮那成佛神變加持經 Dàpílúzhēnà chéngfóshénbiànjiāchí jīng]
[Mahāvairocana Tantra]
[Vairocana Sūtra]

Dàpílúzhēnà chéngfójīngshū > Daibirushanajōbutsukyōshō
Dàpílúzhēnà chéngfóshénbiànjiāchí jīng > Dainichikyō
Daśabhūmikā > Jūjūbibasharon
Daśabhūmika sūtra > Jūjikyō
Daśabhūmikavibhāṣā-śāstra > Jūjūbibasharon
Daśabhūmivibhāṣā-śāstra > Jūjūbibasharon
Deeds and Vows of Monju and Fugen > Monjufugengyōgan
Dīlǐsānmèiyé bùdòngzūnfǎ > Chirisanmayafudōsonbō
Discourse on the Sūtra of the Ten Stages > Jūjikyōron
Document of Protest from Kōfukuji > Kōfukujisōjō
Dvadaśadvāra-śāstra > Jūnimonron
Dvādaśāmukha-śāstra > Jūnimonron

Elaboration of Tract Refuting Heresies > Zaijarinshōgonki
Embodiment of the Way of Enlightenment > Bodhicaryāvatāra
End of Disputes > Vigrahavyāvartanī

Engakukyō 圓覺經 (円覚経) Yuánjüé jīng
Sūtra of Perfect Enlightenment
[Full title: Dàfāngguǎng yuánjüé xiūduōluó liaǒyì jīng 大方廣圓覺修多羅了義經. Translation attributed to Buddhatara at the White Horse Temple in Luoyang but possibly apocryphal.]

Essential Commentary on the Senjakushū > Senjakushūmitsuyōketsu

Fànwǎn jīng > Bonmōkyō
Flower Garland Sūtra > Kegonkyō

Fudōshisha darani himitsuhō 不動使者陀羅尼秘密法 Bùdòngshǐzhě tuóluóní mìmìfǎ
Mystic Rites of the Dhāraṇi of Acala the Messenger
[Mystic Rites of the Dhāraṇi of Acalanātha]

Fugenbosatusgyōgansan 普賢菩薩行願讃 Pǔxiánpúsàxíngyuàn zàn
Hymn on the Deeds and Vows of Fugen Bosatsu
Hymn on the Deeds and Vows of Samantabhadra
Hymn on the Life and Vows of Samantabhadra
[Samantabhadra-praṇidhāna]

Fugengyōganbon 普賢行願品
Chapter on the Practice and Vows of Fugen
[Chapter, in the Kegonkyō, on the Practice and Vows of Samantabhadra]
[=Gaṇḍavyūha]

Further Biographies of Myōkōnin > Myōkōninden zokuhen

Gaṇḍavyūha
Array of Flowers
["Gaṇḍavyūha" usually used in English]
[=Fugengyōganbon, a chapter of the Kegonkyō]

Gāthas on the Two Gates of Entering and Leaving the Pure Land > Nyūshutsunimonge

Godanshō 五段鈔
Book of Five Chapters (by Shōkū)

Godenshō > Honganjishōninden'e
Goichidaikikikigaki > Rennyoshōningoichidaikikikigaki
Guānjīngshù > Kanmuryōjukyōsho
Guānwúliàngshòu jīng > Kanmuryōjukyō
Guānwúliàngshòu jīngshù > Kanmuryōjukyōsho
Guhyakalpa > Himitsugiki

Gutoku-shō 愚禿鈔
Notes by a Simpleton (by Shinran)
[Gutoku is a nickname meaning "simpleton" which Shinran applied to himself]
[The Writing of a Bald-headed Ignoramus]

Hannyakyō 般若經 Bōrě jīng
[collective term for various sutras of the *prajñāpāramitā* group]
[Wisdom Sūtra]
[Prajñāpāramitā Sūtra]

Hannyashingyō 般若心經 Bōrě xīngjīng
Heart of Wisdom Sūtra
[Heart Sūtra]
Prajñāpāramitāhṛdaya-sūtra

Heart Sūtra > Hannyashingyō
Heart of Wisdom Sūtra > Hannyashingyō

Himitsugiki 秘密儀軌 Mìmìyíguǐ
Books of Secret Rites
[Books of Mystic Rituals]
[Guhyakalpa]

Hokekyō > Myōhōrengekyō
Hokkekyō > Myōhōrengekyō
Hokke (sūtra) > Myōhōrengekyō
Honganji Illustrated Scroll of the Shōnin's Life > Honganjishōninden'e

Honganjishōninden'e 本願寺聖人伝絵
The Honganji Illustrated Scroll of the Shōnin's Life (by Kakunyo)
[Godenshō 御伝鈔 is an abbreviated title]

Honganshō 本願鈔
Exposition of the Original Vow (by Kakunyo)

Hṛdaya-sūtra > Hannyashingyō
Húayán jīng > Kegonkyō
Hymn on the Deeds and Vows of Fugen Bosatsu > Fugenbosatusgyōgansan
Hymn on the Deeds and Vows of Samantabhadra > Fugenbosatusgyōgansan
Hymn on the Life and Vows of Samantabhadra > Fugenbosatusgyōgansan
Hymns on the Last Age > Shōzōmatsuwasan
Hymns on the Patriarchs > Kōsōwasan
Hymns on the Ages of Dharma > Shōzōmatsuwasan
Hymns on the Three Dharma-Ages > Shōzōmatsuwasan

Invitation to Understanding > Ryōgemon

Ippengoroku 一遍語録
Ippen's Sermons (by Ippen)

Ippenhijirie 一遍聖絵
Pictures of the Wandering Priest Ippen (pictures by En'i)
(=Ippenshōninerokujōengi)

Ippenshōninerokujōengi 一遍聖人絵六条縁起
Pictorial Record of Ippen Shōnin in Six Sections (text by Shōkai, pictures by En'i)

Ippen's Sayings > Ippengoroku
Ippen's Sermons > Ippengoroku
Itokuki > Rennyoshōninitokuki

Jihitsushō 自筆鈔
Notes Penned by Oneself (by Shōkū)
[Cf. Tahitsushō]

Jīngāng jīng > Kongōkyō
Jīngāngshǒuguānmíngguàndǐng jīng > Kongōshukōmyōkanjōkyō

Jōdoshin'yōshō 浄土真要鈔
Comment on the Essentials of the Pure Land (by Zonkaku)

Jōdowasan 浄土和讃
Songs on the Pure Land (by Shinran)

Jōjumyōhōrengekyōōyugakanchigikikyō 成就妙法蓮華經王瑜伽觀智儀軌經

Chéngjiúmiàofǎliánhuājīngwángyúqiéguānzhìyíguǐ jīng
Ritual Sūtra for the Visualization Wisdom of the King Yoga of the Sūtra of the Lotus Blossom of the Wonderful Dharma

Jūdaifunnumyōōgiki 十大忿怒明王儀軌 Shídàfùnnùmíngwángyíguǐ
Book of Rites Concerning the Ten Gods of Wrath

Jūjihon 十地品
Chapter on the Ten Stages
[15th chapter of Kegonkyō, cf. Jūjikyō]

Jūjikyō (Jutchikyō) 十地経（經）Shídì jīng
Sūtra on the Ten Stages
[Daśabhūmika sūtra]

Jūnimonron 十二門論 Shíèrmén lùn
Twelve Gate Treatise (ascribed to Nāgārjuna)
[Treatise on the Twelve Gates]
[Dvādaśāmukha-śāstra, no known Sanskrit text]
[Dvādaśāmukha-śāstra, no known Sanskrit text]

Jūjikyōron 十地経論 Shídìjīng lùn
Discourse on the Sūtra of the Ten Stages (by Bodhiruci)
[abbreviation: Jūjiron/Jutchiron 十地論 Shídì lùn]

Jutchikyō > Jūjikyō
Jutchiron > Jūjikyōron

Jutsujō 述誠
On Sincerity (by Shōkū)

Kangyōsho > Kanmuryōjukyōsho

Kanmuryōjukyō 觀無量壽經 (観無量寿経) Guānwúliàngshòu jīng
The Sūtra on Visualising [the Buddha of] Immeasurable Life
[The Meditation Sūtra]
[The Sūtra of Meditation on Amida]
[Amitāyurdhyāna-sūtra, N.B. no known Sanskrit text]

Kanmuryōjukyōsho 觀無量壽經疏 (観無量寿経疏) Guānwúliàngshòu jīngshù
Commentary on the Sūtra on Visualising [the Buddha of] Immeasurable Life (by Shàndǎo/Zendō)
[Commentary on the Meditation Sūtra]
[Abbreviation: Kangyōsho]

Kārikā (Madhyamakakārikā) > Chūron

Kegonkyō 華嚴經 (華厳経) Húayán jīng
Flower Garland Sūtra
Avataṃsaka-sūtra
[Daihōkōbutsukegonkyō 大方廣佛華嚴經]

Ketsumyakumonjū > Shinranshōnin Ketsumyakumonjū

Kōfukujisōjō 興福寺奏状
  Document of Protest from Kōfukuji
  [Submitted to the Imperial Court]

Kongōhōkaihiketsushō 金剛宝戒秘決章
  Chapter on the Secret of Diamond-Treasure Precepts (attributed to Hōnen)

Kongōkyō 金剛經 Jīngāng jīng
  The Diamond Sūtra
  Vajracchedikā-sūtra

Kongōshukōmyōkanjōkyō 金剛手光明灌頂經 Jīngāngshǒuguānmíngguàndǐng jīng
  The Sūtra on Vajrapani's Baptism of Light
  [Vajrapani's *Sūtra on the Baptism of Light*]

Konponchūronge > Chūron

Kōsōden 高僧傳 (高僧伝) Gāosēngzhuàn
  Biographies of Eminent Monks (completed in the Sòng Dynasty [988])
  [Biographies of the High Priests]

Kōsōwasan 高僧和讃
  Hymns on the Patriarchs (by Shinran)

Kudenshō 口伝鈔
  Record of Oral Tranmission (by Kakunyo)

Kyakuhaimōki 却廃妄記
  Notes to Avoid Falling into Oblivion (by Jakue-bō Chōen)

Kyōgyōshinshō 教行信証
  Teaching, Practice, Faith and Enlightenment (by Shinran)
  [Doctrine, Practice, Faith, and Attainment]
  [Doctrine-Work-Faith-Attainment]
  [Teaching, Practice, Faith and Realizing of the Pure Land]
  [For full title > Kenjōdoshinjitsukyōgyōshōmonrui]

Laṅkāvatāra-sūtra > Ryōgakyō
Larger Amitāyus > Daimuryōjukyō
Larger Sukhāvatīvyūha-sūtra > Daimuryōjukyō
Larger Sūtra > Daimuryōjukyō
Larger Sūtra of Eternal Life > Daimuryōjukyō
Larger Sūtra of Infinite Life > Daimuryōjukyō
Larger Sūtra on Amitābha > Daimuryōjukyō
Léngqié jīng > Ryōgakyō
Letter in Six Items > Rokujō no ofumi
Letters of Rennyo > Ofumi
Letters to the Cloistered Dowager > Nyoingosho
Life and Vows of Samantabhadra > Bhadracarīpraṇidhāna
Liùshisòngrúlǐ lùn > Rokujūjunyoriro

Lotus Sūtra > Myōhōrengekyō
Lotus of the Good Law > Myōhōrengekyō

Madhyamakakārikā > Chūron
Madhyamaka-śāstra > Chūron
Madhyamika-śāstra > Chūron
Mahāprajñāpāramitā-sūtra >Daihannyakyō
Mahāvairocana Sūtra > Dainichikyō
Mahāvairocana Tantra > Dainichikyō
Mahāyānasaṃgraha > Shōdaijōron

Mahāyānaviṃśaka
Twenty Verses on the Mahāyāna (ascribed to Nāgārjuna)

Mañjuśrīpraṇidhāna-sūtra > Monjushirihotsugankyō
Meditation Sūtra > Kanmuryōjukyō
Miàofǎ liánhuā jīng > Myōhōrengekyō
Middle Treatise > Chūron
Mìmìyíguǐ > Himitsugiki

Monjufugengyōgan 文殊普賢行願 Wénshūpǔxiánxíngyuàn
Deeds and Vows of Monju and Fugen
[cf. Monjushirihotsugan-kyō]

Monjushirihotsugankyō 文殊師利發願經 Wénshūshīlìfāyuàn jīng
The Vows of Mañjuśrī
[Mañjuśrī-praṇidāna sūtra]
[cf. Bhadracarīpraṇidhāna—possible identification]

Mukanshōsōki 夢感聖相記
Record of Perceiving Holy Appearances in a Dream (ascribed to Hōnen)

Mūlamadhyamakakārikā > Chūron
Mūlamadhyamika > Chūron
Muryōjukyō > Daimuryōjukyō

Myōgishingyōshū 明義進行集
Collection for Clarification of Meaning and Advancement of Practice (by Shinzui)
[Collection to Clarify the Meaning and Advance the Practice [of the Nenbutsu]

Myōhōrengekyō 妙法蓮華經 Miàofǎ liánhuā jīng
The Sūtra of the Lotus Blossom of the Wonderful Dharma
[The Lotus Sūtra, The Lotus of the Good Law]
Saddharmapuṇḍarīka-sūtra
[Hokekyō 法華経: widely used shorter name for the Lotus Sūtra]

Myōkōninden 妙好人伝
Biographies of Myōkōnin (compiled by Kōsei and Sōjun)
[published by Sōjun in five volumes 1842–1858]

Myōkōninden zokuhen 妙好人伝続編

Further Biographies of Myōkōnin (compiled by Zō-ō)
[Published by Zō-ō in 1850]

Mystic Rites of the Dharaṇi of Acala the Messenger > Fudōshisha darani himitsuhō

Nehangyō > Daihatsunehangyō
Nirvana Sūtra > see Daihatsunehangyō
Notes by a Simpleton > Gutoku-shō
Notes Lamenting Differences > Tannishō
Notes Penned by Another > Tahitsushō
Notes Penned by Oneself > Jihitsushō
Notes to Avoid Falling into Oblivion > Kyakuhaimōki

Nyoingosho 女院御書
Letters to the Cloistered Dowager (by Shōkū)

Nyūhokkaibon 入法界品
Chapter on Entering the World of Dharma
[Chapter, in the Kegonkyō, on Sudana's entry into the Dharmadhātu]

Nyūshutsunimonge 入出二門偈
Gāthas on the Two Gates of Entering and Leaving the Pure Land (by Shinran)

Ofumi 御文
Letters of Rennyo (by Rennyo)
[Ofumi is the preferred title in the Ōtani-ha, see also Gobunshō]

One Hundred Treatise > Śataka-śāstra
On Sincerity > Jutsujō

Pictures of the Wandering Priest Ippen > Ippenhijirie
Pictorial Record of Ippen Shōnin in Six Sections > Ippenshōninerokujōengi
Plain-wood Nenbutsu > Shiraki no nenbutsu
Praises of Amida > Amidawasan
Prajñāpāramitāhṛdaya-sūtra > Hannyashingyō
Prajñāpāramitā-sūtra > Hannyakyō
Prasannapadā > Chūron
Pulverizing the Categories > Vaidalyaprakaraṇa
Pǔxiánpúsàxíngyuàn zàn > Fugenbosatusgyōgansan

Record of Oral Tranmission > Kudenshō
Record of Dreams > Yumenoki
Record of Perceiving Holy Appearances in a Dream > Mukanshōsōki
Record of Receiving Revelation during Samādhi > Sanmaihottokuki
Record of the Activities of Rennyo Shōnin > Rennyoshōningyōjōki
Record of the Virtues Bequeathed by Rennyo Shōnin > Rennyoshōninitokuki
Record of Western Lands > Saiikiki
Records of the Light in the Japanese Language > Wagotōroku

Rennyoshōningoichidaikikikigaki 蓮如上人御 一代記聞書
Sayings and Doings of the Great Life of Rennyo Shōnin (author unknown)
[Record of Sayings from Rennyo's Life]

Rennyoshōningyōjōki 蓮如上人行状記
Record of the Activities of Rennyo Shōnin (compiled 1716)

Rennyoshōninitokuki 蓮如上人遺徳記
Record of the Virtues Bequeathed by Rennyo Shōnin
[Legacy of Rennyo Shōnin]
[short title: Itokuki]

Rites Concerning the Eight Boy-Attendants... > Shōmudōsonhachidaidōjiki
Ritual Sūtra for the Visualization Wisdom of the King Yoga... > Jōjumyōhōrengekyōōyugakanchigikikyō
Rokujōengi > Ippenshōninerokujōengi

Rokujō no ofumi 六条の御文
Letter in Six Items (by Rennyo, one of the Ofumi)
[Six Item Letter]

Rokujūjunyoriron 六十頌如理論 Liùshisòngrúlǐ lùn
Sixty Verses on Reasoning (by Nāgārjuna)
Yuktiṣaṣṭikā

Ryōgakyō 楞伽經 Léngqié jīng
The Laṅkāvatāra-sūtra

Ryōgemon 領解文
Invitation to Understanding (by Rennyo)

Saddharmapuṇḍarīka-sūtra > Myōhōrengekyō

Saiikiki 西域記 Xīyùjì
Record of Western Lands (by Xuánzàng)
[Record of Travels to Western Lands]
[Hsüang-tsang's Travels to Western Lands]
[Full title (little used): Daitōsaiikiki 大唐西域記]

Saijarin/shōgonki > Zaijarin/shōgonki
Samantabhadra-praṇidhāna > Fugenbosatusgyōgansan

Sanamidabutsuge 讃阿彌陀佛偈 Zàn amítuófó jì
Verses in Praise of Amida Buddha (by Tánluán)

Sanjōwasan 三帖和讃
Threefold Wasan (by Shinran)
[cf. Wasan]

Sanmaihottokuki 三昧発得記
Record of Receiving Revelation during Samādhi (ascribed to Hōnen)

Śataka-śāstra
Treatise in One Hundred Stanzas (by Aryadeva)

[One Hundred Treatise]

Sayings and Doings of the Great Life of Rennyo Shōnin > Rennyoshōningoichidaikikikigaki
Selected Passages on the Nenbutsu of the Original Vow > Senjakuhongannenbutsushū
Senchakushū > Senjakuhongannenbutsushū
Senchakuhongannenbutsushū > Senjakuhongannenbutsushū

Senjakuhongannenbutsushū 選択本願念仏集
Selected Passages on the Nenbutsu of the Original Vow (by Hōnen)
[short form: Senjakushū, pronounced Senchakushū in Jōdo-shū contexts]

Senjakushū > Senjakuhongannenbutsushū

Senjakushūmitsuyōketsu 選択集密要決
Essential Commentary on the Senjakushū (by Shōkū)

Settled Mind and Determined Mind in Summary > Anjinketsujōshō
Seventy Verses on Emptiness > Śūnyatāsaptati
Shèāpídámóyí lùn > Abhidhammattha-saṅgaha
Shèdàshèng lùn > Shōdaijōron
Shèngwúdòngzūnbādàtóngzǐguǐ > Shōmudōsonhachidaidōjiki
Shídàfùnnùmíngwángyíguǐ > Jūdaifunnumyōōgiki
Shídì jīng > Jūjikyō
Shídìjīng lùn > Jūjikyōron
Shíèrmén lùn > Jūnimonron
Shingyō > Hannyashingyō

Shinranshōnin Ketsumyakumonjū 親鸞聖人血脈文集
The Shōnin's Letters on the Tradition (by Shinran)
[compiled anonymously]

Shiraki no nenbutsu 白木の念仏
Plain-wood Nenbutsu (by Shōkū)

Shōabidatsumagiron > Abhidhammattha-saṅgaha

Shōdaijōron 攝大乘論 (摂大乗論) Shèdàshèng lùn
Treatise on the Essentials of the Great Vehicle (by Asaṅga)
Mahāyānasaṃgraha

Shōgonki > Zaijarinshōgonki

Shōmudōsonhachidaidōjiki 聖無動尊八大童子軌 Shèngwúdòngzūnbādàtóngzǐguǐ
Rites Concerning the Eight Boy-Attendants to the Holy Lord of the Immovable
[The Mystic Rites Concerning the Eight Boy-Attendants...]

Shōshinge 正信偈
Verses on True Faith (by Shinran)
[Song of True Faith]
[widely used abbreviation for Shōshinnenbutsuge]

Shōshingetaii 正信偈大意
The Cardinal Meaning of [Shinran's] Verses on True Faith (by Rennyo)

Shōshinnenbutsuge 正信念仏偈
(by Shinran)
Verses on True Faith in the Nenbutsu
[see also Shōshinge]

Shōzōmatsuwasan 正像末和讃
Hymns on the Ages of Dharma (by Shinran)
[Hymns on the three Ages of Dharma]
[Hymns on the Three Periods after Buddha's Demise]

Shūjishō 執持抄
Steadfast Holding [to the Name] (by Kakunyo)

Shutsusanzōkishū 出三藏記集 Chūsānzànjìjí
Collection of Notes on the Tripiṭaka (by Sēngyòu)

Śikṣāsamuccaya
Training Anthology (by Śāntideva)

Six Item Letter > Rokujō no ofumi
Smaller Sukhāvatīvyūha-sūtra > Amidakyō
Songs on the Pure Land > Jōdowasa
Steadfast Holding [to the Name] > Shūjishō
Sukhāvatīvyūha-sūtra > Daimuryōjukyō and/or Amidakyō

Śūnyatāsaptati
Seventy Verses on Emptiness (by Nāgārjuna)

Sūtra of Eternal Life > Daimuryōjukyō
Sūtra of Meditation on Amida > Kanmuryōjukyō
Sūtra of Perfect Enlightenment > Engakukyō
Sūtra of the Last Sermons > Yuikyōgyō
Sūtra of the Lotus Blossom of the Wonderful Dharma > Myōhōrengekyō
Sūtra of the Teaching of Vimalakīrti > Yuimakitsushosetsukyō
Sūtra on Itineration > Yugyōkyō
Sūtra on Meditation on the Buddha of Eternal Life > Kanmuryōjukyō
Sūtra on the Meditation on Amitāyus > Kanmuryōjukyō
Sūtra on the Ten Stages > Jūjikyō
Sūtra on Vajrapani's Baptism of Light > Kongōshukōmyōkanjōkyō

Tahitsushō 他筆鈔
Notes Penned by Another (by a disciple of Shōkū)
[Cf. Jihitsushō]

Tannishō 歎異抄
Notes Lamenting Differences [recording sayings of Shinran] (by Yuien-bō)
[Tract on Deploring Heterodoxies]

Teaching, Practice, Faith and Enlightenment > Kyōgyōshinshō
Threefold *samādhi* for the *kalpa* of Fudōson > Chirisanmayafudōsonbō
Threefold Wasan > Sanjōwasan
Tract on Deploring Heterodoxies > Tannishō
Tract Refuting Heresies > Zaijarin

Training Anthology > Śikṣāsamuccaya
Travels to the Western Countries/Western Lands > Saiikiki

Treatise in One Hundred Stanzas > Śataka-śāstra
Treatise on the Essential Meaning of the Abhidhamma > Abhidhammattha-saṅgaha
Treatise on the Essentials of the Great Vehicle > Shōdaijōron
Trisamaya-acala-kalpa > Chirisanmayafudōsonbō
Twelve Gate Treatise > Jūnimonron
Twenty Verses on the Mahāyāna > Mahāyānaviṃśaka

Vaidalyaprakaraṇa
Pulverizing the Categories (by Nāgārjuna)

Vairocana Sūtra > Dainichikyō
Vajracchedikā-sūtra > Kongōkyō
Verses in Praise of Amida Buddha > Sanamidabutsuge
Verses on True Faith > Shōshinge
Verses on True Faith in the Nenbutsu > Shōshinnenbutsuge

Vigrahavyāvartanī
The End of Disputes (by Nāgārjuna)

Vimalakīrti-nirdeśa > Yuimagyō
Vimalakīrti-sūtra > Yuimagyō

Viṃśakavṛtti
Commentary on the Twenty Verses (by Vasubandhu)

Vows of Mañjuśrī > Monjushirihotsugankyō

Wagotōroku 和語灯録 (和語燈録)
Records of the Light in the Japanese Language (by Hōnen)
[Collected Sayings of Hōnen]
[A Record of the Light]
[Collection of Hōnen's Preachings]

Wasan 和讃
Songs in Japanese
[Sometimes short for Jōdowasan, but at the same time a generic term for the genre which also includes Amida Wasan, Kōsōwasan and Shōzōmatsuwasan by Shinran]
[Psalms]
[cf. Sanjōwasan]

Wéimójié sǔoshūo jīng > Yuimakitsushosetsukyō
Wéimó jīng > Yuimagyō
Wénshūpǔxiánxíngyuàn > Monjufugengyōgan
Wénshūshīlìfāyuàn jīng > Monjushirihotsugan-kyō

Xīyùjì > Saiikiki

Yíjiào jīng > Yuikyōgyō
Yóuxíng jīng > Yugyōkyō

Yuánjüé jīng > Engakukyō

Yugyōkyō 遊行經 Yóuxíng jīng
Sūtra on Itineration
[= Mahāparinibbāna-sutta. The Sino-Japanese name refers to the later journeys of the Buddha]

Yuikyōgyō 遺教經 Yíjiào jīng
Sūtra of the Last Sermons [of the Buddha]

Yuimagyō 維摩經 Wéimó jīng
The Vimalakīrti Sūtra
Vimalakīrti-nirdeśa
[Short for : Yuimakitsushosetsukyō]

Yuimakitsushosetsukyō 維摩詰所説經 Wéimójié sǔoshūo jīng
The Sūtra of the Teaching of Vimalakīrti
Vimalakīrtinirdeśa-sūtra
(cf. Yuimagyō)

Yuktiṣaṣṭikā > Rokujūjunyoriron

Yumenoki 夢之記
Record of Dreams (by Myōe)

Zaijarin 摧邪輪
Tract Refuting Heresies (by Myōe)
[Also pronounced Saijarin]
[Full title: Ikkō senjushū senchakushū no naka ni oite ja wo kudaku rin 於一向専修宗選択集中摧邪輪]

Zaijarinshōgonki 摧邪輪荘厳記
Elaboration of Tract Refuting Heresies (by Myōe)
[Also pronounced Saijarinshōgonki]

Zàn amítuófó jì > Sanamidabutsuge
Zhōng lùn > Chūron

Character List for Historical Persons

The main purpose of this list is to indicate the Sino-Japanese characters used for the names of historical persons mentioned above. It also includes a number of latinized Indian names without Sino-Japanese equivalents, showing the correct accents. Non-historical bodhisattvas and other celestial beings are not listed, but for important cases such as Fugen Bosatsu 普賢菩薩 the characters may be found at the first occurrence. A few figures referred to as bodhisattvas and who may have existed historically are included. All dates given for historical persons, where known, and unless otherwise indicated, are Common Era (CE) dates.

Indian names follow the pattern: Indian / Chinese / characters / Japanese
e.g. Amoghavajra (705–774) Bùkōng 不空 Fukū

Chinese names follow the pattern: Chinese / characters / Japanese
e.g. Shàndǎo 善導 Zendō (613–681)

Korean names follow the pattern: Korean / characters / Japanese
e.g. Beomyeong 法明 Hōmyō (7th century CE)

Japanese names are recognized by having no alternatives
e.g. Kakunyo Shōnin 覚如上人 (1270–1351)

Characters shown in brackets are alternative forms for the same character.

Cross references between languages are shown from the derivatives back to the original:

Chinese to Indian, e.g. Mǎmíng > Aśvaghoṣa

Japanese to Indian, e.g. Memyō > Aśvaghoṣa

Japanese to Chinese, eg. Zendō > Shàndǎo 善導

Cross references to alternative Japanese names for the same person are shown with =
e.g. Dengyō Daishi = Saichō (where the characters will be found).

Amoghavajra (705–774) Bùkōng 不空 Fukū

Anan/Ānàn > Ānanda
Ānanda Ānàn 阿難 Anan
Asahara Saiichi 浅原才市 (1851–1933)
Asaṅga (4th–5th century CE) Wúzhù 無著 Mujaku
Aśoka, King (fl. 3rd century BCE)
Aśvaghoṣa (1st century CE) Mǎmíng 馬鳴 Memyō

Benchō 弁長 (1162–1238) (also Shōkō or Shōkō-bō 聖光房)
Beomyeong 法明 Hōmyō (Korean nun, 7th century CE)
Bhadraśrī Xiánshǒu 賢首 Genju
Bodairushi > Bodhiruci
Bodhiruci (died 527) Pútíliúzhī 菩提流支 Bodairushi
Buddhabhadra (359–429)
Buddhapālita (470–550)
Bùkōng > Amoghavajra

Candrakīrti (seventh century) Yuèchēng 月称 Gesshō
Chéngguān 澄觀 (737–787) Chōkan
Chēyìn 車胤 Sha'in
Chigi > Zhìyí
Chishin > Ippen
Chōen > Jakue-bō Chōen
Chōkan > Chéngguān
Chōsai 長西 (1184–1228)
Cíēn Dàshī 慈恩大師 Jion Daishi (632–682) (also = Kuījī 窺基 Kiki)

Dào'ān 道安 (312–385)
Dàochuò 道綽 Dōshaku (562–645)
Dengyō Daishi 伝教大師 = Saichō
Dharmarakṣa (3rd century CE) Zhú Fǎhù 竺法護 Jiku Hōgo
Dōgen Zenji 道元禅師 (1200–1253)
Donran > Tánluán
Dōshaku > Dàochuò
En'i 円伊 (Kamakura Period)

Ennin 圓仁 (円仁) (794–864) (also Jikaku Daishi 慈覺大師 (慈覚大師))

Enshō Daishi = Ippen Shōnin

Eshin Sōzu = Genshin

Eshinni 恵信尼 (1182–1268)

Eun 慧運 (恵運) (798–869)

Fǎzàng 法蔵 (法藏) Hōzō (643–712)

Fujiwara Kanezane 藤原兼実 (1149–1207) (also Kujō Kanezane 九条兼実)

Fukū > Amoghavajra

Ganchi 願智 (1275–1353)

Gedatsu Shōnin = Jōkei

Genchi > Seikan-bō Genchi
Genjō > Xuánzàng

Genkū 源空 = Hōnen Shōnin

Genshin 源信 (942–1071) (also Eshin Sōzu 恵信僧都)

Gesshō > Candrakīrti

Gijō > Yìjìng

Guīfēng Zōngmì = Zōngmì

Gyōji > Jōgaku-bō Gyōji

Hattō Kokushi = Kakushin

Hōmyō see Beomyeong

Hōnen Shōnin 法然上人 (1133–1212)

Hōzō > Fǎzàng

Ippen Shōnin 一遍上人 (1239–1289) (also Chishin 智真; Enshō Daishi 圓証大師; Yugyō Shōnin 遊行上人)

Jakue-bō Chōen 寂恵房長円

Jiāngliángyēshè > Kālayaśas

Jie Daishi = Ryōgen

Jikaku Daishi = Ennin

Jiku Hōgo > Dharmarakṣa

Jion Daishi > Cíēn Dàshī

Jisshananda > Śikṣānanda
Jitsunyo 実如 (1458–1525)
Jiūmóluóshí > Kumarajīva
Jiun 慈雲 (1718–1804)
Jízàng 吉蔵 Kichizō (549–623)
Jōgaku-bō Gyōji 上覚房行慈
Jōkei 貞慶 (1155–1213) (also Gedatsu Shōnin 解脱上人)
Junnyo 准如 (1442–1483)

Kakunyo Shōnin 覚如上人 (1270–1351)
Kakushin 覺心 (覚心) (1207–1298) (also Hattō Kokushi 法燈国師)
Kālayaśas (4th–5th century) Jiāngliángyēshè 畺良耶舎 Kyōryōyasha
Kanchi Kokushi = Shōkū
Kāng Sēngkǎi = Saṅghavarman
Kaniṣka, King (1st century CE)
Kāśyapa (also Mahākāśyapa, i.e. Great Kāśyapa)
Kedai 華台 (13th century)
Keihō Shūmitsu = Zōngmì
Ken'i 顕意 (12th century)
Kichizō > Jízàng
Kōben 高弁 = Myōe
Kōbō Daishi = Kūkai
Kōsai 幸西 (1163–1247)
Kōsōgai > Saṅghavarman
Kōzen > Rimyō-bō Kōzen
Kuījī 窺基 Kiki (632–682) (also Cíēn Dàshī)
Kujō Kanezane = Fujiwara Kanezane
Kūkai 空海 (774–835) (also Kōbō Daishi 弘法大師)
Kumarajīva (334–413) Jiūmóluóshí 鳩摩羅什 Kumarajū
Kumarajū > Kumarajīva
Kūya Shōnin 空也上人 (903–972)
Kyōryōyasha > Kālayaśas

Lǐ Tōngxuán 李通玄 (635–730 or 646–740)

Lóngshù > Nāgārjuna
Mahākāśyapa > Kāśyapa
Mahāmaudgalyāyana > Maudgalyāyana
Mǎmíng > Aśvaghoṣa
Manjushiri > Mañjuśrī
Mañjuśrī (legendary) Wénshūshīlì 文殊師利 Manjushiri
Maudgalyāyana (also Mahāmaudgalyāyana, i.e. Great Maudgalyāyana)
Memyō > Aśvaghoṣa
Mongaku Shōnin 文覚上人 (文学) (1139–1203)
Mujaku > Asaṅga
Myōe Shōnin 明恵上人 (1173–1232) (also known as Kōben 高弁)

Nāgārjuna (2nd–3rd century CE) Lóngshù 龍樹 (竜樹) Ryūju
Nichiren Shōnin 日蓮聖人 (1222–1282)
Nyoshin Shōnin 如信上人 (1239–1300)

Ōgen 応玄 (1433–1503)
Osono > Tahara no Osono

Prajñā (8th–9th centuries) Bōrě 般若 Hannya
Prince Shōtoku > Shōtoku Taishi
Pútíliúzhī > Bodhiruci

Rennyo Shōnin 蓮如上人 (1415–1499)
Rimyō-bō Kōzen 理明房興然 (1121–1203)
Rinkan-bō Shōsen 林観房聖詮
Ryōgen 良源 (912–985) (also Jie Daishi 慈恵大師)
Ryōken 良顕 (1171–1217)
Ryūju > Nāgārjuna

Saichō 最澄 (767–822) (also Dengyō Daishi 伝教大師)
Saigyō 西行 (1118–1190)
Saimei Tennō 斉明天皇 (Empress, reigned 655–661; also read Saimyō)
Saṅghavarman (3rd century CE) (also Kāng Sēngkǎi 康僧鎧 Kōsōgai)
Śāntideva (11th century)

Śāriputra
Seikan-bō Genchi 勢観房源智 (1183–1238)
Seishimaru 勢至丸 = Hōnen Shōnin (as a child)
Sēngyòu 僧祐 (445–518)
Seshin > Vasubandhu
Sha'in > Chēyìn
Shàndǎo 善導 Zendō (613–681)
Shíchānántúo > Śikṣānanda
Shinkū 信空 (1145–1228)
Shinran Shōnin 親鸞聖人 (1173–1262)
Shìqīn > Vasubandhu
Shōkai 聖戒 (1261–1323)
Shōkō = Benchō
Shōkō-bō = Benchō
Shōkō Tennō (Emperor) 称光天皇 (reigned 1401–1428)
Shōkū 証空 (1177–1247) (also Kanchi Kokushi 鑑智国師)
Shōsen > Rinkan-bō Shōsen
Shōtatsu 聖達 (1203–1279)
Shōtoku Taishi 聖徳太子 (Prince Shōtoku) (574–622) (also Shōtoku Umayado)
Shōtoku Umayado 聖徳馬宿 = Shōtoku Taishi
Shūmitsu > Zōngmì
Śikṣānanda (652–710) Shíchānántuó 實叉難陀 Jisshananda

Tahara no Osono (a *myōkōnin*, name and dates unknown)
Tánluán 曇鸞 Donran (476–542)
Tendai Daishi = Zhìyí

Vasubandhu (4th–5th century) Shìqīn 世親 Seshin
Vimalakīrti (legendary, possibly BCE) Wéimójié 維摩詰 Yuimakitsu

Wéimójié > Vimalakīrti
Wénshūshīlì > Mañjuśrī
Wúzhù > Asaṅga
Xiánshǒu 賢首 Genju (643–712)

Xuánzàng 玄奘 Genjō (602–664)

Yùechēng > Candrakīrti

Yuimakitsu > Vimalakīrti

Yīxíng 一行 Ichigyō (684–727)

Yōmei Tennō (Emperor) 用明天皇 (518–587)

Yugyō Shōnin = Ippen Shōnin

Yuien-bō 唯円房 i.e. Monk Yuien (d. 1290)

Zendō > Shàndǎo

Zhìyí 智顗 Chigi (538–597)

Zhú Fǎhù > Dharmarakṣa

Zōngmì 宗密 Shūmitsu (780–841) (also Guīfēng Zōngmì 圭峰宗密 Keihō Shūmitsu)

Zonkaku Shōnin 存覚上人 (1290–1373)

Zonnyo Shōnin 存如上人 (1396–1457)

Original Publication Details

When the title of an article has been edited for the present volume, the original title is given (with its original orthography) immediately before the other details of the original publication.

Bandō, Shōjun: Myōe's Critique of Hōnen
Original title: Myōe's Criticism of Hōnen
The Eastern Buddhist 1974 New Series Vol VII 1, 37–54

Izumi Hōkei (trans.): Vimalakīrti's Discourse on Emancipation
This was originally published in eight parts as follows:
a) Original title: Vimalakīrti's Discourse on Emancipation (Translation from the Chinese Vimalakīrti-nirdeśa). Introduction
The Eastern Buddhist 1923 Vol II 6, 358–366
b) Original title: Vimalakīrti's Discourse on Emancipation (Translation)
The Eastern Buddhist 1924 Vol III 1, 55–69
c) Original title: Vimalakīrti's Discourse on Emancipation (Continued)
The Eastern Buddhist 1924 Vol III 2, 138–153
d) Original title: Vimalakīrti's Discourse on Emancipation (Continued)
The Eastern Buddhist 1924 Vol III 3, 224–242
e) Original title: Vimalakīrti's Discourse on Emancipation (Continued)
The Eastern Buddhist 1925 Vol III 4, 336–349
f) Original title: Vimalakīrti's Discourse on Emancipation (Continued)
The Eastern Buddhist 1926 Vol IV 1, 48–55
g) Original title: Vimalakīrti's Discourse on Emancipation (Continued)
The Eastern Buddhist 1926 Vol IV 2, 177–190
h) Original title: Vimalakīrti's Discourse on Emancipation (Concluded)
The Eastern Buddhist 1927/8 Vol IV 3/4, 348–366
N.B. Original transcription of author's name: Hokei Idumi.

Izumi Hōkei (trans.): The Hymn on the Life and Vows of Samantabhadra
Original title: The Hymn on the Life and Vows of Samantabhadra, With the Sanskrit Text, Bhadracarīpraṇidhāna
The Eastern Buddhist 1930 Vol V 2/3, 226–241
N.B. Original transcription of author's name: Hokei Idumi.

Kakunyo Shōnin: On Steadfast Holding to the Name
Original title on contents page: The Shūji-shō
Original title at text position: Tract on Steadily Holding to [the Faith]
The Eastern Buddhist 1939 Vol VII 3/4, 363–375

Kaneko Daiei: Rennyo the Restorer
This article originally appeared in two parts as follows:
a) Original title: Rennyo The Restorer (1)
The Eastern Buddhist 1998 New Series XXXI 1, 1–11
b) Original title: Rennyo The Restorer, Part Two
The Eastern Buddhist 1998 New Series XXXI 2, 209–218

Satō, Taira: Asahara Saichi the Myōkōnin
Original title: The Awakening of Faith in the Myokonin Asahara Saichi
The Eastern Buddhist 1985 New Series Vol XVIII 1, 71–89
(Original edition translated by Thomas Kirchner)

Shaku Hannya: The Heart Sūtra (Prajñā-pāramitā-hṛdaya-sūtra)
Original title: The Prajna-paramita-hrdaya-sutra
The Eastern Buddhist 1922 (issued January 1923) Vol II, 3–4, 163–175

Sugihira, Shizutoshi: The Pure Land Doctrine in Shōkū's 'Plain Wood' Nenbutsu
Original title: The Pure Land Doctrine as Illustrated in the "Plain-wood" Nembutsu by Shoku
The Eastern Buddhist 1932 VI 1, 23–39

Suzuki, Beatrice Lane: Outline of the Avataṃsaka Sūtra (*Kegonkyō*)
Original title: An Outline of the Avatamsaka Sutra (Kegonkyo)
The Eastern Buddhist 1934 VI 3, 279–286

Suzuki, Beatrice Lane: Fudō the Immovable
Original title: Fudo the Immovable
The Eastern Buddhist 1922 (issued January 1923) Vol II 3/4, 129–153
(N.B. There is a frontispiece showing Fudō in the same volume)

Suzuki, Beatrice Lane: Ceremonies for Disciples on Mount Kōya
Original title: Ceremonies for Lay Disciples at Kōya-san
The Eastern Buddhist 1933 Vol VI 2, 157–175

Suzuki, Beatrice Lane: Shinran and his Song on Amida
Original title: The Songs of Shinran Shonin
The Eastern Buddhist 1939 VII 3/4, 285–295

Yamaguchi, Susumu (trans.): Nāgārjuna's *Mahāyāna-viṁśaka*
This was originally published in two parts as follows:
a) Original title: Nāgārjuna's Mahāyāna-viṁśaka (Prefatory notes and Tibetan and Chinese texts)
The Eastern Buddhist 1926 Vol IV 1, 56–72
b) Original title: Nāgārjuna's Mahāyāna-viṁśaka (An English Translation with notes)
The Eastern Buddhist 1927 Vol IV 2, 169–176

Original Publication Details

Yanagi, Sōetsu: Ippen Shōnin and the Nenbutsu
Original title: Ippen Shōnin
The Eastern Buddhist 1973 New Series Vol VI 2, 33–57

Index

To reduce complexity, this index does not include: (a) the names of fifty-two bodhisattvas on pages 27–28 (many of whom also appear on pages 73–77); (b) Sanskrit words found in the sūtra text of Chapter 4, on pages 104–105; and (c) Sanskrit and Tibetan terms in Chapter 5, pages 107–114. Please find such items directly in these very concentrated passages.

A

abandoning 6, 26, 46, 39, 50, 53–55, 57, 73, 76, 79, 85–87, 168–169, 175–176, 206, 216, 254, 267, 275
abbot 150, 160–163, 192, 241–242, 245
Abhidharmakośa 183
Abhirati 89–90
absolute (noun or adjective) 26, 37–39, 41, 57, 70, 103, 108, 111, 114, 128, 161, 168, 195–196, 209, 214, 263, 269, 272–274, 276
absorption 186
Acala 133–138, 140
acolyte 266
acquiescence 34–35, 46, 63, 68, 73, 77, 82–83, 93, 95, 160
adamantine 136, 146
adept 186
adhyeṣanā 159
adorning/ment 27–29, 34–35, 47, 49, 51, 55, 57, 59–60, 68, 71, 86, 91, 115, 128, 224
adultery 33, 81, 157, 236
Advaita 203
aesthetics 15
affinity 9
afterlife 254
agate 62
aggregate/s 88, 102
Ajita-Keśakambala 40
Aka-Fudō 145–146
Akaniṣṭha 90
Ākāśagarbha 28
Akizuki Shōken 149
Akṣayamati 75
Akṣobhya 66, 87, 89–90, 134, 138
alms 39–40
altar 150, 160–162, 271
Amida (butsu/nyorai) 4–5, 10–11, 13, 15–18, 168–172, 175–177, 179, 181, 193, 195–196, 199–205, 207–210, 212–219, 221–229, 231–239, 244–245, 250–255, 263–265, 268–278
Amitābha 8–10, 66, 122, 129–130, 168, 221–222, 225, 229
Amitāyurdhyāna Sūtra 225
Amitāyus 10, 134, 222
Amoghasiddhi (Buddha) 134

Amogha/vajra 123–125
Amra fruit 42
Āmrapālī (grove) 25, 82
amṛta 80
amulets (paper) 202
anāgāmin 62
Ānanda 44–45, 82–85, 96, 190
(Paṇḍita) 110
Anāthapiṇḍika 119
Anavataptanāgarāja 143
ancestor 3
anchoretic 186–187, 191–192
Ango (*ango*) 149, 160, 164
Animeṣa 73
Aniruddha 41–42
anjin 211, 250, 255–256
anjinha 211
Anjinketsujōshō 210, 250, 252
annihilated 46, 67, 73, 88, 93, 101, 104, 145
annihilation 41, 53, 57–58, 63, 73, 75–76, 8788, 93, 101, 111, 113
anointing 71, 183
Anokudatsuryūō 143
Anrakuji 266, 270
anutpattika 26
anuttara-samyak-saṃbodhi 23, 85
apparition 66, 251
appearance 29–30, 45, 135, 184–185, 225
Aquinas, Thomas 199
arhat 23, 46, 62–63, 67, 92, 102, 159, 226, 236
Arita 183–184
artha 108
arthacaryā 32
Aruṇa Bodhisattva 75
arūpa 58, 62
arūpa-dhātu 62
Āryadeva 107
Āryāvalokiteśvara 102; see also Avalokiteśvara
Asahara
Saichi 17, 259–276
Saki 269
Setsu 267, 269
Asakura Toshikage 246
asaṃkhyeya 59, 61, 92, 94–95
Asaṅga 108, 221
ascetic 23
Ashikaga 242
Ashuku 134
Aśoka 22
aspirant/s 184, 192
āsrava 27
asura/s 27, 29, 60, 96, 102, 161
ātmabhavaparityaga 159
attachment/s 23, 38, 44, 46, 52, 58, 77, 79, 95, 103, 126, 128, 171, 251, 265, 272, 274
attaining 10, 23–24, 32, 35, 37, 43, 47, 56–57, 62, 67, 86, 91, 129, 150, 153, 175, 179, 205, 211, 215, 232–233, 239, 252
attainment 2, 5, 27, 32, 41, 50, 56, 58, 76, 88, 117, 129, 139, 141, 159, 185, 196, 215, 225, 228, 238, 263, 265, 270–272
auspicious 82, 129, 183–184, 264–265
austerities 168, 170
Avalokiteśvara 28, 101–102, 158, 227
Avataṃsaka Sūtra 8–9, 11, 26, 108–109, 115–120, 150, 183–184, 186
avidyā 103, 133, 237
Avinivartanīya 26
awaken/ed, 31, 39, 41, 43, 45, 51, 69, 71, 73, 112, 126, 129, 153, 155, 158, 163, 169, 172–173, 189, 232, 237–239, 267–268, 278
awakening 17, 71, 139, 153, 186, 202, 204–205, 219, 233–234, 244, 251, 259, 262–263, 276–278
āyatanas 36, 45, 48, 58, 62, 69, 75, 86, 88

B

bala/s 27, 32
Baldheaded 187, 196
Bandō Shōjun 14
baptism 18, 138
Bashō 246
beasts 72, 246
Beck, L. Adams 222
beggar 50–51, 187, 268
beggar-monk 266

begging 39, 45
belief/s 45, 117, 171, 176, 187, 195, 212–213, 232–233, 244
believers 49, 152, 168, 172, 175–176, 178–179, 206, 216, 223, 265
bell 158, 160–161
Bendall, C. 25
benevolence 156, 255
Beomyeong (Hōmyō) 25
beryl 41, 62
Bhadra 122, 124–130
Bhadracarī 121–122, 124–125
Bhadracarīpraṇidhāna 122
Bhadrakalpa 94
Bhadraśrī 124–125
Bhagavat 92, 229
bhagavato 105
Bhaiṣajyarāja 92–94
Bhattacharya, Vidhusekhara 8
bhava 103
Bhikṣu/s 25, 29, 34, 41–43, 45, 94, 102, 119, 151
Bhikṣuṇīs 29
bhūmis 117
bhūta tathatā 186
Bikya 164
Biroshana (Buddha) 134
birth/s 27–28, 31, 38, 45–46, 50, 52–53, 55–56, 58, 63–64, 67, 69, 71, 73, 83–84, 86–88, 93, 103, 111, 113–114, 152, 155, 159–160, 167–168, 170, 179, 194, 196–197, 208, 213, 227, 232, 234–237, 239, 252, 255, 265, 272
Bliss (Land of) 227, 236
blood (paint with) 135
blooming (rare) 225
blossoms (Campaka) 65
blue Fudō 136, 138
Bo-tree 116
bodaishin 139
Bodhi, 30, 32, 46, 50, 55, 61, 63, 67, 70, 84, 89, 91–93, 126, 129, 139, 159–160
bodhi, 101, 105
Bodhicaryāvatāra 159
bodhicitta 139, 152–153, 155, 192–197
Bodhimaṇḍala, 47, 49, 71, 91, 93
bodhipakṣadharmas 32
bodhipākṣika 24
Bodhisattva-hood 49, 95, 108
bodhyaṅga 32
bodies (of bodhisattvas, buddhas) 59, 79, 83–84,
  three (*trīkaya*) 156
bodily 39, 153, 161, 228, 279
bōmori 3
bon 7
Bonmōkyō 150, 158
Bosatsu Precepts 154
bosatsukai 149–151, 154, 159
bōsha 246, 249
bowl 34, 39–41, 44, 79–80
boy/ish 136, 138, 142, 146
Brahma 28, 35, 161
brahmacārin 186, 194
Brahmajāla sūtra 150, 158, 182
Brahman 29, 34, 36, 41–42, 44, 50–52, 57, 59, 61, 65–66, 72, 80, 83, 86, 89, 91
Brahmins 9, 120
bubble/s 36, 62
Buddhabhadra 115, 122–124
Buddha-countries/lands 57, 79, 84
Buddhahood 5, 10, 23, 69–70, 94, 117, 139, 141, 150–152, 158, 162, 168, 174, 202, 205, 223–225, 228, 233, 236, 254, 263, 272
Buddhapālita 107
Bühler, G. 100
Bukkōkan 186
Bunmei (era) 246–248
Bunnan (era) 244
Burma 23
bussetsu 10
Butsu/*butsu*, 11, 205, 209, 23, 263–264, 268–276
  pronunciation 253
  see also Namu Amida Butsu
butsubon ittai 253
Butsugen-Butsumo-Son 184, 186–187
Butsugenhō 183, 186
button 215

C

Cakravāḍa mountains 29, 89
Cakravartin 43–44, 61, 92, 94
Calvin, Jean 182
Campaka blosoms 65
Candracchatra 80, 92–94
Candrakīrti 107, 114
Candrakumāra (Paṇḍita) 110
Candrottama Bodhisattva 76
Canon, Chinese Buddhist 7, 21
carī 122
caryā 117, 122
caste 129
catvāriy apramāṇāni 32
causation 23, 26, 38, 47, 56, 65, 72, 93, 103, 190, 236
  causelessness 28, 57, 87, 93
  cause/s 30, 42, 51, 69, 71, 194, 232, 239
cemetery/ies 3, 12, 266
cessation 2, 37, 58, 228
Ceṭaka 142
Ceylon 23, 125
chanting 15, 53, 160–163, 247, 255, 263
charm/s 216
Chéngguān 124
Chéngjiú miàofǎliánhuājīng wángyúqiéguānzhì yíguǐ jīng 123
Chēyìn 243
chikai no kotoba 277
chiliocosm/s 29, 30, 34, 42, 60–61, 80, 85, 87, 91, 229
Chin Annals 243
China 6, 9, 107, 121, 124–125, 135, 184, 210, 218
Chinese
  patriarchs 185, 221, 235
  texts 4–8, 21, 25, 99–100, 107–115, 122–123, 125, 135, 196, 224–225
  style 189, 243
  vocabulary 15, 22, 27, 59, 103–104, 107–115, 170
Chinkanyōjin 177
Chinzei branch 201, 210
Chion-in 210
Chionji 210
Chirisanmayafudōsonbō 136–137
Chishin 202
Chōen 189, 191–192
Chōsai 201
Christian/ity 3, 17–18, 167–168, 222–223, 232
Chūsānzànjìjí 122
Címǐn 185
Cittānāvaraṇa Bodhisattva 76
cittotpāda 160
clinging 23, 44, 65, 251
cloud/s 36, 62, 118–119, 136, 160, 163, 184–185, 226, 232 clouds, 62, 163, 226, 232
coincidentia oppositorum 272
commentary 236, 243, 260; *Commentary on:*
  Avataṃsaka Sūtra (*Kegonkyō*) 124, 186
  Mahāprajñāpāramitā Sūtra 21, 108–109
  Meditation Sūtra 185, 200, 202, 221, 265
  Shōshinge 249
  Vairocana Sūtra 12, 139–140
  Vasubandhu's Discourse on the Pure Land 221
  Verses on True Shinjin 249
  Vimalakīrtinirdeśa/sutra 24
compassion 2, 4, 23, 30, 32, 37–39, 47, 50–51, 53–55, 63–66, 68, 70, 72, 80–81, 85, 87, 93–94, 119, 152–154, 164, 200, 204, 215, 222–225, 234–235, 264–265, 267, 271–276, 278–279
concentration 27, 32, 37, 128, 176, 187, 264
concept/s 204, 208, 252, 264
  conception/s 5, 24, 63, 75, 88, 95, 100, 168, 187, 196, 203, 268
  conceptual 1–2, 13, 272–273
  deconstruction 2, 8
condition/s 236–238, 253–254,
  mental/karmic 57, 224, 227–228, 232–233, 268
conditionality 103, 108
conditioned 108, 113, 118
confession 42, 120, 126, 154–155, 159–160, 271
confirmation 18, 269, 279

consciousness 27, 46, 58, 62, 75–76, 88, 101–104, 108, 152, 224, 237, 239, 272, 275
jiriki 173
nenbutsu 172
no consciousness 36, 60
of former existence 41
religious/moral 263, 266, 268
six consciousnesses, 103
vijñāna 102–103
contemplation 2, 37, 42, 44, 58, 76, 90, 169–170, 173, 196
conversion 61, 63, 66, 173, 223
cosmology 134, 141, 170
Counter Reformation 182
Court (Buddhism) 24–25, 192, 200
creator 168, 195
Cūḍamaṇirāja Bodhisattva 77

D

Dài Zōng 123
Daiichi Hōetsucho Ubasoku 271
Daiitoku 134
Daimuryōjukyō 10, 235
Daimyōjin (Kasuga) 186
Dainichi 134
Dainichikyō 138
Daizōkyō 7, 21, 139; see also *Taishō* Daizōkyō
dāna 31–32, 153
danka seido 3
Dào'ān 4
Dàochuò 221
daśabhūmi 108
Daśabhūmika 115, 117
Dàwúliàngshòu jīng 10
deai 272
death 27, 30–31, 33, 38, 46–44, 52–53, 55–56, 58, 64, 69, 71, 73, 86–88, 93, 101, 103, 113, 129, 152, 158, 160, 167–170, 174, 176, 179, 181, 185, 189, 195, 202–203, 207, 212–214, 218, 224, 231–234, 236, 238–239, 246, 248, 260–262, 268–269, 271–272
deathbed 212–213, 255
decease 204, 245
defilement/s, 68, 114, 134, 161, 228
deliverance 55–57, 70, 74, 77, 159, 167, 205
delusion/s 151–152, 154–155, 160, 169, 171–172
Demiéville, Paul 6
demon/s, 27, 140, 142, 161, 235, 268
Dengyō Daishi 15
denomination/s 1, 3–4, 16, 18, 99, 241, 247
dependence 17, 104, 225, 237, 272, 276
desire/s 4, 34, 36, 39, 43–44, 46, 49, 57–58, 63–65, 68, 70, 73, 75, 78, 86, 103, 119–120, 140, 152–153, 155, 159, 163, 170–174, 205, 207, 209, 225, 233, 237–239, 243, 252, 263, 267–268, 271
despair 252
destiny 129, 234
destroy/ing 33, 39, 47, 49, 60, 63, 71, 102, 133, 139, 145, 147, 155–158, 173, 193–194, 226, 236
destruction 12, 89, 103, 113–114, 133, 246, 248
detachment 7, 46, 77, 124, 234
deva/s 27, 116, 135
Devarāja 28
devil/s 139, 193, 270
Dhanyākara 119
dhāraṇī/s 35, 70, 92, 94, 100, 136, 150, 158
Dharma 2, 32–33, 38, 58, 152, 158, 163, 187, 189, 191, 201, 208–210, 213–214, 233, 236, 250–254, 271–272, 279
Buddha-Dharma 202
conversation 6,
decline, latter-day 194, 204
name 277
proclamation of 10, 126, 139
refuge 151–153, 163, 278
treasure 170, 227
uncreated 34
wheel of 26, 94, 129
See also: Law
dharmas 27
Dharmadhātu 116–117, 119, 161

Dharmākara 10, 205, 223, 229
Dharmakāya 116–117, 120, 156, 161, 225
Dharmeśvara Bodhisattva 73
dhātu/Dhātu/s 36, 45, 58, 62, 86, 103; see also Dharmadhātu
dhyāna/Dhyāna 32, 57, 152–153, 183
  pāramitā 50
dialectic/al 183, 196
diamond 26, 74, 162–163
directions (ten) 153–154, 162–163
Disciples, 13, 37, disciple/s, 6, 13–14, 24, 26, 29, 35–37, 42–43, 45, 52, 58–55, 64–65, 70, 80, 83, 90, 92, 125, 149–164, 171, 178–179, 183, 185, 189–191, 195–196, 200–202, 206, 210–211, 218, 248–249, 277, 279
discipleship 9, 239
discipline 11, 23, 26, 31, 33, 35, 37, 42–43, 49–50, 71, 73, 75, 80–82, 84, 95, 112, 126–128, 168, 170–171, 173–174, 196, 210, 263; see also Vinaya
  disciplinary 81, 182, 205, 216
discriminate 53, 64, 88, 93, 111, 114
discrimination 10, 38, 51, 53, 64–65, 70, 74, 92, 108, 111–114, 140, 264, 272–276
disease/s 30, 36–37, 44, 54–55, 69, 71–72, 113, 238
divine 43, 101, 159
divinity 12
Dōbō Hōsan 278
Dōgen 199, 202
dogma 175
donation 255
Dōng jìn cháo 115
Donran 15, 221
dorje 162
Dōsai, 246, 250
Dōshaku 221
dōshi 245
dragon/s 142–143
dream/s 8, 36, 43, 63, 84, 108–109, 112, 174, 184–185, 187, 190, 216, 251
dualism 4, 7, 111, 168, 172, 205, 208, 214, 276
duality 6, 9, 13, 42, 46, 63, 73–77, 88, 203–204, 208, 210, 219, 267, 272–273, 275
Durdharṣa (Tathāgata) 51, 66

E

East Asia 1, 4
east/ern
  cosmological 185, 203,
  cultural 99, 200
  Jìn Dynasty 115
Echigo 256
Echizen 246–247
Eckhart, Meister 199
Edo period 260, 262
egg-born 235
Ego/Ego 113–114, 268, 272, 276
egoism/istic 62, 113, 167, 176
egotism/istic 72, 173
Ehime Prefecture 202
eight
  calamities 236
  difficulties 40
  good qualities/merits 161
  misfortunes 33
  points of compass 227
  unobtainables 66
  Vidyarājas 133
eighteen
  avenika dharmas 27
  dhātus/elements 36, 45, 58, 103
  special faculties 27, 47
Eighteenth Vow 10, 205, 224, 233, 235, 237, 254
eightfold
  deliverance/liberation 39, 70, 77
  law 82
  path 23, 32, 57
eighty minor marks 84
eka-kṣaṇa 239
ekō 18, 117, 208, 224, 239, 278
ekstasis 272
elements (four/five) 36, 53–54, 75, 88
elephant/s, 28, 62, 70, 81
eloquence 26, 28, 35, 38–39, 43, 45, 50, 52, 65, 69, 85–86, 94, 127
emakimono 202

embodiment, 185, 239, 276
Emperor 24, 124, 161, 182, 241
Empress 24–25
emptiness 2, 4, 6, 8, 31, 38, 41, 50, 53–56, 61, 63, 70–71, 75–76, 86–87, 93, 99, 101, 103, 108, 228, 173, 204
empty 36, 46–47, 53–54, 56–57, 74–76, 93, 101, 103, 111–112, 114, 194, 206
En'i 202
Engakukyō 186
Engyō 125
enlightenment 1–2, 10, 23–24, 30–34, 37–51, 54, 56–57, 61, 66–67, 69–70, 72–73, 78, 82, 85, 90–91, 94–96, 102, 112, 114–118, 119–120, 126–129, 133, 139, 150, 152–153, 155, 158–159, 161, 167, 169–171, 174–175, 177–178, 186–187, 189, 191–192, 195, 204–205, 210, 214, 216–217, 222, 224, 226, 228, 232–233, 236, 265, 268
Ennin 125
Ennyo Kō'nyū 250
Enō era 201
Enryakuji 222
Entoku era 248
entrusting 104, 204, 207–208, 252, 254, 272–273, 279
Entsūritsuji 149
equality 27, 46–47, 76
equanimity 32, 51
escapism 187
Eshin 199, 213
Eshinni 217
Esoteric/esoteric 17, 116, 123
  Buddhism 11, 125
  esoteric/exoteric 187
  Tendai 12
Etchū 246
eternal/ly 24, 26–27, 35, 46, 48, 68, 82–83, 86, 93, 95, 133, 139–140, 158
  Amida 232, 239
  see also: *Larger* Sūtra of Eternal *Life*
eternity 113–114, 187, 223
ethical 23, 263–265, 267–269
ethics 159, 267
ethnic 187
Eun 125
Europe/an 5, 7, 21, 182, 199
evil 27, 32–33, 35, 40, 43, 48–50, 52–53, 56, 64–65, 68–69, 71–72, 81, 86, 91, 93–94, 96, 103, 109, 112–113, 127–129, 133–135, 138–140, 142–143, 145, 152, 155–156, 158–160, 162, 168, 170–171, 173–175, 177–178, 189, 191, 194, 206–207, 215–216, 226, 232, 234–236, 244, 254, 264, 267, 271–274, 276
  Evil One/s 26, 28, 30, 47, 49, 61, 160
exile of Shinran 187
existential 272
exoteric 116, 187
expedient 22, 32
extinction, 23, 39, 45–46, 57, 74, 76, 94, 101

F

faith 10, 14, 17–18, 22, 24, 26, 32, 35, 71, 94–95, 99, 126, 129, 145, 150, 152, 169, 171–172, 175, 183, 186, 196–197, 205–206, 211–217, 222–226, 228–229, 231–234, 237, 239, 244, 247, 249, 251, 253–254, 256, 259, 262–264, 265, 268–271, 273–276, 279
fāngbiàn 22; see also skilful means
Fànwǎn jīng 182, 191
fearlessness 26–27, 30, 35, 37, 47, 49, 70–71, 73, 79, 85, 95
Fischer, Jakob 5
five
  Buddhas 134
  corruptions 45, 79
  defilements 228, 288
  forms of existence 27
  grave offences/deadly sins 39, 68, 70, 170, 233, 236
  immediate sins 129
  impediments 26
  Indriyas 32
  senses 48, 57, 69, 70, 72

sights 43
skandhas 45, 101–102
strong vegetables 157
supernatural powers 42, 70, 94
unseen teachers 153–154
Vidyārājas 133–134
virtues of rebirth 161
fivefold corruption 45
passion 69
flames, 136, 138, 143, 145, 146, 229, 247
Flaming Light (Buddha) 226
flower/s 28, 34, 64–65, 69, 70, 72, 87, 89, 91, 115, 125, 136–138, 140, 142, 146, 158, 162–163, 200, 225–226, 265, 268
formless/ness 38, 50, 56, 58, 62, 74, 76, 80, 86, 88, 93, 268, 275
forty-eight Vows 168, 205, 224, 236
Fo-shuo 10
founder/s 13, 15–16, 150, 168, 171, 178–179, 199–201, 203, 211, 218, 221, 231, 241–242, 244–245, 248–251, 263, 279
four
arms 137
forms of birth 235
guardian gods 52, 59, 96
kinds of triple jewel 151
noble truths 40
syllables 254,275
ways of acceptance 32
fourfold
acceptance 23, 47, 82, 85
false idea 69
fearlessness 47, 70
Immeasurable Mind 32
Infinite 86
meditation 57
Noble Truth 23, 103
Francis, St. 199
fuda/o-fuda 143, 147
Fudō 12, 133–147
Fudōshisha darani himitsuhō 136
fuekō 209, 214
Fugen Bosatsu 8–9, 16, 124, 227
Fugengyōganbon 115, 120
Fujimoto, R. 15
Fujiwara
Kanezane 189
Period 146, 199
Fukagawa 143
Fukakusa principle 201
Fuke sect 218
Fukui prefecture 246, 248
Fukūjōju 134
funeral 3
funi 203
funnu myōō 133
funnushin 134
furaigō 212–214

G

gaki 161
Gambhīramati 76
gambling 35, 266–267
games 145
Ganchi-bō 231, 240
Gandak (river) 25
Gaṇḍavyūha 9–10, 115–117, 119–120
Gandha mountains 29
Gandhakūṭa 77–80
Gandharvas 29–30, 93–94, 102
Gandhavyūha 78
Ganeṣa 140
Gaṅgā (river)/ Ganges 24, 59–61, 67, 78–79, 229
garbhadhātu 184
garden/s 25, 70, 78, 84, 86, 119
garland/s 71, 90–91
Garuḍas 29
Gautama 24
Gedatsu Shōnin 182
gem/s 28, 138, 238
Genchi 179, 185
gender 3
Genju 26
Genkū 221
Genroku era 247
Genshin 213, 221
gensō ekō 224
German/y 5, 15, 121
geta 260, 270, 275
ghosts 27, 33, 68, 161, 226, 235–236
giant 139

giving 3, 8, 24, 26, 32, 36, 39, 51, 58, 63, 110, 149, 153–155, 157, 167, 190–191, 203, 207, 251, 269
goblins 59–60, 65, 89, 94
God 4, 135, 140, 145, 168
god/s 27, 29–30, 34–36, 45–47, 50, 52, 59–60, 65, 80, 83, 86, 89, 92–94, 96, 102, 126, 128, 133–143, 145, 195, 228, 245, 256
Godenshō 211
Goichidaikikikigaki 250, 257
Gokurakuji 269
gold 51, 62, 146
golden 7, 28, 66, 82, 170, 185
gongyō 277
Gośālīputra 40
Gōsanze 134
Gosōjōshinkan 186
Gōtsu (city) 262
grace 38, 50, 80, 215, 232
gratitude 25, 171–173, 206, 225, 249, 255, 264–265, 278–279
Guāngmíngsì 235
Guānjīngshù 200
Guānpǔxiánpúsà jīng 8–9
Guānwúliàngshòu jīng 9
Guhyakalpa literature 135
guilt 81, 93, 268–269, 272
gutoku 187, 206
Gutokushō 183, 196–197
gyō 17
Gyōji 183

H

Hannen 222
Hannya Shingyō 100
Hansei Zasshi 21
harai 236
Hastings (Encyclopedia) 159
Hattō Kokushi 218
Heart Sūtra 2, 7, 99–105
heaven/s 33, 45, 68, 89–91, 94, 116–117, 140–141, 161, 192, 194, 229, 232, 235–236
Heian period 24, 149, 182–183, 199
heizei gōjō 212–213, 255
hell/s 27, 33, 68, 81, 86, 161, 190, 226, 232, 234–236, 239–240, 256, 270
Henjō Kōngō (Daishi) 163
hereditary 3
heresy/heresies 26–27, 30, 35, 40, 43–44, 46, 49, 53, 55, 69, 72, 91, 93
  heretical 37, 42, 44, 68, 93, 194, 211
  heretics 50, 53, 72, 93, 129
hermit 9, 73, 120
hermitage/s 51, 184, 186–187, 266
heterodox/ies 231, 247
Hida Province 240
Hiei (Mount) 144, 182–183, 197, 222, 245–247
Higashi Honganji 11, 242, 277, 279
hiji 255–256
hijihōmon 247
Himālaya/n 22, 29
Himitsugiki 135
himitsuhō 136
Hīnayāna 22–23, 41, 82, 87, 170–171, 183, 228
Hīnayānists 22–23
hindrances 26–27, 129, 145, 164, 226
Hindu god 141
hinin 187
Hino Arinori 222
Hirota, Dennis 252, 272
hisō hizoku 3
Hitachi province 231
hōben 22
Hōetsucho Ubasoku 271
Hōgenji 247
hōkai (*dharmadh*ātu) 161
Hokekyō 151
Hokuriku region 244, 247, 269
holiness 222
holy 42, 50–51, 93, 133, 140–142, 150–151, 153, 156, 161–162, 164, 174, 184–185, 191, 193–194, 197, 204, 222, 227, 229, 231–234, 237
hōmyō dentatsu 277
Hōmyō (Beomyeong) 25
Hōnen 13–15, 171, 178–179, 181–197, 199–203, 205–211, 213–215, 217–218, 221–222, 224, 234, 244, 265
Honganji 11, 16, 222, 231, 233, 237, 241–249, 269, 277, 279

Hóngfǎ sì 185
Hongwanji 242
Honkō-bō 247
Honpukuji (Katata) 242, 246
honzei 135
honzon 149
horse 62, 70, 81, 145
Hōryūji 100
hōsha 211
Hōshō 134
Hosorogi 246
Hōtoku era 244
household (life) 1–4, 6, 182, 262, 266–267, 269
householder/s 9, 35–38, 43–44, 58–59, 80, 83, 96, 120, 169, 266
hōwa 278
hṛdaya-sūtra 99–105
Hùigǔo 125
hum/*hūṃ* 138, 147
humanistic 212, 267
humility/humble 30, 50, 187, 206, 270–271
Hundred 150
hundred, 12, 29, 31, 34, 36, 38, 40–42, 45–47, 49, 51–52, 59, 82, 91–92, 96, 99, 119, 169, 176, 191, 247
hungry ghosts/spirits 27, 33, 68, 81, 161, 226, 235–236
Hyakumanben 210
hymn/s 7–8, 121–130, 197, 247, 274, 278
Hyōgo Prefecture 202, 248
Hyōsenji 247

I

Ichigyō 12
ichinen 213, 229
ichinen kimyō no kotowari 251
ichinengi 211
ichiyaku hōmon 255
iconic 140
iconography 4, 6, 9, 12, 135, 141
Ida (town) 262
identity of opposites 272
Idumi (= Izumi Hōkei) 5
ignorance 35, 39, 47, 52, 57, 65, 68–69, 75, 81, 89, 93, 101, 103, 108, 112–114, 129, 133, 151, 155, 168, 222–223, 226, 236–237, 252, 272, 278
illness/es 6, 44–45, 78–79
illusion/s 43, 54, 152, 222
  illusory 39–40
immeasurable 10, 27, 32, 37, 92, 118
immortal/ity 26, 41, 71, 80
immovable 12, 38, 47, 133–135, 137, 139–143, 145–147
Imperial 24, 104, 182, 192
impermanence/cy, 53, 61, 111, 113, 244
Inagaki, Hisao 11, 15
incalculable 194, 229
incarnation 22, 78–80, 134, 140, 145, 200, 204, 216
incense 91, 125–126, 153, 158, 163–164
inconceivable/s 58, 60–62, 79, 83, 85, 91–92, 127, 178
India/n 7–8, 21–22, 25, 71, 115, 123–125, 149, 170, 186, 189, 221,
  southern India 125
Indra 28–29, 48, 92–94, 117, 136
Indriyas 32
insight 2, 7, 8, 183, 190, 228, 260, 272
invocation 138, 145–146, 150, 179, 181, 200, 251
Ippen 13, 15–16, 171, 179, 199–203, 205–219
Ippengoroku 179, 206, 218
Ippenhijirie 202
Ishikawa 256
isshin kimyō 251
Iśvara 141
Itokuki 242–243, 249, 251
Iwami province 260
Iyo province, 202
Izumi Hōkei 5, 7–8, 21, 25, 58–59, 63, 121, 147, 248

J

Jaffe, Richard 3
Jakue-bō, 189, 191
Jambudvīpa 59, 89, 94, 170
jarāmaraṇa 103

jāti 103
Jesus (saying) 207
Jetavana Grove 116–117, 119
jewel/s 28–30, 34–35, 91, 128
jeweled 34, 41, 51, 89, 93, 136
Triple Jewel 151–153, 155, 157–158
Ji (Sect, Ji-shū) 114, 171, 179, 199–201, 203, 205, 210, 212, 214, 216, 218
Jiácái 185
Jie 199
jihi 263
Jìn Dynasty 115
Jingoji 183
jiriki 167, 172–174, 176–177, 204, 223–224, 232
Jitsugo 249
Jitsunyo 248
Jiun 121, 125
Jōben 187
Jōdo School/shū 181, 184, 199–201, 203, 205, 210–214, 217–218, 221, 231–233, 238, 244, 255, 269,
Jōdo Shinshū 247, 249, 277–279; see also Shin (-shū, Buddhism), Shinshū
Jōdoshin'yōshō 213
Jōdo Wasan 15
Jōgai ofumi (*jōgai*) 244, 250
Jōgaku-bō 183, 186, 189
jōgyōsanmai 210
Jōkei 182, 192, 197
jōzen 173
jū-kō anjin 255
Jūdaifunnumyōōgiki 138
Jūjikyō 115, 117
Jūjuhon 117
Junnyo 248
Jusha 150, 153–158
Jutsujō 173, 176–177
Jūzenkaikyō 161

K

Kaga province 246, 256
Kai-no-ura 248
Kaji Yōichi 241, 249
Kakuda-Kātyāyana 40
Kakunyo 4, 16, 231, 234, 242–244, 250
Kakushin 218–219
Kakushin-ni 16
Kāla mountains 29
Kālayaśas 225
kalpa/s, 45, 60–61, 72–73, 80–81, 85–86, 91–92, 94–95, 118, 128, 135–136, 137–138, 140, 170, 173–175, 194, 202, 216, 225, 235, 255
kāma 58
Kāmadhātu Heaven 161
Kamakura 12, 145, 181–182, 199–201, 209
Kamatari 24–25
kami 216
kamisori 277
Kanagamori 246, 248
Kanaka mountains 29
kanbun 243
Kaneko Daiei 16, 241
Kaneko Hiroshi 241, 249
Kanfugenbosatsukyō 8
Kangyō 221
Kangyōsho 265
Kaniṣka 22
Kanmu (Emperor) 182
Kanmuryōjukyō 9, 265
Kannon 227
Kanshō period 245–246
Kantō 196, 244
Kārikā 107
karma 27, 30, 36, 103, 113, 127–128, 139, 162, 171, 175, 190, 207, 223, 226, 235–236, 238–239, 254–256, 271–273
karuṇā 32, 200, 204
Kasagi 192
Kasawara Kenju 121
kaṣāya 228
Kasuga Shrine 186–187
Kāśyapa 39–40, 190
Katata Honpukuji 242, 246
Kātyāyana 40–41
Kauśika 48
Kawachi 245, 248
Kawamura, Leslie H. 15
kāya 152; see also bodies
Kedai 202

Kegon
school 183, 186
Sūtra 115, 117–178, 120
Kegonkyō 7, 11, 122, 124, 150
Ken'i 201, 210
Kenjitsu Hakuriku 189
Kenshōji 246
kesō 151–152
ketsumyaku 179
kihō 209–210
kihō ittai 252–253
kimyō 208
kie 277–278
Kierkegaard, Søren 223
kigyōha 211
Kii province 183–184, 186–187, 191–192
kikyōshiki 17–18, 269, 277–279
Kiṃkara 142
Kiṃnaras 29
kimyō 208, 251
Kinai region 245, 250
King/king/s 9, 27, 28, 30, 34, 36, 54, 92, 120,
Aśoka 22
bright king (*myōō*) 12, 133
Cakravartin 43
Kaniṣka 22, 29–30, 133
of deities (Indra) 91–94
of dragons/serpents 59, 143
of mountains 29
of trees (Bodhi tree) 126, 129
Kinki (region) 269
Kirchner, Thomas 259
Kīrtibhūtiprajñā (Bhikṣu) 110
Kobama 260, 266–267
Kōbe 202
Kōben 182
Kōbō Daishi 11–12, 121, 125, 163; see also Kūkai
Kōbukuji 192
Kōfukuji 192
Kōfukujisōjō 192–193
Kōjun 248
Komashi 150
Kōmyōji 235
Kongō Sanmai-in 12
Kongō 134, 163
Kongōge 134
Kongōhōkaihiketsushō 209
Kongōkai 183
Kongōshukōmyōkanjōkyō 138
Kongōyakusha 134
Kongōyasha 134
Kongōzō 134
Korea 25, 269
Kōsai 201, 211
Kōsei 260
Kōsōgai 224
koṭī/s (*koṭi*/s) 129, 236
Kōya (Mount) 12–13, 18, 149, 151, 153, 155, 157, 159, 161, 163–164
Kōyasan, 145
Kōzanji 187
Kōzen 183
Kōzenji 248
Krakucchanda 94
krodhakāya 134
krodharāja 133–134
kṣānti 26, 32, 50, 153
Kṣatriyas 36
Kubono 202
Kudenshō 16
Kūkai 11, 125, 149, 182, 199; see also Kōbō Daishi
Kūlika 143
Kumano Shrine/Myōjin 216
Kumārajīva 8, 25, 71, 100
Kumbhāṇḍas 126
Kunḍalī 134
Kundari 134
Kurikara Fudō 142–143
Kurodani 234
Kurus (country of) 33
Kusunoki, 261, 267, 273
Kuyōjō-dhāraṇi 158
Kūzen 249
Kyakuhaimōki 189, 191
Kyōgyōji 248
Kyōgyōshinshō 3, 10, 183, 196–197, 199, 218, 237, 243, 263–264
Kyōju 150, 153–154
kyōnokuroki 243
Kyōōgokokuji 145

Kyōryōyasha 225
Kyōto 7, 12, 104, 145, 183–184, 186, 191, 196, 210, 222, 245–246, 248, 269, 279
Kyūshū 202

L

laity 1, 11, 12, 24, 131; see also lay
Lake Biwa 246, 248
Lamotte, Étienne 5–6
Laṅkāvatāra Sūtra 10
Larger Sūtra *(of Eternal Life)* 169–170, 176, 200, 205, 224, 235, 238, 263
latter-day Dharma 204
Law (for Dharma) 2, 25–30, 34–35, 37–42, 44, 46–52, 54–55, 57–59, 63–66, 68–73, 76–83, 85–88, 90–96, 120, 159–161, 169, 176, 225, 238
lay 1–6, 8–18, 22, 24, 36, 120, 123, 149–150, 160, 200, 242, 266
  man/men 2, 3, 9, 23–24, 29, 35, 39, 120, 149, 151, 160–161, 203, 215, 225, 271
  persons 2
  women 9, 120, 160
legend 6, 143, 190
letters 10, 63, 65, 67, 77, 84, 178, 217, 244–247, 250–256, 270, 275
Lǐ Tōngxuán 186
lineage/s 241–245, 247–248
lion/s 26–29, 47, 59, 80, 83, 125, 128, 194
  throne 29, 59, 80, 83
liturgy 12, 17, 277
longevity 33, 85, 236
lotus (flower) 29, 31, 34, 69, 72, 89, 127, 129, 136–140, 142, 163, 170, 265
Lotus Sūtra 3, 7–8, 151
Lowrie, Walter 223
Luther, Martin 182

M

Madhyamika 99–100, 107–108, 113–114
Madhyamika Śāstra 100, 113–114
magic 38, 111–112, 140, 255
  magical/ly 62–3 111
  magician 38, 62, 66–67
Mahācakravāḍa mountains 29
Mahākāśyapa 24, 38–39, 61, 69
Mahākātyāyana 41
Mahāmaudgalyāyana 24, 37–38
Mahāmucilinda mountains 29
Mahāsthāmaprapta 227
Mahāvairocana 158, 186
Mahāvyūha 92
Mahāyāna, 1–2, 4, 6–9, 14, 23–24, 31–33, 35, 38, 41, 61, 63, 70, 82–83, 86, 95, 97, 100, 103, 113, 115–116, 119–120, 122–123, 152, 158, 169–171, 174, 182, 186, 203, 222, 224, 227–229
  Mahāyānistic 22
  Mahāyānists 23, 26, 99, 104, 124
Mahāyānaviṃśaka 8, 107–111, 113
Maheśvara 140
Mahoragas 29
maiden/s 9, 48–50, 64–67, 70, 120
Maitrāyaṇīputra 40
Maitreya 45–46, 94–96, 117, 120, 150, 153–154, 192, 234
maitrī 32
Makinoo 184
maladies 87
mamori/o-mamori 143
mandala 184
  maṇḍala 193–194
  mandara 193
manifestation/s 24, 134
manifest/ing 27, 29–30, 35, 50–51, 56–57, 59, 64, 66–67, 69, 72–73, 78, 80–81, 85, 88–90, 111, 118, 193, 216, 222, 260, 265
Manju-in 145
Mañjuśrī 6, 9, 28, 52–57, 59, 62–64, 68–70, 77–78, 82, 91, 96, 110, 117, 119–120, 123–124, 128–129, 134, 150, 153–154
Mañjuśrīpraṇidhāna sūtra 122–123
manovijñāna 103
mantra/s 100–101, 103–104, 140, 146–147, 186
mappō 204
Māra 48–49, 71, 160
marriage 2–3, 241, 244, 266, 269

Maskari-Gośālīputra 40
matricide 236
Māyā 127–128
meat 3, 157
medicine 27, 72, 83, 87, 164
meditate 10–11, 28, 37, 69, 87, 160, 169, 173, 235
  meditation, 9, 11, 13–15, 17, 23, 26–27, 29, 32, 35, 37–39, 41, 43, 47, 49, 51, 55, 57, 63, 68, 70–72, 75, 80, 82, 84–87, 102, 116, 119, 151–153, 163, 169, 171, 173, 176, 179, 182–185, 186–187, 189, 193–194, 200, 202, 221, 265
  meditative/ly 11, 191
Meiji government 3
Meiō era 249
mendicant/s 9, 41, 51, 65, 72, 94, 116, 120, 126
merchant/s 29, 31, 34, 50, 52
mercy 23, 28, 30, 32, 37, 47, 50, 63–64, 66, 70, 72–73, 85, 87, 93, 110, 118, 172, 178, 224, 227
merit 1, 18, 40, 44, 48, 75, 79, 82, 86–89, 91, 114, 117, 120, 127–130, 151, 158, 161–162, 169–170, 173, 175–176, 178–179, 195, 206, 208–209, 211, 214–215, 222, 224–225, 229, 232–233, 238, 255, 268
  merits 21, 32, 36, 39, 43–44, 47, 49, 51, 54, 56, 64, 68, 71, 75, 87, 92, 123, 129, 158–161, 229
  meritorious 29, 41, 76, 90, 118, 177, 239
  transference 214, 239
Michihisa (Ippen) 202
Middle Ages 199
Middle Way 204
middle 112, 114
miei 140
Miidera 144, 246
mikkyō 11–12
mindful/ness 169, 278
mingei 15
miracle/s 29, 58
miraculous, 42, 51, 66, 128, 226, 228, 233
mirage 36, 43, 62
mirror 8, 43, 62, 84, 108, 115
Miyata 248
monastery 23–24, 42, 160
monastic/s 9, 1–3, 6, 8, 16, 22, 35, 183, 245–246
money 143, 243
Mongaku 183
Monju 134
monkey/s, 81, 269
monk/s 1–3, 5–6, 9, 13, 16–17, 24, 120, 149, 160, 164, 185, 187, 189190, 201, 215, 231, 235, 240
  monkhood 2
  monkish 173
monshin 255
monster 112
moon/s 8, 29, 33, 43, 60, 62, 66, 72, 84, 89, 108, 119, 127, 141, 155, 161–162, 227, 243
morality 33, 47, 50, 63, 68, 74, 102, 126, 153, 155, 163, 169–171, 173, 177–178, 182, 228, 262–264, 266–269
Mori, Mrs. 17
Mori Ryūkichi 242
mother/hood 62, 70, 102, 124, 152, 183, 202, 237, 241–242, 271
Mount (Mt.)
  Hiei 144, 182–183, 197, 222, 245–247
  Kōya 12–13, 18, 149
  Meru (= Sumeru) 126
  Sumeru 26, 29, 30, 60, 69, 80, 237
  Vulture 102
mountain/s 12–13, 28–29, 34, 60, 89, 119, 139, 173, 184–185, 191, 203, 237, 246, 276
Mucilinda mountains 29
muditā 32
Mugekō-ryū 245
Mujintō 122
Mukanshōsōki 184
Mūlamadhyamika 107
Müller, Max 7, 100, 104, 121
mumyō 133, 237
Muryōju 134
Muryōjukyō 7

Myōe 14, 181–197
Myōgishingyōshū 217
myōgō 200
Myōhōsan 119
Myōjin (Kumano) 216
myōkōnin 17, 206, 259–267, 269–271, 273, 275–276
Myōō 12, 133–134, 141, 145–146
mystic/al/ism 17, 100, 135–137, 142 146, 184, 259
mythical 2, 6, 276
mythology 14

N

Namu Amida Butsu (Na-mu-a-mi-da-butsu) 5, 11, 200, 205, 208, 217–219, 232–233, 275
Nāgārjuna 8, 21–22, 99–100, 107–109, 111, 113–114, 221
Nāgas 126, 143, 170
naishi 11, 103
nǎizhì 103
nāmarūpa 103
Namas 239
namo 239
Namu (Amida Butsu) 5, 11, 170–171, 176, 179, 199–200, 202–203, 205, 207–210, 212, 214, 217–219, 232–233, 235, 252–254, 263–264, 268–276
  Namu (meaning) 239
Nanjio (= Nanjō) 21
Nanjō, Bun'yū 7, 21, 110, 121
Nara 24, 100, 184, 191
  Buddhism 182–183, 187, 192, 197
Nārāyaṇa Bodhisattva 69, 74
Narita Fudō 143
necklace 51
negation 30, 103
negative 145, 224
negativism 27
Nehan (Nirvāṇa) Sūtra 115
Nehangyō 150
Nehanji 262, 266, 269
nen 10–11, 229
Nenbutsu/Nenbutsu/Nembutsu 4–5, 10–11, 13–15, 17, 165, 167–173, 175–179, 181–183, 184–185, 189, 191–196, 200–201, 203–219, 222, 224–225, 229, 231, 234–238, 240, 253, 255–256, 263–265, 269, 273, 277–279
nenji no gi 250–251, 253–254
Nepal/ese 122, 124
Never Returning 45
Nichiren 14–15, 199–200, 253
Nidāna 103
Niigata Prefecture 256
niji-soku-shiji 254
niji-soku-rokuji 254
Nineteenth Vow 233
Nirgrantha-Jñati-putra 40
Nirmāṇakāya 156
nirvana/*nirvāṇa* 23, 27, 39–40, 43, 46, 53–54, 56–58, 62–63, 69–70, 74, 77, 81, 93, 101, 111–114, 126, 128, 150–152, 159–160, 163, 224, 232–233
  Nirvāṇa Sūtra 115
Nishitani, Keiji 260
nivāraṇa 26
no-birth 45
Nogami Shunjō 10
non-activity 76
non-duality 77, 203–204
non-returners 62
northern (cosmological) 184
nothingness 36, 74
novice/s 17, 40, 59, 78, 86, 95
numberless, 49, 118, 227, 229, 236, 271
nun/s 1, 9, 25, 120, 190
Nyāya 107
Nyoingosho 174, 178
Nyokei 248
Nyorai/*nyorai* 200, 275, 279
Nyorairin Bodhisattva 109
Nyoshin Shōnin 16
Nyūhokkaibon 7, 115, 117
Nyūshutsunimonge 265

O

Obama 248
obedience 139–140
occultism 135

occupation 270
ocean/s, 29–30, 35, 41, 60, 69, 80, 85, 113–115, 118–119, 125, 127–128, 139, 152, 160, 163, 168, 173, 227, 278
Ochi Kōno 202
Ōchō Enichi 4
ōchō 223
Ofumi, 244, 250, 256, 275
ogamazu hiji 255
Ōgen 245
Ōhara 192
Ōhara Kakichi 21
ointments, 125
Ōjō 227, 235
Oku no hosomichi 246
omen 82
Ōmi Province 246
omnipotent 27, 159
omniscience 47, 50, 56, 69, 75, 85–86, 91
Ondoku-san 278–279
oneness 74–75, 88, 210, 275
Ōnin period 246, 248
ontic 228
ontology 24
opposites (identity of) 272
oracles 186
oral tradition 16
ordained 1–3, 10, 24, 123, 183, 243, 266
Order 58, 151, 233, 277
ordination/s, 2, 12, 18, 183
Oriental philosophy 21
Original Vow 169–71, 178–179, 207, 224–225, 227, 232, 234–235, 237–238, 240, 263–265, 279
orthodox/y 22, 211, 231
Ōsaka 183, 245, 248–250
Osono, Tahara no 206
Ōtani-ha (branch) 11, 17, 259, 277
Ōtani Honganji 245–246, 248
Ōtani University 7, 11, 116
Other Power 196, 200, 218–219, 223–224, 233, 236, 251–252, 254, 256, 272–276
otherness 39, 88
Ōtsu 246
Oyasama 271

P

pagoda 12, 169
painting/s 14–15, 112, 133, 145, 187, 202, 213
pañca kaṣāya 228
pantheon 134, 141
Pāpīyas 48–49
parable/s, 84, 202
paradise 224
pāragate 101
pārājika 236
Pāramitās 23, 37, 47, 57, 66, 70, 75, 86, 92, 126, 152–153
Paranirmita heaven 117
pārasaṃgate 101
parent/s 44, 53, 70, 86, 161, 173, 222, 237, 259, 262, 266–267, 271, 273–276
pariṇāmana 117, 159, 239
parinirvāṇa 150
paryavanaddha 26
passions 12, 22, 34, 39–40, 45, 47, 49, 54–56, 62–65, 68–70, 84, 87, 89, 111–113, 127–128, 136, 171, 173, 236, 265
passionlessness 74, 81, 87
path 2, 8, 10, 12, 18, 23, 30–32, 35, 39, 41, 49, 57–58, 69, 90–91, 94, 101, 104, 128, 158, 191, 193–194, 197, 200, 202, 204–205, 213–214, 219, 234, 263, 265–266
paths 27, 43, 69, 93, 111–112, 126–127, 129, 167, 189, 203–204, 226, 235–236, 244, 267
patience 23, 26, 32, 35–37, 47, 63, 73, 75, 82, 153
patriarch/s 14, 16, 185, 200, 203, 221
patricide 236, 271
patron/age 22, 24, 160, 186
peak (Myōhōsan) 119
pearl 4, 62
perfection/s 7–8, 26, 33, 49, 63, 84–85, 118, 156
perfume/s 9, 78–81, 83–84, 87, 120, 157
permanence 50, 71
personifications 135
Petzold, Bruno 15

physician/s 9, 27, 30, 54, 120
pilgrimage 116–117, 120, 186, 202, 244, 247, 269
plain wood *nenbutsu* 168–179, 206
plantain tree 36, 62, 109
poem/s 219, 225, 260–264, 267–271, 273–276
poetic/al 225, 275
poison/ous 36, 72, 84, 112, 190
porcelain 60, 90
Potala 6
powers 27, 42–43, 62, 85, 94, 128, 169–170, 194, 252
  supernatural 6, 22, 24, 29–31, 34–35, 37, 47–48, 50, 52, 57–59, 61, 64, 67, 70, 73, 78–79, 83, 85, 90–92 94, 96
Prabhāvyūha 46
practice/s 68, 183, 193–195, 201, 206, 210–211, 214, 246–247, 250, 254–256
  practitioner 91, 217, 255
  practicer/ practiser 182, 194–195, 210, 263–265
practise/practising, 23, 30, 47, 49–51, 68, 72, 82, 86–87,90–92, 94, 96, 102, 118, 126, 129, 152, 155, 159, 163, 168–170, 173, 175, 178–179, 235, 259, 265
Pradhānakuśala Bodhisattva 76
Prajñā/prajñā
  bodhisattva 134
  (person) 115, 124,
  (concept) 32, 103, 117, 152–153, 161, 204, 226, 228
Prajñāpāramitā 50, 70, 101–102, 104
  literature 7, 138
  Prajñāpāramitāhṛdaya sūtra 8, 121
  Prajñāpāramitā sūtra 21, 99 102, 108, 138
praṇidhi 160
Prāsaṅgika school 107
Pratisthāna world 119
pratītya utpanna 111
pratītya samutpāda 103, 112
Pratyakṣa 74
pratyeka/buddha 23, 39, 57, 61, 65–66, 68, 78, 85, 94, 126, 152, 226
pray/er 78–79, 135, 143, 153, 158, 160, 201, 207, 213–214, 216
preach/ing 23, 25, 29–31, 33, 35–38, 38, 40–42, 43, 45–48, 51–53, 55, 61, 63–65, 68, 77–82, 86–87, 88–93, 95–96, 102, 116–117, 119, 124, 129, 150–151, 158–161, 192, 202, 214–215, 217, 222, 248
precept/s, 2–3, 13, 33, 35, 81, 86, 88, 93, 149–158, 161–164, 182, 184, 186, 191–192, 194, 203, 215
preta 27
priest/s 16, 24, 123, 125, 143, 149–150, 153, 156, 160–162, 164, 185, 187, 199, 201–203, 213, 215–216, 222, 225, 246, 249, 260, 270, 275, 279
prince/s, 24, 28, 36, 92–94, 199
Priyadarśana Bodhisattva 75
priyavacana 32
prophecy 94
psalm 222
pūjā 159
Puṇyakṣetra Bodhisattva 76
puṇyānumodanā 159
Pūraṇa-Kāśyapa 40
pure 26, 29–35, 37, 40, 42–44, 46, 50, 54, 56–57, 59, 63, 66, 68, 70–71, 74, 82, 84, 86, 88–90, 92, 95, 111, 113, 117–118, 123, 125–126, 128–129, 139, 154, 159, 161–162, 172, 186, 194, 206, 212, 216, 223, 260, 263, 265, 273, 275
  purify/ication 33, 43, 49, 51, 85–86, 127–128, 143, 154, 161–162
  purity/pureness 31, 34, 43, 49, 51, 57, 63, 70–71, 73, 79, 81, 94, 127–128, 134, 162, 168, 203, 211, 216, 218, 227, 231–233, 265, 276
Pure Land 4–5, 7, 9–16, 99, 120, 122, 140, 167–179, 181–185, 193–194, 196–197, 199–219, 221–229, 232–238, 244–245, 255, 265, 271
purgatories 111
Pūrṇa 40–41
Pūrṇa -Maitrāyaṇīputra 40
Purple cloud 184, 232
purvapranidhāna 227

Puṣpavyūha 28, 76
Puṣya 74
Pŭxiánpúsà-xíngyuàn zàn 123–124
Pŭxián púsà, 124

Q

quarter/s 10, 26, 29, 44, 59–61, 66, 70–71, 78–79, 89, 93, 96, 118–119, 124–129, 158, 168, 205, 227–229, 233, 236, 239, 246–249
Queen Vaidehī 9, 225

R

raft of the Mahāyāna 113
Rahder, Johannes 4
Rāhula 43
raigō 212, 255
Rājagṛha 102
Rakṣasas 94
Ratna mountains 29
Ratnacandra 66
Ratnacchatra 92, 94
Ratnakūṭa 28–29, 31, 33–34
Ratnamudrāhasta 77
Ratnasaṃbhava 134
Ratnaśrī 66
Ratnatejas 66, 94
Ratnavyūha 66
rebirth 4, 62–63, 122, 168–169, 171–177, 179, 185, 200, 202, 205, 207–208, 211–217, 223, 227–229, 231–240
reborn 57, 62, 67, 82, 120, 168–170, 172, 175–179, 212, 224, 232, 234–235, 238
recitation 9, 11, 24–25, 42, 90–93, 95–96, 99, 122–124, 129, 140, 163, 168–169, 170–179, 184, 205, 208, 210–211, 214–215, 217, 219, 234–235, 237–238, 240, 269, 274, 273, 277–278
recompense 50, 212, 235, 237
Record
  of Dreams 184–185, 187, 190
  of Oral Transmisson 16
  of Sayings from Rennyō's Life 242, 249
  of Way of Life of Shōma 260
Reformation
  Buddhist 182
  Protestant 182
refuge/s 16, 30, 58, 64, 87, 93, 119, 151–153, 158–159, 163–164, 205–207, 209, 222–223, 225–229, 236, 251–254, 273, 277–278
regulations 247, 256–257
reincarnation 241
rekishi 241, 249
religion/s 1, 6, 11, 18, 21, 23–24, 78–79, 159, 199, 215, 242, 244, 247, 252, 259
religionists 223
religious 2, 12, 15, 17, 22–23, 78–79, 84, 89, 119–20, 135, 145, 154, 162, 172, 182–185, 187, 196, 199–200, 202, 205–207, 209, 217–218, 223, 225, 242, 244, 247, 252, 256, 260, 262–269, 271, 276
Rengo 249
Rennyadai 186
Rennyo Shōnin 13, 16, 215, 241–257, 275
Rennyoshōningoichidaikikigaki 242, 249
Rennyoshōningyōjōki 242
Rennyoshōninitokuki 242, 251
renunciation 1, 43–44, 56, 86, 187, 266
Riddhis 32
righteous/ness 27, 29–30, 32, 35, 37, 70, 77, 126, 194, 197, 267
Rimyō-bō 183
rinjūraigō 212–213
Rinkan-bō 183
Rinzai Zen 199
Rishukyō 7
ritai 151
rite/s 3, 17–18, 136–138, 142, 277, 279
ritual/s 2–3, 12–13, 17, 135, 145, 150, 160, 183, 242
ritualism 135, 224
Rogers, Ann T. 242, 245–246, 249–250, 252–256
Rogers, Minor L. 242, 245–246, 249–250, 252–256
rokuji-soku-rokuji 254
Rokujō no ofumi 256
Rokujōengi 202
Rokujūshōnyoriron 114

rope 135–139
rosary 210
Ruci (Tathāgata) 94
rūpa 58, 102
Ryōgemon 250
Ryōken 247
Ryūju 221; see also Nāgārjuna
Ryūkan Risshi 201, 211
Ryūkoku 15, 222, 228

S

sacred, 22, 44–45, 61, 100, 137, 159, 243–244, 269, 278
sacrifice 22, 188
ṣaḍāyatana 103
Saddharmapuṇḍarīka (Sūtra) 115, 123 151
Sadho 164
Sādhumati Boddhisattva 74
Sāgaramegha 119
Sahā world 78–79, 81, 90
Sahāṃpati 61
Saichi (Asahara) 17, 259–276
Saichō 182, 199
Saigyō 246
Saijarin/shōgonki 181
Saikyō (Asahara) 266–269
Saimei (Tennō) 24
Saimyō (Empress) 24
saint/ly 15 40, 43, 56, 93, 160, 199, 204, 222, 225
Sakaki Ryōsaburō 104
Śākhayaprabhā (Bhikṣu) 110
Śakra 35–36, 59, 61, 65–66, 72, 83, 91–92
śakti 134
Śākyamuni 10, 24, 34, 42, 48, 66, 79, 81, 87, 90, 115–117, 149–150, 153–154, 158, 160, 163, 186, 225–229, 236
salvation, 8, 16, 23, 50, 112, 117–118, 152, 159–160, 167–169, 176, 178, 181, 202, 204–205, 207–208, 212, 214–215, 217, 222, 224, 227, 232, 250, 253, 255–256, 264–265, 269–270
samādhi/Samādhi 27, 37, 40, 57, 78, 81, 102, 119, 161, 184–188, 196, 210, 269
samānārthatā 32
Samantabhadra 2, 7–10, 16, 115–125, 127–129, 227
Samantabhadracaryāpraṇidhāna 123
Samantadarśanarūpakāya 70
Samantagupta 75
samaya 135
Saṃbhogakāya 156
saṃbodhi 23
saṃgha 2, 26
saṃgraha 23
saṃjñā 102
saṃparigrahavastu 32
saṃsāra 74
saṃskāra 102–103
samudaya 103
samyakprahāṇa 32
samyak saṃbodhi 23, 85
Sanamidabutsuge 221
Sangha 151–152, 163–164, 170, 277–278
Sanghavarman 224
Sanjōwasan 247
Sanjujōkai 151
Sañjya-Vairāṣṭrikaputra 40
Śaṅkhacūḍa 34
Sānlùn zōng 107
Sanmaihottokuki 185
Sanronshū 107
Śāntendriya Bodhisattva 76
Śāntideva 25, 122, 159
sanzen 173
Sanzenbutsumyō 149–150
Śāriputra 24, 33–34, 37, 58–61, 64–67, 77, 80, 83, 88–90, 96, 101–102, 151
Sarvagandhasugandha 78–80, 83, 85
Sarvārthasiddha 66
Sarvasukhamaṇḍita world 80
śāstra/s, 100, 107, 113–114, 170–171
Śataka 107
Satō Taira 17, 259
satori 168
satya 103
saviour 31, 239
savour 71
sebutsu danomi 255
secular 14, 94, 247, 236, 266
seed/s 60–2, 69–70, 114, 139, 160, 195, 236–237, 252

Seikan-bō 185
Seiren-in 145
Seishi 227
Seizan 14, 168, 171, 201, 252
Sekisui-in 186
self 26, 35, 38, 41, 47, 50, 54, 65, 75–76, 79, 81, 86, 91, 93, 102, 111–114, 152, 167–169, 172, 176, 178–179, 187, 195, 197, 200, 204–9, 216, 219, 223–225, 228, 232–234, 237, 251–252, 264–265, 267–268, 272–276, 279
selfhood 38, 88
self reflection 257
self power 204
self sacrifice 22
selfish/ness 22, 30, 69 133
selfless/ness 41, 47, 50, 53, 56, 61, 63, 75, 87, 93
Sen'yū 245
Senchakushū 181
Senjakuhongannenbutsushū 200, 218
Senjakushū 181–185, 189–193, 195–196, 207
senses 46, 48–49, 57, 65, 69–70, 72, 102–103, 173
sentient (beings) 111–112, 114, 136, 139–140, 150–153, 157, 161–164, 168, 174–175, 195, 202, 204–205, 207–208, 210, 213–214, 216–218, 224, 232, 238–239, 253–254, 275
sermon/s 26, 151, 183, 206, 267, 269, 274, 278–279
serpent/s 29–30, 59, 65, 89, 93–94, 268
Seshin 221
sesshu fusha 193
settled 111, 149, 160, 164, 238, 246, 252–253, 255–256, 267
Settsu Province 245, 248–249
seven
patriarchs of Shin 235 precious jewels 29, 91 constituents of Bodhi 32
sevenfold purity 70 sevenfold treasure 71 seven sins 155
sevenfold abode 69
Shaku 279
Hannya 7, 99
Shūso 269
Shakuni 279
Shakuni Kōryū 269
Shàndǎo 184–186, 193, 196, 200, 202, 206, 221, 235, 253, 265, 274; see also Zendō
shànqiǎo fāngbiàn 22; see also skilful means
Sharihotsu 151
shaven/shaving 173, 262, 266
Shido kegyō 149
Shiga prefecture 246
shijū 236
Shikoku 202
Shimane Prefecture 260, 262
Shimotsuma Hōgen 248
Shin (-shū, Buddhism) 2–4, 9–18, 99, 115, 178, 181, 199, 201, 203, 205, 210–216, 218, 221–225, 231–232, 235, 238–239, 241–248, 250–251, 255, 257, 259–260, 262–263, 265, 272, 274–275
Shinano 269
Shinbessho 149–150
Shingon 2, 4, 11–13, 17–18, 100, 125, 133–135, 141, 145, 149, 162, 182, 186, 199, 224
shinjin 11, 244, 249, 251, 256
Shinkū 196
Shinnō-in 145
shinnyo 152, 161
Shinnyokan 186
shinpi 17
Shinran, 2, 4, 10, 13, 15–16, 18, 178–179, 183, 187, 196–197, 199, 201–203, 205–209, 211–215, 217–218, 221–225, 227–229, 231, 235, 241, 243–244, 246–247, 249–252, 259, 263–266, 269, 278–279
Shinshō-in 248–249
Shinshōji Jōson 248
Shinshū 7, 11, 21, 241–243, 247, 249, 252, 259, 263, 277–279; see also Shin (-shū, Buddhism)
Shinshū hōyō 243
Shinshū kana shōgyō 242–243
Shinshū seiten (etc.) 242–243

Shintō 187, 192
shiraki 168, 206
shishin ekō 208–209
shōdōmon 255
Shōgonki 181, 183, 191–194, 197
Shōja 150
shōjō no gō 207
Shōju 154
Shōkai 202
Shōkō 201, 241
Shōkū 13–14, 167–169, 171–179, 201, 206
Shōma arinomama no ki 260
Shōmitsu-in Sen'yū 245
Shōmudōsonhachidaidōjiki 142
Shōmyō (witness) 150, 154
shōmyōnin 150
shōmyō (recitation) 195, 205, 255
Shōō era 201
Shōraku 119
Shōrin-in 192
Shōsen 183
Shōshinge 225, 247, 249, 277
Shōshingetaii, 249
Shōtatsu 201–202
Shōtoku (Prince Umayado) 24, 199
Shōzōmatsuwasan 197
shrine/s 187, 216, 256
shūgaku 252
shugyō 149
shūji 231
Shūjishō 4, 16, 231
Shūka 277–278
shukke 2, 4
Shūso 269
sick/ness 6, 25, 36–367, 52–56, 164
siddham style 146–147
Śikhins 29
Śikṣananda 115
Śikṣāsamuccaya 25, 122
śīla 31, 150, 152–153
silence, 37, 42, 44, 65, 77–78, 84, 99, 116, 191
Siṃhaghoṣa Buddha 66
Siṃhamati Bodhsattva 74
similes 8, 108
Śiva 141
six
  āyatanas 69, 88
  heretics 40
  kinds of consciousness 102
  pāramitās (perfections) 23, 26, 57, 63, 92, 118, 153
  paths of existence 111, 167, 235
  sense organs/objects 38, 103
  Six Item Letter 256
  six character/syllable name 170, 200, 203, 205, 218, 253–254, 274
  supernatural powers 37, 57
sixty-two heresies 43, 53, 69
skandhas 36, 45, 48, 62, 75, 86, 101–103, 109
skilful/skillful
  expedient 22
  means 22, 26, 127
  necessary 33, 35–37, 62–63
  skill 22
  skilfulness 22
smṛtyupasthāna 32
snake/s 36, 48, 142
sō ni arazu zoku ni arazu 3
Soga Ryōjin 253
Sōjun 260
sokutokuōjō 213
solitary 187–188, 208, 226, 267
solitude 187, 266
Sòng (dynasty) 123
song/s 15, 70, 221–222, 224–225, 229
  Song of True Faith 247, 249
  Song on Amida 13, 221–229
Sonshō-in 183, 187
Sōtō Zen 199
soul/s, 100, 117, 252, 254, 273
southward (cosmological) 184, 237
space 76, 78, 91, 102, 128, 192, 222, 226, 253
sparśa 103
spells 72
spirits 65, 72, 78–79, 81, 139, 143
spiritual charity festival 50–51
Śramaṇa/s 48, 50
Śrāvaka/s 23, 39, 41, 43, 52, 56–57, 61, 65–66, 68, 70, 78, 80, 82, 83, 85, 89–90, 94, 151–152, 226, 228

Śrāvakayāna 34
Śrāvaka-mind, 74
Śravasti 119
Śrīgarbha Bodhisattva 76
Śrīgupta Bodhisattva 73
Śrīsiras Bodhisattva 73
srotāpanna 62
stage 6–8, 22, 26, 116, 205, 229, 233, 239, 263–265, 267
steadfast/ness 16, 68, 83, 229, 231–239, 254
Stūpa of seven jewels 91
Subāhu 74
Subhūti 39–40
suchness 45–46, 63, 111, 161, 168, 186, 204
Sudatta 50
Śuddha 42
Śuddhamati 74
Sudhana 9, 116–117, 119–120
Sugata, 92
Sugi 271
Sugihira Shizutoshi 14–16, 168
Sukhāvatīvyūha 120–121, 169–170, 176, 224, 235, 238
Sumati 75
Sumeru 26, 29–30, 60, 69, 80, 237
Sumerudhvaja 59
Sumerupradīparāja, Buddha 59
Sumida (river) 143
Sunakṣatra Bodhisattva 74
Sunetra Bodhisattva 74
śūnya/*tā* 8, 99–101, 103–104, 108–109, 113, 228
supernatural
  beings 11, 24
  power/s 6, 22, 24, 29–31, 34–35, 37, 47–48, 50, 52, 57–59, 61, 64, 67, 70, 73, 78–79, 83, 85, 90–92 94, 96
  sight 42
  wisdom 86
superstitions 141, 244
Susa Shinryū 4
sutehijiri 203
Suzuki, Daisetsu Teitarō (also Daisetz) 9–11, 17, 21, 110, 116, 147, 199, 259–261, 273–276
Suzuki, Beatrice Lane 9, 11–13, 15, 115, 118, 133, 145, 149–150, 221
svāhā 101
syllable/s 112–113, 146, 200, 203, 205, 218, 253, 274–275
symbol/ic/ism 122, 134–136, 138, 140, 142, 160, 193

T

Tahara no Osono 206
Tahitsushō 176
Taishō (Shinshū) Daizōkyō 7, 21, 139, 243
Taizōkai 184
Takada-ha 247–248
Takao 183–184, 186–188, 192
Takejizaiten 117
Taketsu 117
Tamayama Keiho 149
Tanaka, Kenneth K. 249
Tanba 248
tanenbutsu 210–211
Táng (China, Dynasty) 115, 123, 184–185, 200, 217, 235
Tánluán 15, 221
Tannishō 16, 178, 265, 272
Tantric literature/doctrines 184, 186
Tao-an 4
tariki 167–169, 172–178, 204–205, 223, 232, 244, 250–251
Tathāgata 34, 37, 40, 43–45, 51, 59, 63–64, 78–80, 85, 87–96, 139–140, 205, 225, 227, 229, 252–255
Tathāgatahood 69–70, 227
Tathāgatas 71, 84–85, 91, 102, 120, 147, 162
tathatā 152, 161, 168
Tattvarata Bodhisattva 77
ten
  bhūmis 117
  evil deeds 236
  kalpas 225, 255
  pāramitās 23, 37, 63
  powers (*bala*) 27, 47, 70
  quarters 66
  stages 117
  vows 120, 122

Tendai school 125 182, 199, 222
doctrine 14
Mikkyō 12
Teramoto, Yenga 100, 104, 110
Teramoto, Edatsu 261, 266–268, 270–271
Theosophist/s 12
Theravāda 1
thirty-two signs of perfection 84
thirty-seven requisites 32, 37, 47
three
bodies of Buddha 156
chiliocosms 42, 60, 85, 87
divisions of time 128
evil paths of existence 226, 235–236
passions 62
Pure Land Sūtras 200
refuges 151, 153, 278
states of existence 44, 47
treasures 26, 38, 76, 110, 170–171, 277–278
treatises 107
worlds of existence 88, 93
threefold
activity 174
emancipation 49
intelligence 37
knowledge 47
law of permancy
see also triple
throne/s 29, 43, 59, 80, 83
thunder 27–28
thunderbolt 136
Tibet/an 5, 6, 8, 12, 99–104, 107–111, 113–114, 122, 162
Tinsley, Elizabeth 149
Tōdaiji 183
Toganoo 183–184, 186, 189–190
Togashi Masachika 248
Tōji 12, 145
Tokugawa Period 3, 242–243, 247
shogunate 203
Tokuun 119
Trailokyavijaya 134
transcendent/ce 16, 103, 128, 139, 167–168, 178, 197, 226–227, 233, 253, 264, 267, 273–274, 276
transgression/s 162, 182, 191
transience 34, 36, 43, 48, 56, 69, 71, 75, 87, 93, 202
transitoriness 41
translator/s 4–5, 7, 11, 21, 27, 110–111, 123, 199–200, 202, 204, 206, 209–210, 241, 249
transmigration 74, 111–113, 127, 152, 154, 158, 167, 175–176, 202
Trayastriṃśa heaven 60, 89
treasure/s (three etc) 26–29, 30, 34, 38, 66, 69, 70–72, 76, 90, 92, 10, 139, 170–171, 227, 229, 277–278
Treatise on Peace and Joy 221
trikāya 156
Tripiṭaka 109, 110, 122, 124; see also Taishō (Shinshū) Daizōkyō
Triple/triple
activity/non-activity 76
Jewel 151–153, 155, 157–158
Mind 197
world 37, 108–109, 129
see also: threefold
triratna 151
Trisamaya-acala-kalpa 136, 138, 140
tṛṣnā 103
Tsa 110–114
turtles 60
Tuṣita Heaven 45, 117, 192
Twelfth Vow 236
twelve āyatanas 36, 45, 48, 58, 75
twelvefold chain of causation 23, 47, 93, 103
Twenty Verses on the Mahāyāna 8

U

Ucchuṣma-Vidyārāja 141
udumbara 225
Uji 248
Umayado, see Shōtoku
Umeda Kenkyō 270
unclean 43
uncreated 26, 34, 43, 45–46, 59, 69, 73–74, 76–77, 81, 84–88
undefiled 26, 110, 206
Unimpeded Light Lineage 245
unimpeded 26, 49, 52, 94, 117

universal/ity 3–4, 8, 39, 49, 103, 118, 163, 167, 197, 214, 222
universe 60, 71, 115–119, 125, 134, 140, 158–159, 161–161, 185
unlimited 7, 10, 85
unobstructed 84, 229
unworldliness 74, 259
upādāna 103
Upāli 42–43, 163
upāsaka/s 29
upāsikā/s 29
upāya 22, 26, 32–33, 70; see also skilful means
  kauśalya, 22
upekṣā 32
Ususama Myōō 141

V

Vaidalya 107
Vairāṣṭrikaputra 40
Vairocana 12, 116–118, 134, 138–140, 158
  Vairochana 116
Vaiśālī 25, 29, 35, 38, 43, 46, 52, 59, 80
vaiśāradya 27
Vajra 134, 147, 162
vajra 123, 134, 136–138, 142
Vajracchedikā 121
vajradhātu 183
Vajragarbha 134
Vajrapāṇi 138
Vajrayakṣa 134
vandana 159
vārṣika 160
Vaśavartin deities 34
Vasubandhu 108, 221
Vasuṃdhara Bodhisattva 48
vedanā 102–103
vehicle/s 70, 128, 140
  great 1, 14,
  three 65, 134, 226
verse/s 8, 17, 29, 31, 99, 108–110, 113, 119, 202, 219, 247, 249, 260–261, 269, 274–275, 277
vidyā 133
vidyārāja/ Vidyārāja 133–135, 141
Vidyuddeva Bodhisattva 75
Vihar 25
vihāras 160
vijñāna 102–103
Vimalakīrti 2, 4–7, 9, 19, 27, 29, 31, 33, 35–55, 57–65, 67–71, 73, 75, 77–83, 85, 87–91, 93, 95–96
Vimalakīrtinirdeśa/sūtra 6, 21, 24–25, 96
Viṃśakavṛtti 109
Vinaya/s 149, 170
Vinayaka 140
vipāka 113
vīrya 32
  pāramitā 50, 153
visions 8, 63, 108, 183–185
visualization
  meditation 9
  sūtras 9
void/ness 88, 228
vow 4–5, 17, 43, 153, 156, 172–173, 177, 204, 215, 225, 228, 232–240, 244, 251, 253–254, 277–279
  Eighteenth 10, 254, 263
  not to enter Nirvana 152
  original 16, 87, 135, 139–140, 169–171, 178, 207, 224, 227, 232, 251, 263–265
vows 2, 4–5, 7–8, 10, 14, 18, 35, 47, 68, 115–117, 119–130, 152, 159, 168, 175, 178, 205, 213, 224, 236, 263
Vulture Mount 102
Vyūha-Śuddha 42

W

Wagotōroku 178, 196
Wajō 150, 153–159
Wakasa province 248
Wakayama Prefecture 183
Wasan 15–16, 221–225, 233, 278
Watanabe Kaikyoku 121–122
way/s 32, 35, 68, 163, 189, 195–196, 204, 260, 278
Wénshūshīlìfāyuàn jīng 122–123
west/ern
  cosmological 168, 184, 203, 228, 255
  cultural 1, 21, 167, 200, 259, 260
wheel 26, 30, 57, 93–94, 113, 126–129, 226

white
body 142,
lotus 265
path 202
will of Amida 251, 253
wisdom, 23, 25–28, 31–37, 43, 45, 47, 49, 51–52, 55–57, 62–63, 68, 70–77, 80, 82, 84–87, 93, 101–102, 112, 117, 127–129, 139, 142, 151–153, 158, 161, 163, 171, 178, 182, 194–195, 204, 215, 222, 225, 227, 229, 232–235, 239, 269, 278
women 29, 67, 89, 143, 149, 152, 195, 200, 215, 260, 279
worldliness 74
worldly 1, 26, 30, 33, 35, 114, 133, 139, 152, 169, 172–173, 177, 187–188, 203, 252
worlds 29–30, 51, 56–57, 59–61, 67, 78, 80, 88, 91–93, 116, 119, 145, 155–156, 158, 224, 228, 236, 252
Wŭ pronunciation 217
wu wei 27

X

Xiánjíxiáng púsà 124
Xiánshǒu 26, 124
Xuánzàng 186

Y

yācanā 159
Yakṣa/s 29–30, 126, 134–135
Yama 117
Yamabe Shūgaku 15, 222
Yamagoe Amida 213
Yamaguchi Susumu 8
Yamamoto Ine 271
Yamamoto Kōshō 250
Yamamoto Wahei 266
Yamāntaka 134
Yamashina 245, 248–249
Yamashiro (province) 248
Yanagi Sōetsu 15–16, 199
yellow Fudō 136, 138, 145–146
Yīxíng 12, 139–140
Yogācāra 8, 221
yojanas 59, 96
Yokogawa Kenshō 11
Yokota Takezō 5
Yōmei (Emperor) 24
Yoritsune 175
Yoshizaki 245–248, 250
Yuasa Munemitsu 186
Yuien(-bō) 16
Yuikyōgyō 151, 183
Yuima 24
yuishin 263
Yumenoki 184–185

Z

zài *jiā* chū jiā 4
Zaijarin/shōgonki 181, 183, 187, 189–193, 196–197
zaike bukkyō 2–4
Zàn amítuófó jì 221
Zen 3, 10–11, 14, 116, 168, 199, 218–219, 223–224, 259
zenchishiki 206, 255
Zendō 169, 174, 200, 221, 235–237, 239; see also Shàndǎo
zengyō hōben 22; see also skilful means
Zenjū (=Dōsai) 246, 248, 250
Zenkōji 202
Zenmyōji 190
Zhēn Yuán 124
Zō-ō 260
Zōngmì 125
Zonkaku 213
Zonnyo Shōnin 241

www.ingramcontent.com/pod-product-compliance
Lightning Source LLC
Chambersburg PA
CBHW070011010526
44117CB00011B/1521